GCC 7.0 GNU Compiler Collection Internals 2/2

A catalogue record for this book is available from the Hong Kong Public Libraries.

Published in Hong Kong by Samurai Media Limited.

Email: info@samuraimedia.org

ISBN 978-988-8406-99-9

Short Contents

Table of Contents

17 Target Description Macros and Functions

17 Target Description Macros and Functions

In addition to the file 'machine.md', a machine description includes a C header file conventionally given the name 'machine.h' and a C source file named 'machine.c'. The header file defines numerous macros that convey the information about the target machine that does not fit into the scheme of the '.md' file. The file 'tm.h' should be a link to 'machine.h'. The header file 'config.h' includes 'tm.h' and most compiler source files include 'config.h'. The source file defines a variable targetm, which is a structure containing pointers to functions and data relating to the target machine. 'machine.c' should also contain their definitions, if they are not defined elsewhere in GCC, and other functions called through the macros defined in the '.h' file.

17.1 The Global targetm Variable

struct gcc_target targetm   [Variable]

The target '.c' file must define the global targetm variable which contains pointers to functions and data relating to the target machine. The variable is declared in 'target.h'; 'target-def.h' defines the macro TARGET_INITIALIZER which is used to initialize the variable, and macros for the default initializers for elements of the structure. The '.c' file should override those macros for which the default definition is inappropriate. For example:

```
#include "target.h"
#include "target-def.h"

/* Initialize the GCC target structure.  */

#undef TARGET_COMP_TYPE_ATTRIBUTES
#define TARGET_COMP_TYPE_ATTRIBUTES machine_comp_type_attributes

struct gcc_target targetm = TARGET_INITIALIZER;
```

Where a macro should be defined in the '.c' file in this manner to form part of the targetm structure, it is documented below as a "Target Hook" with a prototype. Many macros will change in future from being defined in the '.h' file to being part of the targetm structure.

Similarly, there is a targetcm variable for hooks that are specific to front ends for C-family languages, documented as "C Target Hook". This is declared in 'c-family/c-target.h', the initializer TARGETCM_INITIALIZER in 'c-family/c-target-def.h'. If targets initialize targetcm themselves, they should set target_has_targetcm=yes in 'config.gcc'; otherwise a default definition is used.

Similarly, there is a targetm_common variable for hooks that are shared between the compiler driver and the compilers proper, documented as "Common Target Hook". This is declared in 'common/common-target.h', the initializer TARGETM_COMMON_INITIALIZER in 'common/common-target-def.h'. If targets initialize targetm_common themselves, they should set target_has_targetm_common=yes in 'config.gcc'; otherwise a default definition is used.

17.2 Controlling the Compilation Driver, 'gcc'

You can control the compilation driver.

DRIVER_SELF_SPECS   [Macro]
:   A list of specs for the driver itself. It should be a suitable initializer for an array of strings, with no surrounding braces.

    The driver applies these specs to its own command line between loading default 'specs' files (but not command-line specified ones) and choosing the multilib directory or running any subcommands. It applies them in the order given, so each spec can depend on the options added by earlier ones. It is also possible to remove options using '%<option' in the usual way.

    This macro can be useful when a port has several interdependent target options. It provides a way of standardizing the command line so that the other specs are easier to write.

    Do not define this macro if it does not need to do anything.

OPTION_DEFAULT_SPECS   [Macro]
:   A list of specs used to support configure-time default options (i.e. '--with' options) in the driver. It should be a suitable initializer for an array of structures, each containing two strings, without the outermost pair of surrounding braces.

    The first item in the pair is the name of the default. This must match the code in 'config.gcc' for the target. The second item is a spec to apply if a default with this name was specified. The string '%(VALUE)' in the spec will be replaced by the value of the default everywhere it occurs.

    The driver will apply these specs to its own command line between loading default 'specs' files and processing DRIVER_SELF_SPECS, using the same mechanism as DRIVER_SELF_SPECS.

    Do not define this macro if it does not need to do anything.

CPP_SPEC   [Macro]
:   A C string constant that tells the GCC driver program options to pass to CPP. It can also specify how to translate options you give to GCC into options for GCC to pass to the CPP.

    Do not define this macro if it does not need to do anything.

CPLUSPLUS_CPP_SPEC   [Macro]
:   This macro is just like CPP_SPEC, but is used for C++, rather than C. If you do not define this macro, then the value of CPP_SPEC (if any) will be used instead.

CC1_SPEC   [Macro]
:   A C string constant that tells the GCC driver program options to pass to cc1, cc1plus, f771, and the other language front ends. It can also specify how to translate options you give to GCC into options for GCC to pass to front ends.

    Do not define this macro if it does not need to do anything.

CC1PLUS_SPEC   [Macro]

>   A C string constant that tells the GCC driver program options to pass to `cc1plus`. It can also specify how to translate options you give to GCC into options for GCC to pass to the `cc1plus`.
>
>   Do not define this macro if it does not need to do anything. Note that everything defined in CC1_SPEC is already passed to `cc1plus` so there is no need to duplicate the contents of CC1_SPEC in CC1PLUS_SPEC.

ASM_SPEC   [Macro]

>   A C string constant that tells the GCC driver program options to pass to the assembler. It can also specify how to translate options you give to GCC into options for GCC to pass to the assembler. See the file 'sun3.h' for an example of this.
>
>   Do not define this macro if it does not need to do anything.

ASM_FINAL_SPEC   [Macro]

>   A C string constant that tells the GCC driver program how to run any programs which cleanup after the normal assembler. Normally, this is not needed. See the file 'mips.h' for an example of this.
>
>   Do not define this macro if it does not need to do anything.

AS_NEEDS_DASH_FOR_PIPED_INPUT   [Macro]

>   Define this macro, with no value, if the driver should give the assembler an argument consisting of a single dash, '-', to instruct it to read from its standard input (which will be a pipe connected to the output of the compiler proper). This argument is given after any '-o' option specifying the name of the output file.
>
>   If you do not define this macro, the assembler is assumed to read its standard input if given no non-option arguments. If your assembler cannot read standard input at all, use a '%{pipe:%e}' construct; see 'mips.h' for instance.

LINK_SPEC   [Macro]

>   A C string constant that tells the GCC driver program options to pass to the linker. It can also specify how to translate options you give to GCC into options for GCC to pass to the linker.
>
>   Do not define this macro if it does not need to do anything.

LIB_SPEC   [Macro]

>   Another C string constant used much like LINK_SPEC. The difference between the two is that LIB_SPEC is used at the end of the command given to the linker.
>
>   If this macro is not defined, a default is provided that loads the standard C library from the usual place. See 'gcc.c'.

LIBGCC_SPEC   [Macro]

>   Another C string constant that tells the GCC driver program how and when to place a reference to 'libgcc.a' into the linker command line. This constant is placed both before and after the value of LIB_SPEC.
>
>   If this macro is not defined, the GCC driver provides a default that passes the string '-lgcc' to the linker.

REAL_LIBGCC_SPEC   [Macro]

> By default, if ENABLE_SHARED_LIBGCC is defined, the LIBGCC_SPEC is not directly used by the driver program but is instead modified to refer to different versions of 'libgcc.a' depending on the values of the command line flags '-static', '-shared', '-static-libgcc', and '-shared-libgcc'. On targets where these modifications are inappropriate, define REAL_LIBGCC_SPEC instead. REAL_LIBGCC_SPEC tells the driver how to place a reference to 'libgcc' on the link command line, but, unlike LIBGCC_SPEC, it is used unmodified.

USE_LD_AS_NEEDED   [Macro]

> A macro that controls the modifications to LIBGCC_SPEC mentioned in REAL_LIBGCC_SPEC. If nonzero, a spec will be generated that uses '--as-needed' or equivalent options and the shared 'libgcc' in place of the static exception handler library, when linking without any of -static, -static-libgcc, or -shared-libgcc.

LINK_EH_SPEC   [Macro]

> If defined, this C string constant is added to LINK_SPEC. When USE_LD_AS_NEEDED is zero or undefined, it also affects the modifications to LIBGCC_SPEC mentioned in REAL_LIBGCC_SPEC.

STARTFILE_SPEC   [Macro]

> Another C string constant used much like LINK_SPEC. The difference between the two is that STARTFILE_SPEC is used at the very beginning of the command given to the linker.

> If this macro is not defined, a default is provided that loads the standard C startup file from the usual place. See 'gcc.c'.

ENDFILE_SPEC   [Macro]

> Another C string constant used much like LINK_SPEC. The difference between the two is that ENDFILE_SPEC is used at the very end of the command given to the linker.

> Do not define this macro if it does not need to do anything.

THREAD_MODEL_SPEC   [Macro]

> GCC -v will print the thread model GCC was configured to use. However, this doesn't work on platforms that are multilibbed on thread models, such as AIX 4.3. On such platforms, define THREAD_MODEL_SPEC such that it evaluates to a string without blanks that names one of the recognized thread models. %*, the default value of this macro, will expand to the value of thread_file set in 'config.gcc'.

SYSROOT_SUFFIX_SPEC   [Macro]

> Define this macro to add a suffix to the target sysroot when GCC is configured with a sysroot. This will cause GCC to search for usr/lib, et al, within sysroot+suffix.

SYSROOT_HEADERS_SUFFIX_SPEC   [Macro]

> Define this macro to add a headers_suffix to the target sysroot when GCC is configured with a sysroot. This will cause GCC to pass the updated sysroot+headers_suffix to CPP, causing it to search for usr/include, et al, within sysroot+headers_suffix.

EXTRA_SPECS   [Macro]

> Define this macro to provide additional specifications to put in the 'specs' file that can be used in various specifications like CC1_SPEC.
>
> The definition should be an initializer for an array of structures, containing a string constant, that defines the specification name, and a string constant that provides the specification.
>
> Do not define this macro if it does not need to do anything.
>
> EXTRA_SPECS is useful when an architecture contains several related targets, which have various ..._SPECS which are similar to each other, and the maintainer would like one central place to keep these definitions.
>
> For example, the PowerPC System V.4 targets use EXTRA_SPECS to define either _CALL_SYSV when the System V calling sequence is used or _CALL_AIX when the older AIX-based calling sequence is used.
>
> The 'config/rs6000/rs6000.h' target file defines:
>
> ```
> #define EXTRA_SPECS \
>   { "cpp_sysv_default", CPP_SYSV_DEFAULT },
>
> #define CPP_SYS_DEFAULT ""
> ```
>
> The 'config/rs6000/sysv.h' target file defines:
>
> ```
> #undef CPP_SPEC
> #define CPP_SPEC \
> "%{posix: -D_POSIX_SOURCE } \
> %{mcall-sysv: -D_CALL_SYSV } \
> %{!mcall-sysv: %(cpp_sysv_default) } \
> %{msoft-float: -D_SOFT_FLOAT} %{mcpu=403: -D_SOFT_FLOAT}"
>
> #undef CPP_SYSV_DEFAULT
> #define CPP_SYSV_DEFAULT "-D_CALL_SYSV"
> ```
>
> while the 'config/rs6000/eabiaix.h' target file defines CPP_SYSV_DEFAULT as:
>
> ```
> #undef CPP_SYSV_DEFAULT
> #define CPP_SYSV_DEFAULT "-D_CALL_AIX"
> ```

LINK_LIBGCC_SPECIAL_1   [Macro]

> Define this macro if the driver program should find the library 'libgcc.a'. If you do not define this macro, the driver program will pass the argument '-lgcc' to tell the linker to do the search.

LINK_GCC_C_SEQUENCE_SPEC   [Macro]

> The sequence in which libgcc and libc are specified to the linker. By default this is %G %L %G.

POST_LINK_SPEC   [Macro]

> Define this macro to add additional steps to be executed after linker. The default value of this macro is empty string.

LINK_COMMAND_SPEC   [Macro]

> A C string constant giving the complete command line need to execute the linker. When you do this, you will need to update your port each time a change is made to the link command line within 'gcc.c'. Therefore, define this macro only if you need

to completely redefine the command line for invoking the linker and there is no other way to accomplish the effect you need. Overriding this macro may be avoidable by overriding `LINK_GCC_C_SEQUENCE_SPEC` instead.

`bool TARGET_ALWAYS_STRIP_DOTDOT`   [Common Target Hook]

True if '`..`' components should always be removed from directory names computed relative to GCC's internal directories, false (default) if such components should be preserved and directory names containing them passed to other tools such as the linker.

`MULTILIB_DEFAULTS`   [Macro]

Define this macro as a C expression for the initializer of an array of string to tell the driver program which options are defaults for this target and thus do not need to be handled specially when using `MULTILIB_OPTIONS`.

Do not define this macro if `MULTILIB_OPTIONS` is not defined in the target makefile fragment or if none of the options listed in `MULTILIB_OPTIONS` are set by default. See Section 19.1 [Target Fragment], page 617.

`RELATIVE_PREFIX_NOT_LINKDIR`   [Macro]

Define this macro to tell `gcc` that it should only translate a '`-B`' prefix into a '`-L`' linker option if the prefix indicates an absolute file name.

`MD_EXEC_PREFIX`   [Macro]

If defined, this macro is an additional prefix to try after `STANDARD_EXEC_PREFIX`. `MD_EXEC_PREFIX` is not searched when the compiler is built as a cross compiler. If you define `MD_EXEC_PREFIX`, then be sure to add it to the list of directories used to find the assembler in '`configure.ac`'.

`STANDARD_STARTFILE_PREFIX`   [Macro]

Define this macro as a C string constant if you wish to override the standard choice of `libdir` as the default prefix to try when searching for startup files such as '`crt0.o`'. `STANDARD_STARTFILE_PREFIX` is not searched when the compiler is built as a cross compiler.

`STANDARD_STARTFILE_PREFIX_1`   [Macro]

Define this macro as a C string constant if you wish to override the standard choice of `/lib` as a prefix to try after the default prefix when searching for startup files such as '`crt0.o`'. `STANDARD_STARTFILE_PREFIX_1` is not searched when the compiler is built as a cross compiler.

`STANDARD_STARTFILE_PREFIX_2`   [Macro]

Define this macro as a C string constant if you wish to override the standard choice of `/lib` as yet another prefix to try after the default prefix when searching for startup files such as '`crt0.o`'. `STANDARD_STARTFILE_PREFIX_2` is not searched when the compiler is built as a cross compiler.

`MD_STARTFILE_PREFIX`   [Macro]

If defined, this macro supplies an additional prefix to try after the standard prefixes. `MD_EXEC_PREFIX` is not searched when the compiler is built as a cross compiler.

MD_STARTFILE_PREFIX_1   [Macro]
> If defined, this macro supplies yet another prefix to try after the standard prefixes.
> It is not searched when the compiler is built as a cross compiler.

INIT_ENVIRONMENT   [Macro]
> Define this macro as a C string constant if you wish to set environment variables for
> programs called by the driver, such as the assembler and loader. The driver passes
> the value of this macro to `putenv` to initialize the necessary environment variables.

LOCAL_INCLUDE_DIR   [Macro]
> Define this macro as a C string constant if you wish to override the standard choice
> of '/usr/local/include' as the default prefix to try when searching for local
> header files. LOCAL_INCLUDE_DIR comes before NATIVE_SYSTEM_HEADER_DIR (set in
> 'config.gcc', normally '/usr/include') in the search order.
>
> Cross compilers do not search either '/usr/local/include' or its replacement.

NATIVE_SYSTEM_HEADER_COMPONENT   [Macro]
> The "component" corresponding to NATIVE_SYSTEM_HEADER_DIR. See INCLUDE_
> DEFAULTS, below, for the description of components. If you do not define this macro,
> no component is used.

INCLUDE_DEFAULTS   [Macro]
> Define this macro if you wish to override the entire default search path for include
> files. For a native compiler, the default search path usually consists of GCC_INCLUDE_
> DIR, LOCAL_INCLUDE_DIR, GPLUSPLUS_INCLUDE_DIR, and NATIVE_SYSTEM_HEADER_
> DIR. In addition, GPLUSPLUS_INCLUDE_DIR and GCC_INCLUDE_DIR are defined auto-
> matically by 'Makefile', and specify private search areas for GCC. The directory
> GPLUSPLUS_INCLUDE_DIR is used only for C++ programs.
>
> The definition should be an initializer for an array of structures. Each array element
> should have four elements: the directory name (a string constant), the component
> name (also a string constant), a flag for C++-only directories, and a flag showing that
> the includes in the directory don't need to be wrapped in `extern` 'C' when compiling
> C++. Mark the end of the array with a null element.
>
> The component name denotes what GNU package the include file is part of, if any,
> in all uppercase letters. For example, it might be 'GCC' or 'BINUTILS'. If the package
> is part of a vendor-supplied operating system, code the component name as '0'.
>
> For example, here is the definition used for VAX/VMS:
>
> ```
> #define INCLUDE_DEFAULTS \
> {                                            \
>   { "GNU_GXX_INCLUDE:", "G++", 1, 1},        \
>   { "GNU_CC_INCLUDE:", "GCC", 0, 0},         \
>   { "SYS$SYSROOT:[SYSLIB.]", 0, 0, 0},       \
>   { ".", 0, 0, 0},                           \
>   { 0, 0, 0, 0}                              \
> }
> ```

Here is the order of prefixes tried for exec files:

1. Any prefixes specified by the user with '-B'.

2. The environment variable `GCC_EXEC_PREFIX` or, if `GCC_EXEC_PREFIX` is not set and the compiler has not been installed in the configure-time *prefix*, the location in which the compiler has actually been installed.

3. The directories specified by the environment variable `COMPILER_PATH`.

4. The macro `STANDARD_EXEC_PREFIX`, if the compiler has been installed in the configured-time *prefix*.

5. The location '`/usr/libexec/gcc/`', but only if this is a native compiler.

6. The location '`/usr/lib/gcc/`', but only if this is a native compiler.

7. The macro `MD_EXEC_PREFIX`, if defined, but only if this is a native compiler.

Here is the order of prefixes tried for startfiles:

1. Any prefixes specified by the user with '`-B`'.

2. The environment variable `GCC_EXEC_PREFIX` or its automatically determined value based on the installed toolchain location.

3. The directories specified by the environment variable `LIBRARY_PATH` (or port-specific name; native only, cross compilers do not use this).

4. The macro `STANDARD_EXEC_PREFIX`, but only if the toolchain is installed in the configured *prefix* or this is a native compiler.

5. The location '`/usr/lib/gcc/`', but only if this is a native compiler.

6. The macro `MD_EXEC_PREFIX`, if defined, but only if this is a native compiler.

7. The macro `MD_STARTFILE_PREFIX`, if defined, but only if this is a native compiler, or we have a target system root.

8. The macro `MD_STARTFILE_PREFIX_1`, if defined, but only if this is a native compiler, or we have a target system root.

9. The macro `STANDARD_STARTFILE_PREFIX`, with any sysroot modifications. If this path is relative it will be prefixed by `GCC_EXEC_PREFIX` and the machine suffix or `STANDARD_EXEC_PREFIX` and the machine suffix.

10. The macro `STANDARD_STARTFILE_PREFIX_1`, but only if this is a native compiler, or we have a target system root. The default for this macro is '`/lib/`'.

11. The macro `STANDARD_STARTFILE_PREFIX_2`, but only if this is a native compiler, or we have a target system root. The default for this macro is '`/usr/lib/`'.

17.3 Run-time Target Specification

Here are run-time target specifications.

`TARGET_CPU_CPP_BUILTINS ()`   [Macro]

> This function-like macro expands to a block of code that defines built-in preprocessor macros and assertions for the target CPU, using the functions `builtin_define`, `builtin_define_std` and `builtin_assert`. When the front end calls this macro it provides a trailing semicolon, and since it has finished command line option processing your code can use those results freely.
>
> `builtin_assert` takes a string in the form you pass to the command-line option '`-A`', such as `cpu=mips`, and creates the assertion. `builtin_define` takes a string in the form accepted by option '`-D`' and unconditionally defines the macro.

`builtin_define_std` takes a string representing the name of an object-like macro. If it doesn't lie in the user's namespace, `builtin_define_std` defines it unconditionally. Otherwise, it defines a version with two leading underscores, and another version with two leading and trailing underscores, and defines the original only if an ISO standard was not requested on the command line. For example, passing `unix` defines `__unix`, `__unix__` and possibly `unix`; passing `_mips` defines `__mips`, `__mips__` and possibly `_mips`, and passing `_ABI64` defines only `_ABI64`.

You can also test for the C dialect being compiled. The variable `c_language` is set to one of `clk_c`, `clk_cplusplus` or `clk_objective_c`. Note that if we are preprocessing assembler, this variable will be `clk_c` but the function-like macro `preprocessing_asm_p()` will return true, so you might want to check for that first. If you need to check for strict ANSI, the variable `flag_iso` can be used. The function-like macro `preprocessing_trad_p()` can be used to check for traditional preprocessing.

`TARGET_OS_CPP_BUILTINS ()`   [Macro]

> Similarly to `TARGET_CPU_CPP_BUILTINS` but this macro is optional and is used for the target operating system instead.

`TARGET_OBJFMT_CPP_BUILTINS ()`   [Macro]

> Similarly to `TARGET_CPU_CPP_BUILTINS` but this macro is optional and is used for the target object format. 'elfos.h' uses this macro to define `__ELF__`, so you probably do not need to define it yourself.

`extern int target_flags`   [Variable]

> This variable is declared in 'options.h', which is included before any target-specific headers.

`int TARGET_DEFAULT_TARGET_FLAGS`   [Common Target Hook]

> This variable specifies the initial value of `target_flags`. Its default setting is 0.

`bool TARGET_HANDLE_OPTION (`*struct gcc_options* `*opts,`   [Common Target Hook]
>   *struct gcc_options* `*opts_set,` *const struct cl_decoded_option* `*decoded,`
>   *location_t* `loc)`

> This hook is called whenever the user specifies one of the target-specific options described by the '.opt' definition files (see Chapter 8 [Options], page 107). It has the opportunity to do some option-specific processing and should return true if the option is valid. The default definition does nothing but return true.
>
> *decoded* specifies the option and its arguments. *opts* and *opts_set* are the `gcc_options` structures to be used for storing option state, and *loc* is the location at which the option was passed (`UNKNOWN_LOCATION` except for options passed via attributes).

`bool TARGET_HANDLE_C_OPTION (`*size_t* `code,` *const char* `*arg,` *int*   [C Target Hook]
>   `value)`

> This target hook is called whenever the user specifies one of the target-specific C language family options described by the '.opt' definition files(see Chapter 8 [Options], page 107). It has the opportunity to do some option-specific processing and should return true if the option is valid. The arguments are like for `TARGET_HANDLE_OPTION`. The default definition does nothing but return false.

In general, you should use `TARGET_HANDLE_OPTION` to handle options. However, if processing an option requires routines that are only available in the C (and related language) front ends, then you should use `TARGET_HANDLE_C_OPTION` instead.

`tree TARGET_OBJC_CONSTRUCT_STRING_OBJECT (tree string)` [C Target Hook]
Targets may provide a string object type that can be used within and between C, C++ and their respective Objective-C dialects. A string object might, for example, embed encoding and length information. These objects are considered opaque to the compiler and handled as references. An ideal implementation makes the composition of the string object match that of the Objective-C `NSString` (`NXString` for GNUStep), allowing efficient interworking between C-only and Objective-C code. If a target implements string objects then this hook should return a reference to such an object constructed from the normal 'C' string representation provided in *string*. At present, the hook is used by Objective-C only, to obtain a common-format string object when the target provides one.

`void TARGET_OBJC_DECLARE_UNRESOLVED_CLASS_REFERENCE` [C Target Hook]
`(const char *classname)`
Declare that Objective C class *classname* is referenced by the current TU.

`void TARGET_OBJC_DECLARE_CLASS_DEFINITION (const char` [C Target Hook]
`*classname)`
Declare that Objective C class *classname* is defined by the current TU.

`bool TARGET_STRING_OBJECT_REF_TYPE_P (const_tree` [C Target Hook]
`stringref)`
If a target implements string objects then this hook should return `true` if *stringref* is a valid reference to such an object.

`void TARGET_CHECK_STRING_OBJECT_FORMAT_ARG (tree` [C Target Hook]
`format_arg, tree args_list)`
If a target implements string objects then this hook should should provide a facility to check the function arguments in *args_list* against the format specifiers in *format_arg* where the type of *format_arg* is one recognized as a valid string reference type.

`void TARGET_OVERRIDE_OPTIONS_AFTER_CHANGE (void)` [Target Hook]
This target function is similar to the hook `TARGET_OPTION_OVERRIDE` but is called when the optimize level is changed via an attribute or pragma or when it is reset at the end of the code affected by the attribute or pragma. It is not called at the beginning of compilation when `TARGET_OPTION_OVERRIDE` is called so if you want to perform these actions then, you should have `TARGET_OPTION_OVERRIDE` call `TARGET_OVERRIDE_OPTIONS_AFTER_CHANGE`.

`C_COMMON_OVERRIDE_OPTIONS` [Macro]
This is similar to the `TARGET_OPTION_OVERRIDE` hook but is only used in the C language frontends (C, Objective-C, C++, Objective-C++) and so can be used to alter option flag variables which only exist in those frontends.

const struct default_options *   [Common Target Hook]
      TARGET_OPTION_OPTIMIZATION_TABLE

> Some machines may desire to change what optimizations are performed for various optimization levels. This variable, if defined, describes options to enable at particular sets of optimization levels. These options are processed once just after the optimization level is determined and before the remainder of the command options have been parsed, so may be overridden by other options passed explicitly.
>
> This processing is run once at program startup and when the optimization options are changed via #pragma GCC optimize or by using the optimize attribute.

void TARGET_OPTION_INIT_STRUCT (*struct gcc_options*   [Common Target Hook]
      *opts)

> Set target-dependent initial values of fields in *opts*.

void TARGET_OPTION_DEFAULT_PARAMS (*void*)   [Common Target Hook]

> Set target-dependent default values for '--param' settings, using calls to set_default_param_value.

SWITCHABLE_TARGET   [Macro]

> Some targets need to switch between substantially different subtargets during compilation. For example, the MIPS target has one subtarget for the traditional MIPS architecture and another for MIPS16. Source code can switch between these two subarchitectures using the mips16 and nomips16 attributes.
>
> Such subtargets can differ in things like the set of available registers, the set of available instructions, the costs of various operations, and so on. GCC caches a lot of this type of information in global variables, and recomputing them for each subtarget takes a significant amount of time. The compiler therefore provides a facility for maintaining several versions of the global variables and quickly switching between them; see 'target-globals.h' for details.
>
> Define this macro to 1 if your target needs this facility. The default is 0.

bool TARGET_FLOAT_EXCEPTIONS_ROUNDING_SUPPORTED_P (*void*)   [Target Hook]

> Returns true if the target supports IEEE 754 floating-point exceptions and rounding modes, false otherwise. This is intended to relate to the float and double types, but not necessarily long double. By default, returns true if the adddf3 instruction pattern is available and false otherwise, on the assumption that hardware floating point supports exceptions and rounding modes but software floating point does not.

17.4 Defining data structures for per-function information.

If the target needs to store information on a per-function basis, GCC provides a macro and a couple of variables to allow this. Note, just using statics to store the information is a bad idea, since GCC supports nested functions, so you can be halfway through encoding one function when another one comes along.

GCC defines a data structure called struct function which contains all of the data specific to an individual function. This structure contains a field called machine whose type is struct machine_function *, which can be used by targets to point to their own specific data.

If a target needs per-function specific data it should define the type **struct machine_function** and also the macro INIT_EXPANDERS. This macro should be used to initialize the function pointer **init_machine_status**. This pointer is explained below.

One typical use of per-function, target specific data is to create an RTX to hold the register containing the function's return address. This RTX can then be used to implement the **__builtin_return_address** function, for level 0.

Note—earlier implementations of GCC used a single data area to hold all of the per-function information. Thus when processing of a nested function began the old per-function data had to be pushed onto a stack, and when the processing was finished, it had to be popped off the stack. GCC used to provide function pointers called **save_machine_status** and **restore_machine_status** to handle the saving and restoring of the target specific information. Since the single data area approach is no longer used, these pointers are no longer supported.

INIT_EXPANDERS   [Macro]
  Macro called to initialize any target specific information. This macro is called once per function, before generation of any RTL has begun. The intention of this macro is to allow the initialization of the function pointer **init_machine_status**.

void (*)(struct function *) init_machine_status   [Variable]
  If this function pointer is non-NULL it will be called once per function, before function compilation starts, in order to allow the target to perform any target specific initialization of the **struct function** structure. It is intended that this would be used to initialize the **machine** of that structure.

  struct machine_function structures are expected to be freed by GC. Generally, any memory that they reference must be allocated by using GC allocation, including the structure itself.

17.5 Storage Layout

Note that the definitions of the macros in this table which are sizes or alignments measured in bits do not need to be constant. They can be C expressions that refer to static variables, such as the **target_flags**. See Section 17.3 [Run-time Target], page 440.

BITS_BIG_ENDIAN   [Macro]
  Define this macro to have the value 1 if the most significant bit in a byte has the lowest number; otherwise define it to have the value zero. This means that bit-field instructions count from the most significant bit. If the machine has no bit-field instructions, then this must still be defined, but it doesn't matter which value it is defined to. This macro need not be a constant.

  This macro does not affect the way structure fields are packed into bytes or words; that is controlled by BYTES_BIG_ENDIAN.

BYTES_BIG_ENDIAN   [Macro]
  Define this macro to have the value 1 if the most significant byte in a word has the lowest number. This macro need not be a constant.

WORDS_BIG_ENDIAN   [Macro]

>   Define this macro to have the value 1 if, in a multiword object, the most significant
>   word has the lowest number. This applies to both memory locations and registers;
>   see REG_WORDS_BIG_ENDIAN if the order of words in memory is not the same as the
>   order in registers. This macro need not be a constant.

REG_WORDS_BIG_ENDIAN   [Macro]

>   On some machines, the order of words in a multiword object differs between registers
>   in memory. In such a situation, define this macro to describe the order of words in a
>   register. The macro WORDS_BIG_ENDIAN controls the order of words in memory.

FLOAT_WORDS_BIG_ENDIAN   [Macro]

>   Define this macro to have the value 1 if DFmode, XFmode or TFmode floating point
>   numbers are stored in memory with the word containing the sign bit at the lowest
>   address; otherwise define it to have the value 0. This macro need not be a constant.
>
>   You need not define this macro if the ordering is the same as for multi-word integers.

BITS_PER_WORD   [Macro]

>   Number of bits in a word. If you do not define this macro, the default is BITS_PER_
>   UNIT * UNITS_PER_WORD.

MAX_BITS_PER_WORD   [Macro]

>   Maximum number of bits in a word. If this is undefined, the default is BITS_PER_
>   WORD. Otherwise, it is the constant value that is the largest value that BITS_PER_WORD
>   can have at run-time.

UNITS_PER_WORD   [Macro]

>   Number of storage units in a word; normally the size of a general-purpose register, a
>   power of two from 1 or 8.

MIN_UNITS_PER_WORD   [Macro]

>   Minimum number of units in a word. If this is undefined, the default is UNITS_PER_
>   WORD. Otherwise, it is the constant value that is the smallest value that UNITS_PER_
>   WORD can have at run-time.

POINTER_SIZE   [Macro]

>   Width of a pointer, in bits. You must specify a value no wider than the width of
>   Pmode. If it is not equal to the width of Pmode, you must define POINTERS_EXTEND_
>   UNSIGNED. If you do not specify a value the default is BITS_PER_WORD.

POINTERS_EXTEND_UNSIGNED   [Macro]

>   A C expression that determines how pointers should be extended from ptr_mode to
>   either Pmode or word_mode. It is greater than zero if pointers should be zero-extended,
>   zero if they should be sign-extended, and negative if some other sort of conversion is
>   needed. In the last case, the extension is done by the target's ptr_extend instruction.
>
>   You need not define this macro if the ptr_mode, Pmode and word_mode are all the
>   same width.

PROMOTE_MODE (*m*, *unsignedp*, *type*)   [Macro]

A macro to update *m* and *unsignedp* when an object whose type is *type* and which has the specified mode and signedness is to be stored in a register. This macro is only called when *type* is a scalar type.

On most RISC machines, which only have operations that operate on a full register, define this macro to set *m* to `word_mode` if *m* is an integer mode narrower than `BITS_PER_WORD`. In most cases, only integer modes should be widened because wider-precision floating-point operations are usually more expensive than their narrower counterparts.

For most machines, the macro definition does not change *unsignedp*. However, some machines, have instructions that preferentially handle either signed or unsigned quantities of certain modes. For example, on the DEC Alpha, 32-bit loads from memory and 32-bit add instructions sign-extend the result to 64 bits. On such machines, set *unsignedp* according to which kind of extension is more efficient.

Do not define this macro if it would never modify *m*.

enum flt_eval_method TARGET_C_EXCESS_PRECISION (*enum*   [Target Hook]
        excess_precision_type **type**)

Return a value, with the same meaning as the C99 macro `FLT_EVAL_METHOD` that describes which excess precision should be applied. *type* is either `EXCESS_PRECISION_TYPE_IMPLICIT`, `EXCESS_PRECISION_TYPE_FAST`, or `EXCESS_PRECISION_TYPE_STANDARD`. For `EXCESS_PRECISION_TYPE_IMPLICIT`, the target should return which precision and range operations will be implictly evaluated in regardless of the excess precision explicitly added. For `EXCESS_PRECISION_TYPE_STANDARD` and `EXCESS_PRECISION_TYPE_FAST`, the target should return the explicit excess precision that should be added depending on the value set for '-fexcess-precision=[standard|fast]'. Note that unpredictable explicit excess precision does not make sense, so a target should never return `FLT_EVAL_METHOD_UNPREDICTABLE` when *type* is `EXCESS_PRECISION_TYPE_STANDARD` or `EXCESS_PRECISION_TYPE_FAST`.

machine_mode TARGET_PROMOTE_FUNCTION_MODE (*const_tree* **type**,   [Target Hook]
        machine_mode **mode**, *int* ***punsignedp**, *const_tree* **funtype**, *int* **for_return**)

Like `PROMOTE_MODE`, but it is applied to outgoing function arguments or function return values. The target hook should return the new mode and possibly change ***punsignedp** if the promotion should change signedness. This function is called only for scalar *or pointer* types.

for_return allows to distinguish the promotion of arguments and return values. If it is 1, a return value is being promoted and `TARGET_FUNCTION_VALUE` must perform the same promotions done here. If it is 2, the returned mode should be that of the register in which an incoming parameter is copied, or the outgoing result is computed; then the hook should return the same mode as `promote_mode`, though the signedness may be different.

type can be NULL when promoting function arguments of libcalls.

The default is to not promote arguments and return values. You can also define the hook to `default_promote_function_mode_always_promote` if you would like to apply the same rules given by `PROMOTE_MODE`.

PARM_BOUNDARY   [Macro]

Normal alignment required for function parameters on the stack, in bits. All stack parameters receive at least this much alignment regardless of data type. On most machines, this is the same as the size of an integer.

STACK_BOUNDARY   [Macro]

Define this macro to the minimum alignment enforced by hardware for the stack pointer on this machine. The definition is a C expression for the desired alignment (measured in bits). This value is used as a default if PREFERRED_STACK_BOUNDARY is not defined. On most machines, this should be the same as PARM_BOUNDARY.

PREFERRED_STACK_BOUNDARY   [Macro]

Define this macro if you wish to preserve a certain alignment for the stack pointer, greater than what the hardware enforces. The definition is a C expression for the desired alignment (measured in bits). This macro must evaluate to a value equal to or larger than STACK_BOUNDARY.

INCOMING_STACK_BOUNDARY   [Macro]

Define this macro if the incoming stack boundary may be different from PREFERRED_STACK_BOUNDARY. This macro must evaluate to a value equal to or larger than STACK_BOUNDARY.

FUNCTION_BOUNDARY   [Macro]

Alignment required for a function entry point, in bits.

BIGGEST_ALIGNMENT   [Macro]

Biggest alignment that any data type can require on this machine, in bits. Note that this is not the biggest alignment that is supported, just the biggest alignment that, when violated, may cause a fault.

HOST_WIDE_INT TARGET_ABSOLUTE_BIGGEST_ALIGNMENT   [Target Hook]

If defined, this target hook specifies the absolute biggest alignment that a type or variable can have on this machine, otherwise, BIGGEST_ALIGNMENT is used.

MALLOC_ABI_ALIGNMENT   [Macro]

Alignment, in bits, a C conformant malloc implementation has to provide. If not defined, the default value is BITS_PER_WORD.

ATTRIBUTE_ALIGNED_VALUE   [Macro]

Alignment used by the __attribute__ ((aligned)) construct. If not defined, the default value is BIGGEST_ALIGNMENT.

MINIMUM_ATOMIC_ALIGNMENT   [Macro]

If defined, the smallest alignment, in bits, that can be given to an object that can be referenced in one operation, without disturbing any nearby object. Normally, this is BITS_PER_UNIT, but may be larger on machines that don't have byte or half-word store operations.

BIGGEST_FIELD_ALIGNMENT   [Macro]

Biggest alignment that any structure or union field can require on this machine, in bits. If defined, this overrides BIGGEST_ALIGNMENT for structure and union fields

only, unless the field alignment has been set by the `__attribute__ ((aligned (n)))`
construct.

`ADJUST_FIELD_ALIGN (field, computed)`   [Macro]

An expression for the alignment of a structure field *field* if the alignment computed
in the usual way (including applying of `BIGGEST_ALIGNMENT` and `BIGGEST_FIELD_`
`ALIGNMENT` to the alignment) is *computed*. It overrides alignment only if the field
alignment has not been set by the `__attribute__ ((aligned (n)))` construct.

`MAX_STACK_ALIGNMENT`   [Macro]

Biggest stack alignment guaranteed by the backend. Use this macro to specify the
maximum alignment of a variable on stack.

If not defined, the default value is `STACK_BOUNDARY`.

`MAX_OFILE_ALIGNMENT`   [Macro]

Biggest alignment supported by the object file format of this machine. Use this macro
to limit the alignment which can be specified using the `__attribute__ ((aligned`
`(n)))` construct. If not defined, the default value is `BIGGEST_ALIGNMENT`.

On systems that use ELF, the default (in 'config/elfos.h') is the largest supported
32-bit ELF section alignment representable on a 32-bit host e.g. '(((uint64_t)
1 << 28) * 8)'. On 32-bit ELF the largest supported section alignment in bits is
'(0x80000000 * 8)', but this is not representable on 32-bit hosts.

`DATA_ALIGNMENT (type, basic-align)`   [Macro]

If defined, a C expression to compute the alignment for a variable in the static store.
type is the data type, and *basic-align* is the alignment that the object would ordinarily
have. The value of this macro is used instead of that alignment to align the object.

If this macro is not defined, then *basic-align* is used.

One use of this macro is to increase alignment of medium-size data to make it all fit
in fewer cache lines. Another is to cause character arrays to be word-aligned so that
`strcpy` calls that copy constants to character arrays can be done inline.

`DATA_ABI_ALIGNMENT (type, basic-align)`   [Macro]

Similar to `DATA_ALIGNMENT`, but for the cases where the ABI mandates some alignment increase, instead of optimization only purposes. E.g. AMD x86-64 psABI says
that variables with array type larger than 15 bytes must be aligned to 16 byte boundaries.

If this macro is not defined, then *basic-align* is used.

`CONSTANT_ALIGNMENT (constant, basic-align)`   [Macro]

If defined, a C expression to compute the alignment given to a constant that is being
placed in memory. *constant* is the constant and *basic-align* is the alignment that
the object would ordinarily have. The value of this macro is used instead of that
alignment to align the object.

The default definition just returns *basic-align*.

The typical use of this macro is to increase alignment for string constants to be word
aligned so that `strcpy` calls that copy constants can be done inline.

LOCAL_ALIGNMENT (*type, basic-align***)** [Macro]

> If defined, a C expression to compute the alignment for a variable in the local store. *type* is the data type, and *basic-align* is the alignment that the object would ordinarily have. The value of this macro is used instead of that alignment to align the object.
>
> If this macro is not defined, then *basic-align* is used.
>
> One use of this macro is to increase alignment of medium-size data to make it all fit in fewer cache lines.
>
> If the value of this macro has a type, it should be an unsigned type.

HOST_WIDE_INT TARGET_VECTOR_ALIGNMENT (*const_tree type***)** [Target Hook]

> This hook can be used to define the alignment for a vector of type *type*, in order to comply with a platform ABI. The default is to require natural alignment for vector types. The alignment returned by this hook must be a power-of-two multiple of the default alignment of the vector element type.

STACK_SLOT_ALIGNMENT (*type, mode, basic-align***)** [Macro]

> If defined, a C expression to compute the alignment for stack slot. *type* is the data type, *mode* is the widest mode available, and *basic-align* is the alignment that the slot would ordinarily have. The value of this macro is used instead of that alignment to align the slot.
>
> If this macro is not defined, then *basic-align* is used when *type* is NULL. Otherwise, LOCAL_ALIGNMENT will be used.
>
> This macro is to set alignment of stack slot to the maximum alignment of all possible modes which the slot may have.
>
> If the value of this macro has a type, it should be an unsigned type.

LOCAL_DECL_ALIGNMENT (*decl***)** [Macro]

> If defined, a C expression to compute the alignment for a local variable *decl*.
>
> If this macro is not defined, then LOCAL_ALIGNMENT (TREE_TYPE (*decl*), DECL_ALIGN (*decl*)) is used.
>
> One use of this macro is to increase alignment of medium-size data to make it all fit in fewer cache lines.
>
> If the value of this macro has a type, it should be an unsigned type.

MINIMUM_ALIGNMENT (*exp, mode, align***)** [Macro]

> If defined, a C expression to compute the minimum required alignment for dynamic stack realignment purposes for *exp* (a type or decl), *mode*, assuming normal alignment *align*.
>
> If this macro is not defined, then *align* will be used.

EMPTY_FIELD_BOUNDARY [Macro]

> Alignment in bits to be given to a structure bit-field that follows an empty field such as int : 0;.
>
> If PCC_BITFIELD_TYPE_MATTERS is true, it overrides this macro.

STRUCTURE_SIZE_BOUNDARY   [Macro]

> Number of bits which any structure or union's size must be a multiple of. Each structure or union's size is rounded up to a multiple of this.

> If you do not define this macro, the default is the same as BITS_PER_UNIT.

STRICT_ALIGNMENT   [Macro]

> Define this macro to be the value 1 if instructions will fail to work if given data not on the nominal alignment. If instructions will merely go slower in that case, define this macro as 0.

PCC_BITFIELD_TYPE_MATTERS   [Macro]

> Define this if you wish to imitate the way many other C compilers handle alignment of bit-fields and the structures that contain them.

> The behavior is that the type written for a named bit-field (int, short, or other integer type) imposes an alignment for the entire structure, as if the structure really did contain an ordinary field of that type. In addition, the bit-field is placed within the structure so that it would fit within such a field, not crossing a boundary for it.

> Thus, on most machines, a named bit-field whose type is written as int would not cross a four-byte boundary, and would force four-byte alignment for the whole structure. (The alignment used may not be four bytes; it is controlled by the other alignment parameters.)

> An unnamed bit-field will not affect the alignment of the containing structure.

> If the macro is defined, its definition should be a C expression; a nonzero value for the expression enables this behavior.

> Note that if this macro is not defined, or its value is zero, some bit-fields may cross more than one alignment boundary. The compiler can support such references if there are 'insv', 'extv', and 'extzv' insns that can directly reference memory.

> The other known way of making bit-fields work is to define STRUCTURE_SIZE_ BOUNDARY as large as BIGGEST_ALIGNMENT. Then every structure can be accessed with fullwords.

> Unless the machine has bit-field instructions or you define STRUCTURE_SIZE_BOUNDARY that way, you must define PCC_BITFIELD_TYPE_MATTERS to have a nonzero value.

> If your aim is to make GCC use the same conventions for laying out bit-fields as are used by another compiler, here is how to investigate what the other compiler does. Compile and run this program:

```
struct foo1
{
  char x;
  char :0;
  char y;
};

struct foo2
{
  char x;
  int :0;
  char y;
};
```

```
main ()
{
  printf ("Size of foo1 is %d\n",
          sizeof (struct foo1));
  printf ("Size of foo2 is %d\n",
          sizeof (struct foo2));
  exit (0);
}
```

If this prints 2 and 5, then the compiler's behavior is what you would get from `PCC_BITFIELD_TYPE_MATTERS`.

`BITFIELD_NBYTES_LIMITED`   [Macro]

> Like `PCC_BITFIELD_TYPE_MATTERS` except that its effect is limited to aligning a bitfield within the structure.

`bool TARGET_ALIGN_ANON_BITFIELD (`*void*`)`   [Target Hook]

> When `PCC_BITFIELD_TYPE_MATTERS` is true this hook will determine whether unnamed bitfields affect the alignment of the containing structure. The hook should return true if the structure should inherit the alignment requirements of an unnamed bitfield's type.

`bool TARGET_NARROW_VOLATILE_BITFIELD (`*void*`)`   [Target Hook]

> This target hook should return `true` if accesses to volatile bitfields should use the narrowest mode possible. It should return `false` if these accesses should use the bitfield container type.
>
> The default is `false`.

`bool TARGET_MEMBER_TYPE_FORCES_BLK (`*const_tree* `field`,   [Target Hook]
>   *machine_mode* `mode`)`

> Return true if a structure, union or array containing *field* should be accessed using `BLKMODE`.
>
> If *field* is the only field in the structure, *mode* is its mode, otherwise *mode* is VOIDmode. *mode* is provided in the case where structures of one field would require the structure's mode to retain the field's mode.
>
> Normally, this is not needed.

`ROUND_TYPE_ALIGN (`*type*`,` *computed*`,` *specified*`)`   [Macro]

> Define this macro as an expression for the alignment of a type (given by *type* as a tree node) if the alignment computed in the usual way is *computed* and the alignment explicitly specified was *specified*.
>
> The default is to use *specified* if it is larger; otherwise, use the smaller of *computed* and `BIGGEST_ALIGNMENT`

`MAX_FIXED_MODE_SIZE`   [Macro]

> An integer expression for the size in bits of the largest integer machine mode that should actually be used. All integer machine modes of this size or smaller can be used for structures and unions with the appropriate sizes. If this macro is undefined, `GET_MODE_BITSIZE (DImode)` is assumed.

STACK_SAVEAREA_MODE (*save_level*)   [Macro]

> If defined, an expression of type `machine_mode` that specifies the mode of the save area operand of a `save_stack_level` named pattern (see Section 16.9 [Standard Names], page 356). *save_level* is one of `SAVE_BLOCK`, `SAVE_FUNCTION`, or `SAVE_NONLOCAL` and selects which of the three named patterns is having its mode specified.

> You need not define this macro if it always returns `Pmode`. You would most commonly define this macro if the `save_stack_level` patterns need to support both a 32- and a 64-bit mode.

STACK_SIZE_MODE   [Macro]

> If defined, an expression of type `machine_mode` that specifies the mode of the size increment operand of an `allocate_stack` named pattern (see Section 16.9 [Standard Names], page 356).

> You need not define this macro if it always returns `word_mode`. You would most commonly define this macro if the `allocate_stack` pattern needs to support both a 32- and a 64-bit mode.

machine_mode TARGET_LIBGCC_CMP_RETURN_MODE (*void*)   [Target Hook]

> This target hook should return the mode to be used for the return value of compare instructions expanded to libgcc calls. If not defined `word_mode` is returned which is the right choice for a majority of targets.

machine_mode TARGET_LIBGCC_SHIFT_COUNT_MODE (*void*)   [Target Hook]

> This target hook should return the mode to be used for the shift count operand of shift instructions expanded to libgcc calls. If not defined `word_mode` is returned which is the right choice for a majority of targets.

machine_mode TARGET_UNWIND_WORD_MODE (*void*)   [Target Hook]

> Return machine mode to be used for `_Unwind_Word` type. The default is to use `word_mode`.

bool TARGET_MS_BITFIELD_LAYOUT_P (*const_tree* record_type)   [Target Hook]

> This target hook returns `true` if bit-fields in the given *record_type* are to be laid out following the rules of Microsoft Visual C/C++, namely: (i) a bit-field won't share the same storage unit with the previous bit-field if their underlying types have different sizes, and the bit-field will be aligned to the highest alignment of the underlying types of itself and of the previous bit-field; (ii) a zero-sized bit-field will affect the alignment of the whole enclosing structure, even if it is unnamed; except that (iii) a zero-sized bit-field will be disregarded unless it follows another bit-field of nonzero size. If this hook returns `true`, other macros that control bit-field layout are ignored.

> When a bit-field is inserted into a packed record, the whole size of the underlying type is used by one or more same-size adjacent bit-fields (that is, if its long:3, 32 bits is used in the record, and any additional adjacent long bit-fields are packed into the same chunk of 32 bits. However, if the size changes, a new field of that size is allocated). In an unpacked record, this is the same as using alignment, but not equivalent when packing.

If both MS bit-fields and '`__attribute__((packed))`' are used, the latter will take precedence. If '`__attribute__((packed))`' is used on a single field when MS bit-fields are in use, it will take precedence for that field, but the alignment of the rest of the structure may affect its placement.

bool **TARGET_DECIMAL_FLOAT_SUPPORTED_P** (*void*)   [Target Hook]
 Returns true if the target supports decimal floating point.

bool **TARGET_FIXED_POINT_SUPPORTED_P** (*void*)   [Target Hook]
 Returns true if the target supports fixed-point arithmetic.

void **TARGET_EXPAND_TO_RTL_HOOK** (*void*)   [Target Hook]
 This hook is called just before expansion into rtl, allowing the target to perform additional initializations or analysis before the expansion. For example, the rs6000 port uses it to allocate a scratch stack slot for use in copying SDmode values between memory and floating point registers whenever the function being expanded has any SDmode usage.

void **TARGET_INSTANTIATE_DECLS** (*void*)   [Target Hook]
 This hook allows the backend to perform additional instantiations on rtl that are not actually in any insns yet, but will be later.

const char * **TARGET_MANGLE_TYPE** (*const_tree* **type**)   [Target Hook]
 If your target defines any fundamental types, or any types your target uses should be mangled differently from the default, define this hook to return the appropriate encoding for these types as part of a C++ mangled name. The *type* argument is the tree structure representing the type to be mangled. The hook may be applied to trees which are not target-specific fundamental types; it should return `NULL` for all such types, as well as arguments it does not recognize. If the return value is not `NULL`, it must point to a statically-allocated string constant.

 Target-specific fundamental types might be new fundamental types or qualified versions of ordinary fundamental types. Encode new fundamental types as '**u** *n* **name**', where *name* is the name used for the type in source code, and *n* is the length of *name* in decimal. Encode qualified versions of ordinary types as '**U** *n* **name** **code**', where *name* is the name used for the type qualifier in source code, *n* is the length of *name* as above, and *code* is the code used to represent the unqualified version of this type. (See `write_builtin_type` in '`cp/mangle.c`' for the list of codes.) In both cases the spaces are for clarity; do not include any spaces in your string.

 This hook is applied to types prior to typedef resolution. If the mangled name for a particular type depends only on that type's main variant, you can perform typedef resolution yourself using `TYPE_MAIN_VARIANT` before mangling.

 The default version of this hook always returns `NULL`, which is appropriate for a target that does not define any new fundamental types.

17.6 Layout of Source Language Data Types

These macros define the sizes and other characteristics of the standard basic data types used in programs being compiled. Unlike the macros in the previous section, these apply to specific features of C and related languages, rather than to fundamental aspects of storage layout.

INT_TYPE_SIZE   [Macro]
    A C expression for the size in bits of the type int on the target machine. If you don't define this, the default is one word.

SHORT_TYPE_SIZE   [Macro]
    A C expression for the size in bits of the type short on the target machine. If you don't define this, the default is half a word. (If this would be less than one storage unit, it is rounded up to one unit.)

LONG_TYPE_SIZE   [Macro]
    A C expression for the size in bits of the type long on the target machine. If you don't define this, the default is one word.

ADA_LONG_TYPE_SIZE   [Macro]
    On some machines, the size used for the Ada equivalent of the type long by a native Ada compiler differs from that used by C. In that situation, define this macro to be a C expression to be used for the size of that type. If you don't define this, the default is the value of LONG_TYPE_SIZE.

LONG_LONG_TYPE_SIZE   [Macro]
    A C expression for the size in bits of the type long long on the target machine. If you don't define this, the default is two words. If you want to support GNU Ada on your machine, the value of this macro must be at least 64.

CHAR_TYPE_SIZE   [Macro]
    A C expression for the size in bits of the type char on the target machine. If you don't define this, the default is BITS_PER_UNIT.

BOOL_TYPE_SIZE   [Macro]
    A C expression for the size in bits of the C++ type bool and C99 type _Bool on the target machine. If you don't define this, and you probably shouldn't, the default is CHAR_TYPE_SIZE.

FLOAT_TYPE_SIZE   [Macro]
    A C expression for the size in bits of the type float on the target machine. If you don't define this, the default is one word.

DOUBLE_TYPE_SIZE   [Macro]
    A C expression for the size in bits of the type double on the target machine. If you don't define this, the default is two words.

LONG_DOUBLE_TYPE_SIZE   [Macro]
    A C expression for the size in bits of the type long double on the target machine. If you don't define this, the default is two words.

SHORT_FRACT_TYPE_SIZE   [Macro]
    A C expression for the size in bits of the type short _Fract on the target machine. If you don't define this, the default is BITS_PER_UNIT.

FRACT_TYPE_SIZE   [Macro]
> A C expression for the size in bits of the type `_Fract` on the target machine. If you don't define this, the default is `BITS_PER_UNIT * 2`.

LONG_FRACT_TYPE_SIZE   [Macro]
> A C expression for the size in bits of the type `long _Fract` on the target machine. If you don't define this, the default is `BITS_PER_UNIT * 4`.

LONG_LONG_FRACT_TYPE_SIZE   [Macro]
> A C expression for the size in bits of the type `long long _Fract` on the target machine. If you don't define this, the default is `BITS_PER_UNIT * 8`.

SHORT_ACCUM_TYPE_SIZE   [Macro]
> A C expression for the size in bits of the type `short _Accum` on the target machine. If you don't define this, the default is `BITS_PER_UNIT * 2`.

ACCUM_TYPE_SIZE   [Macro]
> A C expression for the size in bits of the type `_Accum` on the target machine. If you don't define this, the default is `BITS_PER_UNIT * 4`.

LONG_ACCUM_TYPE_SIZE   [Macro]
> A C expression for the size in bits of the type `long _Accum` on the target machine. If you don't define this, the default is `BITS_PER_UNIT * 8`.

LONG_LONG_ACCUM_TYPE_SIZE   [Macro]
> A C expression for the size in bits of the type `long long _Accum` on the target machine. If you don't define this, the default is `BITS_PER_UNIT * 16`.

LIBGCC2_GNU_PREFIX   [Macro]
> This macro corresponds to the `TARGET_LIBFUNC_GNU_PREFIX` target hook and should be defined if that hook is overriden to be true. It causes function names in libgcc to be changed to use a `__gnu_` prefix for their name rather than the default `__`. A port which uses this macro should also arrange to use 't-gnu-prefix' in the libgcc 'config.host'.

WIDEST_HARDWARE_FP_SIZE   [Macro]
> A C expression for the size in bits of the widest floating-point format supported by the hardware. If you define this macro, you must specify a value less than or equal to the value of `LONG_DOUBLE_TYPE_SIZE`. If you do not define this macro, the value of `LONG_DOUBLE_TYPE_SIZE` is the default.

DEFAULT_SIGNED_CHAR   [Macro]
> An expression whose value is 1 or 0, according to whether the type `char` should be signed or unsigned by default. The user can always override this default with the options '-fsigned-char' and '-funsigned-char'.

bool TARGET_DEFAULT_SHORT_ENUMS (*void*)   [Target Hook]
> This target hook should return true if the compiler should give an `enum` type only as many bytes as it takes to represent the range of possible values of that type. It should return false if all `enum` types should be allocated like `int`.
>
> The default is to return false.

SIZE_TYPE   [Macro]

> A C expression for a string describing the name of the data type to use for size values. The typedef name `size_t` is defined using the contents of the string.
>
> The string can contain more than one keyword. If so, separate them with spaces, and write first any length keyword, then `unsigned` if appropriate, and finally `int`. The string must exactly match one of the data type names defined in the function `c_common_nodes_and_builtins` in the file 'c-family/c-common.c'. You may not omit `int` or change the order—that would cause the compiler to crash on startup.
>
> If you don't define this macro, the default is `"long unsigned int"`.

SIZETYPE   [Macro]

> GCC defines internal types (`sizetype`, `ssizetype`, `bitsizetype` and `sbitsizetype`) for expressions dealing with size. This macro is a C expression for a string describing the name of the data type from which the precision of `sizetype` is extracted.
>
> The string has the same restrictions as `SIZE_TYPE` string.
>
> If you don't define this macro, the default is `SIZE_TYPE`.

PTRDIFF_TYPE   [Macro]

> A C expression for a string describing the name of the data type to use for the result of subtracting two pointers. The typedef name `ptrdiff_t` is defined using the contents of the string. See `SIZE_TYPE` above for more information.
>
> If you don't define this macro, the default is `"long int"`.

WCHAR_TYPE   [Macro]

> A C expression for a string describing the name of the data type to use for wide characters. The typedef name `wchar_t` is defined using the contents of the string. See `SIZE_TYPE` above for more information.
>
> If you don't define this macro, the default is `"int"`.

WCHAR_TYPE_SIZE   [Macro]

> A C expression for the size in bits of the data type for wide characters. This is used in `cpp`, which cannot make use of `WCHAR_TYPE`.

WINT_TYPE   [Macro]

> A C expression for a string describing the name of the data type to use for wide characters passed to `printf` and returned from `getwc`. The typedef name `wint_t` is defined using the contents of the string. See `SIZE_TYPE` above for more information.
>
> If you don't define this macro, the default is `"unsigned int"`.

INTMAX_TYPE   [Macro]

> A C expression for a string describing the name of the data type that can represent any value of any standard or extended signed integer type. The typedef name `intmax_t` is defined using the contents of the string. See `SIZE_TYPE` above for more information.
>
> If you don't define this macro, the default is the first of `"int"`, `"long int"`, or `"long long int"` that has as much precision as `long long int`.

UINTMAX_TYPE   [Macro]
> A C expression for a string describing the name of the data type that can represent
> any value of any standard or extended unsigned integer type. The typedef name
> uintmax_t is defined using the contents of the string. See SIZE_TYPE above for more
> information.
>
> If you don't define this macro, the default is the first of "unsigned int", "long
> unsigned int", or "long long unsigned int" that has as much precision as long
> long unsigned int.

SIG_ATOMIC_TYPE   [Macro]
INT8_TYPE   [Macro]
INT16_TYPE   [Macro]
INT32_TYPE   [Macro]
INT64_TYPE   [Macro]
UINT8_TYPE   [Macro]
UINT16_TYPE   [Macro]
UINT32_TYPE   [Macro]
UINT64_TYPE   [Macro]
INT_LEAST8_TYPE   [Macro]
INT_LEAST16_TYPE   [Macro]
INT_LEAST32_TYPE   [Macro]
INT_LEAST64_TYPE   [Macro]
UINT_LEAST8_TYPE   [Macro]
UINT_LEAST16_TYPE   [Macro]
UINT_LEAST32_TYPE   [Macro]
UINT_LEAST64_TYPE   [Macro]
INT_FAST8_TYPE   [Macro]
INT_FAST16_TYPE   [Macro]
INT_FAST32_TYPE   [Macro]
INT_FAST64_TYPE   [Macro]
UINT_FAST8_TYPE   [Macro]
UINT_FAST16_TYPE   [Macro]
UINT_FAST32_TYPE   [Macro]
UINT_FAST64_TYPE   [Macro]
INTPTR_TYPE   [Macro]
UINTPTR_TYPE   [Macro]
> C expressions for the standard types sig_atomic_t, int8_t, int16_t, int32_t,
> int64_t, uint8_t, uint16_t, uint32_t, uint64_t, int_least8_t, int_least16_t,
> int_least32_t, int_least64_t, uint_least8_t, uint_least16_t, uint_least32_
> t, uint_least64_t, int_fast8_t, int_fast16_t, int_fast32_t, int_fast64_t,
> uint_fast8_t, uint_fast16_t, uint_fast32_t, uint_fast64_t, intptr_t, and
> uintptr_t. See SIZE_TYPE above for more information.
>
> If any of these macros evaluates to a null pointer, the corresponding type is not
> supported; if GCC is configured to provide <stdint.h> in such a case, the header
> provided may not conform to C99, depending on the type in question. The defaults
> for all of these macros are null pointers.

TARGET_PTRMEMFUNC_VBIT_LOCATION   [Macro]

The C++ compiler represents a pointer-to-member-function with a struct that looks
like:

```
struct {
  union {
    void (*fn)();
    ptrdiff_t vtable_index;
  };
  ptrdiff_t delta;
};
```

The C++ compiler must use one bit to indicate whether the function that will be
called through a pointer-to-member-function is virtual. Normally, we assume that
the low-order bit of a function pointer must always be zero. Then, by ensuring that
the vtable_index is odd, we can distinguish which variant of the union is in use. But,
on some platforms function pointers can be odd, and so this doesn't work. In that
case, we use the low-order bit of the `delta` field, and shift the remainder of the `delta`
field to the left.

GCC will automatically make the right selection about where to store this bit using
the `FUNCTION_BOUNDARY` setting for your platform. However, some platforms such as
ARM/Thumb have `FUNCTION_BOUNDARY` set such that functions always start at even
addresses, but the lowest bit of pointers to functions indicate whether the function at
that address is in ARM or Thumb mode. If this is the case of your architecture, you
should define this macro to `ptrmemfunc_vbit_in_delta`.

In general, you should not have to define this macro. On architectures in which
function addresses are always even, according to `FUNCTION_BOUNDARY`, GCC will automatically define this macro to `ptrmemfunc_vbit_in_pfn`.

TARGET_VTABLE_USES_DESCRIPTORS   [Macro]

Normally, the C++ compiler uses function pointers in vtables. This macro allows the
target to change to use "function descriptors" instead. Function descriptors are found
on targets for whom a function pointer is actually a small data structure. Normally
the data structure consists of the actual code address plus a data pointer to which
the function's data is relative.

If vtables are used, the value of this macro should be the number of words that the
function descriptor occupies.

TARGET_VTABLE_ENTRY_ALIGN   [Macro]

By default, the vtable entries are void pointers, the so the alignment is the same as
pointer alignment. The value of this macro specifies the alignment of the vtable entry
in bits. It should be defined only when special alignment is necessary. */

TARGET_VTABLE_DATA_ENTRY_DISTANCE   [Macro]

There are a few non-descriptor entries in the vtable at offsets below zero. If these
entries must be padded (say, to preserve the alignment specified by `TARGET_VTABLE_
ENTRY_ALIGN`), set this to the number of words in each data entry.

17.7 Register Usage

This section explains how to describe what registers the target machine has, and how (in general) they can be used.

The description of which registers a specific instruction can use is done with register classes; see Section 17.8 [Register Classes], page 465. For information on using registers to access a stack frame, see Section 17.9.4 [Frame Registers], page 483. For passing values in registers, see Section 17.9.7 [Register Arguments], page 489. For returning values in registers, see Section 17.9.8 [Scalar Return], page 496.

17.7.1 Basic Characteristics of Registers

Registers have various characteristics.

FIRST_PSEUDO_REGISTER   [Macro]
      Number of hardware registers known to the compiler. They receive numbers 0 through
      FIRST_PSEUDO_REGISTER-1; thus, the first pseudo register's number really is assigned
      the number FIRST_PSEUDO_REGISTER.

FIXED_REGISTERS   [Macro]
      An initializer that says which registers are used for fixed purposes all throughout the
      compiled code and are therefore not available for general allocation. These would
      include the stack pointer, the frame pointer (except on machines where that can be
      used as a general register when no frame pointer is needed), the program counter
      on machines where that is considered one of the addressable registers, and any other
      numbered register with a standard use.

      This information is expressed as a sequence of numbers, separated by commas and
      surrounded by braces. The nth number is 1 if register n is fixed, 0 otherwise.

      The table initialized from this macro, and the table initialized by the following
      one, may be overridden at run time either automatically, by the actions of the
      macro CONDITIONAL_REGISTER_USAGE, or by the user with the command options
      '-ffixed-reg', '-fcall-used-reg' and '-fcall-saved-reg'.

CALL_USED_REGISTERS   [Macro]
      Like FIXED_REGISTERS but has 1 for each register that is clobbered (in general) by
      function calls as well as for fixed registers. This macro therefore identifies the registers
      that are not available for general allocation of values that must live across function
      calls.

      If a register has 0 in CALL_USED_REGISTERS, the compiler automatically saves it on
      function entry and restores it on function exit, if the register is used within the
      function.

CALL_REALLY_USED_REGISTERS   [Macro]
      Like CALL_USED_REGISTERS except this macro doesn't require that the entire set of
      FIXED_REGISTERS be included. (CALL_USED_REGISTERS must be a superset of FIXED_
      REGISTERS). This macro is optional. If not specified, it defaults to the value of
      CALL_USED_REGISTERS.

HARD_REGNO_CALL_PART_CLOBBERED (*regno*, *mode*)   [Macro]
 A C expression that is nonzero if it is not permissible to store a value of mode *mode*
 in hard register number *regno* across a call without some part of it being clobbered.
 For most machines this macro need not be defined. It is only required for machines
 that do not preserve the entire contents of a register across a call.

void TARGET_CONDITIONAL_REGISTER_USAGE (*void*)   [Target Hook]
 This hook may conditionally modify five variables `fixed_regs`, `call_used_regs`,
 `global_regs`, `reg_names`, and `reg_class_contents`, to take into account any
 dependence of these register sets on target flags. The first three of these are of
 type `char []` (interpreted as boolean vectors). `global_regs` is a `const char`
 `*[]`, and `reg_class_contents` is a `HARD_REG_SET`. Before the macro is called,
 `fixed_regs`, `call_used_regs`, `reg_class_contents`, and `reg_names` have been
 initialized from `FIXED_REGISTERS`, `CALL_USED_REGISTERS`, `REG_CLASS_CONTENTS`,
 and `REGISTER_NAMES`, respectively. `global_regs` has been cleared, and any
 '`-ffixed-`*reg*', '`-fcall-used-`*reg*' and '`-fcall-saved-`*reg*' command options have
 been applied.

 If the usage of an entire class of registers depends on the target flags, you may indicate
 this to GCC by using this macro to modify `fixed_regs` and `call_used_regs` to 1
 for each of the registers in the classes which should not be used by GCC. Also
 make `define_register_constraints` return `NO_REGS` for constraints that shouldn't
 be used.

 (However, if this class is not included in `GENERAL_REGS` and all of the insn patterns
 whose constraints permit this class are controlled by target switches, then GCC will
 automatically avoid using these registers when the target switches are opposed to
 them.)

INCOMING_REGNO (*out*)   [Macro]
 Define this macro if the target machine has register windows. This C expression
 returns the register number as seen by the called function corresponding to the register
 number *out* as seen by the calling function. Return *out* if register number *out* is not
 an outbound register.

OUTGOING_REGNO (*in*)   [Macro]
 Define this macro if the target machine has register windows. This C expression
 returns the register number as seen by the calling function corresponding to the
 register number *in* as seen by the called function. Return *in* if register number *in* is
 not an inbound register.

LOCAL_REGNO (*regno*)   [Macro]
 Define this macro if the target machine has register windows. This C expression
 returns true if the register is call-saved but is in the register window. Unlike most
 call-saved registers, such registers need not be explicitly restored on function exit or
 during non-local gotos.

PC_REGNUM   [Macro]
 If the program counter has a register number, define this as that register number.
 Otherwise, do not define it.

17.7.2 Order of Allocation of Registers

Registers are allocated in order.

REG_ALLOC_ORDER   [Macro]

    If defined, an initializer for a vector of integers, containing the numbers of hard registers in the order in which GCC should prefer to use them (from most preferred to least).

    If this macro is not defined, registers are used lowest numbered first (all else being equal).

    One use of this macro is on machines where the highest numbered registers must always be saved and the save-multiple-registers instruction supports only sequences of consecutive registers. On such machines, define `REG_ALLOC_ORDER` to be an initializer that lists the highest numbered allocable register first.

ADJUST_REG_ALLOC_ORDER   [Macro]

    A C statement (sans semicolon) to choose the order in which to allocate hard registers for pseudo-registers local to a basic block.

    Store the desired register order in the array `reg_alloc_order`. Element 0 should be the register to allocate first; element 1, the next register; and so on.

    The macro body should not assume anything about the contents of `reg_alloc_order` before execution of the macro.

    On most machines, it is not necessary to define this macro.

HONOR_REG_ALLOC_ORDER   [Macro]

    Normally, IRA tries to estimate the costs for saving a register in the prologue and restoring it in the epilogue. This discourages it from using call-saved registers. If a machine wants to ensure that IRA allocates registers in the order given by REG_ALLOC_ORDER even if some call-saved registers appear earlier than call-used ones, then define this macro as a C expression to nonzero. Default is 0.

IRA_HARD_REGNO_ADD_COST_MULTIPLIER (*regno*)   [Macro]

    In some case register allocation order is not enough for the Integrated Register Allocator (IRA) to generate a good code. If this macro is defined, it should return a floating point value based on *regno*. The cost of using *regno* for a pseudo will be increased by approximately the pseudo's usage frequency times the value returned by this macro. Not defining this macro is equivalent to having it always return `0.0`.

    On most machines, it is not necessary to define this macro.

17.7.3 How Values Fit in Registers

This section discusses the macros that describe which kinds of values (specifically, which machine modes) each register can hold, and how many consecutive registers are needed for a given mode.

HARD_REGNO_NREGS (*regno*, *mode*)   [Macro]

    A C expression for the number of consecutive hard registers, starting at register number *regno*, required to hold a value of mode *mode*. This macro must never return zero, even if a register cannot hold the requested mode - indicate that with HARD_REGNO_MODE_OK and/or CANNOT_CHANGE_MODE_CLASS instead.

On a machine where all registers are exactly one word, a suitable definition of this macro is

```
#define HARD_REGNO_NREGS(REGNO, MODE)            \
  ((GET_MODE_SIZE (MODE) + UNITS_PER_WORD - 1)   \
   / UNITS_PER_WORD)
```

HARD_REGNO_NREGS_HAS_PADDING (*regno, mode*)   [Macro]

A C expression that is nonzero if a value of mode *mode*, stored in memory, ends with padding that causes it to take up more space than in registers starting at register number *regno* (as determined by multiplying GCC's notion of the size of the register when containing this mode by the number of registers returned by HARD_REGNO_NREGS). By default this is zero.

For example, if a floating-point value is stored in three 32-bit registers but takes up 128 bits in memory, then this would be nonzero.

This macros only needs to be defined if there are cases where subreg_get_info would otherwise wrongly determine that a subreg can be represented by an offset to the register number, when in fact such a subreg would contain some of the padding not stored in registers and so not be representable.

HARD_REGNO_NREGS_WITH_PADDING (*regno, mode*)   [Macro]

For values of *regno* and *mode* for which HARD_REGNO_NREGS_HAS_PADDING returns nonzero, a C expression returning the greater number of registers required to hold the value including any padding. In the example above, the value would be four.

REGMODE_NATURAL_SIZE (*mode*)   [Macro]

Define this macro if the natural size of registers that hold values of mode *mode* is not the word size. It is a C expression that should give the natural size in bytes for the specified mode. It is used by the register allocator to try to optimize its results. This happens for example on SPARC 64-bit where the natural size of floating-point registers is still 32-bit.

HARD_REGNO_MODE_OK (*regno, mode*)   [Macro]

A C expression that is nonzero if it is permissible to store a value of mode *mode* in hard register number *regno* (or in several registers starting with that one). For a machine where all registers are equivalent, a suitable definition is

```
#define HARD_REGNO_MODE_OK(REGNO, MODE) 1
```

You need not include code to check for the numbers of fixed registers, because the allocation mechanism considers them to be always occupied.

On some machines, double-precision values must be kept in even/odd register pairs. You can implement that by defining this macro to reject odd register numbers for such modes.

The minimum requirement for a mode to be OK in a register is that the 'mov*mode*' instruction pattern support moves between the register and other hard register in the same class and that moving a value into the register and back out not alter it.

Since the same instruction used to move word_mode will work for all narrower integer modes, it is not necessary on any machine for HARD_REGNO_MODE_OK to distinguish between these modes, provided you define patterns 'movhi', etc., to take advantage of this. This is useful because of the interaction between HARD_REGNO_MODE_OK and MODES_TIEABLE_P; it is very desirable for all integer modes to be tieable.

Many machines have special registers for floating point arithmetic. Often people assume that floating point machine modes are allowed only in floating point registers. This is not true. Any registers that can hold integers can safely *hold* a floating point machine mode, whether or not floating arithmetic can be done on it in those registers. Integer move instructions can be used to move the values.

On some machines, though, the converse is true: fixed-point machine modes may not go in floating registers. This is true if the floating registers normalize any value stored in them, because storing a non-floating value there would garble it. In this case, HARD_REGNO_MODE_OK should reject fixed-point machine modes in floating registers. But if the floating registers do not automatically normalize, if you can store any bit pattern in one and retrieve it unchanged without a trap, then any machine mode may go in a floating register, so you can define this macro to say so.

The primary significance of special floating registers is rather that they are the registers acceptable in floating point arithmetic instructions. However, this is of no concern to HARD_REGNO_MODE_OK. You handle it by writing the proper constraints for those instructions.

On some machines, the floating registers are especially slow to access, so that it is better to store a value in a stack frame than in such a register if floating point arithmetic is not being done. As long as the floating registers are not in class GENERAL_REGS, they will not be used unless some pattern's constraint asks for one.

HARD_REGNO_RENAME_OK (*from*, *to*)   [Macro]
A C expression that is nonzero if it is OK to rename a hard register *from* to another hard register *to*.

One common use of this macro is to prevent renaming of a register to another register that is not saved by a prologue in an interrupt handler.

The default is always nonzero.

MODES_TIEABLE_P (*mode1*, *mode2*)   [Macro]
A C expression that is nonzero if a value of mode *mode1* is accessible in mode *mode2* without copying.

If HARD_REGNO_MODE_OK (*r*, *mode1*) and HARD_REGNO_MODE_OK (*r*, *mode2*) are always the same for any *r*, then MODES_TIEABLE_P (*mode1*, *mode2*) should be nonzero. If they differ for any *r*, you should define this macro to return zero unless some other mechanism ensures the accessibility of the value in a narrower mode.

You should define this macro to return nonzero in as many cases as possible since doing so will allow GCC to perform better register allocation.

bool TARGET_HARD_REGNO_SCRATCH_OK (*unsigned int* **regno**)   [Target Hook]
This target hook should return **true** if it is OK to use a hard register *regno* as scratch reg in peephole2.

One common use of this macro is to prevent using of a register that is not saved by a prologue in an interrupt handler.

The default version of this hook always returns **true**.

AVOID_CCMODE_COPIES   [Macro]

>   Define this macro if the compiler should avoid copies to/from **CCmode** registers. You should only define this macro if support for copying to/from **CCmode** is incomplete.

17.7.4 Handling Leaf Functions

On some machines, a leaf function (i.e., one which makes no calls) can run more efficiently if it does not make its own register window. Often this means it is required to receive its arguments in the registers where they are passed by the caller, instead of the registers where they would normally arrive.

The special treatment for leaf functions generally applies only when other conditions are met; for example, often they may use only those registers for its own variables and temporaries. We use the term "leaf function" to mean a function that is suitable for this special handling, so that functions with no calls are not necessarily "leaf functions".

GCC assigns register numbers before it knows whether the function is suitable for leaf function treatment. So it needs to renumber the registers in order to output a leaf function. The following macros accomplish this.

LEAF_REGISTERS   [Macro]

>   Name of a char vector, indexed by hard register number, which contains 1 for a register that is allowable in a candidate for leaf function treatment.
>
>   If leaf function treatment involves renumbering the registers, then the registers marked here should be the ones before renumbering—those that GCC would ordinarily allocate. The registers which will actually be used in the assembler code, after renumbering, should not be marked with 1 in this vector.
>
>   Define this macro only if the target machine offers a way to optimize the treatment of leaf functions.

LEAF_REG_REMAP (*regno*)   [Macro]

>   A C expression whose value is the register number to which *regno* should be renumbered, when a function is treated as a leaf function.
>
>   If *regno* is a register number which should not appear in a leaf function before renumbering, then the expression should yield −1, which will cause the compiler to abort.
>
>   Define this macro only if the target machine offers a way to optimize the treatment of leaf functions, and registers need to be renumbered to do this.

TARGET_ASM_FUNCTION_PROLOGUE and **TARGET_ASM_FUNCTION_EPILOGUE** must usually treat leaf functions specially. They can test the C variable **current_function_is_leaf** which is nonzero for leaf functions. **current_function_is_leaf** is set prior to local register allocation and is valid for the remaining compiler passes. They can also test the C variable **current_function_uses_only_leaf_regs** which is nonzero for leaf functions which only use leaf registers. **current_function_uses_only_leaf_regs** is valid after all passes that modify the instructions have been run and is only useful if **LEAF_REGISTERS** is defined.

17.7.5 Registers That Form a Stack

There are special features to handle computers where some of the "registers" form a stack. Stack registers are normally written by pushing onto the stack, and are numbered relative to the top of the stack.

Currently, GCC can only handle one group of stack-like registers, and they must be consecutively numbered. Furthermore, the existing support for stack-like registers is specific to the 80387 floating point coprocessor. If you have a new architecture that uses stack-like registers, you will need to do substantial work on 'reg-stack.c' and write your machine description to cooperate with it, as well as defining these macros.

STACK_REGS   [Macro]
    Define this if the machine has any stack-like registers.

STACK_REG_COVER_CLASS   [Macro]
    This is a cover class containing the stack registers. Define this if the machine has any stack-like registers.

FIRST_STACK_REG   [Macro]
    The number of the first stack-like register. This one is the top of the stack.

LAST_STACK_REG   [Macro]
    The number of the last stack-like register. This one is the bottom of the stack.

17.8 Register Classes

On many machines, the numbered registers are not all equivalent. For example, certain registers may not be allowed for indexed addressing; certain registers may not be allowed in some instructions. These machine restrictions are described to the compiler using *register classes*.

You define a number of register classes, giving each one a name and saying which of the registers belong to it. Then you can specify register classes that are allowed as operands to particular instruction patterns.

In general, each register will belong to several classes. In fact, one class must be named ALL_REGS and contain all the registers. Another class must be named NO_REGS and contain no registers. Often the union of two classes will be another class; however, this is not required.

One of the classes must be named GENERAL_REGS. There is nothing terribly special about the name, but the operand constraint letters 'r' and 'g' specify this class. If GENERAL_REGS is the same as ALL_REGS, just define it as a macro which expands to ALL_REGS.

Order the classes so that if class x is contained in class y then x has a lower class number than y.

The way classes other than GENERAL_REGS are specified in operand constraints is through machine-dependent operand constraint letters. You can define such letters to correspond to various classes, then use them in operand constraints.

You must define the narrowest register classes for allocatable registers, so that each class either has no subclasses, or that for some mode, the move cost between registers within the class is cheaper than moving a register in the class to or from memory (see Section 17.16 [Costs], page 525).

You should define a class for the union of two classes whenever some instruction allows both classes. For example, if an instruction allows either a floating point (coprocessor) register or a general register for a certain operand, you should define a class FLOAT_OR_GENERAL_REGS which includes both of them. Otherwise you will get suboptimal code, or even internal compiler errors when reload cannot find a register in the class computed via reg_class_subunion.

You must also specify certain redundant information about the register classes: for each class, which classes contain it and which ones are contained in it; for each pair of classes, the largest class contained in their union.

When a value occupying several consecutive registers is expected in a certain class, all the registers used must belong to that class. Therefore, register classes cannot be used to enforce a requirement for a register pair to start with an even-numbered register. The way to specify this requirement is with HARD_REGNO_MODE_OK.

Register classes used for input-operands of bitwise-and or shift instructions have a special requirement: each such class must have, for each fixed-point machine mode, a subclass whose registers can transfer that mode to or from memory. For example, on some machines, the operations for single-byte values (QImode) are limited to certain registers. When this is so, each register class that is used in a bitwise-and or shift instruction must have a subclass consisting of registers from which single-byte values can be loaded or stored. This is so that PREFERRED_RELOAD_CLASS can always have a possible value to return.

enum reg_class   [Data type]
    An enumerated type that must be defined with all the register class names as enumerated values. NO_REGS must be first. ALL_REGS must be the last register class, followed by one more enumerated value, LIM_REG_CLASSES, which is not a register class but rather tells how many classes there are.

    Each register class has a number, which is the value of casting the class name to type int. The number serves as an index in many of the tables described below.

N_REG_CLASSES   [Macro]
    The number of distinct register classes, defined as follows:

```
#define N_REG_CLASSES (int) LIM_REG_CLASSES
```

REG_CLASS_NAMES   [Macro]
    An initializer containing the names of the register classes as C string constants. These names are used in writing some of the debugging dumps.

REG_CLASS_CONTENTS   [Macro]
    An initializer containing the contents of the register classes, as integers which are bit masks. The nth integer specifies the contents of class n. The way the integer mask is interpreted is that register r is in the class if mask & (1 << r) is 1.

    When the machine has more than 32 registers, an integer does not suffice. Then the integers are replaced by sub-initializers, braced groupings containing several integers. Each sub-initializer must be suitable as an initializer for the type HARD_REG_SET which is defined in 'hard-reg-set.h'. In this situation, the first integer in each sub-initializer corresponds to registers 0 through 31, the second integer to registers 32 through 63, and so on.

REGNO_REG_CLASS (*regno*)   [Macro]

> A C expression whose value is a register class containing hard register *regno*. In general there is more than one such class; choose a class which is *minimal*, meaning that no smaller class also contains the register.

BASE_REG_CLASS   [Macro]

> A macro whose definition is the name of the class to which a valid base register must belong. A base register is one used in an address which is the register value plus a displacement.

MODE_BASE_REG_CLASS (*mode*)   [Macro]

> This is a variation of the BASE_REG_CLASS macro which allows the selection of a base register in a mode dependent manner. If *mode* is VOIDmode then it should return the same value as BASE_REG_CLASS.

MODE_BASE_REG_REG_CLASS (*mode*)   [Macro]

> A C expression whose value is the register class to which a valid base register must belong in order to be used in a base plus index register address. You should define this macro if base plus index addresses have different requirements than other base register uses.

MODE_CODE_BASE_REG_CLASS (*mode*, *address_space*, *outer_code*,   [Macro]
    index_code)

> A C expression whose value is the register class to which a valid base register for a memory reference in mode *mode* to address space *address_space* must belong. *outer_code* and *index_code* define the context in which the base register occurs. *outer_code* is the code of the immediately enclosing expression (MEM for the top level of an address, ADDRESS for something that occurs in an address_operand). *index_code* is the code of the corresponding index expression if *outer_code* is PLUS; SCRATCH otherwise.

INDEX_REG_CLASS   [Macro]

> A macro whose definition is the name of the class to which a valid index register must belong. An index register is one used in an address where its value is either multiplied by a scale factor or added to another register (as well as added to a displacement).

REGNO_OK_FOR_BASE_P (*num*)   [Macro]

> A C expression which is nonzero if register number *num* is suitable for use as a base register in operand addresses.

REGNO_MODE_OK_FOR_BASE_P (*num*, *mode*)   [Macro]

> A C expression that is just like REGNO_OK_FOR_BASE_P, except that that expression may examine the mode of the memory reference in *mode*. You should define this macro if the mode of the memory reference affects whether a register may be used as a base register. If you define this macro, the compiler will use it instead of REGNO_OK_FOR_BASE_P. The mode may be VOIDmode for addresses that appear outside a MEM, i.e., as an address_operand.

`REGNO_MODE_OK_FOR_REG_BASE_P` (*num*, *mode*)   [Macro]

>   A C expression which is nonzero if register number *num* is suitable for use as a base register in base plus index operand addresses, accessing memory in mode *mode*. It may be either a suitable hard register or a pseudo register that has been allocated such a hard register. You should define this macro if base plus index addresses have different requirements than other base register uses.
>
>   Use of this macro is deprecated; please use the more general `REGNO_MODE_CODE_OK_FOR_BASE_P`.

`REGNO_MODE_CODE_OK_FOR_BASE_P` (*num*, *mode*, *address_space*,   [Macro]
    outer_code, *index_code*)

>   A C expression which is nonzero if register number *num* is suitable for use as a base register in operand addresses, accessing memory in mode *mode* in address space *address_space*. This is similar to `REGNO_MODE_OK_FOR_BASE_P`, except that that expression may examine the context in which the register appears in the memory reference. *outer_code* is the code of the immediately enclosing expression (`MEM` if at the top level of the address, `ADDRESS` for something that occurs in an `address_operand`). *index_code* is the code of the corresponding index expression if *outer_code* is `PLUS`; `SCRATCH` otherwise. The mode may be `VOIDmode` for addresses that appear outside a `MEM`, i.e., as an `address_operand`.

`REGNO_OK_FOR_INDEX_P` (*num*)   [Macro]

>   A C expression which is nonzero if register number *num* is suitable for use as an index register in operand addresses. It may be either a suitable hard register or a pseudo register that has been allocated such a hard register.
>
>   The difference between an index register and a base register is that the index register may be scaled. If an address involves the sum of two registers, neither one of them scaled, then either one may be labeled the "base" and the other the "index"; but whichever labeling is used must fit the machine's constraints of which registers may serve in each capacity. The compiler will try both labelings, looking for one that is valid, and will reload one or both registers only if neither labeling works.

`reg_class_t TARGET_PREFERRED_RENAME_CLASS` (*reg_class_t*   [Target Hook]
    rclass)

>   A target hook that places additional preference on the register class to use when it is necessary to rename a register in class *rclass* to another class, or perhaps *NO_REGS*, if no preferred register class is found or hook `preferred_rename_class` is not implemented. Sometimes returning a more restrictive class makes better code. For example, on ARM, thumb-2 instructions using `LO_REGS` may be smaller than instructions using `GENERIC_REGS`. By returning `LO_REGS` from `preferred_rename_class`, code size can be reduced.

`reg_class_t TARGET_PREFERRED_RELOAD_CLASS` (*rtx x*, *reg_class_t*   [Target Hook]
    rclass)

>   A target hook that places additional restrictions on the register class to use when it is necessary to copy value *x* into a register in class *rclass*. The value is a register class; perhaps *rclass*, or perhaps another, smaller class.
>
>   The default version of this hook always returns value of `rclass` argument.

Sometimes returning a more restrictive class makes better code. For example, on the 68000, when *x* is an integer constant that is in range for a 'moveq' instruction, the value of this macro is always DATA_REGS as long as *rclass* includes the data registers. Requiring a data register guarantees that a 'moveq' will be used.

One case where TARGET_PREFERRED_RELOAD_CLASS must not return *rclass* is if *x* is a legitimate constant which cannot be loaded into some register class. By returning NO_REGS you can force *x* into a memory location. For example, rs6000 can load immediate values into general-purpose registers, but does not have an instruction for loading an immediate value into a floating-point register, so TARGET_PREFERRED_ RELOAD_CLASS returns NO_REGS when *x* is a floating-point constant. If the constant can't be loaded into any kind of register, code generation will be better if TARGET_ LEGITIMATE_CONSTANT_P makes the constant illegitimate instead of using TARGET_ PREFERRED_RELOAD_CLASS.

If an insn has pseudos in it after register allocation, reload will go through the alternatives and call repeatedly TARGET_PREFERRED_RELOAD_CLASS to find the best one. Returning NO_REGS, in this case, makes reload add a ! in front of the constraint: the x86 back-end uses this feature to discourage usage of 387 registers when math is done in the SSE registers (and vice versa).

PREFERRED_RELOAD_CLASS (*x*, *class*) [Macro]

A C expression that places additional restrictions on the register class to use when it is necessary to copy value *x* into a register in class *class*. The value is a register class; perhaps *class*, or perhaps another, smaller class. On many machines, the following definition is safe:

```
#define PREFERRED_RELOAD_CLASS(X,CLASS) CLASS
```

Sometimes returning a more restrictive class makes better code. For example, on the 68000, when *x* is an integer constant that is in range for a 'moveq' instruction, the value of this macro is always DATA_REGS as long as *class* includes the data registers. Requiring a data register guarantees that a 'moveq' will be used.

One case where PREFERRED_RELOAD_CLASS must not return *class* is if *x* is a legitimate constant which cannot be loaded into some register class. By returning NO_REGS you can force *x* into a memory location. For example, rs6000 can load immediate values into general-purpose registers, but does not have an instruction for loading an immediate value into a floating-point register, so PREFERRED_RELOAD_CLASS returns NO_REGS when *x* is a floating-point constant. If the constant can't be loaded into any kind of register, code generation will be better if TARGET_LEGITIMATE_CONSTANT_P makes the constant illegitimate instead of using TARGET_PREFERRED_RELOAD_CLASS.

If an insn has pseudos in it after register allocation, reload will go through the alternatives and call repeatedly PREFERRED_RELOAD_CLASS to find the best one. Returning NO_REGS, in this case, makes reload add a ! in front of the constraint: the x86 back-end uses this feature to discourage usage of 387 registers when math is done in the SSE registers (and vice versa).

reg_class_t TARGET_PREFERRED_OUTPUT_RELOAD_CLASS (*rtx x,* [Target Hook]
    reg_class_t **rclass**)

Like TARGET_PREFERRED_RELOAD_CLASS, but for output reloads instead of input reloads.

The default version of this hook always returns value of `rclass` argument.

You can also use `TARGET_PREFERRED_OUTPUT_RELOAD_CLASS` to discourage reload from using some alternatives, like `TARGET_PREFERRED_RELOAD_CLASS`.

`LIMIT_RELOAD_CLASS (mode, class)`   [Macro]

A C expression that places additional restrictions on the register class to use when it is necessary to be able to hold a value of mode *mode* in a reload register for which class *class* would ordinarily be used.

Unlike `PREFERRED_RELOAD_CLASS`, this macro should be used when there are certain modes that simply can't go in certain reload classes.

The value is a register class; perhaps *class*, or perhaps another, smaller class.

Don't define this macro unless the target machine has limitations which require the macro to do something nontrivial.

`reg_class_t TARGET_SECONDARY_RELOAD (bool in_p, rtx x,`   [Target Hook]
        `reg_class_t reload_class, machine_mode reload_mode,`
        `secondary_reload_info *sri)`

Many machines have some registers that cannot be copied directly to or from memory or even from other types of registers. An example is the 'MQ' register, which on most machines, can only be copied to or from general registers, but not memory. Below, we shall be using the term 'intermediate register' when a move operation cannot be performed directly, but has to be done by copying the source into the intermediate register first, and then copying the intermediate register to the destination. An intermediate register always has the same mode as source and destination. Since it holds the actual value being copied, reload might apply optimizations to re-use an intermediate register and eliding the copy from the source when it can determine that the intermediate register still holds the required value.

Another kind of secondary reload is required on some machines which allow copying all registers to and from memory, but require a scratch register for stores to some memory locations (e.g., those with symbolic address on the RT, and those with certain symbolic address on the SPARC when compiling PIC). Scratch registers need not have the same mode as the value being copied, and usually hold a different value than that being copied. Special patterns in the md file are needed to describe how the copy is performed with the help of the scratch register; these patterns also describe the number, register class(es) and mode(s) of the scratch register(s).

In some cases, both an intermediate and a scratch register are required.

For input reloads, this target hook is called with nonzero *in_p*, and *x* is an rtx that needs to be copied to a register of class *reload_class* in *reload_mode*. For output reloads, this target hook is called with zero *in_p*, and a register of class *reload_class* needs to be copied to rtx *x* in *reload_mode*.

If copying a register of *reload_class* from/to *x* requires an intermediate register, the hook `secondary_reload` should return the register class required for this intermediate register. If no intermediate register is required, it should return NO_REGS. If more than one intermediate register is required, describe the one that is closest in the copy chain to the reload register.

If scratch registers are needed, you also have to describe how to perform the copy from/to the reload register to/from this closest intermediate register. Or if no intermediate register is required, but still a scratch register is needed, describe the copy from/to the reload register to/from the reload operand x.

You do this by setting `sri->icode` to the instruction code of a pattern in the md file which performs the move. Operands 0 and 1 are the output and input of this copy, respectively. Operands from operand 2 onward are for scratch operands. These scratch operands must have a mode, and a single-register-class output constraint.

When an intermediate register is used, the `secondary_reload` hook will be called again to determine how to copy the intermediate register to/from the reload operand x, so your hook must also have code to handle the register class of the intermediate operand.

x might be a pseudo-register or a `subreg` of a pseudo-register, which could either be in a hard register or in memory. Use `true_regnum` to find out; it will return −1 if the pseudo is in memory and the hard register number if it is in a register.

Scratch operands in memory (constraint `"=m"` / `"=&m"`) are currently not supported. For the time being, you will have to continue to use `SECONDARY_MEMORY_NEEDED` for that purpose.

`copy_cost` also uses this target hook to find out how values are copied. If you want it to include some extra cost for the need to allocate (a) scratch register(s), set `sri->extra_cost` to the additional cost. Or if two dependent moves are supposed to have a lower cost than the sum of the individual moves due to expected fortuitous scheduling and/or special forwarding logic, you can set `sri->extra_cost` to a negative amount.

SECONDARY_RELOAD_CLASS (*class*, *mode*, x)   [Macro]
SECONDARY_INPUT_RELOAD_CLASS (*class*, *mode*, x)   [Macro]
SECONDARY_OUTPUT_RELOAD_CLASS (*class*, *mode*, x)   [Macro]
  These macros are obsolete, new ports should use the target hook `TARGET_SECONDARY_RELOAD` instead.

  These are obsolete macros, replaced by the `TARGET_SECONDARY_RELOAD` target hook. Older ports still define these macros to indicate to the reload phase that it may need to allocate at least one register for a reload in addition to the register to contain the data. Specifically, if copying x to a register *class* in *mode* requires an intermediate register, you were supposed to define `SECONDARY_INPUT_RELOAD_CLASS` to return the largest register class all of whose registers can be used as intermediate registers or scratch registers.

  If copying a register *class* in *mode* to x requires an intermediate or scratch register, `SECONDARY_OUTPUT_RELOAD_CLASS` was supposed to be defined be defined to return the largest register class required. If the requirements for input and output reloads were the same, the macro `SECONDARY_RELOAD_CLASS` should have been used instead of defining both macros identically.

  The values returned by these macros are often `GENERAL_REGS`. Return `NO_REGS` if no spare register is needed; i.e., if x can be directly copied to or from a register of *class* in *mode* without requiring a scratch register. Do not define this macro if it would always return `NO_REGS`.

If a scratch register is required (either with or without an intermediate register),
you were supposed to define patterns for 'reload_in*m*' or 'reload_out*m*', as required
(see Section 16.9 [Standard Names], page 356. These patterns, which were normally
implemented with a **define_expand**, should be similar to the 'mov*m*' patterns, except
that operand 2 is the scratch register.

These patterns need constraints for the reload register and scratch register that contain a single register class. If the original reload register (whose class is *class*) can
meet the constraint given in the pattern, the value returned by these macros is used
for the class of the scratch register. Otherwise, two additional reload registers are
required. Their classes are obtained from the constraints in the insn pattern.

x might be a pseudo-register or a **subreg** of a pseudo-register, which could either be
in a hard register or in memory. Use **true_regnum** to find out; it will return −1 if
the pseudo is in memory and the hard register number if it is in a register.

These macros should not be used in the case where a particular class of registers
can only be copied to memory and not to another class of registers. In that case,
secondary reload registers are not needed and would not be helpful. Instead, a stack
location must be used to perform the copy and the mov*m* pattern should use memory
as an intermediate storage. This case often occurs between floating-point and general
registers.

SECONDARY_MEMORY_NEEDED (*class1*, *class2*, *m*)   [Macro]
Certain machines have the property that some registers cannot be copied to some
other registers without using memory. Define this macro on those machines to be
a C expression that is nonzero if objects of mode *m* in registers of *class1* can only
be copied to registers of class *class2* by storing a register of *class1* into memory and
loading that memory location into a register of *class2*.

Do not define this macro if its value would always be zero.

SECONDARY_MEMORY_NEEDED_RTX (*mode*)   [Macro]
Normally when **SECONDARY_MEMORY_NEEDED** is defined, the compiler allocates a stack
slot for a memory location needed for register copies. If this macro is defined, the
compiler instead uses the memory location defined by this macro.

Do not define this macro if you do not define **SECONDARY_MEMORY_NEEDED**.

SECONDARY_MEMORY_NEEDED_MODE (*mode*)   [Macro]
When the compiler needs a secondary memory location to copy between two registers
of mode *mode*, it normally allocates sufficient memory to hold a quantity of **BITS_
PER_WORD** bits and performs the store and load operations in a mode that many bits
wide and whose class is the same as that of *mode*.

This is right thing to do on most machines because it ensures that all bits of the
register are copied and prevents accesses to the registers in a narrower mode, which
some machines prohibit for floating-point registers.

However, this default behavior is not correct on some machines, such as the DEC
Alpha, that store short integers in floating-point registers differently than in integer
registers. On those machines, the default widening will not work correctly and you
must define this macro to suppress that widening in some cases. See the file 'alpha.h'
for details.

Do not define this macro if you do not define SECONDARY_MEMORY_NEEDED or if widening *mode* to a mode that is BITS_PER_WORD bits wide is correct for your machine.

bool TARGET_CLASS_LIKELY_SPILLED_P (*reg_class_t rclass*)   [Target Hook]
A target hook which returns **true** if pseudos that have been assigned to registers of class *rclass* would likely be spilled because registers of *rclass* are needed for spill registers.

The default version of this target hook returns **true** if *rclass* has exactly one register and **false** otherwise. On most machines, this default should be used. For generally register-starved machines, such as i386, or machines with right register constraints, such as SH, this hook can be used to avoid excessive spilling.

This hook is also used by some of the global intra-procedural code transformations to throtle code motion, to avoid increasing register pressure.

unsigned char TARGET_CLASS_MAX_NREGS (*reg_class_t rclass*,   [Target Hook]
        machine_mode mode)
A target hook returns the maximum number of consecutive registers of class *rclass* needed to hold a value of mode *mode*.

This is closely related to the macro HARD_REGNO_NREGS. In fact, the value returned by **TARGET_CLASS_MAX_NREGS** (*rclass, mode*) target hook should be the maximum value of HARD_REGNO_NREGS (*regno, mode*) for all *regno* values in the class *rclass*.

This target hook helps control the handling of multiple-word values in the reload pass.

The default version of this target hook returns the size of *mode* in words.

CLASS_MAX_NREGS (*class, mode*)   [Macro]
A C expression for the maximum number of consecutive registers of class *class* needed to hold a value of mode *mode*.

This is closely related to the macro HARD_REGNO_NREGS. In fact, the value of the macro **CLASS_MAX_NREGS** (*class, mode*) should be the maximum value of HARD_REGNO_NREGS (*regno, mode*) for all *regno* values in the class *class*.

This macro helps control the handling of multiple-word values in the reload pass.

CANNOT_CHANGE_MODE_CLASS (*from, to, class*)   [Macro]
If defined, a C expression that returns nonzero for a *class* for which a change from mode *from* to mode *to* is invalid.

For example, loading 32-bit integer or floating-point objects into floating-point registers on Alpha extends them to 64 bits. Therefore loading a 64-bit object and then storing it as a 32-bit object does not store the low-order 32 bits, as would be the case for a normal register. Therefore, 'alpha.h' defines CANNOT_CHANGE_MODE_CLASS as below:

```
#define CANNOT_CHANGE_MODE_CLASS(FROM, TO, CLASS) \
  (GET_MODE_SIZE (FROM) != GET_MODE_SIZE (TO) \
   ? reg_classes_intersect_p (FLOAT_REGS, (CLASS)) : 0)
```

Even if storing from a register in mode *to* would be valid, if both *from* and **raw_reg_mode** for *class* are wider than **word_mode**, then we must prevent *to* narrowing the mode. This happens when the middle-end assumes that it can load or store pieces of an *N*-word pseudo, and that the pseudo will eventually be allocated to *N* `word_mode` hard registers. Failure to prevent this kind of mode change will result in the entire `raw_reg_mode` being modified instead of the partial value that the middle-end intended.

`reg_class_t TARGET_IRA_CHANGE_PSEUDO_ALLOCNO_CLASS` (*int*,   [Target Hook]
    reg_class_t, *reg_class_t*)
A target hook which can change allocno class for given pseudo from allocno and best class calculated by IRA.

The default version of this target hook always returns given class.

`bool TARGET_LRA_P` (*void*)   [Target Hook]
A target hook which returns true if we use LRA instead of reload pass. The default version of this target hook returns true. New ports should use LRA, and existing ports are encouraged to convert.

`int TARGET_REGISTER_PRIORITY` (*int*)   [Target Hook]
A target hook which returns the register priority number to which the register *hard_regno* belongs to. The bigger the number, the more preferable the hard register usage (when all other conditions are the same). This hook can be used to prefer some hard register over others in LRA. For example, some x86-64 register usage needs additional prefix which makes instructions longer. The hook can return lower priority number for such registers make them less favorable and as result making the generated code smaller. The default version of this target hook returns always zero.

`bool TARGET_REGISTER_USAGE_LEVELING_P` (*void*)   [Target Hook]
A target hook which returns true if we need register usage leveling. That means if a few hard registers are equally good for the assignment, we choose the least used hard register. The register usage leveling may be profitable for some targets. Don't use the usage leveling for targets with conditional execution or targets with big register files as it hurts if-conversion and cross-jumping optimizations. The default version of this target hook returns always false.

`bool TARGET_DIFFERENT_ADDR_DISPLACEMENT_P` (*void*)   [Target Hook]
A target hook which returns true if an address with the same structure can have different maximal legitimate displacement. For example, the displacement can depend on memory mode or on operand combinations in the insn. The default version of this target hook returns always false.

`bool TARGET_CANNOT_SUBSTITUTE_MEM_EQUIV_P` (*rtx* `subst`)   [Target Hook]
A target hook which returns `true` if *subst* can't substitute safely pseudos with equivalent memory values during register allocation. The default version of this target hook returns `false`. On most machines, this default should be used. For generally machines with non orthogonal register usage for addressing, such as SH, this hook can be used to avoid excessive spilling.

`bool TARGET_LEGITIMIZE_ADDRESS_DISPLACEMENT` (*rtx* `*disp`,   [Target Hook]
    rtx `*offset`, *machine_mode* `mode`)
A target hook which returns `true` if **disp* is legitimezed to valid address displacement with subtracting **offset* at memory mode *mode*. The default version of this

target hook returns `false`. This hook will benefit machines with limited base plus displacement addressing.

reg_class_t TARGET_SPILL_CLASS (*reg_class_t*, *machine_mode*)   [Target Hook]
> This hook defines a class of registers which could be used for spilling pseudos of the given mode and class, or `NO_REGS` if only memory should be used. Not defining this hook is equivalent to returning `NO_REGS` for all inputs.

bool TARGET_ADDITIONAL_ALLOCNO_CLASS_P (*reg_class_t*)   [Target Hook]
> This hook should return `true` if given class of registers should be an allocno class in any way. Usually RA uses only one register class from all classes containing the same register set. In some complicated cases, you need to have two or more such classes as allocno ones for RA correct work. Not defining this hook is equivalent to returning `false` for all inputs.

machine_mode TARGET_CSTORE_MODE (*enum insn_code* `icode`)   [Target Hook]
> This hook defines the machine mode to use for the boolean result of conditional store patterns. The ICODE argument is the instruction code for the cstore being performed. Not definiting this hook is the same as accepting the mode encoded into operand 0 of the cstore expander patterns.

int TARGET_COMPUTE_PRESSURE_CLASSES (*enum reg_class*   [Target Hook]
        pressure_classes)
> A target hook which lets a backend compute the set of pressure classes to be used by those optimization passes which take register pressure into account, as opposed to letting IRA compute them. It returns the number of register classes stored in the array *pressure_classes*.

17.9 Stack Layout and Calling Conventions

This describes the stack layout and calling conventions.

17.9.1 Basic Stack Layout

Here is the basic stack layout.

STACK_GROWS_DOWNWARD   [Macro]
> Define this macro to be true if pushing a word onto the stack moves the stack pointer to a smaller address, and false otherwise.

STACK_PUSH_CODE   [Macro]
> This macro defines the operation used when something is pushed on the stack. In RTL, a push operation will be (`set` (`mem` (STACK_PUSH_CODE (`reg sp`))) ...)
>
> The choices are `PRE_DEC`, `POST_DEC`, `PRE_INC`, and `POST_INC`. Which of these is correct depends on the stack direction and on whether the stack pointer points to the last item on the stack or whether it points to the space for the next item on the stack.
>
> The default is `PRE_DEC` when `STACK_GROWS_DOWNWARD` is true, which is almost always right, and `PRE_INC` otherwise, which is often wrong.

FRAME_GROWS_DOWNWARD [Macro]

Define this macro to nonzero value if the addresses of local variable slots are at negative offsets from the frame pointer.

ARGS_GROW_DOWNWARD [Macro]

Define this macro if successive arguments to a function occupy decreasing addresses on the stack.

STARTING_FRAME_OFFSET [Macro]

Offset from the frame pointer to the first local variable slot to be allocated.

If FRAME_GROWS_DOWNWARD, find the next slot's offset by subtracting the first slot's length from STARTING_FRAME_OFFSET. Otherwise, it is found by adding the length of the first slot to the value STARTING_FRAME_OFFSET.

STACK_ALIGNMENT_NEEDED [Macro]

Define to zero to disable final alignment of the stack during reload. The nonzero default for this macro is suitable for most ports.

On ports where STARTING_FRAME_OFFSET is nonzero or where there is a register save block following the local block that doesn't require alignment to STACK_BOUNDARY, it may be beneficial to disable stack alignment and do it in the backend.

STACK_POINTER_OFFSET [Macro]

Offset from the stack pointer register to the first location at which outgoing arguments are placed. If not specified, the default value of zero is used. This is the proper value for most machines.

If ARGS_GROW_DOWNWARD, this is the offset to the location above the first location at which outgoing arguments are placed.

FIRST_PARM_OFFSET (*fundecl*) [Macro]

Offset from the argument pointer register to the first argument's address. On some machines it may depend on the data type of the function.

If ARGS_GROW_DOWNWARD, this is the offset to the location above the first argument's address.

STACK_DYNAMIC_OFFSET (*fundecl*) [Macro]

Offset from the stack pointer register to an item dynamically allocated on the stack, e.g., by alloca.

The default value for this macro is STACK_POINTER_OFFSET plus the length of the outgoing arguments. The default is correct for most machines. See 'function.c' for details.

INITIAL_FRAME_ADDRESS_RTX [Macro]

A C expression whose value is RTL representing the address of the initial stack frame. This address is passed to RETURN_ADDR_RTX and DYNAMIC_CHAIN_ADDRESS. If you don't define this macro, a reasonable default value will be used. Define this macro in order to make frame pointer elimination work in the presence of __builtin_frame_address (count) and __builtin_return_address (count) for count not equal to zero.

DYNAMIC_CHAIN_ADDRESS (*frameaddr*)   [Macro]

A C expression whose value is RTL representing the address in a stack frame where the pointer to the caller's frame is stored. Assume that *frameaddr* is an RTL expression for the address of the stack frame itself.

If you don't define this macro, the default is to return the value of *frameaddr*—that is, the stack frame address is also the address of the stack word that points to the previous frame.

SETUP_FRAME_ADDRESSES   [Macro]

A C expression that produces the machine-specific code to setup the stack so that arbitrary frames can be accessed. For example, on the SPARC, we must flush all of the register windows to the stack before we can access arbitrary stack frames. You will seldom need to define this macro. The default is to do nothing.

rtx TARGET_BUILTIN_SETJMP_FRAME_VALUE (*void*)   [Target Hook]

This target hook should return an rtx that is used to store the address of the current frame into the built in `setjmp` buffer. The default value, `virtual_stack_vars_rtx`, is correct for most machines. One reason you may need to define this target hook is if `hard_frame_pointer_rtx` is the appropriate value on your machine.

FRAME_ADDR_RTX (*frameaddr*)   [Macro]

A C expression whose value is RTL representing the value of the frame address for the current frame. *frameaddr* is the frame pointer of the current frame. This is used for __builtin_frame_address. You need only define this macro if the frame address is not the same as the frame pointer. Most machines do not need to define it.

RETURN_ADDR_RTX (*count, frameaddr*)   [Macro]

A C expression whose value is RTL representing the value of the return address for the frame *count* steps up from the current frame, after the prologue. *frameaddr* is the frame pointer of the *count* frame, or the frame pointer of the *count* − 1 frame if `RETURN_ADDR_IN_PREVIOUS_FRAME` is nonzero.

The value of the expression must always be the correct address when *count* is zero, but may be `NULL_RTX` if there is no way to determine the return address of other frames.

RETURN_ADDR_IN_PREVIOUS_FRAME   [Macro]

Define this macro to nonzero value if the return address of a particular stack frame is accessed from the frame pointer of the previous stack frame. The zero default for this macro is suitable for most ports.

INCOMING_RETURN_ADDR_RTX   [Macro]

A C expression whose value is RTL representing the location of the incoming return address at the beginning of any function, before the prologue. This RTL is either a `REG`, indicating that the return value is saved in 'REG', or a `MEM` representing a location in the stack.

You only need to define this macro if you want to support call frame debugging information like that provided by DWARF 2.

If this RTL is a `REG`, you should also define `DWARF_FRAME_RETURN_COLUMN` to `DWARF_FRAME_REGNUM (REGNO)`.

DWARF_ALT_FRAME_RETURN_COLUMN   [Macro]

A C expression whose value is an integer giving a DWARF 2 column number that
may be used as an alternative return column. The column must not correspond to
any gcc hard register (that is, it must not be in the range of `DWARF_FRAME_REGNUM`).

This macro can be useful if `DWARF_FRAME_RETURN_COLUMN` is set to a general register,
but an alternative column needs to be used for signal frames. Some targets have also
used different frame return columns over time.

DWARF_ZERO_REG   [Macro]

A C expression whose value is an integer giving a DWARF 2 register number that is
considered to always have the value zero. This should only be defined if the target
has an architected zero register, and someone decided it was a good idea to use that
register number to terminate the stack backtrace. New ports should avoid this.

void TARGET_DWARF_HANDLE_FRAME_UNSPEC (*const char *label*,   [Target Hook]
     rtx pattern, *int index*)

This target hook allows the backend to emit frame-related insns that contain UN-
SPECs or UNSPEC_VOLATILEs. The DWARF 2 call frame debugging info engine
will invoke it on insns of the form

```
(set (reg) (unspec [...] UNSPEC_INDEX))
```

and

```
(set (reg) (unspec_volatile [...] UNSPECV_INDEX)).
```

to let the backend emit the call frame instructions. *label* is the CFI label attached to
the insn, *pattern* is the pattern of the insn and *index* is `UNSPEC_INDEX` or `UNSPECV_INDEX`.

INCOMING_FRAME_SP_OFFSET   [Macro]

A C expression whose value is an integer giving the offset, in bytes, from the value
of the stack pointer register to the top of the stack frame at the beginning of any
function, before the prologue. The top of the frame is defined to be the value of the
stack pointer in the previous frame, just before the call instruction.

You only need to define this macro if you want to support call frame debugging
information like that provided by DWARF 2.

ARG_POINTER_CFA_OFFSET (*fundecl*)   [Macro]

A C expression whose value is an integer giving the offset, in bytes, from the argument
pointer to the canonical frame address (cfa). The final value should coincide with that
calculated by `INCOMING_FRAME_SP_OFFSET`. Which is unfortunately not usable during
virtual register instantiation.

The default value for this macro is `FIRST_PARM_OFFSET (fundecl) + crtl->args.pretend_args_size`, which is correct for most machines; in general, the
arguments are found immediately before the stack frame. Note that this is not the
case on some targets that save registers into the caller's frame, such as SPARC and
rs6000, and so such targets need to define this macro.

You only need to define this macro if the default is incorrect, and you want to support
call frame debugging information like that provided by DWARF 2.

FRAME_POINTER_CFA_OFFSET (*fundecl*) [Macro]

If defined, a C expression whose value is an integer giving the offset in bytes from the frame pointer to the canonical frame address (cfa). The final value should coincide with that calculated by `INCOMING_FRAME_SP_OFFSET`.

Normally the CFA is calculated as an offset from the argument pointer, via `ARG_POINTER_CFA_OFFSET`, but if the argument pointer is variable due to the ABI, this may not be possible. If this macro is defined, it implies that the virtual register instantiation should be based on the frame pointer instead of the argument pointer. Only one of `FRAME_POINTER_CFA_OFFSET` and `ARG_POINTER_CFA_OFFSET` should be defined.

CFA_FRAME_BASE_OFFSET (*fundecl*) [Macro]

If defined, a C expression whose value is an integer giving the offset in bytes from the canonical frame address (cfa) to the frame base used in DWARF 2 debug information. The default is zero. A different value may reduce the size of debug information on some ports.

17.9.2 Exception Handling Support

EH_RETURN_DATA_REGNO (*N*) [Macro]

A C expression whose value is the Nth register number used for data by exception handlers, or `INVALID_REGNUM` if fewer than N registers are usable.

The exception handling library routines communicate with the exception handlers via a set of agreed upon registers. Ideally these registers should be call-clobbered; it is possible to use call-saved registers, but may negatively impact code size. The target must support at least 2 data registers, but should define 4 if there are enough free registers.

You must define this macro if you want to support call frame exception handling like that provided by DWARF 2.

EH_RETURN_STACKADJ_RTX [Macro]

A C expression whose value is RTL representing a location in which to store a stack adjustment to be applied before function return. This is used to unwind the stack to an exception handler's call frame. It will be assigned zero on code paths that return normally.

Typically this is a call-clobbered hard register that is otherwise untouched by the epilogue, but could also be a stack slot.

Do not define this macro if the stack pointer is saved and restored by the regular prolog and epilog code in the call frame itself; in this case, the exception handling library routines will update the stack location to be restored in place. Otherwise, you must define this macro if you want to support call frame exception handling like that provided by DWARF 2.

EH_RETURN_HANDLER_RTX [Macro]

A C expression whose value is RTL representing a location in which to store the address of an exception handler to which we should return. It will not be assigned on code paths that return normally.

Typically this is the location in the call frame at which the normal return address is stored. For targets that return by popping an address off the stack, this might be a memory address just below the *target* call frame rather than inside the current call frame. If defined, `EH_RETURN_STACKADJ_RTX` will have already been assigned, so it may be used to calculate the location of the target call frame.

Some targets have more complex requirements than storing to an address calculable during initial code generation. In that case the `eh_return` instruction pattern should be used instead.

If you want to support call frame exception handling, you must define either this macro or the `eh_return` instruction pattern.

`RETURN_ADDR_OFFSET`   [Macro]
    If defined, an integer-valued C expression for which rtl will be generated to add it to the exception handler address before it is searched in the exception handling tables, and to subtract it again from the address before using it to return to the exception handler.

`ASM_PREFERRED_EH_DATA_FORMAT (code, global)`   [Macro]
    This macro chooses the encoding of pointers embedded in the exception handling sections. If at all possible, this should be defined such that the exception handling section will not require dynamic relocations, and so may be read-only.

    code is 0 for data, 1 for code labels, 2 for function pointers. *global* is true if the symbol may be affected by dynamic relocations. The macro should return a combination of the `DW_EH_PE_*` defines as found in 'dwarf2.h'.

    If this macro is not defined, pointers will not be encoded but represented directly.

`ASM_MAYBE_OUTPUT_ENCODED_ADDR_RTX (file, encoding, size, addr,`   [Macro]
        `done)`
    This macro allows the target to emit whatever special magic is required to represent the encoding chosen by `ASM_PREFERRED_EH_DATA_FORMAT`. Generic code takes care of pc-relative and indirect encodings; this must be defined if the target uses text-relative or data-relative encodings.

    This is a C statement that branches to *done* if the format was handled. *encoding* is the format chosen, *size* is the number of bytes that the format occupies, *addr* is the `SYMBOL_REF` to be emitted.

`MD_FALLBACK_FRAME_STATE_FOR (context, fs)`   [Macro]
    This macro allows the target to add CPU and operating system specific code to the call-frame unwinder for use when there is no unwind data available. The most common reason to implement this macro is to unwind through signal frames.

    This macro is called from `uw_frame_state_for` in 'unwind-dw2.c', 'unwind-dw2-xtensa.c' and 'unwind-ia64.c'. *context* is an `_Unwind_Context`; *fs* is an `_Unwind_FrameState`. Examine `context->ra` for the address of the code being executed and `context->cfa` for the stack pointer value. If the frame can be decoded, the register save addresses should be updated in *fs* and the macro should evaluate to `_URC_NO_REASON`. If the frame cannot be decoded, the macro should evaluate to `_URC_END_OF_STACK`.

For proper signal handling in Java this macro is accompanied by `MAKE_THROW_FRAME`, defined in 'libjava/include/*-signal.h' headers.

MD_HANDLE_UNWABI (*context*, *fs*)   [Macro]

This macro allows the target to add operating system specific code to the call-frame unwinder to handle the IA-64 `.unwabi` unwinding directive, usually used for signal or interrupt frames.

This macro is called from `uw_update_context` in libgcc's 'unwind-ia64.c'. *context* is an `_Unwind_Context`; *fs* is an `_Unwind_FrameState`. Examine `fs->unwabi` for the abi and context in the `.unwabi` directive. If the `.unwabi` directive can be handled, the register save addresses should be updated in *fs*.

TARGET_USES_WEAK_UNWIND_INFO   [Macro]

A C expression that evaluates to true if the target requires unwind info to be given comdat linkage. Define it to be 1 if comdat linkage is necessary. The default is 0.

17.9.3 Specifying How Stack Checking is Done

GCC will check that stack references are within the boundaries of the stack, if the option '-fstack-check' is specified, in one of three ways:

1. If the value of the `STACK_CHECK_BUILTIN` macro is nonzero, GCC will assume that you have arranged for full stack checking to be done at appropriate places in the configuration files. GCC will not do other special processing.

2. If `STACK_CHECK_BUILTIN` is zero and the value of the `STACK_CHECK_STATIC_BUILTIN` macro is nonzero, GCC will assume that you have arranged for static stack checking (checking of the static stack frame of functions) to be done at appropriate places in the configuration files. GCC will only emit code to do dynamic stack checking (checking on dynamic stack allocations) using the third approach below.

3. If neither of the above are true, GCC will generate code to periodically "probe" the stack pointer using the values of the macros defined below.

If neither STACK_CHECK_BUILTIN nor STACK_CHECK_STATIC_BUILTIN is defined, GCC will change its allocation strategy for large objects if the option '-fstack-check' is specified: they will always be allocated dynamically if their size exceeds `STACK_CHECK_MAX_VAR_SIZE` bytes.

STACK_CHECK_BUILTIN   [Macro]

A nonzero value if stack checking is done by the configuration files in a machine-dependent manner. You should define this macro if stack checking is required by the ABI of your machine or if you would like to do stack checking in some more efficient way than the generic approach. The default value of this macro is zero.

STACK_CHECK_STATIC_BUILTIN   [Macro]

A nonzero value if static stack checking is done by the configuration files in a machine-dependent manner. You should define this macro if you would like to do static stack checking in some more efficient way than the generic approach. The default value of this macro is zero.

STACK_CHECK_PROBE_INTERVAL_EXP   [Macro]

>   An integer specifying the interval at which GCC must generate stack probe instruc-
>   tions, defined as 2 raised to this integer. You will normally define this macro so that
>   the interval be no larger than the size of the "guard pages" at the end of a stack area.
>   The default value of 12 (4096-byte interval) is suitable for most systems.

STACK_CHECK_MOVING_SP   [Macro]

>   An integer which is nonzero if GCC should move the stack pointer page by page when
>   doing probes. This can be necessary on systems where the stack pointer contains the
>   bottom address of the memory area accessible to the executing thread at any point
>   in time. In this situation an alternate signal stack is required in order to be able to
>   recover from a stack overflow. The default value of this macro is zero.

STACK_CHECK_PROTECT   [Macro]

>   The number of bytes of stack needed to recover from a stack overflow, for lan-
>   guages where such a recovery is supported. The default value of 4KB/8KB with the
>   setjmp/longjmp-based exception handling mechanism and 8KB/12KB with other ex-
>   ception handling mechanisms should be adequate for most architectures and operating
>   systems.

The following macros are relevant only if neither STACK_CHECK_BUILTIN nor
STACK_CHECK_STATIC_BUILTIN is defined; you can omit them altogether in the
opposite case.

STACK_CHECK_MAX_FRAME_SIZE   [Macro]

>   The maximum size of a stack frame, in bytes. GCC will generate probe instructions
>   in non-leaf functions to ensure at least this many bytes of stack are available. If a
>   stack frame is larger than this size, stack checking will not be reliable and GCC will
>   issue a warning. The default is chosen so that GCC only generates one instruction
>   on most systems. You should normally not change the default value of this macro.

STACK_CHECK_FIXED_FRAME_SIZE   [Macro]

>   GCC uses this value to generate the above warning message. It represents the amount
>   of fixed frame used by a function, not including space for any callee-saved registers,
>   temporaries and user variables. You need only specify an upper bound for this amount
>   and will normally use the default of four words.

STACK_CHECK_MAX_VAR_SIZE   [Macro]

>   The maximum size, in bytes, of an object that GCC will place in the fixed area of
>   the stack frame when the user specifies '-fstack-check'. GCC computed the default
>   from the values of the above macros and you will normally not need to override that
>   default.

17.9.4 Registers That Address the Stack Frame

This discusses registers that address the stack frame.

STACK_POINTER_REGNUM   [Macro]

>   The register number of the stack pointer register, which must also be a fixed register
>   according to FIXED_REGISTERS. On most machines, the hardware determines which
>   register this is.

FRAME_POINTER_REGNUM   [Macro]

>   The register number of the frame pointer register, which is used to access automatic
>   variables in the stack frame. On some machines, the hardware determines which
>   register this is. On other machines, you can choose any register you wish for this
>   purpose.

HARD_FRAME_POINTER_REGNUM   [Macro]

>   On some machines the offset between the frame pointer and starting offset of the
>   automatic variables is not known until after register allocation has been done (for
>   example, because the saved registers are between these two locations). On those
>   machines, define FRAME_POINTER_REGNUM the number of a special, fixed register to be
>   used internally until the offset is known, and define HARD_FRAME_POINTER_REGNUM to
>   be the actual hard register number used for the frame pointer.
>
>   You should define this macro only in the very rare circumstances when it is not possi-
>   ble to calculate the offset between the frame pointer and the automatic variables until
>   after register allocation has been completed. When this macro is defined, you must
>   also indicate in your definition of ELIMINABLE_REGS how to eliminate FRAME_POINTER_
>   REGNUM into either HARD_FRAME_POINTER_REGNUM or STACK_POINTER_REGNUM.
>
>   Do not define this macro if it would be the same as FRAME_POINTER_REGNUM.

ARG_POINTER_REGNUM   [Macro]

>   The register number of the arg pointer register, which is used to access the function's
>   argument list. On some machines, this is the same as the frame pointer register.
>   On some machines, the hardware determines which register this is. On other ma-
>   chines, you can choose any register you wish for this purpose. If this is not the same
>   register as the frame pointer register, then you must mark it as a fixed register ac-
>   cording to FIXED_REGISTERS, or arrange to be able to eliminate it (see Section 17.9.5
>   [Elimination], page 485).

HARD_FRAME_POINTER_IS_FRAME_POINTER   [Macro]

>   Define this to a preprocessor constant that is nonzero if hard_frame_pointer_
>   rtx and frame_pointer_rtx should be the same. The default definition is
>   '(HARD_FRAME_POINTER_REGNUM == FRAME_POINTER_REGNUM)'; you only need to
>   define this macro if that definition is not suitable for use in preprocessor conditionals.

HARD_FRAME_POINTER_IS_ARG_POINTER   [Macro]

>   Define this to a preprocessor constant that is nonzero if hard_frame_pointer_
>   rtx and arg_pointer_rtx should be the same. The default definition is
>   '(HARD_FRAME_POINTER_REGNUM == ARG_POINTER_REGNUM)'; you only need to define
>   this macro if that definition is not suitable for use in preprocessor conditionals.

RETURN_ADDRESS_POINTER_REGNUM   [Macro]

> The register number of the return address pointer register, which is used to access the current function's return address from the stack. On some machines, the return address is not at a fixed offset from the frame pointer or stack pointer or argument pointer. This register can be defined to point to the return address on the stack, and then be converted by **ELIMINABLE_REGS** into either the frame pointer or stack pointer.
>
> Do not define this macro unless there is no other way to get the return address from the stack.

STATIC_CHAIN_REGNUM   [Macro]
STATIC_CHAIN_INCOMING_REGNUM   [Macro]

> Register numbers used for passing a function's static chain pointer. If register windows are used, the register number as seen by the called function is **STATIC_CHAIN_INCOMING_REGNUM**, while the register number as seen by the calling function is **STATIC_CHAIN_REGNUM**. If these registers are the same, **STATIC_CHAIN_INCOMING_REGNUM** need not be defined.
>
> The static chain register need not be a fixed register.
>
> If the static chain is passed in memory, these macros should not be defined; instead, the **TARGET_STATIC_CHAIN** hook should be used.

rtx TARGET_STATIC_CHAIN (*const_tree* **fndecl_or_type**, *bool*   [Target Hook]
      incoming_p)

> This hook replaces the use of **STATIC_CHAIN_REGNUM** et al for targets that may use different static chain locations for different nested functions. This may be required if the target has function attributes that affect the calling conventions of the function and those calling conventions use different static chain locations.
>
> The default version of this hook uses **STATIC_CHAIN_REGNUM** et al.
>
> If the static chain is passed in memory, this hook should be used to provide rtx giving **mem** expressions that denote where they are stored. Often the **mem** expression as seen by the caller will be at an offset from the stack pointer and the **mem** expression as seen by the callee will be at an offset from the frame pointer. The variables **stack_pointer_rtx**, **frame_pointer_rtx**, and **arg_pointer_rtx** will have been initialized and should be used to refer to those items.

DWARF_FRAME_REGISTERS   [Macro]

> This macro specifies the maximum number of hard registers that can be saved in a call frame. This is used to size data structures used in DWARF2 exception handling.
>
> Prior to GCC 3.0, this macro was needed in order to establish a stable exception handling ABI in the face of adding new hard registers for ISA extensions. In GCC 3.0 and later, the EH ABI is insulated from changes in the number of hard registers. Nevertheless, this macro can still be used to reduce the runtime memory requirements of the exception handling routines, which can be substantial if the ISA contains a lot of registers that are not call-saved.
>
> If this macro is not defined, it defaults to **FIRST_PSEUDO_REGISTER**.

PRE_GCC3_DWARF_FRAME_REGISTERS   [Macro]

    This macro is similar to `DWARF_FRAME_REGISTERS`, but is provided for backward compatibility in pre GCC 3.0 compiled code.

    If this macro is not defined, it defaults to `DWARF_FRAME_REGISTERS`.

DWARF_REG_TO_UNWIND_COLUMN (*regno*)   [Macro]

    Define this macro if the target's representation for dwarf registers is different than the internal representation for unwind column. Given a dwarf register, this macro should return the internal unwind column number to use instead.

    See the PowerPC's SPE target for an example.

DWARF_FRAME_REGNUM (*regno*)   [Macro]

    Define this macro if the target's representation for dwarf registers used in .eh_frame or .debug_frame is different from that used in other debug info sections. Given a GCC hard register number, this macro should return the .eh_frame register number. The default is `DBX_REGISTER_NUMBER (*regno*)`.

DWARF2_FRAME_REG_OUT (*regno*, *for_eh*)   [Macro]

    Define this macro to map register numbers held in the call frame info that GCC has collected using `DWARF_FRAME_REGNUM` to those that should be output in .debug_frame (*for_eh* is zero) and .eh_frame (*for_eh* is nonzero). The default is to return *regno*.

REG_VALUE_IN_UNWIND_CONTEXT   [Macro]

    Define this macro if the target stores register values as `_Unwind_Word` type in unwind context. It should be defined if target register size is larger than the size of `void *`. The default is to store register values as `void *` type.

ASSUME_EXTENDED_UNWIND_CONTEXT   [Macro]

    Define this macro to be 1 if the target always uses extended unwind context with version, args_size and by_value fields. If it is undefined, it will be defined to 1 when `REG_VALUE_IN_UNWIND_CONTEXT` is defined and 0 otherwise.

17.9.5 Eliminating Frame Pointer and Arg Pointer

This is about eliminating the frame pointer and arg pointer.

bool TARGET_FRAME_POINTER_REQUIRED (*void*)   [Target Hook]

    This target hook should return **true** if a function must have and use a frame pointer. This target hook is called in the reload pass. If its return value is **true** the function will have a frame pointer.

    This target hook can in principle examine the current function and decide according to the facts, but on most machines the constant **false** or the constant **true** suffices. Use **false** when the machine allows code to be generated with no frame pointer, and doing so saves some time or space. Use **true** when there is no possible advantage to avoiding a frame pointer.

    In certain cases, the compiler does not know how to produce valid code without a frame pointer. The compiler recognizes those cases and automatically gives the function a frame pointer regardless of what `targetm.frame_pointer_required` returns. You don't need to worry about them.

In a function that does not require a frame pointer, the frame pointer register can be allocated for ordinary usage, unless you mark it as a fixed register. See FIXED_REGISTERS for more information.

Default return value is `false`.

ELIMINABLE_REGS   [Macro]

This macro specifies a table of register pairs used to eliminate unneeded registers that point into the stack frame.

The definition of this macro is a list of structure initializations, each of which specifies an original and replacement register.

On some machines, the position of the argument pointer is not known until the compilation is completed. In such a case, a separate hard register must be used for the argument pointer. This register can be eliminated by replacing it with either the frame pointer or the argument pointer, depending on whether or not the frame pointer has been eliminated.

In this case, you might specify:

```
#define ELIMINABLE_REGS  \
{{ARG_POINTER_REGNUM, STACK_POINTER_REGNUM}, \
 {ARG_POINTER_REGNUM, FRAME_POINTER_REGNUM}, \
 {FRAME_POINTER_REGNUM, STACK_POINTER_REGNUM}}
```

Note that the elimination of the argument pointer with the stack pointer is specified first since that is the preferred elimination.

bool TARGET_CAN_ELIMINATE (*const int* **from_reg**, *const int*   [Target Hook]
         to_reg)

This target hook should return `true` if the compiler is allowed to try to replace register number *from_reg* with register number *to_reg*. This target hook will usually be `true`, since most of the cases preventing register elimination are things that the compiler already knows about.

Default return value is `true`.

INITIAL_ELIMINATION_OFFSET (*from-reg*, *to-reg*, *offset-var*)   [Macro]

This macro returns the initial difference between the specified pair of registers. The value would be computed from information such as the result of `get_frame_size ()` and the tables of registers `df_regs_ever_live_p` and `call_used_regs`.

17.9.6 Passing Function Arguments on the Stack

The macros in this section control how arguments are passed on the stack. See the following section for other macros that control passing certain arguments in registers.

bool TARGET_PROMOTE_PROTOTYPES (*const_tree* **fntype**)   [Target Hook]

This target hook returns `true` if an argument declared in a prototype as an integral type smaller than `int` should actually be passed as an `int`. In addition to avoiding errors in certain cases of mismatch, it also makes for better code on certain machines. The default is to not promote prototypes.

PUSH_ARGS [Macro]

> A C expression. If nonzero, push insns will be used to pass outgoing arguments. If the target machine does not have a push instruction, set it to zero. That directs GCC to use an alternate strategy: to allocate the entire argument block and then store the arguments into it. When `PUSH_ARGS` is nonzero, `PUSH_ROUNDING` must be defined too.

PUSH_ARGS_REVERSED [Macro]

> A C expression. If nonzero, function arguments will be evaluated from last to first, rather than from first to last. If this macro is not defined, it defaults to `PUSH_ARGS` on targets where the stack and args grow in opposite directions, and 0 otherwise.

PUSH_ROUNDING (*npushed***)** [Macro]

> A C expression that is the number of bytes actually pushed onto the stack when an instruction attempts to push *npushed* bytes.
>
> On some machines, the definition
>
> ```
> #define PUSH_ROUNDING(BYTES) (BYTES)
> ```
>
> will suffice. But on other machines, instructions that appear to push one byte actually push two bytes in an attempt to maintain alignment. Then the definition should be
>
> ```
> #define PUSH_ROUNDING(BYTES) (((BYTES) + 1) & ~1)
> ```
>
> If the value of this macro has a type, it should be an unsigned type.

ACCUMULATE_OUTGOING_ARGS [Macro]

> A C expression. If nonzero, the maximum amount of space required for outgoing arguments will be computed and placed into `crtl->outgoing_args_size`. No space will be pushed onto the stack for each call; instead, the function prologue should increase the stack frame size by this amount.
>
> Setting both `PUSH_ARGS` and `ACCUMULATE_OUTGOING_ARGS` is not proper.

REG_PARM_STACK_SPACE (*fndecl***)** [Macro]

> Define this macro if functions should assume that stack space has been allocated for arguments even when their values are passed in registers.
>
> The value of this macro is the size, in bytes, of the area reserved for arguments passed in registers for the function represented by *fndecl*, which can be zero if GCC is calling a library function. The argument *fndecl* can be the FUNCTION_DECL, or the type itself of the function.
>
> This space can be allocated by the caller, or be a part of the machine-dependent stack frame: `OUTGOING_REG_PARM_STACK_SPACE` says which.

INCOMING_REG_PARM_STACK_SPACE (*fndecl***)** [Macro]

> Like `REG_PARM_STACK_SPACE`, but for incoming register arguments. Define this macro if space guaranteed when compiling a function body is different to space required when making a call, a situation that can arise with K&R style function definitions.

OUTGOING_REG_PARM_STACK_SPACE (*fntype***)** [Macro]

> Define this to a nonzero value if it is the responsibility of the caller to allocate the area reserved for arguments passed in registers when calling a function of *fntype*. *fntype* may be NULL if the function called is a library function.
>
> If `ACCUMULATE_OUTGOING_ARGS` is defined, this macro controls whether the space for these arguments counts in the value of `crtl->outgoing_args_size`.

`STACK_PARMS_IN_REG_PARM_AREA`   [Macro]

> Define this macro if `REG_PARM_STACK_SPACE` is defined, but the stack parameters don't skip the area specified by it.
>
> Normally, when a parameter is not passed in registers, it is placed on the stack beyond the `REG_PARM_STACK_SPACE` area. Defining this macro suppresses this behavior and causes the parameter to be passed on the stack in its natural location.

`int TARGET_RETURN_POPS_ARGS (`*tree* `fundecl`*, tree* `funtype`*, int*   [Target Hook]
     `size`*)*

> This target hook returns the number of bytes of its own arguments that a function pops on returning, or 0 if the function pops no arguments and the caller must therefore pop them all after the function returns.
>
> *fundecl* is a C variable whose value is a tree node that describes the function in question. Normally it is a node of type `FUNCTION_DECL` that describes the declaration of the function. From this you can obtain the `DECL_ATTRIBUTES` of the function.
>
> *funtype* is a C variable whose value is a tree node that describes the function in question. Normally it is a node of type `FUNCTION_TYPE` that describes the data type of the function. From this it is possible to obtain the data types of the value and arguments (if known).
>
> When a call to a library function is being considered, *fundecl* will contain an identifier node for the library function. Thus, if you need to distinguish among various library functions, you can do so by their names. Note that "library function" in this context means a function used to perform arithmetic, whose name is known specially in the compiler and was not mentioned in the C code being compiled.
>
> *size* is the number of bytes of arguments passed on the stack. If a variable number of bytes is passed, it is zero, and argument popping will always be the responsibility of the calling function.
>
> On the VAX, all functions always pop their arguments, so the definition of this macro is *size*. On the 68000, using the standard calling convention, no functions pop their arguments, so the value of the macro is always 0 in this case. But an alternative calling convention is available in which functions that take a fixed number of arguments pop them but other functions (such as `printf`) pop nothing (the caller pops all). When this convention is in use, *funtype* is examined to determine whether a function takes a fixed number of arguments.

`CALL_POPS_ARGS (`*cum*`)`   [Macro]

> A C expression that should indicate the number of bytes a call sequence pops off the stack. It is added to the value of `RETURN_POPS_ARGS` when compiling a function call.
>
> *cum* is the variable in which all arguments to the called function have been accumulated.
>
> On certain architectures, such as the SH5, a call trampoline is used that pops certain registers off the stack, depending on the arguments that have been passed to the function. Since this is a property of the call site, not of the called function, `RETURN_POPS_ARGS` is not appropriate.

17.9.7 Passing Arguments in Registers

This section describes the macros which let you control how various types of arguments are passed in registers or how they are arranged in the stack.

rtx TARGET_FUNCTION_ARG (*cumulative_args_t* ca, *machine_mode*   [Target Hook]
       mode, *const_tree* type, *bool* named)

Return an RTX indicating whether a function argument is passed in a register and if so, which register.

The arguments are *ca*, which summarizes all the previous arguments; *mode*, the machine mode of the argument; *type*, the data type of the argument as a tree node or 0 if that is not known (which happens for C support library functions); and *named*, which is true for an ordinary argument and false for nameless arguments that correspond to '...' in the called function's prototype. *type* can be an incomplete type if a syntax error has previously occurred.

The return value is usually either a reg RTX for the hard register in which to pass the argument, or zero to pass the argument on the stack.

The return value can be a const_int which means argument is passed in a target specific slot with specified number. Target hooks should be used to store or load argument in such case. See TARGET_STORE_BOUNDS_FOR_ARG and TARGET_LOAD_BOUNDS_FOR_ARG for more information.

The value of the expression can also be a parallel RTX. This is used when an argument is passed in multiple locations. The mode of the parallel should be the mode of the entire argument. The parallel holds any number of expr_list pairs; each one describes where part of the argument is passed. In each expr_list the first operand must be a reg RTX for the hard register in which to pass this part of the argument, and the mode of the register RTX indicates how large this part of the argument is. The second operand of the expr_list is a const_int which gives the offset in bytes into the entire argument of where this part starts. As a special exception the first expr_list in the parallel RTX may have a first operand of zero. This indicates that the entire argument is also stored on the stack.

The last time this hook is called, it is called with MODE == VOIDmode, and its result is passed to the call or call_value pattern as operands 2 and 3 respectively.

The usual way to make the ISO library 'stdarg.h' work on a machine where some arguments are usually passed in registers, is to cause nameless arguments to be passed on the stack instead. This is done by making TARGET_FUNCTION_ARG return 0 whenever *named* is false.

You may use the hook targetm.calls.must_pass_in_stack in the definition of this macro to determine if this argument is of a type that must be passed in the stack. If REG_PARM_STACK_SPACE is not defined and TARGET_FUNCTION_ARG returns nonzero for such an argument, the compiler will abort. If REG_PARM_STACK_SPACE is defined, the argument will be computed in the stack and then loaded into a register.

bool TARGET_MUST_PASS_IN_STACK (*machine_mode* **mode**,   [Target Hook]
     const_tree **type**)

This target hook should return **true** if we should not pass *type* solely in registers. The file 'expr.h' defines a definition that is usually appropriate, refer to 'expr.h' for additional documentation.

rtx TARGET_FUNCTION_INCOMING_ARG (*cumulative_args_t* **ca**,   [Target Hook]
     machine_mode **mode**, *const_tree* **type**, *bool* **named**)

Define this hook if the caller and callee on the target have different views of where arguments are passed. Also define this hook if there are functions that are never directly called, but are invoked by the hardware and which have nonstandard calling conventions.

In this case **TARGET_FUNCTION_ARG** computes the register in which the caller passes the value, and **TARGET_FUNCTION_INCOMING_ARG** should be defined in a similar fashion to tell the function being called where the arguments will arrive.

TARGET_FUNCTION_INCOMING_ARG can also return arbitrary address computation using hard register, which can be forced into a register, so that it can be used to pass special arguments.

If **TARGET_FUNCTION_INCOMING_ARG** is not defined, **TARGET_FUNCTION_ARG** serves both purposes.

bool TARGET_USE_PSEUDO_PIC_REG (*void*)   [Target Hook]

This hook should return 1 in case pseudo register should be created for pic_offset_table_rtx during function expand.

void TARGET_INIT_PIC_REG (*void*)   [Target Hook]

Perform a target dependent initialization of pic_offset_table_rtx. This hook is called at the start of register allocation.

int TARGET_ARG_PARTIAL_BYTES (*cumulative_args_t* **cum**,   [Target Hook]
     machine_mode **mode**, *tree* **type**, *bool* **named**)

This target hook returns the number of bytes at the beginning of an argument that must be put in registers. The value must be zero for arguments that are passed entirely in registers or that are entirely pushed on the stack.

On some machines, certain arguments must be passed partially in registers and partially in memory. On these machines, typically the first few words of arguments are passed in registers, and the rest on the stack. If a multi-word argument (a **double** or a structure) crosses that boundary, its first few words must be passed in registers and the rest must be pushed. This macro tells the compiler when this occurs, and how many bytes should go in registers.

TARGET_FUNCTION_ARG for these arguments should return the first register to be used by the caller for this argument; likewise **TARGET_FUNCTION_INCOMING_ARG**, for the called function.

bool **TARGET_PASS_BY_REFERENCE** (*cumulative_args_t* **cum**,   [Target Hook]
    machine_mode **mode**, *const_tree* **type**, *bool* **named**)

> This target hook should return **true** if an argument at the position indicated by *cum* should be passed by reference. This predicate is queried after target independent reasons for being passed by reference, such as **TREE_ADDRESSABLE (type)**.

> If the hook returns true, a copy of that argument is made in memory and a pointer to the argument is passed instead of the argument itself. The pointer is passed in whatever way is appropriate for passing a pointer to that type.

bool **TARGET_CALLEE_COPIES** (*cumulative_args_t* **cum**,   [Target Hook]
    machine_mode **mode**, *const_tree* **type**, *bool* **named**)

> The function argument described by the parameters to this hook is known to be passed by reference. The hook should return true if the function argument should be copied by the callee instead of copied by the caller.

> For any argument for which the hook returns true, if it can be determined that the argument is not modified, then a copy need not be generated.

> The default version of this hook always returns false.

CUMULATIVE_ARGS   [Macro]

> A C type for declaring a variable that is used as the first argument of **TARGET_FUNCTION_ARG** and other related values. For some target machines, the type **int** suffices and can hold the number of bytes of argument so far.

> There is no need to record in **CUMULATIVE_ARGS** anything about the arguments that have been passed on the stack. The compiler has other variables to keep track of that. For target machines on which all arguments are passed on the stack, there is no need to store anything in **CUMULATIVE_ARGS**; however, the data structure must exist and should not be empty, so use **int**.

OVERRIDE_ABI_FORMAT (*fndecl*)   [Macro]

> If defined, this macro is called before generating any code for a function, but after the *cfun* descriptor for the function has been created. The back end may use this macro to update *cfun* to reflect an ABI other than that which would normally be used by default. If the compiler is generating code for a compiler-generated function, *fndecl* may be **NULL**.

INIT_CUMULATIVE_ARGS (*cum*, *fntype*, *libname*, *fndecl*,   [Macro]
    n_named_args)

> A C statement (sans semicolon) for initializing the variable *cum* for the state at the beginning of the argument list. The variable has type **CUMULATIVE_ARGS**. The value of *fntype* is the tree node for the data type of the function which will receive the args, or 0 if the args are to a compiler support library function. For direct calls that are not libcalls, *fndecl* contain the declaration node of the function. *fndecl* is also set when **INIT_CUMULATIVE_ARGS** is used to find arguments for the function being compiled. *n_named_args* is set to the number of named arguments, including a structure return address if it is passed as a parameter, when making a call. When processing incoming arguments, *n_named_args* is set to −1.

> When processing a call to a compiler support library function, *libname* identifies which one. It is a **symbol_ref** rtx which contains the name of the function, as a

string. *libname* is 0 when an ordinary C function call is being processed. Thus, each time this macro is called, either *libname* or *fntype* is nonzero, but never both of them at once.

INIT_CUMULATIVE_LIBCALL_ARGS (*cum*, *mode*, *libname*)   [Macro]
    Like INIT_CUMULATIVE_ARGS but only used for outgoing libcalls, it gets a MODE argument instead of *fntype*, that would be NULL. *indirect* would always be zero, too. If this macro is not defined, INIT_CUMULATIVE_ARGS (cum, NULL_RTX, libname, 0) is used instead.

INIT_CUMULATIVE_INCOMING_ARGS (*cum*, *fntype*, *libname*)   [Macro]
    Like INIT_CUMULATIVE_ARGS but overrides it for the purposes of finding the arguments for the function being compiled. If this macro is undefined, INIT_CUMULATIVE_ARGS is used instead.

    The value passed for *libname* is always 0, since library routines with special calling conventions are never compiled with GCC. The argument *libname* exists for symmetry with INIT_CUMULATIVE_ARGS.

void TARGET_FUNCTION_ARG_ADVANCE (*cumulative_args_t* ca,   [Target Hook]
      machine_mode mode, *const_tree* type, *bool* named)
    This hook updates the summarizer variable pointed to by *ca* to advance past an argument in the argument list. The values *mode*, *type* and *named* describe that argument. Once this is done, the variable *cum* is suitable for analyzing the *following* argument with TARGET_FUNCTION_ARG, etc.

    This hook need not do anything if the argument in question was passed on the stack. The compiler knows how to track the amount of stack space used for arguments without any special help.

FUNCTION_ARG_OFFSET (*mode*, *type*)   [Macro]
    If defined, a C expression that is the number of bytes to add to the offset of the argument passed in memory. This is needed for the SPU, which passes **char** and **short** arguments in the preferred slot that is in the middle of the quad word instead of starting at the top.

FUNCTION_ARG_PADDING (*mode*, *type*)   [Macro]
    If defined, a C expression which determines whether, and in which direction, to pad out an argument with extra space. The value should be of type **enum direction**: either **upward** to pad above the argument, **downward** to pad below, or **none** to inhibit padding.

    The *amount* of padding is not controlled by this macro, but by the target hook TARGET_FUNCTION_ARG_ROUND_BOUNDARY. It is always just enough to reach the next multiple of that boundary.

    This macro has a default definition which is right for most systems. For little-endian machines, the default is to pad upward. For big-endian machines, the default is to pad downward for an argument of constant size shorter than an **int**, and upward otherwise.

PAD_VARARGS_DOWN [Macro]

If defined, a C expression which determines whether the default implementation of va_arg will attempt to pad down before reading the next argument, if that argument is smaller than its aligned space as controlled by `PARM_BOUNDARY`. If this macro is not defined, all such arguments are padded down if `BYTES_BIG_ENDIAN` is true.

BLOCK_REG_PADDING (*mode*, *type*, *first*) [Macro]

Specify padding for the last element of a block move between registers and memory. *first* is nonzero if this is the only element. Defining this macro allows better control of register function parameters on big-endian machines, without using `PARALLEL` rtl. In particular, `MUST_PASS_IN_STACK` need not test padding and mode of types in registers, as there is no longer a "wrong" part of a register; For example, a three byte aggregate may be passed in the high part of a register if so required.

unsigned int TARGET_FUNCTION_ARG_BOUNDARY (*machine_mode* *mode*, *const_tree* *type*) [Target Hook]

This hook returns the alignment boundary, in bits, of an argument with the specified mode and type. The default hook returns `PARM_BOUNDARY` for all arguments.

unsigned int TARGET_FUNCTION_ARG_ROUND_BOUNDARY (*machine_mode* *mode*, *const_tree* *type*) [Target Hook]

Normally, the size of an argument is rounded up to `PARM_BOUNDARY`, which is the default value for this hook. You can define this hook to return a different value if an argument size must be rounded to a larger value.

FUNCTION_ARG_REGNO_P (*regno*) [Macro]

A C expression that is nonzero if *regno* is the number of a hard register in which function arguments are sometimes passed. This does *not* include implicit arguments such as the static chain and the structure-value address. On many machines, no registers can be used for this purpose since all function arguments are pushed on the stack.

bool TARGET_SPLIT_COMPLEX_ARG (*const_tree* *type*) [Target Hook]

This hook should return true if parameter of type *type* are passed as two scalar parameters. By default, GCC will attempt to pack complex arguments into the target's word size. Some ABIs require complex arguments to be split and treated as their individual components. For example, on AIX64, complex floats should be passed in a pair of floating point registers, even though a complex float would fit in one 64-bit floating point register.

The default value of this hook is `NULL`, which is treated as always false.

tree TARGET_BUILD_BUILTIN_VA_LIST (*void*) [Target Hook]

This hook returns a type node for `va_list` for the target. The default version of the hook returns `void*`.

int TARGET_ENUM_VA_LIST_P (*int* *idx*, *const char* **pname*, *tree* **ptree*) [Target Hook]

This target hook is used in function `c_common_nodes_and_builtins` to iterate through the target specific builtin types for va_list. The variable *idx* is used as iterator. *pname* has to be a pointer to a `const char *` and *ptree* a pointer to a `tree` typed variable. The arguments *pname* and *ptree* are used to store the result of this macro and are set to the name of the va_list builtin type and its internal type. If the return value of this macro is zero, then there is no more element. Otherwise the *IDX* should be increased for the next call of this macro to iterate through all types.

`tree TARGET_FN_ABI_VA_LIST (tree fndecl)`   [Target Hook]
This hook returns the va_list type of the calling convention specified by *fndecl*. The default version of this hook returns `va_list_type_node`.

`tree TARGET_CANONICAL_VA_LIST_TYPE (tree type)`   [Target Hook]
This hook returns the va_list type of the calling convention specified by the type of *type*. If *type* is not a valid va_list type, it returns `NULL_TREE`.

`tree TARGET_GIMPLIFY_VA_ARG_EXPR (tree valist, tree type,`   [Target Hook]
`        gimple_seq *pre_p, gimple_seq *post_p)`
This hook performs target-specific gimplification of `VA_ARG_EXPR`. The first two parameters correspond to the arguments to `va_arg`; the latter two are as in `gimplify.c:gimplify_expr`.

`bool TARGET_VALID_POINTER_MODE (machine_mode mode)`   [Target Hook]
Define this to return nonzero if the port can handle pointers with machine mode *mode*. The default version of this hook returns true for both `ptr_mode` and `Pmode`.

`bool TARGET_REF_MAY_ALIAS_ERRNO (struct ao_ref *ref)`   [Target Hook]
Define this to return nonzero if the memory reference *ref* may alias with the system C library errno location. The default version of this hook assumes the system C library errno location is either a declaration of type int or accessed by dereferencing a pointer to int.

`bool TARGET_SCALAR_MODE_SUPPORTED_P (machine_mode mode)`   [Target Hook]
Define this to return nonzero if the port is prepared to handle insns involving scalar mode *mode*. For a scalar mode to be considered supported, all the basic arithmetic and comparisons must work.

The default version of this hook returns true for any mode required to handle the basic C types (as defined by the port). Included here are the double-word arithmetic supported by the code in 'optabs.c'.

`bool TARGET_VECTOR_MODE_SUPPORTED_P (machine_mode mode)`   [Target Hook]
Define this to return nonzero if the port is prepared to handle insns involving vector mode *mode*. At the very least, it must have move patterns for this mode.

`bool TARGET_ARRAY_MODE_SUPPORTED_P (machine_mode mode,`   [Target Hook]
`        unsigned HOST_WIDE_INT nelems)`
Return true if GCC should try to use a scalar mode to store an array of *nelems* elements, given that each element has mode *mode*. Returning true here overrides the usual `MAX_FIXED_MODE` limit and allows GCC to use any defined integer mode.

One use of this hook is to support vector load and store operations that operate on several homogeneous vectors. For example, ARM NEON has operations like:

```
int8x8x3_t vld3_s8 (const int8_t *)
```

where the return type is defined as:

```
typedef struct int8x8x3_t
{
   int8x8_t val[3];
} int8x8x3_t;
```

If this hook allows `val` to have a scalar mode, then `int8x8x3_t` can have the same mode. GCC can then store `int8x8x3_t`s in registers rather than forcing them onto the stack.

bool TARGET_LIBGCC_FLOATING_MODE_SUPPORTED_P   [Target Hook]
      (*machine_mode* **mode**)

Define this to return nonzero if libgcc provides support for the floating-point mode *mode*, which is known to pass `TARGET_SCALAR_MODE_SUPPORTED_P`. The default version of this hook returns true for all of `SFmode`, `DFmode`, `XFmode` and `TFmode`, if such modes exist.

machine_mode TARGET_FLOATN_MODE (*int* **n**, *bool* **extended**)   [Target Hook]

Define this to return the machine mode to use for the type `_Floatn`, if *extended* is false, or the type `_Floatnx`, if *extended* is true. If such a type is not supported, return `VOIDmode`. The default version of this hook returns `SFmode` for `_Float32`, `DFmode` for `_Float64` and `_Float32x` and `TFmode` for `_Float128`, if those modes exist and satisfy the requirements for those types and pass `TARGET_SCALAR_MODE_SUPPORTED_P` and `TARGET_LIBGCC_FLOATING_MODE_SUPPORTED_P`; for `_Float64x`, it returns the first of `XFmode` and `TFmode` that exists and satisfies the same requirements; for other types, it returns `VOIDmode`. The hook is only called for values of n and *extended* that are valid according to ISO/IEC TS 18661-3:2015; that is, n is one of 32, 64, 128, or, if *extended* is false, 16 or greater than 128 and a multiple of 32.

bool TARGET_SMALL_REGISTER_CLASSES_FOR_MODE_P   [Target Hook]
      (*machine_mode* **mode**)

Define this to return nonzero for machine modes for which the port has small register classes. If this target hook returns nonzero for a given *mode*, the compiler will try to minimize the lifetime of registers in *mode*. The hook may be called with `VOIDmode` as argument. In this case, the hook is expected to return nonzero if it returns nonzero for any mode.

On some machines, it is risky to let hard registers live across arbitrary insns. Typically, these machines have instructions that require values to be in specific registers (like an accumulator), and reload will fail if the required hard register is used for another purpose across such an insn.

Passes before reload do not know which hard registers will be used in an instruction, but the machine modes of the registers set or used in the instruction are already known. And for some machines, register classes are small for, say, integer registers but not for floating point registers. For example, the AMD x86-64 architecture requires specific registers for the legacy x86 integer instructions, but there are many SSE registers for floating point operations. On such targets, a good strategy may be to return nonzero from this hook for `INTEGRAL_MODE_P` machine modes but zero for the SSE register classes.

The default version of this hook returns false for any mode. It is always safe to redefine this hook to return with a nonzero value. But if you unnecessarily define it, you will reduce the amount of optimizations that can be performed in some cases. If you do not define this hook to return a nonzero value when it is required, the compiler will run out of spill registers and print a fatal error message.

17.9.8 How Scalar Function Values Are Returned

This section discusses the macros that control returning scalars as values—values that can fit in registers.

rtx **TARGET_FUNCTION_VALUE** (*const_tree* **ret_type**, *const_tree*   [Target Hook]
     fn_decl_or_type, *bool* **outgoing**)

Define this to return an RTX representing the place where a function returns or receives a value of data type *ret_type*, a tree node representing a data type. *fn_decl_or_type* is a tree node representing FUNCTION_DECL or FUNCTION_TYPE of a function being called. If *outgoing* is false, the hook should compute the register in which the caller will see the return value. Otherwise, the hook should return an RTX representing the place where a function returns a value.

On many machines, only TYPE_MODE (**ret_type**) is relevant. (Actually, on most machines, scalar values are returned in the same place regardless of mode.) The value of the expression is usually a **reg** RTX for the hard register where the return value is stored. The value can also be a **parallel** RTX, if the return value is in multiple places. See TARGET_FUNCTION_ARG for an explanation of the **parallel** form. Note that the callee will populate every location specified in the **parallel**, but if the first element of the **parallel** contains the whole return value, callers will use that element as the canonical location and ignore the others. The m68k port uses this type of **parallel** to return pointers in both '%a0' (the canonical location) and '%d0'.

If TARGET_PROMOTE_FUNCTION_RETURN returns true, you must apply the same promotion rules specified in PROMOTE_MODE if *valtype* is a scalar type.

If the precise function being called is known, *func* is a tree node (FUNCTION_DECL) for it; otherwise, *func* is a null pointer. This makes it possible to use a different value-returning convention for specific functions when all their calls are known.

Some target machines have "register windows" so that the register in which a function returns its value is not the same as the one in which the caller sees the value. For such machines, you should return different RTX depending on *outgoing*.

TARGET_FUNCTION_VALUE is not used for return values with aggregate data types, because these are returned in another way. See TARGET_STRUCT_VALUE_RTX and related macros, below.

FUNCTION_VALUE (*valtype*, *func*)   [Macro]

This macro has been deprecated. Use TARGET_FUNCTION_VALUE for a new target instead.

LIBCALL_VALUE (*mode*)   [Macro]

A C expression to create an RTX representing the place where a library function returns a value of mode *mode*.

Note that "library function" in this context means a compiler support routine, used to perform arithmetic, whose name is known specially by the compiler and was not mentioned in the C code being compiled.

rtx TARGET_LIBCALL_VALUE (*machine_mode* **mode**, *const_rtx* **fun**)   [Target Hook]
> Define this hook if the back-end needs to know the name of the libcall function in order to determine where the result should be returned.
>
> The mode of the result is given by *mode* and the name of the called library function is given by *fun*. The hook should return an RTX representing the place where the library function result will be returned.
>
> If this hook is not defined, then LIBCALL_VALUE will be used.

FUNCTION_VALUE_REGNO_P (*regno*)   [Macro]
> A C expression that is nonzero if *regno* is the number of a hard register in which the values of called function may come back.
>
> A register whose use for returning values is limited to serving as the second of a pair (for a value of type **double**, say) need not be recognized by this macro. So for most machines, this definition suffices:
>
> ```
> #define FUNCTION_VALUE_REGNO_P(N) ((N) == 0)
> ```
>
> If the machine has register windows, so that the caller and the called function use different registers for the return value, this macro should recognize only the caller's register numbers.
>
> This macro has been deprecated. Use TARGET_FUNCTION_VALUE_REGNO_P for a new target instead.

bool TARGET_FUNCTION_VALUE_REGNO_P (*const unsigned int*   [Target Hook]
>   *regno*)
> A target hook that return **true** if *regno* is the number of a hard register in which the values of called function may come back.
>
> A register whose use for returning values is limited to serving as the second of a pair (for a value of type **double**, say) need not be recognized by this target hook.
>
> If the machine has register windows, so that the caller and the called function use different registers for the return value, this target hook should recognize only the caller's register numbers.
>
> If this hook is not defined, then FUNCTION_VALUE_REGNO_P will be used.

APPLY_RESULT_SIZE   [Macro]
> Define this macro if 'untyped_call' and 'untyped_return' need more space than is implied by FUNCTION_VALUE_REGNO_P for saving and restoring an arbitrary return value.

bool TARGET_OMIT_STRUCT_RETURN_REG   [Target Hook]
> Normally, when a function returns a structure by memory, the address is passed as an invisible pointer argument, but the compiler also arranges to return the address from the function like it would a normal pointer return value. Define this to true if that behavior is undesirable on your target.

bool **TARGET_RETURN_IN_MSB** (*const_tree* **type**)   [Target Hook]

> This hook should return true if values of type *type* are returned at the most significant end of a register (in other words, if they are padded at the least significant end). You can assume that *type* is returned in a register; the caller is required to check this.
>
> Note that the register provided by **TARGET_FUNCTION_VALUE** must be able to hold the complete return value. For example, if a 1-, 2- or 3-byte structure is returned at the most significant end of a 4-byte register, **TARGET_FUNCTION_VALUE** should provide an **SImode** rtx.

17.9.9 How Large Values Are Returned

When a function value's mode is **BLKmode** (and in some other cases), the value is not returned according to **TARGET_FUNCTION_VALUE** (see Section 17.9.8 [Scalar Return], page 496). Instead, the caller passes the address of a block of memory in which the value should be stored. This address is called the *structure value address*.

This section describes how to control returning structure values in memory.

bool **TARGET_RETURN_IN_MEMORY** (*const_tree* **type**, *const_tree*   [Target Hook]
     fntype)

> This target hook should return a nonzero value to say to return the function value in memory, just as large structures are always returned. Here *type* will be the data type of the value, and *fntype* will be the type of the function doing the returning, or **NULL** for libcalls.
>
> Note that values of mode **BLKmode** must be explicitly handled by this function. Also, the option '**-fpcc-struct-return**' takes effect regardless of this macro. On most systems, it is possible to leave the hook undefined; this causes a default definition to be used, whose value is the constant 1 for **BLKmode** values, and 0 otherwise.
>
> Do not use this hook to indicate that structures and unions should always be returned in memory. You should instead use **DEFAULT_PCC_STRUCT_RETURN** to indicate this.

DEFAULT_PCC_STRUCT_RETURN   [Macro]

> Define this macro to be 1 if all structure and union return values must be in memory. Since this results in slower code, this should be defined only if needed for compatibility with other compilers or with an ABI. If you define this macro to be 0, then the conventions used for structure and union return values are decided by the **TARGET_RETURN_IN_MEMORY** target hook.
>
> If not defined, this defaults to the value 1.

rtx **TARGET_STRUCT_VALUE_RTX** (*tree* **fndecl**, *int* **incoming**)   [Target Hook]

> This target hook should return the location of the structure value address (normally a **mem** or **reg**), or 0 if the address is passed as an "invisible" first argument. Note that *fndecl* may be **NULL**, for libcalls. You do not need to define this target hook if the address is always passed as an "invisible" first argument.
>
> On some architectures the place where the structure value address is found by the called function is not the same place that the caller put it. This can be due to register windows, or it could be because the function prologue moves it to a different place. *incoming* is **1** or **2** when the location is needed in the context of the called function, and **0** in the context of the caller.

If *incoming* is nonzero and the address is to be found on the stack, return a `mem` which refers to the frame pointer. If *incoming* is 2, the result is being used to fetch the structure value address at the beginning of a function. If you need to emit adjusting code, you should do it at this point.

PCC_STATIC_STRUCT_RETURN   [Macro]
> Define this macro if the usual system convention on the target machine for returning structures and unions is for the called function to return the address of a static variable containing the value.
>
> Do not define this if the usual system convention is for the caller to pass an address to the subroutine.
>
> This macro has effect in '`-fpcc-struct-return`' mode, but it does nothing when you use '`-freg-struct-return`' mode.

machine_mode TARGET_GET_RAW_RESULT_MODE (*int regno*)   [Target Hook]
> This target hook returns the mode to be used when accessing raw return registers in `__builtin_return`. Define this macro if the value in *reg_raw_mode* is not correct.

machine_mode TARGET_GET_RAW_ARG_MODE (*int regno*)   [Target Hook]
> This target hook returns the mode to be used when accessing raw argument registers in `__builtin_apply_args`. Define this macro if the value in *reg_raw_mode* is not correct.

17.9.10 Caller-Saves Register Allocation

If you enable it, GCC can save registers around function calls. This makes it possible to use call-clobbered registers to hold variables that must live across calls.

HARD_REGNO_CALLER_SAVE_MODE (*regno*, *nregs*)   [Macro]
> A C expression specifying which mode is required for saving *nregs* of a pseudo-register in call-clobbered hard register *regno*. If *regno* is unsuitable for caller save, `VOIDmode` should be returned. For most machines this macro need not be defined since GCC will select the smallest suitable mode.

17.9.11 Function Entry and Exit

This section describes the macros that output function entry (*prologue*) and exit (*epilogue*) code.

void TARGET_ASM_FUNCTION_PROLOGUE (*FILE *file*,   [Target Hook]
        HOST_WIDE_INT size)
> If defined, a function that outputs the assembler code for entry to a function. The prologue is responsible for setting up the stack frame, initializing the frame pointer register, saving registers that must be saved, and allocating *size* additional bytes of storage for the local variables. *size* is an integer. *file* is a stdio stream to which the assembler code should be output.
>
> The label for the beginning of the function need not be output by this macro. That has already been done when the macro is run.
>
> To determine which registers to save, the macro can refer to the array `regs_ever_live`: element *r* is nonzero if hard register *r* is used anywhere within the function.

This implies the function prologue should save register *r*, provided it is not one of the call-used registers. (`TARGET_ASM_FUNCTION_EPILOGUE` must likewise use `regs_ever_live`.)

On machines that have "register windows", the function entry code does not save on the stack the registers that are in the windows, even if they are supposed to be preserved by function calls; instead it takes appropriate steps to "push" the register stack, if any non-call-used registers are used in the function.

On machines where functions may or may not have frame-pointers, the function entry code must vary accordingly; it must set up the frame pointer if one is wanted, and not otherwise. To determine whether a frame pointer is in wanted, the macro can refer to the variable `frame_pointer_needed`. The variable's value will be 1 at run time in a function that needs a frame pointer. See Section 17.9.5 [Elimination], page 485.

The function entry code is responsible for allocating any stack space required for the function. This stack space consists of the regions listed below. In most cases, these regions are allocated in the order listed, with the last listed region closest to the top of the stack (the lowest address if `STACK_GROWS_DOWNWARD` is defined, and the highest address if it is not defined). You can use a different order for a machine if doing so is more convenient or required for compatibility reasons. Except in cases where required by standard or by a debugger, there is no reason why the stack layout used by GCC need agree with that used by other compilers for a machine.

void **TARGET_ASM_FUNCTION_END_PROLOGUE** (*FILE *file*)   [Target Hook]
> If defined, a function that outputs assembler code at the end of a prologue. This should be used when the function prologue is being emitted as RTL, and you have some extra assembler that needs to be emitted. See [prologue instruction pattern], page 383.

void **TARGET_ASM_FUNCTION_BEGIN_EPILOGUE** (*FILE *file*)   [Target Hook]
> If defined, a function that outputs assembler code at the start of an epilogue. This should be used when the function epilogue is being emitted as RTL, and you have some extra assembler that needs to be emitted. See [epilogue instruction pattern], page 383.

void **TARGET_ASM_FUNCTION_EPILOGUE** (*FILE *file*,   [Target Hook]
> *HOST_WIDE_INT size*)
> If defined, a function that outputs the assembler code for exit from a function. The epilogue is responsible for restoring the saved registers and stack pointer to their values when the function was called, and returning control to the caller. This macro takes the same arguments as the macro `TARGET_ASM_FUNCTION_PROLOGUE`, and the registers to restore are determined from `regs_ever_live` and `CALL_USED_REGISTERS` in the same way.

> On some machines, there is a single instruction that does all the work of returning from the function. On these machines, give that instruction the name 'return' and do not define the macro `TARGET_ASM_FUNCTION_EPILOGUE` at all.

> Do not define a pattern named 'return' if you want the `TARGET_ASM_FUNCTION_EPILOGUE` to be used. If you want the target switches to control whether return

instructions or epilogues are used, define a 'return' pattern with a validity condition that tests the target switches appropriately. If the 'return' pattern's validity condition is false, epilogues will be used.

On machines where functions may or may not have frame-pointers, the function exit code must vary accordingly. Sometimes the code for these two cases is completely different. To determine whether a frame pointer is wanted, the macro can refer to the variable `frame_pointer_needed`. The variable's value will be 1 when compiling a function that needs a frame pointer.

Normally, `TARGET_ASM_FUNCTION_PROLOGUE` and `TARGET_ASM_FUNCTION_EPILOGUE` must treat leaf functions specially. The C variable `current_function_is_leaf` is nonzero for such a function. See Section 17.7.4 [Leaf Functions], page 464.

On some machines, some functions pop their arguments on exit while others leave that for the caller to do. For example, the 68020 when given '-mrtd' pops arguments in functions that take a fixed number of arguments.

Your definition of the macro `RETURN_POPS_ARGS` decides which functions pop their own arguments. `TARGET_ASM_FUNCTION_EPILOGUE` needs to know what was decided. The number of bytes of the current function's arguments that this function should pop is available in `crtl->args.pops_args`. See Section 17.9.8 [Scalar Return], page 496.

- A region of `crtl->args.pretend_args_size` bytes of uninitialized space just underneath the first argument arriving on the stack. (This may not be at the very start of the allocated stack region if the calling sequence has pushed anything else since pushing the stack arguments. But usually, on such machines, nothing else has been pushed yet, because the function prologue itself does all the pushing.) This region is used on machines where an argument may be passed partly in registers and partly in memory, and, in some cases to support the features in `<stdarg.h>`.

- An area of memory used to save certain registers used by the function. The size of this area, which may also include space for such things as the return address and pointers to previous stack frames, is machine-specific and usually depends on which registers have been used in the function. Machines with register windows often do not require a save area.

- A region of at least *size* bytes, possibly rounded up to an allocation boundary, to contain the local variables of the function. On some machines, this region and the save area may occur in the opposite order, with the save area closer to the top of the stack.

- Optionally, when `ACCUMULATE_OUTGOING_ARGS` is defined, a region of `crtl->outgoing_args_size` bytes to be used for outgoing argument lists of the function. See Section 17.9.6 [Stack Arguments], page 486.

`EXIT_IGNORE_STACK`   [Macro]
Define this macro as a C expression that is nonzero if the return instruction or the function epilogue ignores the value of the stack pointer; in other words, if it is safe to delete an instruction to adjust the stack pointer before a return from the function. The default is 0.

Note that this macro's value is relevant only for functions for which frame pointers are maintained. It is never safe to delete a final stack adjustment in a function that has no frame pointer, and the compiler knows this regardless of `EXIT_IGNORE_STACK`.

EPILOGUE_USES (*regno*)   [Macro]
> Define this macro as a C expression that is nonzero for registers that are used by the epilogue or the 'return' pattern. The stack and frame pointer registers are already assumed to be used as needed.

EH_USES (*regno*)   [Macro]
> Define this macro as a C expression that is nonzero for registers that are used by the exception handling mechanism, and so should be considered live on entry to an exception edge.

void TARGET_ASM_OUTPUT_MI_THUNK (*FILE *file*, *tree*   [Target Hook]
> thunk_fndecl, *HOST_WIDE_INT* delta, *HOST_WIDE_INT*
> vcall_offset, *tree* function)

> A function that outputs the assembler code for a thunk function, used to implement C++ virtual function calls with multiple inheritance. The thunk acts as a wrapper around a virtual function, adjusting the implicit object parameter before handing control off to the real function.

> First, emit code to add the integer *delta* to the location that contains the incoming first argument. Assume that this argument contains a pointer, and is the one used to pass the this pointer in C++. This is the incoming argument *before* the function prologue, e.g. '%o0' on a sparc. The addition must preserve the values of all other incoming arguments.

> Then, if *vcall_offset* is nonzero, an additional adjustment should be made after adding delta. In particular, if *p* is the adjusted pointer, the following adjustment should be made:

> p += (*((ptrdiff_t **)p))[vcall_offset/sizeof(ptrdiff_t)]

> After the additions, emit code to jump to *function*, which is a FUNCTION_DECL. This is a direct pure jump, not a call, and does not touch the return address. Hence returning from *FUNCTION* will return to whoever called the current 'thunk'.

> The effect must be as if *function* had been called directly with the adjusted first argument. This macro is responsible for emitting all of the code for a thunk function; TARGET_ASM_FUNCTION_PROLOGUE and TARGET_ASM_FUNCTION_EPILOGUE are not invoked.

> The *thunk_fndecl* is redundant. (*delta* and *function* have already been extracted from it.) It might possibly be useful on some targets, but probably not.

> If you do not define this macro, the target-independent code in the C++ front end will generate a less efficient heavyweight thunk that calls *function* instead of jumping to it. The generic approach does not support varargs.

bool TARGET_ASM_CAN_OUTPUT_MI_THUNK (*const_tree*   [Target Hook]
> thunk_fndecl, *HOST_WIDE_INT* delta, *HOST_WIDE_INT*
> vcall_offset, *const_tree* function)

> A function that returns true if TARGET_ASM_OUTPUT_MI_THUNK would be able to output the assembler code for the thunk function specified by the arguments it is passed, and false otherwise. In the latter case, the generic approach will be used by the C++ front end, with the limitations previously exposed.

17.9.12 Generating Code for Profiling

These macros will help you generate code for profiling.

FUNCTION_PROFILER (`file`, `labelno`)   [Macro]

    A C statement or compound statement to output to *file* some assembler code to call the profiling subroutine `mcount`.

    The details of how `mcount` expects to be called are determined by your operating system environment, not by GCC. To figure them out, compile a small program for profiling using the system's installed C compiler and look at the assembler code that results.

    Older implementations of `mcount` expect the address of a counter variable to be loaded into some register. The name of this variable is 'LP' followed by the number *labelno*, so you would generate the name using 'LP%d' in a `fprintf`.

PROFILE_HOOK   [Macro]

    A C statement or compound statement to output to *file* some assembly code to call the profiling subroutine `mcount` even the target does not support profiling.

NO_PROFILE_COUNTERS   [Macro]

    Define this macro to be an expression with a nonzero value if the `mcount` subroutine on your system does not need a counter variable allocated for each function. This is true for almost all modern implementations. If you define this macro, you must not use the *labelno* argument to `FUNCTION_PROFILER`.

PROFILE_BEFORE_PROLOGUE   [Macro]

    Define this macro if the code for function profiling should come before the function prologue. Normally, the profiling code comes after.

bool TARGET_KEEP_LEAF_WHEN_PROFILED (*void*)   [Target Hook]

    This target hook returns true if the target wants the leaf flag for the current function to stay true even if it calls mcount. This might make sense for targets using the leaf flag only to determine whether a stack frame needs to be generated or not and for which the call to mcount is generated before the function prologue.

17.9.13 Permitting tail calls

bool TARGET_FUNCTION_OK_FOR_SIBCALL (*tree decl*, *tree exp*)   [Target Hook]

    True if it is OK to do sibling call optimization for the specified call expression *exp*. *decl* will be the called function, or `NULL` if this is an indirect call.

    It is not uncommon for limitations of calling conventions to prevent tail calls to functions outside the current unit of translation, or during PIC compilation. The hook is used to enforce these restrictions, as the `sibcall` md pattern can not fail, or fall over to a "normal" call. The criteria for successful sibling call optimization may vary greatly between different architectures.

void TARGET_EXTRA_LIVE_ON_ENTRY (*bitmap regs*)   [Target Hook]

    Add any hard registers to *regs* that are live on entry to the function. This hook only needs to be defined to provide registers that cannot be found by examination of FUNCTION_ARG_REGNO_P, the callee saved registers, STATIC_CHAIN_INCOMING_REGNUM, STATIC_CHAIN_REGNUM, TARGET_STRUCT_VALUE_RTX, FRAME_POINTER_REGNUM, EH_USES, FRAME_POINTER_REGNUM, ARG_POINTER_REGNUM, and the PIC_OFFSET_TABLE_REGNUM.

void TARGET_SET_UP_BY_PROLOGUE (*struct hard_reg_set_container* [Target Hook]
      *)

This hook should add additional registers that are computed by the prologue to the hard regset for shrink-wrapping optimization purposes.

bool TARGET_WARN_FUNC_RETURN (*tree*)   [Target Hook]

True if a function's return statements should be checked for matching the function's return type. This includes checking for falling off the end of a non-void function. Return false if no such check should be made.

17.9.14 Shrink-wrapping separate components

The prologue may perform a variety of target dependent tasks such as saving callee-saved registers, saving the return address, aligning the stack, creating a stack frame, initializing the PIC register, setting up the static chain, etc.

On some targets some of these tasks may be independent of others and thus may be shrink-wrapped separately. These independent tasks are referred to as components and are handled generically by the target independent parts of GCC.

Using the following hooks those prologue or epilogue components can be shrink-wrapped separately, so that the initialization (and possibly teardown) those components do is not done as frequently on execution paths where this would unnecessary.

What exactly those components are is up to the target code; the generic code treats them abstractly, as a bit in an sbitmap. These sbitmaps are allocated by the shrink_wrap.get_separate_components and shrink_wrap.components_for_bb hooks, and deallocated by the generic code.

sbitmap TARGET_SHRINK_WRAP_GET_SEPARATE_COMPONENTS (*void*)   [Target Hook]

This hook should return an sbitmap with the bits set for those components that can be separately shrink-wrapped in the current function. Return NULL if the current function should not get any separate shrink-wrapping. Don't define this hook if it would always return NULL. If it is defined, the other hooks in this group have to be defined as well.

sbitmap TARGET_SHRINK_WRAP_COMPONENTS_FOR_BB (*basic_block*)   [Target Hook]

This hook should return an sbitmap with the bits set for those components where either the prologue component has to be executed before the basic_block, or the epilogue component after it, or both.

void TARGET_SHRINK_WRAP_DISQUALIFY_COMPONENTS (*sbitmap*   [Target Hook]
      components, *edge* e, *sbitmap* edge_components, *bool* is_prologue)

This hook should clear the bits in the *components* bitmap for those components in *edge_components* that the target cannot handle on edge *e*, where *is_prologue* says if this is for a prologue or an epilogue instead.

void `TARGET_SHRINK_WRAP_EMIT_PROLOGUE_COMPONENTS`   [Target Hook]
    (*sbitmap*)
    Emit prologue insns for the components indicated by the parameter.

void `TARGET_SHRINK_WRAP_EMIT_EPILOGUE_COMPONENTS`   [Target Hook]
    (*sbitmap*)
    Emit epilogue insns for the components indicated by the parameter.

void `TARGET_SHRINK_WRAP_SET_HANDLED_COMPONENTS` (*sbitmap*)   [Target Hook]
    Mark the components in the parameter as handled, so that the `prologue` and
    `epilogue` named patterns know to ignore those components. The target code should
    not hang on to the `sbitmap`, it will be deleted after this call.

17.9.15 Stack smashing protection

tree `TARGET_STACK_PROTECT_GUARD` (*void*)   [Target Hook]
    This hook returns a `DECL` node for the external variable to use for the stack protection
    guard. This variable is initialized by the runtime to some random value and is used
    to initialize the guard value that is placed at the top of the local stack frame. The
    type of this variable must be `ptr_type_node`.

    The default version of this hook creates a variable called '`__stack_chk_guard`', which
    is normally defined in '`libgcc2.c`'.

tree `TARGET_STACK_PROTECT_FAIL` (*void*)   [Target Hook]
    This hook returns a `CALL_EXPR` that alerts the runtime that the stack protect guard
    variable has been modified. This expression should involve a call to a `noreturn`
    function.

    The default version of this hook invokes a function called '`__stack_chk_fail`', taking
    no arguments. This function is normally defined in '`libgcc2.c`'.

bool `TARGET_STACK_PROTECT_RUNTIME_ENABLED_P` (*void*)   [Target Hook]
    Returns true if the target wants GCC's default stack protect runtime support, oth-
    erwise return false. The default implementation always returns true.

bool `TARGET_SUPPORTS_SPLIT_STACK` (*bool* **report**,   [Common Target Hook]
    struct gcc_options ***opts**)
    Whether this target supports splitting the stack when the options described in *opts*
    have been passed. This is called after options have been parsed, so the target may
    reject splitting the stack in some configurations. The default version of this hook
    returns false. If *report* is true, this function may issue a warning or error; if *report* is
    false, it must simply return a value

17.9.16 Miscellaneous register hooks

bool `TARGET_CALL_FUSAGE_CONTAINS_NON_CALLEE_CLOBBERS`   [Target Hook]
    Set to true if each call that binds to a local definition explicitly clobbers or sets
    all non-fixed registers modified by performing the call. That is, by the call pat-
    tern itself, or by code that might be inserted by the linker (e.g. stubs, veneers,

branch islands), but not including those modifiable by the callee. The affected registers may be mentioned explicitly in the call pattern, or included as clobbers in CALL_INSN_FUNCTION_USAGE. The default version of this hook is set to false. The purpose of this hook is to enable the fipa-ra optimization.

17.10 Implementing the Varargs Macros

GCC comes with an implementation of `<varargs.h>` and `<stdarg.h>` that work without change on machines that pass arguments on the stack. Other machines require their own implementations of varargs, and the two machine independent header files must have conditionals to include it.

ISO `<stdarg.h>` differs from traditional `<varargs.h>` mainly in the calling convention for `va_start`. The traditional implementation takes just one argument, which is the variable in which to store the argument pointer. The ISO implementation of `va_start` takes an additional second argument. The user is supposed to write the last named argument of the function here.

However, `va_start` should not use this argument. The way to find the end of the named arguments is with the built-in functions described below.

`__builtin_saveregs ()`   [Macro]
> Use this built-in function to save the argument registers in memory so that the varargs mechanism can access them. Both ISO and traditional versions of `va_start` must use `__builtin_saveregs`, unless you use `TARGET_SETUP_INCOMING_VARARGS` (see below) instead.
>
> On some machines, `__builtin_saveregs` is open-coded under the control of the target hook `TARGET_EXPAND_BUILTIN_SAVEREGS`. On other machines, it calls a routine written in assembler language, found in 'libgcc2.c'.
>
> Code generated for the call to `__builtin_saveregs` appears at the beginning of the function, as opposed to where the call to `__builtin_saveregs` is written, regardless of what the code is. This is because the registers must be saved before the function starts to use them for its own purposes.

`__builtin_next_arg (lastarg)`   [Macro]
> This builtin returns the address of the first anonymous stack argument, as type `void *`. If `ARGS_GROW_DOWNWARD`, it returns the address of the location above the first anonymous stack argument. Use it in `va_start` to initialize the pointer for fetching arguments from the stack. Also use it in `va_start` to verify that the second parameter *lastarg* is the last named argument of the current function.

`__builtin_classify_type (object)`   [Macro]
> Since each machine has its own conventions for which data types are passed in which kind of register, your implementation of `va_arg` has to embody these conventions. The easiest way to categorize the specified data type is to use `__builtin_classify_type` together with `sizeof` and `__alignof__`.
>
> `__builtin_classify_type` ignores the value of *object*, considering only its data type. It returns an integer describing what kind of type that is—integer, floating, pointer, structure, and so on.

The file 'typeclass.h' defines an enumeration that you can use to interpret the values of __builtin_classify_type.

These machine description macros help implement varargs:

rtx TARGET_EXPAND_BUILTIN_SAVEREGS (*void*)   [Target Hook]
    If defined, this hook produces the machine-specific code for a call to __builtin_saveregs. This code will be moved to the very beginning of the function, before any parameter access are made. The return value of this function should be an RTX that contains the value to use as the return of __builtin_saveregs.

void TARGET_SETUP_INCOMING_VARARGS (*cumulative_args_t*   [Target Hook]
        args_so_far, *machine_mode* mode, *tree* type, *int* *pretend_args_size*, *int*
        second_time)
    This target hook offers an alternative to using __builtin_saveregs and defining the hook TARGET_EXPAND_BUILTIN_SAVEREGS. Use it to store the anonymous register arguments into the stack so that all the arguments appear to have been passed consecutively on the stack. Once this is done, you can use the standard implementation of varargs that works for machines that pass all their arguments on the stack.

    The argument *args_so_far* points to the CUMULATIVE_ARGS data structure, containing the values that are obtained after processing the named arguments. The arguments *mode* and *type* describe the last named argument—its machine mode and its data type as a tree node.

    The target hook should do two things: first, push onto the stack all the argument registers *not* used for the named arguments, and second, store the size of the data thus pushed into the int-valued variable pointed to by *pretend_args_size*. The value that you store here will serve as additional offset for setting up the stack frame.

    Because you must generate code to push the anonymous arguments at compile time without knowing their data types, TARGET_SETUP_INCOMING_VARARGS is only useful on machines that have just a single category of argument register and use it uniformly for all data types.

    If the argument *second_time* is nonzero, it means that the arguments of the function are being analyzed for the second time. This happens for an inline function, which is not actually compiled until the end of the source file. The hook TARGET_SETUP_INCOMING_VARARGS should not generate any instructions in this case.

bool TARGET_STRICT_ARGUMENT_NAMING (*cumulative_args_t* ca)   [Target Hook]
    Define this hook to return **true** if the location where a function argument is passed depends on whether or not it is a named argument.

    This hook controls how the *named* argument to TARGET_FUNCTION_ARG is set for varargs and stdarg functions. If this hook returns **true**, the *named* argument is always true for named arguments, and false for unnamed arguments. If it returns **false**, but TARGET_PRETEND_OUTGOING_VARARGS_NAMED returns **true**, then all arguments are treated as named. Otherwise, all named arguments except the last are treated as named.

    You need not define this hook if it always returns **false**.

`void TARGET_CALL_ARGS (`*rtx*`, tree)`   [Target Hook]

> While generating RTL for a function call, this target hook is invoked once for each argument passed to the function, either a register returned by `TARGET_FUNCTION_ARG` or a memory location. It is called just before the point where argument registers are stored. The type of the function to be called is also passed as the second argument; it is `NULL_TREE` for libcalls. The `TARGET_END_CALL_ARGS` hook is invoked just after the code to copy the return reg has been emitted. This functionality can be used to perform special setup of call argument registers if a target needs it. For functions without arguments, the hook is called once with `pc_rtx` passed instead of an argument register. Most ports do not need to implement anything for this hook.

`void TARGET_END_CALL_ARGS (`*void*`)`   [Target Hook]

> This target hook is invoked while generating RTL for a function call, just after the point where the return reg is copied into a pseudo. It signals that all the call argument and return registers for the just emitted call are now no longer in use. Most ports do not need to implement anything for this hook.

`bool TARGET_PRETEND_OUTGOING_VARARGS_NAMED`   [Target Hook]
      `(`*cumulative_args_t* `ca)`

> If you need to conditionally change ABIs so that one works with `TARGET_SETUP_INCOMING_VARARGS`, but the other works like neither `TARGET_SETUP_INCOMING_VARARGS` nor `TARGET_STRICT_ARGUMENT_NAMING` was defined, then define this hook to return **true** if `TARGET_SETUP_INCOMING_VARARGS` is used, **false** otherwise. Otherwise, you should not define this hook.

`rtx TARGET_LOAD_BOUNDS_FOR_ARG (`*rtx* `slot,` *rtx* `arg,` *rtx*   [Target Hook]
      `slot_no)`

> This hook is used by expand pass to emit insn to load bounds of *arg* passed in *slot*. Expand pass uses this hook in case bounds of *arg* are not passed in register. If *slot* is a memory, then bounds are loaded as for regular pointer loaded from memory. If *slot* is not a memory then *slot_no* is an integer constant holding number of the target dependent special slot which should be used to obtain bounds. Hook returns RTX holding loaded bounds.

`void TARGET_STORE_BOUNDS_FOR_ARG (`*rtx* `arg,` *rtx* `slot,` *rtx*   [Target Hook]
      `bounds,` *rtx* `slot_no)`

> This hook is used by expand pass to emit insns to store *bounds* of *arg* passed in *slot*. Expand pass uses this hook in case *bounds* of *arg* are not passed in register. If *slot* is a memory, then *bounds* are stored as for regular pointer stored in memory. If *slot* is not a memory then *slot_no* is an integer constant holding number of the target dependent special slot which should be used to store *bounds*.

`rtx TARGET_LOAD_RETURNED_BOUNDS (`*rtx* `slot)`   [Target Hook]

> This hook is used by expand pass to emit insn to load bounds returned by function call in *slot*. Hook returns RTX holding loaded bounds.

`void TARGET_STORE_RETURNED_BOUNDS (`*rtx* `slot,` *rtx* `bounds)`   [Target Hook]

> This hook is used by expand pass to emit insn to store *bounds* returned by function call into *slot*.

rtx **TARGET_CHKP_FUNCTION_VALUE_BOUNDS** (*const_tree* **ret_type**,   [Target Hook]
     const_tree **fn_decl_or_type**, *bool* **outgoing**)

> Define this to return an RTX representing the place where a function returns bounds for returned pointers. Arguments meaning is similar to **TARGET_FUNCTION_VALUE**.

void **TARGET_SETUP_INCOMING_VARARG_BOUNDS** (*cumulative_args_t*   [Target Hook]
     args_so_far, *enum machine_mode* **mode**, *tree* **type**, *int*
     ***pretend_args_size**, *int* **second_time**)

> Use it to store bounds for anonymous register arguments stored into the stack. Arguments meaning is similar to **TARGET_SETUP_INCOMING_VARARGS**.

17.11 Trampolines for Nested Functions

A *trampoline* is a small piece of code that is created at run time when the address of a nested function is taken. It normally resides on the stack, in the stack frame of the containing function. These macros tell GCC how to generate code to allocate and initialize a trampoline.

The instructions in the trampoline must do two things: load a constant address into the static chain register, and jump to the real address of the nested function. On CISC machines such as the m68k, this requires two instructions, a move immediate and a jump. Then the two addresses exist in the trampoline as word-long immediate operands. On RISC machines, it is often necessary to load each address into a register in two parts. Then pieces of each address form separate immediate operands.

The code generated to initialize the trampoline must store the variable parts—the static chain value and the function address—into the immediate operands of the instructions. On a CISC machine, this is simply a matter of copying each address to a memory reference at the proper offset from the start of the trampoline. On a RISC machine, it may be necessary to take out pieces of the address and store them separately.

void **TARGET_ASM_TRAMPOLINE_TEMPLATE** (*FILE *f*)   [Target Hook]

> This hook is called by **assemble_trampoline_template** to output, on the stream *f*, assembler code for a block of data that contains the constant parts of a trampoline. This code should not include a label—the label is taken care of automatically.

> If you do not define this hook, it means no template is needed for the target. Do not define this hook on systems where the block move code to copy the trampoline into place would be larger than the code to generate it on the spot.

TRAMPOLINE_SECTION   [Macro]

> Return the section into which the trampoline template is to be placed (see Section 17.18 [Sections], page 539). The default value is **readonly_data_section**.

TRAMPOLINE_SIZE   [Macro]

> A C expression for the size in bytes of the trampoline, as an integer.

TRAMPOLINE_ALIGNMENT   [Macro]

> Alignment required for trampolines, in bits.

> If you don't define this macro, the value of **FUNCTION_ALIGNMENT** is used for aligning trampolines.

void TARGET_TRAMPOLINE_INIT (*rtx* **m_tramp**, *tree* **fndecl**, *rtx*   [Target Hook]
    static_chain)

> This hook is called to initialize a trampoline. *m_tramp* is an RTX for the memory block for the trampoline; *fndecl* is the FUNCTION_DECL for the nested function; *static_chain* is an RTX for the static chain value that should be passed to the function when it is called.
>
> If the target defines TARGET_ASM_TRAMPOLINE_TEMPLATE, then the first thing this hook should do is emit a block move into *m_tramp* from the memory block returned by assemble_trampoline_template. Note that the block move need only cover the constant parts of the trampoline. If the target isolates the variable parts of the trampoline to the end, not all TRAMPOLINE_SIZE bytes need be copied.
>
> If the target requires any other actions, such as flushing caches or enabling stack execution, these actions should be performed after initializing the trampoline proper.

rtx TARGET_TRAMPOLINE_ADJUST_ADDRESS (*rtx* **addr**)   [Target Hook]

> This hook should perform any machine-specific adjustment in the address of the trampoline. Its argument contains the address of the memory block that was passed to TARGET_TRAMPOLINE_INIT. In case the address to be used for a function call should be different from the address at which the template was stored, the different address should be returned; otherwise *addr* should be returned unchanged. If this hook is not defined, *addr* will be used for function calls.

int TARGET_CUSTOM_FUNCTION_DESCRIPTORS   [Target Hook]

> This hook should be defined to a power of 2 if the target will benefit from the use of custom descriptors for nested functions instead of the standard trampolines. Such descriptors are created at run time on the stack and made up of data only, but they are non-standard so the generated code must be prepared to deal with them. This hook should be defined to 0 if the target uses function descriptors for its standard calling sequence, like for example HP-PA or IA-64. Using descriptors for nested functions eliminates the need for trampolines that reside on the stack and require it to be made executable.
>
> The value of the macro is used to parameterize the run-time identification scheme implemented to distinguish descriptors from function addresses: it gives the number of bytes by which their address is misaligned compared with function addresses. The value of 1 will generally work, unless it is already reserved by the target for another purpose, like for example on ARM.

Implementing trampolines is difficult on many machines because they have separate instruction and data caches. Writing into a stack location fails to clear the memory in the instruction cache, so when the program jumps to that location, it executes the old contents.

Here are two possible solutions. One is to clear the relevant parts of the instruction cache whenever a trampoline is set up. The other is to make all trampolines identical, by having them jump to a standard subroutine. The former technique makes trampoline execution faster; the latter makes initialization faster.

To clear the instruction cache when a trampoline is initialized, define the following macro.

CLEAR_INSN_CACHE (*beg*, *end*) [Macro]

> If defined, expands to a C expression clearing the *instruction cache* in the specified interval. The definition of this macro would typically be a series of **asm** statements. Both *beg* and *end* are both pointer expressions.

To use a standard subroutine, define the following macro. In addition, you must make sure that the instructions in a trampoline fill an entire cache line with identical instructions, or else ensure that the beginning of the trampoline code is always aligned at the same point in its cache line. Look in 'm68k.h' as a guide.

TRANSFER_FROM_TRAMPOLINE [Macro]

> Define this macro if trampolines need a special subroutine to do their work. The macro should expand to a series of **asm** statements which will be compiled with GCC. They go in a library function named __transfer_from_trampoline.

> If you need to avoid executing the ordinary prologue code of a compiled C function when you jump to the subroutine, you can do so by placing a special label of your own in the assembler code. Use one **asm** statement to generate an assembler label, and another to make the label global. Then trampolines can use that label to jump directly to your special assembler code.

17.12 Implicit Calls to Library Routines

Here is an explanation of implicit calls to library routines.

DECLARE_LIBRARY_RENAMES [Macro]

> This macro, if defined, should expand to a piece of C code that will get expanded when compiling functions for libgcc.a. It can be used to provide alternate names for GCC's internal library functions if there are ABI-mandated names that the compiler should provide.

void TARGET_INIT_LIBFUNCS (*void*) [Target Hook]

> This hook should declare additional library routines or rename existing ones, using the functions set_optab_libfunc and init_one_libfunc defined in 'optabs.c'. init_optabs calls this macro after initializing all the normal library routines.

> The default is to do nothing. Most ports don't need to define this hook.

bool TARGET_LIBFUNC_GNU_PREFIX [Target Hook]

> If false (the default), internal library routines start with two underscores. If set to true, these routines start with __gnu_ instead. E.g., __muldi3 changes to __gnu_muldi3. This currently only affects functions defined in 'libgcc2.c'. If this is set to true, the 'tm.h' file must also #define LIBGCC2_GNU_PREFIX.

FLOAT_LIB_COMPARE_RETURNS_BOOL (*mode*, *comparison*) [Macro]

> This macro should return **true** if the library routine that implements the floating point comparison operator *comparison* in mode *mode* will return a boolean, and *false* if it will return a tristate.

> GCC's own floating point libraries return tristates from the comparison operators, so the default returns false always. Most ports don't need to define this macro.

TARGET_LIB_INT_CMP_BIASED   [Macro]

    This macro should evaluate to **true** if the integer comparison functions (like **__ cmpdi2**) return 0 to indicate that the first operand is smaller than the second, 1 to indicate that they are equal, and 2 to indicate that the first operand is greater than the second. If this macro evaluates to **false** the comparison functions return -1, 0, and 1 instead of 0, 1, and 2. If the target uses the routines in 'libgcc.a', you do not need to define this macro.

TARGET_HAS_NO_HW_DIVIDE   [Macro]

    This macro should be defined if the target has no hardware divide instructions. If this macro is defined, GCC will use an algorithm which make use of simple logical and arithmetic operations for 64-bit division. If the macro is not defined, GCC will use an algorithm which make use of a 64-bit by 32-bit divide primitive.

TARGET_EDOM   [Macro]

    The value of **EDOM** on the target machine, as a C integer constant expression. If you don't define this macro, GCC does not attempt to deposit the value of **EDOM** into **errno** directly. Look in '/usr/include/errno.h' to find the value of **EDOM** on your system.

    If you do not define **TARGET_EDOM**, then compiled code reports domain errors by calling the library function and letting it report the error. If mathematical functions on your system use **matherr** when there is an error, then you should leave **TARGET_ EDOM** undefined so that **matherr** is used normally.

GEN_ERRNO_RTX   [Macro]

    Define this macro as a C expression to create an rtl expression that refers to the global "variable" **errno**. (On certain systems, **errno** may not actually be a variable.) If you don't define this macro, a reasonable default is used.

bool TARGET_LIBC_HAS_FUNCTION (*enum function_class* **fn_class**)   [Target Hook]

    This hook determines whether a function from a class of functions *fn_class* is present at the runtime.

NEXT_OBJC_RUNTIME   [Macro]

    Set this macro to 1 to use the "NeXT" Objective-C message sending conventions by default. This calling convention involves passing the object, the selector and the method arguments all at once to the method-lookup library function. This is the usual setting when targeting Darwin/Mac OS X systems, which have the NeXT runtime installed.

    If the macro is set to 0, the "GNU" Objective-C message sending convention will be used by default. This convention passes just the object and the selector to the method-lookup function, which returns a pointer to the method.

    In either case, it remains possible to select code-generation for the alternate scheme, by means of compiler command line switches.

17.13 Addressing Modes

This is about addressing modes.

`HAVE_PRE_INCREMENT`   [Macro]
`HAVE_PRE_DECREMENT`   [Macro]
`HAVE_POST_INCREMENT`   [Macro]
`HAVE_POST_DECREMENT`   [Macro]

> A C expression that is nonzero if the machine supports pre-increment, pre-decrement, post-increment, or post-decrement addressing respectively.

`HAVE_PRE_MODIFY_DISP`   [Macro]
`HAVE_POST_MODIFY_DISP`   [Macro]

> A C expression that is nonzero if the machine supports pre- or post-address side-effect generation involving constants other than the size of the memory operand.

`HAVE_PRE_MODIFY_REG`   [Macro]
`HAVE_POST_MODIFY_REG`   [Macro]

> A C expression that is nonzero if the machine supports pre- or post-address side-effect generation involving a register displacement.

`CONSTANT_ADDRESS_P (x)`   [Macro]

> A C expression that is 1 if the RTX x is a constant which is a valid address. On most machines the default definition of `(CONSTANT_P (x) && GET_CODE (x) != CONST_DOUBLE)` is acceptable, but a few machines are more restrictive as to which constant addresses are supported.

`CONSTANT_P (x)`   [Macro]

> `CONSTANT_P`, which is defined by target-independent code, accepts integer-values expressions whose values are not explicitly known, such as `symbol_ref`, `label_ref`, and `high` expressions and `const` arithmetic expressions, in addition to `const_int` and `const_double` expressions.

`MAX_REGS_PER_ADDRESS`   [Macro]

> A number, the maximum number of registers that can appear in a valid memory address. Note that it is up to you to specify a value equal to the maximum number that `TARGET_LEGITIMATE_ADDRESS_P` would ever accept.

`bool TARGET_LEGITIMATE_ADDRESS_P (`*machine_mode* `mode,` *rtx* `x,`   [Target Hook]
     bool `strict)`

> A function that returns whether x (an RTX) is a legitimate memory address on the target machine for a memory operand of mode *mode*.
>
> Legitimate addresses are defined in two variants: a strict variant and a non-strict one. The *strict* parameter chooses which variant is desired by the caller.
>
> The strict variant is used in the reload pass. It must be defined so that any pseudo-register that has not been allocated a hard register is considered a memory reference. This is because in contexts where some kind of register is required, a pseudo-register with no hard register must be rejected. For non-hard registers, the strict variant should look up the `reg_renumber` array; it should then proceed using the hard register number in the array, or treat the pseudo as a memory reference if the array holds -1.

The non-strict variant is used in other passes. It must be defined to accept all pseudo-registers in every context where some kind of register is required.

Normally, constant addresses which are the sum of a `symbol_ref` and an integer are stored inside a `const` RTX to mark them as constant. Therefore, there is no need to recognize such sums specifically as legitimate addresses. Normally you would simply recognize any `const` as legitimate.

Usually `PRINT_OPERAND_ADDRESS` is not prepared to handle constant sums that are not marked with `const`. It assumes that a naked `plus` indicates indexing. If so, then you *must* reject such naked constant sums as illegitimate addresses, so that none of them will be given to `PRINT_OPERAND_ADDRESS`.

On some machines, whether a symbolic address is legitimate depends on the section that the address refers to. On these machines, define the target hook `TARGET_ENCODE_SECTION_INFO` to store the information into the `symbol_ref`, and then check for it here. When you see a `const`, you will have to look inside it to find the `symbol_ref` in order to determine the section. See Section 17.20 [Assembler Format], page 545.

Some ports are still using a deprecated legacy substitute for this hook, the `GO_IF_LEGITIMATE_ADDRESS` macro. This macro has this syntax:

```
#define GO_IF_LEGITIMATE_ADDRESS (mode, x, label)
```

and should `goto` *label* if the address *x* is a valid address on the target machine for a memory operand of mode *mode*.

Compiler source files that want to use the strict variant of this macro define the macro `REG_OK_STRICT`. You should use an `#ifdef REG_OK_STRICT` conditional to define the strict variant in that case and the non-strict variant otherwise.

Using the hook is usually simpler because it limits the number of files that are recompiled when changes are made.

TARGET_MEM_CONSTRAINT   [Macro]

A single character to be used instead of the default 'm' character for general memory addresses. This defines the constraint letter which matches the memory addresses accepted by `TARGET_LEGITIMATE_ADDRESS_P`. Define this macro if you want to support new address formats in your back end without changing the semantics of the 'm' constraint. This is necessary in order to preserve functionality of inline assembly constructs using the 'm' constraint.

FIND_BASE_TERM (*x*)   [Macro]

A C expression to determine the base term of address *x*, or to provide a simplified version of *x* from which 'alias.c' can easily find the base term. This macro is used in only two places: `find_base_value` and `find_base_term` in 'alias.c'.

It is always safe for this macro to not be defined. It exists so that alias analysis can understand machine-dependent addresses.

The typical use of this macro is to handle addresses containing a label_ref or symbol_ref within an UNSPEC.

rtx TARGET_LEGITIMIZE_ADDRESS (*rtx x*, *rtx oldx*, *machine_mode*   [Target Hook]
       mode)

This hook is given an invalid memory address *x* for an operand of mode *mode* and should try to return a valid memory address.

x will always be the result of a call to `break_out_memory_refs`, and *oldx* will be the operand that was given to that function to produce *x*.

The code of the hook should not alter the substructure of *x*. If it transforms *x* into a more legitimate form, it should return the new *x*.

It is not necessary for this hook to come up with a legitimate address, with the exception of native TLS addresses (see Section 17.25 [Emulated TLS], page 585). The compiler has standard ways of doing so in all cases. In fact, if the target supports only emulated TLS, it is safe to omit this hook or make it return *x* if it cannot find a valid way to legitimize the address. But often a machine-dependent strategy can generate better code.

LEGITIMIZE_RELOAD_ADDRESS (*x*, *mode*, *opnum*, *type*, *ind_levels*, *win*)   [Macro]
  A C compound statement that attempts to replace *x*, which is an address that needs reloading, with a valid memory address for an operand of mode *mode*. *win* will be a C statement label elsewhere in the code. It is not necessary to define this macro, but it might be useful for performance reasons.

  For example, on the i386, it is sometimes possible to use a single reload register instead of two by reloading a sum of two pseudo registers into a register. On the other hand, for number of RISC processors offsets are limited so that often an intermediate address needs to be generated in order to address a stack slot. By defining **LEGITIMIZE_RELOAD_ADDRESS** appropriately, the intermediate addresses generated for adjacent some stack slots can be made identical, and thus be shared.

  Note: This macro should be used with caution. It is necessary to know something of how reload works in order to effectively use this, and it is quite easy to produce macros that build in too much knowledge of reload internals.

  Note: This macro must be able to reload an address created by a previous invocation of this macro. If it fails to handle such addresses then the compiler may generate incorrect code or abort.

  The macro definition should use `push_reload` to indicate parts that need reloading; *opnum*, *type* and *ind_levels* are usually suitable to be passed unaltered to `push_reload`.

  The code generated by this macro must not alter the substructure of *x*. If it transforms *x* into a more legitimate form, it should assign *x* (which will always be a C variable) a new value. This also applies to parts that you change indirectly by calling `push_reload`.

  The macro definition may use `strict_memory_address_p` to test if the address has become legitimate.

  If you want to change only a part of *x*, one standard way of doing this is to use `copy_rtx`. Note, however, that it unshares only a single level of rtl. Thus, if the part to be changed is not at the top level, you'll need to replace first the top level. It is not necessary for this macro to come up with a legitimate address; but often a machine-dependent strategy can generate better code.

`bool TARGET_MODE_DEPENDENT_ADDRESS_P` (*const_rtx* **addr**,   [Target Hook]
  addr_space_t **addrspace**)

> This hook returns `true` if memory address *addr* in address space *addrspace* can have different meanings depending on the machine mode of the memory reference it is used for or if the address is valid for some modes but not others.
>
> Autoincrement and autodecrement addresses typically have mode-dependent effects because the amount of the increment or decrement is the size of the operand being addressed. Some machines have other mode-dependent addresses. Many RISC machines have no mode-dependent addresses.
>
> You may assume that *addr* is a valid address for the machine.
>
> The default version of this hook returns `false`.

`bool TARGET_LEGITIMATE_CONSTANT_P` (*machine_mode* **mode**, *rtx*   [Target Hook]
  x)

> This hook returns true if *x* is a legitimate constant for a *mode*-mode immediate operand on the target machine. You can assume that *x* satisfies `CONSTANT_P`, so you need not check this.
>
> The default definition returns true.

`rtx TARGET_DELEGITIMIZE_ADDRESS` (*rtx* **x**)   [Target Hook]

> This hook is used to undo the possibly obfuscating effects of the `LEGITIMIZE_ADDRESS` and `LEGITIMIZE_RELOAD_ADDRESS` target macros. Some backend implementations of these macros wrap symbol references inside an `UNSPEC` rtx to represent PIC or similar addressing modes. This target hook allows GCC's optimizers to understand the semantics of these opaque `UNSPEC`s by converting them back into their original form.

`bool TARGET_CONST_NOT_OK_FOR_DEBUG_P` (*rtx* **x**)   [Target Hook]

> This hook should return true if *x* should not be emitted into debug sections.

`bool TARGET_CANNOT_FORCE_CONST_MEM` (*machine_mode* **mode**, *rtx*   [Target Hook]
  x)

> This hook should return true if *x* is of a form that cannot (or should not) be spilled to the constant pool. *mode* is the mode of *x*.
>
> The default version of this hook returns false.
>
> The primary reason to define this hook is to prevent reload from deciding that a non-legitimate constant would be better reloaded from the constant pool instead of spilling and reloading a register holding the constant. This restriction is often true of addresses of TLS symbols for various targets.

`bool TARGET_USE_BLOCKS_FOR_CONSTANT_P` (*machine_mode* **mode**,   [Target Hook]
  const_rtx **x**)

> This hook should return true if pool entries for constant *x* can be placed in an `object_block` structure. *mode* is the mode of *x*.
>
> The default version returns false for all constants.

bool TARGET_USE_BLOCKS_FOR_DECL_P (*const_tree* **decl**)   [Target Hook]

This hook should return true if pool entries for *decl* should be placed in an object_block structure.

The default version returns true for all decls.

tree TARGET_BUILTIN_RECIPROCAL (*tree* **fndecl**)   [Target Hook]

This hook should return the DECL of a function that implements the reciprocal of the machine-specific builtin function *fndecl*, or NULL_TREE if such a function is not available.

tree TARGET_VECTORIZE_BUILTIN_MASK_FOR_LOAD (*void*)   [Target Hook]

This hook should return the DECL of a function f that given an address *addr* as an argument returns a mask m that can be used to extract from two vectors the relevant data that resides in *addr* in case *addr* is not properly aligned.

The autovectorizer, when vectorizing a load operation from an address *addr* that may be unaligned, will generate two vector loads from the two aligned addresses around *addr*. It then generates a REALIGN_LOAD operation to extract the relevant data from the two loaded vectors. The first two arguments to REALIGN_LOAD, *v1* and *v2*, are the two vectors, each of size *VS*, and the third argument, *OFF*, defines how the data will be extracted from these two vectors: if *OFF* is 0, then the returned vector is *v2*; otherwise, the returned vector is composed from the last *VS-OFF* elements of *v1* concatenated to the first *OFF* elements of *v2*.

If this hook is defined, the autovectorizer will generate a call to f (using the DECL tree that this hook returns) and will use the return value of f as the argument *OFF* to REALIGN_LOAD. Therefore, the mask m returned by f should comply with the semantics expected by REALIGN_LOAD described above. If this hook is not defined, then *addr* will be used as the argument *OFF* to REALIGN_LOAD, in which case the low $\log2(VS) - 1$ bits of *addr* will be considered.

int TARGET_VECTORIZE_BUILTIN_VECTORIZATION_COST (*enum*   [Target Hook]
        vect_cost_for_stmt **type_of_cost**, *tree* **vectype**, *int* **misalign**)

Returns cost of different scalar or vector statements for vectorization cost model. For vector memory operations the cost may depend on type (*vectype*) and misalignment value (*misalign*).

bool TARGET_VECTORIZE_VECTOR_ALIGNMENT_REACHABLE   [Target Hook]
        (*const_tree* **type**, *bool* **is_packed**)

Return true if vector alignment is reachable (by peeling N iterations) for the given type.

bool TARGET_VECTORIZE_VEC_PERM_CONST_OK (*machine_mode*,   [Target Hook]
        const unsigned char ***sel**)

Return true if a vector created for vec_perm_const is valid.

tree TARGET_VECTORIZE_BUILTIN_CONVERSION (*unsigned* **code**,   [Target Hook]
        tree **dest_type**, *tree* **src_type**)

This hook should return the DECL of a function that implements conversion of the input vector of type *src_type* to type *dest_type*. The value of *code* is one of the enumerators in `enum tree_code` and specifies how the conversion is to be applied (truncation, rounding, etc.).

If this hook is defined, the autovectorizer will use the `TARGET_VECTORIZE_BUILTIN_CONVERSION` target hook when vectorizing conversion. Otherwise, it will return `NULL_TREE`.

`tree TARGET_VECTORIZE_BUILTIN_VECTORIZED_FUNCTION`   [Target Hook]
        (*unsigned* `code`, *tree* `vec_type_out`, *tree* `vec_type_in`)

This hook should return the decl of a function that implements the vectorized variant of the function with the `combined_fn` code *code* or `NULL_TREE` if such a function is not available. The return type of the vectorized function shall be of vector type *vec_type_out* and the argument types should be *vec_type_in*.

`tree TARGET_VECTORIZE_BUILTIN_MD_VECTORIZED_FUNCTION`   [Target Hook]
        (*tree* `fndecl`, *tree* `vec_type_out`, *tree* `vec_type_in`)

This hook should return the decl of a function that implements the vectorized variant of target built-in function `fndecl`. The return type of the vectorized function shall be of vector type *vec_type_out* and the argument types should be *vec_type_in*.

`bool TARGET_VECTORIZE_SUPPORT_VECTOR_MISALIGNMENT`   [Target Hook]
        (*machine_mode* `mode`, *const_tree* `type`, *int* `misalignment`, *bool* `is_packed`)

This hook should return true if the target supports misaligned vector store/load of a specific factor denoted in the *misalignment* parameter. The vector store/load should be of machine mode *mode* and the elements in the vectors should be of type *type*. *is_packed* parameter is true if the memory access is defined in a packed struct.

`machine_mode TARGET_VECTORIZE_PREFERRED_SIMD_MODE`   [Target Hook]
        (*machine_mode* `mode`)

This hook should return the preferred mode for vectorizing scalar mode *mode*. The default is equal to `word_mode`, because the vectorizer can do some transformations even in absence of specialized SIMD hardware.

`unsigned int`   [Target Hook]
        `TARGET_VECTORIZE_AUTOVECTORIZE_VECTOR_SIZES` (*void*)

This hook should return a mask of sizes that should be iterated over after trying to autovectorize using the vector size derived from the mode returned by `TARGET_VECTORIZE_PREFERRED_SIMD_MODE`. The default is zero which means to not iterate over other vector sizes.

`machine_mode TARGET_VECTORIZE_GET_MASK_MODE` (*unsigned*   [Target Hook]
        `nunits`, *unsigned* `length`)

This hook returns mode to be used for a mask to be used for a vector of specified *length* with *nunits* elements. By default an integer vector mode of a proper size is returned.

`void * TARGET_VECTORIZE_INIT_COST` (*struct loop* `*loop_info`)   [Target Hook]

This hook should initialize target-specific data structures in preparation for modeling the costs of vectorizing a loop or basic block. The default allocates three unsigned integers for accumulating costs for the prologue, body, and epilogue of the loop or basic block. If *loop_info* is non-NULL, it identifies the loop being vectorized; otherwise a single block is being vectorized.

unsigned TARGET_VECTORIZE_ADD_STMT_COST (*void **data*, *int*   [Target Hook]
    count, *enum vect_cost_for_stmt* **kind**, *struct _stmt_vec_info* ***stmt_info***, *int*
    misalign, *enum vect_cost_model_location* **where**)
    This hook should update the target-specific *data* in response to adding *count* copies
    of the given *kind* of statement to a loop or basic block. The default adds the builtin
    vectorizer cost for the copies of the statement to the accumulator specified by *where*,
    (the prologue, body, or epilogue) and returns the amount added. The return value
    should be viewed as a tentative cost that may later be revised.

void TARGET_VECTORIZE_FINISH_COST (*void **data*, *unsigned*   [Target Hook]
    prologue_cost, *unsigned **body_cost**, *unsigned **epilogue_cost**)
    This hook should complete calculations of the cost of vectorizing a loop or basic block
    based on *data*, and return the prologue, body, and epilogue costs as unsigned integers.
    The default returns the value of the three accumulators.

void TARGET_VECTORIZE_DESTROY_COST_DATA (*void **data*)   [Target Hook]
    This hook should release *data* and any related data structures allocated by TAR-
    GET_VECTORIZE_INIT_COST. The default releases the accumulator.

tree TARGET_VECTORIZE_BUILTIN_GATHER (*const_tree*   [Target Hook]
    mem_vectype, *const_tree* ***index_type***, *int* ***scale***)
    Target builtin that implements vector gather operation. *mem_vectype* is the vector
    type of the load and *index_type* is scalar type of the index, scaled by *scale*. The
    default is NULL_TREE which means to not vectorize gather loads.

tree TARGET_VECTORIZE_BUILTIN_SCATTER (*const_tree* ***vectype***,   [Target Hook]
    const_tree ***index_type***, *int* ***scale***)
    Target builtin that implements vector scatter operation. *vectype* is the vector type
    of the store and *index_type* is scalar type of the index, scaled by *scale*. The default
    is NULL_TREE which means to not vectorize scatter stores.

int TARGET_SIMD_CLONE_COMPUTE_VECSIZE_AND_SIMDLEN (*struct*   [Target Hook]
    *cgraph_node **, *struct cgraph_simd_clone **, **tree**, **int**)
    This hook should set *vecsize_mangle*, *vecsize_int*, *vecsize_float* fields in *simd_clone*
    structure pointed by *clone_info* argument and also *simdlen* field if it was previously
    0. The hook should return 0 if SIMD clones shouldn't be emitted, or number of
    vecsize_mangle variants that should be emitted.

void TARGET_SIMD_CLONE_ADJUST (*struct cgraph_node **)   [Target Hook]
    This hook should add implicit **attribute(target("..."))** attribute to SIMD clone
    node if needed.

int TARGET_SIMD_CLONE_USABLE (*struct cgraph_node **)   [Target Hook]
    This hook should return -1 if SIMD clone *node* shouldn't be used in vectorized loops
    in current function, or non-negative number if it is usable. In that case, the smaller
    the number is, the more desirable it is to use it.

`int TARGET_SIMT_VF (`*void*`)`   [Target Hook]
> Return number of threads in SIMT thread group on the target.

`bool TARGET_GOACC_VALIDATE_DIMS (`*tree* `decl,` *int* `*dims,` *int*   [Target Hook]
>   `fn_level)`
> This hook should check the launch dimensions provided for an OpenACC compute
> region, or routine. Defaulted values are represented as -1 and non-constant values as
> 0. The *fn_level* is negative for the function corresponding to the compute region. For
> a routine is is the outermost level at which partitioned execution may be spawned.
> The hook should verify non-default values. If DECL is NULL, global defaults are
> being validated and unspecified defaults should be filled in. Diagnostics should be
> issued as appropriate. Return true, if changes have been made. You must override
> this hook to provide dimensions larger than 1.

`int TARGET_GOACC_DIM_LIMIT (`*int* `axis)`   [Target Hook]
> This hook should return the maximum size of a particular dimension, or zero if
> unbounded.

`bool TARGET_GOACC_FORK_JOIN (`*gcall* `*call,` *const int* `*dims,` *bool*   [Target Hook]
>   `is_fork)`
> This hook can be used to convert IFN_GOACC_FORK and IFN_GOACC_JOIN func-
> tion calls to target-specific gimple, or indicate whether they should be retained. It is
> executed during the oacc_device_lower pass. It should return true, if the call should
> be retained. It should return false, if it is to be deleted (either because target-specific
> gimple has been inserted before it, or there is no need for it). The default hook returns
> false, if there are no RTL expanders for them.

`void TARGET_GOACC_REDUCTION (`*gcall* `*call)`   [Target Hook]
> This hook is used by the oacc_transform pass to expand calls to the
> *GOACC_REDUCTION* internal function, into a sequence of gimple instructions.
> *call* is gimple statement containing the call to the function. This hook removes
> statement *call* after the expanded sequence has been inserted. This hook is also
> responsible for allocating any storage for reductions when necessary.

17.14 Anchored Addresses

GCC usually addresses every static object as a separate entity. For example, if we have:

```
static int a, b, c;
int foo (void) { return a + b + c; }
```

the code for `foo` will usually calculate three separate symbolic addresses: those of `a`, `b`
and `c`. On some targets, it would be better to calculate just one symbolic address and access
the three variables relative to it. The equivalent pseudocode would be something like:

```
int foo (void)
{
  register int *xr = &x;
  return xr[&a - &x] + xr[&b - &x] + xr[&c - &x];
}
```

(which isn't valid C). We refer to shared addresses like `x` as "section anchors". Their use
is controlled by '`-fsection-anchors`'.

The hooks below describe the target properties that GCC needs to know in order to make effective use of section anchors. It won't use section anchors at all unless either TARGET_MIN_ANCHOR_OFFSET or TARGET_MAX_ANCHOR_OFFSET is set to a nonzero value.

HOST_WIDE_INT TARGET_MIN_ANCHOR_OFFSET   [Target Hook]

> The minimum offset that should be applied to a section anchor. On most targets, it should be the smallest offset that can be applied to a base register while still giving a legitimate address for every mode. The default value is 0.

HOST_WIDE_INT TARGET_MAX_ANCHOR_OFFSET   [Target Hook]

> Like TARGET_MIN_ANCHOR_OFFSET, but the maximum (inclusive) offset that should be applied to section anchors. The default value is 0.

void TARGET_ASM_OUTPUT_ANCHOR (rtx x)   [Target Hook]

> Write the assembly code to define section anchor x, which is a SYMBOL_REF for which 'SYMBOL_REF_ANCHOR_P (x)' is true. The hook is called with the assembly output position set to the beginning of SYMBOL_REF_BLOCK (x).
>
> If ASM_OUTPUT_DEF is available, the hook's default definition uses it to define the symbol as '. + SYMBOL_REF_BLOCK_OFFSET (x)'. If ASM_OUTPUT_DEF is not available, the hook's default definition is NULL, which disables the use of section anchors altogether.

bool TARGET_USE_ANCHORS_FOR_SYMBOL_P (const_rtx x)   [Target Hook]

> Return true if GCC should attempt to use anchors to access SYMBOL_REF x. You can assume 'SYMBOL_REF_HAS_BLOCK_INFO_P (x)' and '!SYMBOL_REF_ANCHOR_P (x)'.
>
> The default version is correct for most targets, but you might need to intercept this hook to handle things like target-specific attributes or target-specific sections.

17.15 Condition Code Status

The macros in this section can be split in two families, according to the two ways of representing condition codes in GCC.

The first representation is the so called (cc0) representation (see Section 16.12 [Jump Patterns], page 390), where all instructions can have an implicit clobber of the condition codes. The second is the condition code register representation, which provides better schedulability for architectures that do have a condition code register, but on which most instructions do not affect it. The latter category includes most RISC machines.

The implicit clobbering poses a strong restriction on the placement of the definition and use of the condition code. In the past the definition and use were always adjacent. However, recent changes to support trapping arithmatic may result in the definition and user being in different blocks. Thus, there may be a NOTE_INSN_BASIC_BLOCK between them. Additionally, the definition may be the source of exception handling edges.

These restrictions can prevent important optimizations on some machines. For example, on the IBM RS/6000, there is a delay for taken branches unless the condition code register is set three instructions earlier than the conditional branch. The instruction scheduler cannot perform this optimization if it is not permitted to separate the definition and use of the condition code register.

For this reason, it is possible and suggested to use a register to represent the condition code for new ports. If there is a specific condition code register in the machine, use a hard register. If the condition code or comparison result can be placed in any general register, or if there are multiple condition registers, use a pseudo register. Registers used to store the condition code value will usually have a mode that is in class MODE_CC.

Alternatively, you can use BImode if the comparison operator is specified already in the compare instruction. In this case, you are not interested in most macros in this section.

17.15.1 Representation of condition codes using (cc0)

The file 'conditions.h' defines a variable cc_status to describe how the condition code was computed (in case the interpretation of the condition code depends on the instruction that it was set by). This variable contains the RTL expressions on which the condition code is currently based, and several standard flags.

Sometimes additional machine-specific flags must be defined in the machine description header file. It can also add additional machine-specific information by defining CC_STATUS_MDEP.

CC_STATUS_MDEP   [Macro]
    C code for a data type which is used for declaring the mdep component of cc_status. It defaults to int.

    This macro is not used on machines that do not use cc0.

CC_STATUS_MDEP_INIT   [Macro]
    A C expression to initialize the mdep field to "empty". The default definition does nothing, since most machines don't use the field anyway. If you want to use the field, you should probably define this macro to initialize it.

    This macro is not used on machines that do not use cc0.

NOTICE_UPDATE_CC (exp, insn)   [Macro]
    A C compound statement to set the components of cc_status appropriately for an insn insn whose body is exp. It is this macro's responsibility to recognize insns that set the condition code as a byproduct of other activity as well as those that explicitly set (cc0).

    This macro is not used on machines that do not use cc0.

    If there are insns that do not set the condition code but do alter other machine registers, this macro must check to see whether they invalidate the expressions that the condition code is recorded as reflecting. For example, on the 68000, insns that store in address registers do not set the condition code, which means that usually NOTICE_UPDATE_CC can leave cc_status unaltered for such insns. But suppose that the previous insn set the condition code based on location 'a4@(102)' and the current insn stores a new value in 'a4'. Although the condition code is not changed by this, it will no longer be true that it reflects the contents of 'a4@(102)'. Therefore, NOTICE_UPDATE_CC must alter cc_status in this case to say that nothing is known about the condition code value.

    The definition of NOTICE_UPDATE_CC must be prepared to deal with the results of peephole optimization: insns whose patterns are parallel RTXs containing various reg, mem or constants which are just the operands. The RTL structure of these insns is not sufficient to indicate what the insns actually do. What `NOTICE_UPDATE_CC` should do when it sees one is just to run `CC_STATUS_INIT`.

A possible definition of `NOTICE_UPDATE_CC` is to call a function that looks at an attribute (see Section 16.19 [Insn Attributes], page 405) named, for example, 'cc'. This avoids having detailed information about patterns in two places, the 'md' file and in `NOTICE_UPDATE_CC`.

17.15.2 Representation of condition codes using registers

SELECT_CC_MODE (*op, x, y*)   [Macro]

On many machines, the condition code may be produced by other instructions than compares, for example the branch can use directly the condition code set by a subtract instruction. However, on some machines when the condition code is set this way some bits (such as the overflow bit) are not set in the same way as a test instruction, so that a different branch instruction must be used for some conditional branches. When this happens, use the machine mode of the condition code register to record different formats of the condition code register. Modes can also be used to record which compare instruction (e.g. a signed or an unsigned comparison) produced the condition codes.

If other modes than `CCmode` are required, add them to 'machine-modes.def' and define `SELECT_CC_MODE` to choose a mode given an operand of a compare. This is needed because the modes have to be chosen not only during RTL generation but also, for example, by instruction combination. The result of `SELECT_CC_MODE` should be consistent with the mode used in the patterns; for example to support the case of the add on the SPARC discussed above, we have the pattern

```
(define_insn ""
  [(set (reg:CCNZ 0)
        (compare:CCNZ
          (plus:SI (match_operand:SI 0 "register_operand" "%r")
                   (match_operand:SI 1 "arith_operand" "rI"))
          (const_int 0)))]
  ""
  "...")
```

together with a `SELECT_CC_MODE` that returns `CCNZmode` for comparisons whose argument is a `plus`:

```
#define SELECT_CC_MODE(OP,X,Y) \
  (GET_MODE_CLASS (GET_MODE (X)) == MODE_FLOAT          \
   ? ((OP == LT || OP == LE || OP == GT || OP == GE)    \
      ? CCFPEmode : CCFPmode)                           \
   : ((GET_CODE (X) == PLUS || GET_CODE (X) == MINUS    \
       || GET_CODE (X) == NEG || GET_CODE (x) == ASHIFT) \
      ? CCNZmode : CCmode))
```

Another reason to use modes is to retain information on which operands were used by the comparison; see `REVERSIBLE_CC_MODE` later in this section.

You should define this macro if and only if you define extra CC modes in 'machine-modes.def'.

void **TARGET_CANONICALIZE_COMPARISON** (*int *code*, *rtx *op0*, *rtx*   [Target Hook]
        op1, *bool op0_preserve_value*)

On some machines not all possible comparisons are defined, but you can convert an invalid comparison into a valid one. For example, the Alpha does not have a GT comparison, but you can use an LT comparison instead and swap the order of the operands.

On such machines, implement this hook to do any required conversions. *code* is the initial comparison code and *op0* and *op1* are the left and right operands of the comparison, respectively. If *op0_preserve_value* is **true** the implementation is not allowed to change the value of *op0* since the value might be used in RTXs which aren't comparisons. E.g. the implementation is not allowed to swap operands in that case.

GCC will not assume that the comparison resulting from this macro is valid but will see if the resulting insn matches a pattern in the 'md' file.

You need not to implement this hook if it would never change the comparison code or operands.

REVERSIBLE_CC_MODE (*mode*)   [Macro]

A C expression whose value is one if it is always safe to reverse a comparison whose mode is *mode*. If SELECT_CC_MODE can ever return *mode* for a floating-point inequality comparison, then REVERSIBLE_CC_MODE (*mode*) must be zero.

You need not define this macro if it would always returns zero or if the floating-point format is anything other than **IEEE_FLOAT_FORMAT**. For example, here is the definition used on the SPARC, where floating-point inequality comparisons are given either **CCFPEmode** or **CCFPmode**:

```
#define REVERSIBLE_CC_MODE(MODE) \
    ((MODE) != CCFPEmode && (MODE) != CCFPmode)
```

REVERSE_CONDITION (*code, mode*)   [Macro]

A C expression whose value is reversed condition code of the *code* for comparison done in CC_MODE *mode*. The macro is used only in case REVERSIBLE_CC_MODE (*mode*) is nonzero. Define this macro in case machine has some non-standard way how to reverse certain conditionals. For instance in case all floating point conditions are non-trapping, compiler may freely convert unordered compares to ordered ones. Then definition may look like:

```
#define REVERSE_CONDITION(CODE, MODE) \
    ((MODE) != CCFPmode ? reverse_condition (CODE) \
     : reverse_condition_maybe_unordered (CODE))
```

bool **TARGET_FIXED_CONDITION_CODE_REGS** (*unsigned int *p1*,   [Target Hook]
        *unsigned int *p2*)

On targets which do not use (cc0), and which use a hard register rather than a pseudo-register to hold condition codes, the regular CSE passes are often not able to identify cases in which the hard register is set to a common value. Use this hook to enable a small pass which optimizes such cases. This hook should return true to enable this pass, and it should set the integers to which its arguments point to the hard register numbers used for condition codes. When there is only one such register, as is true on most systems, the integer pointed to by *p2* should be set to `INVALID_REGNUM`.

The default version of this hook returns false.

machine_mode TARGET_CC_MODES_COMPATIBLE (*machine_mode* **m1**,   [Target Hook]
    machine_mode **m2**)

On targets which use multiple condition code modes in class `MODE_CC`, it is sometimes the case that a comparison can be validly done in more than one mode. On such a system, define this target hook to take two mode arguments and to return a mode in which both comparisons may be validly done. If there is no such mode, return `VOIDmode`.

The default version of this hook checks whether the modes are the same. If they are, it returns that mode. If they are different, it returns `VOIDmode`.

unsigned int TARGET_FLAGS_REGNUM   [Target Hook]

If the target has a dedicated flags register, and it needs to use the post-reload comparison elimination pass, then this value should be set appropriately.

17.16 Describing Relative Costs of Operations

These macros let you describe the relative speed of various operations on the target machine.

REGISTER_MOVE_COST (*mode*, *from*, *to*)   [Macro]

A C expression for the cost of moving data of mode *mode* from a register in class *from* to one in class *to*. The classes are expressed using the enumeration values such as `GENERAL_REGS`. A value of 2 is the default; other values are interpreted relative to that.

It is not required that the cost always equal 2 when *from* is the same as *to*; on some machines it is expensive to move between registers if they are not general registers.

If reload sees an insn consisting of a single **set** between two hard registers, and if `REGISTER_MOVE_COST` applied to their classes returns a value of 2, reload does not check to ensure that the constraints of the insn are met. Setting a cost of other than 2 will allow reload to verify that the constraints are met. You should do this if the 'movm' pattern's constraints do not allow such copying.

These macros are obsolete, new ports should use the target hook `TARGET_REGISTER_MOVE_COST` instead.

int TARGET_REGISTER_MOVE_COST (*machine_mode* **mode**, *reg_class_t*   [Target Hook]
    from, *reg_class_t* **to**)

This target hook should return the cost of moving data of mode *mode* from a register in class *from* to one in class *to*. The classes are expressed using the enumeration values such as `GENERAL_REGS`. A value of 2 is the default; other values are interpreted relative to that.

It is not required that the cost always equal 2 when *from* is the same as *to*; on some machines it is expensive to move between registers if they are not general registers.

If reload sees an insn consisting of a single **set** between two hard registers, and if `TARGET_REGISTER_MOVE_COST` applied to their classes returns a value of 2, reload does not check to ensure that the constraints of the insn are met. Setting a cost of other than 2 will allow reload to verify that the constraints are met. You should do this if the 'movm' pattern's constraints do not allow such copying.

The default version of this function returns 2.

MEMORY_MOVE_COST (*mode*, *class*, *in*)   [Macro]

A C expression for the cost of moving data of mode *mode* between a register of class *class* and memory; *in* is zero if the value is to be written to memory, nonzero if it is to be read in. This cost is relative to those in REGISTER_MOVE_COST. If moving between registers and memory is more expensive than between two registers, you should define this macro to express the relative cost.

If you do not define this macro, GCC uses a default cost of 4 plus the cost of copying via a secondary reload register, if one is needed. If your machine requires a secondary reload register to copy between memory and a register of *class* but the reload mechanism is more complex than copying via an intermediate, define this macro to reflect the actual cost of the move.

GCC defines the function memory_move_secondary_cost if secondary reloads are needed. It computes the costs due to copying via a secondary register. If your machine copies from memory using a secondary register in the conventional way but the default base value of 4 is not correct for your machine, define this macro to add some other value to the result of that function. The arguments to that function are the same as to this macro.

These macros are obsolete, new ports should use the target hook TARGET_MEMORY_MOVE_COST instead.

int TARGET_MEMORY_MOVE_COST (*machine_mode* mode, *reg_class_t*   [Target Hook]
**   *rclass*, *bool* in)**

This target hook should return the cost of moving data of mode *mode* between a register of class *rclass* and memory; *in* is false if the value is to be written to memory, true if it is to be read in. This cost is relative to those in TARGET_REGISTER_MOVE_COST. If moving between registers and memory is more expensive than between two registers, you should add this target hook to express the relative cost.

If you do not add this target hook, GCC uses a default cost of 4 plus the cost of copying via a secondary reload register, if one is needed. If your machine requires a secondary reload register to copy between memory and a register of *rclass* but the reload mechanism is more complex than copying via an intermediate, use this target hook to reflect the actual cost of the move.

GCC defines the function memory_move_secondary_cost if secondary reloads are needed. It computes the costs due to copying via a secondary register. If your machine copies from memory using a secondary register in the conventional way but the default base value of 4 is not correct for your machine, use this target hook to add some other value to the result of that function. The arguments to that function are the same as to this target hook.

BRANCH_COST (*speed_p*, *predictable_p*)   [Macro]

A C expression for the cost of a branch instruction. A value of 1 is the default; other values are interpreted relative to that. Parameter *speed_p* is true when the branch in question should be optimized for speed. When it is false, `BRANCH_COST` should return a value optimal for code size rather than performance. *predictable_p* is true for well-predicted branches. On many architectures the `BRANCH_COST` can be reduced then.

Here are additional macros which do not specify precise relative costs, but only that certain actions are more expensive than GCC would ordinarily expect.

`SLOW_BYTE_ACCESS`   [Macro]

Define this macro as a C expression which is nonzero if accessing less than a word of memory (i.e. a `char` or a `short`) is no faster than accessing a word of memory, i.e., if such access require more than one instruction or if there is no difference in cost between byte and (aligned) word loads.

When this macro is not defined, the compiler will access a field by finding the smallest containing object; when it is defined, a fullword load will be used if alignment permits. Unless bytes accesses are faster than word accesses, using word accesses is preferable since it may eliminate subsequent memory access if subsequent accesses occur to other fields in the same word of the structure, but to different bytes.

`SLOW_UNALIGNED_ACCESS (mode, alignment)`   [Macro]

Define this macro to be the value 1 if memory accesses described by the *mode* and *alignment* parameters have a cost many times greater than aligned accesses, for example if they are emulated in a trap handler. This macro is invoked only for unaligned accesses, i.e. when `alignment < GET_MODE_ALIGNMENT (mode)`.

When this macro is nonzero, the compiler will act as if `STRICT_ALIGNMENT` were nonzero when generating code for block moves. This can cause significantly more instructions to be produced. Therefore, do not set this macro nonzero if unaligned accesses only add a cycle or two to the time for a memory access.

If the value of this macro is always zero, it need not be defined. If this macro is defined, it should produce a nonzero value when `STRICT_ALIGNMENT` is nonzero.

`MOVE_RATIO (speed)`   [Macro]

The threshold of number of scalar memory-to-memory move insns, *below* which a sequence of insns should be generated instead of a string move insn or a library call. Increasing the value will always make code faster, but eventually incurs high cost in increased code size.

Note that on machines where the corresponding move insn is a `define_expand` that emits a sequence of insns, this macro counts the number of such sequences.

The parameter *speed* is true if the code is currently being optimized for speed rather than size.

If you don't define this, a reasonable default is used.

`bool TARGET_USE_BY_PIECES_INFRASTRUCTURE_P (unsigned`   [Target Hook]
`      HOST_WIDE_INT size, unsigned int alignment, enum by_pieces_operation`
`      op, bool speed_p)`

GCC will attempt several strategies when asked to copy between two areas of memory, or to set, clear or store to memory, for example when copying a `struct`. The `by_pieces` infrastructure implements such memory operations as a sequence of load, store or move insns. Alternate strategies are to expand the `movmem` or `setmem` optabs, to emit a library call, or to emit unit-by-unit, loop-based operations.

This target hook should return true if, for a memory operation with a given *size* and *alignment*, using the `by_pieces` infrastructure is expected to result in better code generation. Both *size* and *alignment* are measured in terms of storage units.

The parameter *op* is one of: `CLEAR_BY_PIECES`, `MOVE_BY_PIECES`, `SET_BY_PIECES`, `STORE_BY_PIECES` or `COMPARE_BY_PIECES`. These describe the type of memory operation under consideration.

The parameter *speed_p* is true if the code is currently being optimized for speed rather than size.

Returning true for higher values of *size* can improve code generation for speed if the target does not provide an implementation of the `movmem` or `setmem` standard names, if the `movmem` or `setmem` implementation would be more expensive than a sequence of insns, or if the overhead of a library call would dominate that of the body of the memory operation.

Returning true for higher values of `size` may also cause an increase in code size, for example where the number of insns emitted to perform a move would be greater than that of a library call.

int TARGET_COMPARE_BY_PIECES_BRANCH_RATIO (*machine_mode*   [Target Hook]
      mode)

When expanding a block comparison in MODE, gcc can try to reduce the number of branches at the expense of more memory operations. This hook allows the target to override the default choice. It should return the factor by which branches should be reduced over the plain expansion with one comparison per *mode*-sized piece. A port can also prevent a particular mode from being used for block comparisons by returning a negative number from this hook.

MOVE_MAX_PIECES   [Macro]

A C expression used by `move_by_pieces` to determine the largest unit a load or store used to copy memory is. Defaults to `MOVE_MAX`.

STORE_MAX_PIECES   [Macro]

A C expression used by `store_by_pieces` to determine the largest unit a store used to memory is. Defaults to `MOVE_MAX_PIECES`, or two times the size of `HOST_WIDE_INT`, whichever is smaller.

COMPARE_MAX_PIECES   [Macro]

A C expression used by `compare_by_pieces` to determine the largest unit a load or store used to compare memory is. Defaults to `MOVE_MAX_PIECES`.

CLEAR_RATIO (*speed*)   [Macro]

The threshold of number of scalar move insns, *below* which a sequence of insns should be generated to clear memory instead of a string clear insn or a library call. Increasing the value will always make code faster, but eventually incurs high cost in increased code size.

The parameter *speed* is true if the code is currently being optimized for speed rather than size.

If you don't define this, a reasonable default is used.

SET_RATIO (*speed*) [Macro]

The threshold of number of scalar move insns, *below* which a sequence of insns should be generated to set memory to a constant value, instead of a block set insn or a library call. Increasing the value will always make code faster, but eventually incurs high cost in increased code size.

The parameter *speed* is true if the code is currently being optimized for speed rather than size.

If you don't define this, it defaults to the value of MOVE_RATIO.

USE_LOAD_POST_INCREMENT (*mode*) [Macro]

A C expression used to determine whether a load postincrement is a good thing to use for a given mode. Defaults to the value of HAVE_POST_INCREMENT.

USE_LOAD_POST_DECREMENT (*mode*) [Macro]

A C expression used to determine whether a load postdecrement is a good thing to use for a given mode. Defaults to the value of HAVE_POST_DECREMENT.

USE_LOAD_PRE_INCREMENT (*mode*) [Macro]

A C expression used to determine whether a load preincrement is a good thing to use for a given mode. Defaults to the value of HAVE_PRE_INCREMENT.

USE_LOAD_PRE_DECREMENT (*mode*) [Macro]

A C expression used to determine whether a load predecrement is a good thing to use for a given mode. Defaults to the value of HAVE_PRE_DECREMENT.

USE_STORE_POST_INCREMENT (*mode*) [Macro]

A C expression used to determine whether a store postincrement is a good thing to use for a given mode. Defaults to the value of HAVE_POST_INCREMENT.

USE_STORE_POST_DECREMENT (*mode*) [Macro]

A C expression used to determine whether a store postdecrement is a good thing to use for a given mode. Defaults to the value of HAVE_POST_DECREMENT.

USE_STORE_PRE_INCREMENT (*mode*) [Macro]

This macro is used to determine whether a store preincrement is a good thing to use for a given mode. Defaults to the value of HAVE_PRE_INCREMENT.

USE_STORE_PRE_DECREMENT (*mode*) [Macro]

This macro is used to determine whether a store predecrement is a good thing to use for a given mode. Defaults to the value of HAVE_PRE_DECREMENT.

NO_FUNCTION_CSE [Macro]

Define this macro to be true if it is as good or better to call a constant function address than to call an address kept in a register.

LOGICAL_OP_NON_SHORT_CIRCUIT [Macro]

Define this macro if a non-short-circuit operation produced by 'fold_range_test ()' is optimal. This macro defaults to true if BRANCH_COST is greater than or equal to the value 2.

bool TARGET_OPTAB_SUPPORTED_P (*int op, machine_mode* **mode1**,   [Target Hook]
        machine_mode **mode2**, *optimization_type* **opt_type**)

Return true if the optimizers should use optab *op* with modes *mode1* and *mode2* for optimization type *opt_type*. The optab is known to have an associated '.md' instruction whose C condition is true. *mode2* is only meaningful for conversion optabs; for direct optabs it is a copy of *mode1*.

For example, when called with *op* equal to `rint_optab` and *mode1* equal to `DFmode`, the hook should say whether the optimizers should use optab `rintdf2`.

The default hook returns true for all inputs.

bool TARGET_RTX_COSTS (*rtx* **x**, *machine_mode* **mode**, *int*   [Target Hook]
        outer_code, *int* **opno**, *int* ***total**, *bool* **speed**)

This target hook describes the relative costs of RTL expressions.

The cost may depend on the precise form of the expression, which is available for examination in *x*, and the fact that *x* appears as operand *opno* of an expression with rtx code *outer_code*. That is, the hook can assume that there is some rtx *y* such that 'GET_CODE (*y*) == **outer_code**' and such that either (a) 'XEXP (*y*, **opno**) == *x*' or (b) 'XVEC (*y*, **opno**)' contains *x*.

mode is *x*'s machine mode, or for cases like `const_int` that do not have a mode, the mode in which *x* is used.

In implementing this hook, you can use the construct `COSTS_N_INSNS (n)` to specify a cost equal to *n* fast instructions.

On entry to the hook, ***total** contains a default estimate for the cost of the expression. The hook should modify this value as necessary. Traditionally, the default costs are `COSTS_N_INSNS (5)` for multiplications, `COSTS_N_INSNS (7)` for division and modulus operations, and `COSTS_N_INSNS (1)` for all other operations.

When optimizing for code size, i.e. when **speed** is false, this target hook should be used to estimate the relative size cost of an expression, again relative to `COSTS_N_INSNS`.

The hook returns true when all subexpressions of *x* have been processed, and false when `rtx_cost` should recurse.

int TARGET_ADDRESS_COST (*rtx* **address**, *machine_mode* **mode**,   [Target Hook]
        addr_space_t **as**, *bool* **speed**)

This hook computes the cost of an addressing mode that contains *address*. If not defined, the cost is computed from the *address* expression and the `TARGET_RTX_COST` hook.

For most CISC machines, the default cost is a good approximation of the true cost of the addressing mode. However, on RISC machines, all instructions normally have the same length and execution time. Hence all addresses will have equal costs.

In cases where more than one form of an address is known, the form with the lowest cost will be used. If multiple forms have the same, lowest, cost, the one that is the most complex will be used.

For example, suppose an address that is equal to the sum of a register and a constant is used twice in the same basic block. When this macro is not defined, the address will be computed in a register and memory references will be indirect through that register. On machines where the cost of the addressing mode containing the sum is no higher than that of a simple indirect reference, this will produce an additional instruction and possibly require an additional register. Proper specification of this macro eliminates this overhead for such machines.

This hook is never called with an invalid address.

On machines where an address involving more than one register is as cheap as an address computation involving only one register, defining `TARGET_ADDRESS_COST` to reflect this can cause two registers to be live over a region of code where only one would have been if `TARGET_ADDRESS_COST` were not defined in that manner. This effect should be considered in the definition of this macro. Equivalent costs should probably only be given to addresses with different numbers of registers on machines with lots of registers.

unsigned int TARGET_MAX_NOCE_IFCVT_SEQ_COST (*edge e*)   [Target Hook]
This hook returns a value in the same units as `TARGET_RTX_COSTS`, giving the maximum acceptable cost for a sequence generated by the RTL if-conversion pass when conditional execution is not available. The RTL if-conversion pass attempts to convert conditional operations that would require a branch to a series of unconditional operations and `movmodecc` insns. This hook returns the maximum cost of the unconditional instructions and the `movmodecc` insns. RTL if-conversion is cancelled if the cost of the converted sequence is greater than the value returned by this hook.

e is the edge between the basic block containing the conditional branch to the basic block which would be executed if the condition were true.

The default implementation of this hook uses the `max-rtl-if-conversion-[un]predictable` parameters if they are set, and uses a multiple of `BRANCH_COST` otherwise.

bool TARGET_NO_SPECULATION_IN_DELAY_SLOTS_P (*void*)   [Target Hook]
This predicate controls the use of the eager delay slot filler to disallow speculatively executed instructions being placed in delay slots. Targets such as certain MIPS architectures possess both branches with and without delay slots. As the eager delay slot filler can decrease performance, disabling it is beneficial when ordinary branches are available. Use of delay slot branches filled using the basic filler is often still desirable as the delay slot can hide a pipeline bubble.

17.17 Adjusting the Instruction Scheduler

The instruction scheduler may need a fair amount of machine-specific adjustment in order to produce good code. GCC provides several target hooks for this purpose. It is usually enough to define just a few of them: try the first ones in this list first.

int TARGET_SCHED_ISSUE_RATE (*void*)   [Target Hook]
This hook returns the maximum number of instructions that can ever issue at the same time on the target machine. The default is one. Although the insn scheduler can define itself the possibility of issue an insn on the same cycle, the value can serve as an additional constraint to issue insns on the same simulated processor cycle (see hooks '`TARGET_SCHED_REORDER`' and '`TARGET_SCHED_REORDER2`'). This value must be

constant over the entire compilation. If you need it to vary depending on what the instructions are, you must use 'TARGET_SCHED_VARIABLE_ISSUE'.

int TARGET_SCHED_VARIABLE_ISSUE (*FILE *file*, *int* verbose,   [Target Hook]
    *rtx_insn *insn*, *int* more)

This hook is executed by the scheduler after it has scheduled an insn from the ready list. It should return the number of insns which can still be issued in the current cycle. The default is 'more - 1' for insns other than CLOBBER and USE, which normally are not counted against the issue rate. You should define this hook if some insns take more machine resources than others, so that fewer insns can follow them in the same cycle. *file* is either a null pointer, or a stdio stream to write any debug output to. *verbose* is the verbose level provided by '-fsched-verbose-*n*'. *insn* is the instruction that was scheduled.

int TARGET_SCHED_ADJUST_COST (*rtx_insn *insn*, *int* dep_type1,   [Target Hook]
    *rtx_insn *dep_insn*, *int* cost, *unsigned int* dw)

This function corrects the value of *cost* based on the relationship between *insn* and *dep_insn* through a dependence of type dep_type, and strength *dw*. It should return the new value. The default is to make no adjustment to *cost*. This can be used for example to specify to the scheduler using the traditional pipeline description that an output- or anti-dependence does not incur the same cost as a data-dependence. If the scheduler using the automaton based pipeline description, the cost of anti-dependence is zero and the cost of output-dependence is maximum of one and the difference of latency times of the first and the second insns. If these values are not acceptable, you could use the hook to modify them too. See also see Section 16.19.9 [Processor pipeline description], page 414.

int TARGET_SCHED_ADJUST_PRIORITY (*rtx_insn *insn*, *int*   [Target Hook]
    priority)

This hook adjusts the integer scheduling priority *priority* of *insn*. It should return the new priority. Increase the priority to execute *insn* earlier, reduce the priority to execute *insn* later. Do not define this hook if you do not need to adjust the scheduling priorities of insns.

int TARGET_SCHED_REORDER (*FILE *file*, *int* verbose, *rtx_insn*   [Target Hook]
    **ready, *int* *n_readyp, *int* clock)

This hook is executed by the scheduler after it has scheduled the ready list, to allow the machine description to reorder it (for example to combine two small instructions together on 'VLIW' machines). *file* is either a null pointer, or a stdio stream to write any debug output to. *verbose* is the verbose level provided by '-fsched-verbose-*n*'. *ready* is a pointer to the ready list of instructions that are ready to be scheduled. *n_readyp* is a pointer to the number of elements in the ready list. The scheduler reads the ready list in reverse order, starting with ready[*n_readyp* − 1] and going to ready[0]. *clock* is the timer tick of the scheduler. You may modify the ready list and the number of ready insns. The return value is the number of insns that can issue this cycle; normally this is just issue_rate. See also 'TARGET_SCHED_REORDER2'.

int TARGET_SCHED_REORDER2 (*FILE *file*, *int* **verbose**, *rtx_insn*   [Target Hook]
    ready*, *int *n_readyp*, *int* **clock)
> Like 'TARGET_SCHED_REORDER', but called at a different time. That function is called
> whenever the scheduler starts a new cycle. This one is called once per iteration over
> a cycle, immediately after 'TARGET_SCHED_VARIABLE_ISSUE'; it can reorder the ready
> list and return the number of insns to be scheduled in the same cycle. Defining this
> hook can be useful if there are frequent situations where scheduling one insn causes
> other insns to become ready in the same cycle. These other insns can then be taken
> into account properly.

bool TARGET_SCHED_MACRO_FUSION_P (*void*)   [Target Hook]
> This hook is used to check whether target platform supports macro fusion.

bool TARGET_SCHED_MACRO_FUSION_PAIR_P (*rtx_insn* **prev**,   [Target Hook]
    rtx_insn **curr**)
> This hook is used to check whether two insns should be macro fused for a target
> microarchitecture. If this hook returns true for the given insn pair (*prev* and *curr*),
> the scheduler will put them into a sched group, and they will not be scheduled apart.
> The two insns will be either two SET insns or a compare and a conditional jump and
> this hook should validate any dependencies needed to fuse the two insns together.

void TARGET_SCHED_DEPENDENCIES_EVALUATION_HOOK (*rtx_insn*   [Target Hook]
    **head*, *rtx_insn *tail*)
> This hook is called after evaluation forward dependencies of insns in chain given by
> two parameter values (*head* and *tail* correspondingly) but before insns scheduling of
> the insn chain. For example, it can be used for better insn classification if it requires
> analysis of dependencies. This hook can use backward and forward dependencies of
> the insn scheduler because they are already calculated.

void TARGET_SCHED_INIT (*FILE *file*, *int* **verbose**, *int*   [Target Hook]
    max_ready)
> This hook is executed by the scheduler at the beginning of each block of instructions
> that are to be scheduled. *file* is either a null pointer, or a stdio stream to write
> any debug output to. *verbose* is the verbose level provided by '-fsched-verbose-*n*'.
> *max_ready* is the maximum number of insns in the current scheduling region that can
> be live at the same time. This can be used to allocate scratch space if it is needed,
> e.g. by 'TARGET_SCHED_REORDER'.

void TARGET_SCHED_FINISH (*FILE *file*, *int* **verbose**)   [Target Hook]
> This hook is executed by the scheduler at the end of each block of instructions that
> are to be scheduled. It can be used to perform cleanup of any actions done by the
> other scheduling hooks. *file* is either a null pointer, or a stdio stream to write any
> debug output to. *verbose* is the verbose level provided by '-fsched-verbose-*n*'.

void TARGET_SCHED_INIT_GLOBAL (*FILE *file*, *int* **verbose**, *int*   [Target Hook]
    old_max_uid)
> This hook is executed by the scheduler after function level initializations. *file* is either
> a null pointer, or a stdio stream to write any debug output to. *verbose* is the verbose
> level provided by '-fsched-verbose-*n*'. *old_max_uid* is the maximum insn uid when
> scheduling begins.

void TARGET_SCHED_FINISH_GLOBAL (*FILE *file*, *int verbose*)   [Target Hook]
     This is the cleanup hook corresponding to TARGET_SCHED_INIT_GLOBAL. *file* is either
     a null pointer, or a stdio stream to write any debug output to. *verbose* is the verbose
     level provided by '-fsched-verbose-*n*'.

rtx TARGET_SCHED_DFA_PRE_CYCLE_INSN (*void*)   [Target Hook]
     The hook returns an RTL insn. The automaton state used in the pipeline hazard
     recognizer is changed as if the insn were scheduled when the new simulated processor
     cycle starts. Usage of the hook may simplify the automaton pipeline description for
     some VLIW processors. If the hook is defined, it is used only for the automaton based
     pipeline description. The default is not to change the state when the new simulated
     processor cycle starts.

void TARGET_SCHED_INIT_DFA_PRE_CYCLE_INSN (*void*)   [Target Hook]
     The hook can be used to initialize data used by the previous hook.

rtx_insn * TARGET_SCHED_DFA_POST_CYCLE_INSN (*void*)   [Target Hook]
     The hook is analogous to 'TARGET_SCHED_DFA_PRE_CYCLE_INSN' but used to changed
     the state as if the insn were scheduled when the new simulated processor cycle finishes.

void TARGET_SCHED_INIT_DFA_POST_CYCLE_INSN (*void*)   [Target Hook]
     The hook is analogous to 'TARGET_SCHED_INIT_DFA_PRE_CYCLE_INSN' but used to
     initialize data used by the previous hook.

void TARGET_SCHED_DFA_PRE_ADVANCE_CYCLE (*void*)   [Target Hook]
     The hook to notify target that the current simulated cycle is about to finish. The
     hook is analogous to 'TARGET_SCHED_DFA_PRE_CYCLE_INSN' but used to change the
     state in more complicated situations - e.g., when advancing state on a single insn is
     not enough.

void TARGET_SCHED_DFA_POST_ADVANCE_CYCLE (*void*)   [Target Hook]
     The hook to notify target that new simulated cycle has just started. The hook is
     analogous to 'TARGET_SCHED_DFA_POST_CYCLE_INSN' but used to change the state
     in more complicated situations - e.g., when advancing state on a single insn is not
     enough.

int TARGET_SCHED_FIRST_CYCLE_MULTIPASS_DFA_LOOKAHEAD   [Target Hook]
          (*void*)
     This hook controls better choosing an insn from the ready insn queue for the DFA-
     based insn scheduler. Usually the scheduler chooses the first insn from the queue.
     If the hook returns a positive value, an additional scheduler code tries all permu-
     tations of 'TARGET_SCHED_FIRST_CYCLE_MULTIPASS_DFA_LOOKAHEAD ()' subsequent
     ready insns to choose an insn whose issue will result in maximal number of issued
     insns on the same cycle. For the VLIW processor, the code could actually solve the
     problem of packing simple insns into the VLIW insn. Of course, if the rules of VLIW
     packing are described in the automaton.

     This code also could be used for superscalar RISC processors. Let us consider a
     superscalar RISC processor with 3 pipelines. Some insns can be executed in pipelines
     A or *B*, some insns can be executed only in pipelines *B* or *C*, and one insn can be

executed in pipeline B. The processor may issue the 1st insn into A and the 2nd one into B. In this case, the 3rd insn will wait for freeing B until the next cycle. If the scheduler issues the 3rd insn the first, the processor could issue all 3 insns per cycle.

Actually this code demonstrates advantages of the automaton based pipeline hazard recognizer. We try quickly and easy many insn schedules to choose the best one.

The default is no multipass scheduling.

int   [Target Hook]
       `TARGET_SCHED_FIRST_CYCLE_MULTIPASS_DFA_LOOKAHEAD_GUARD`
       (*rtx_insn* `*insn`, *int* `ready_index`)
This hook controls what insns from the ready insn queue will be considered for the multipass insn scheduling. If the hook returns zero for *insn*, the insn will be considered in multipass scheduling. Positive return values will remove *insn* from consideration on the current round of multipass scheduling. Negative return values will remove *insn* from consideration for given number of cycles. Backends should be careful about returning non-zero for highest priority instruction at position 0 in the ready list. *ready_index* is passed to allow backends make correct judgements.

The default is that any ready insns can be chosen to be issued.

void `TARGET_SCHED_FIRST_CYCLE_MULTIPASS_BEGIN` (*void*   [Target Hook]
      `*data`, *signed char* `*ready_try`, *int* `n_ready`, *bool* `first_cycle_insn_p`)
This hook prepares the target backend for a new round of multipass scheduling.

void `TARGET_SCHED_FIRST_CYCLE_MULTIPASS_ISSUE` (*void*   [Target Hook]
      `*data`, *signed char* `*ready_try`, *int* `n_ready`, *rtx_insn* `*insn`, *const void*
      `*prev_data`)
This hook is called when multipass scheduling evaluates instruction INSN.

void `TARGET_SCHED_FIRST_CYCLE_MULTIPASS_BACKTRACK` (*const*   [Target Hook]
      void `*data`, *signed char* `*ready_try`, *int* `n_ready`)
This is called when multipass scheduling backtracks from evaluation of an instruction.

void `TARGET_SCHED_FIRST_CYCLE_MULTIPASS_END` (*const void*   [Target Hook]
      `*data`)
This hook notifies the target about the result of the concluded current round of multipass scheduling.

void `TARGET_SCHED_FIRST_CYCLE_MULTIPASS_INIT` (*void* `*data`)   [Target Hook]
This hook initializes target-specific data used in multipass scheduling.

void `TARGET_SCHED_FIRST_CYCLE_MULTIPASS_FINI` (*void* `*data`)   [Target Hook]
This hook finalizes target-specific data used in multipass scheduling.

int `TARGET_SCHED_DFA_NEW_CYCLE` (*FILE* `*dump`, *int* `verbose`,   [Target Hook]
      rtx_insn `*insn`, *int* `last_clock`, *int* `clock`, *int* `*sort_p`)
This hook is called by the insn scheduler before issuing *insn* on cycle *clock*. If the hook returns nonzero, *insn* is not issued on this processor cycle. Instead, the processor cycle is advanced. If **sort_p* is zero, the insn ready queue is not sorted on the new cycle start as usually. *dump* and *verbose* specify the file and verbosity level to use

for debugging output. *last_clock* and *clock* are, respectively, the processor cycle on which the previous insn has been issued, and the current processor cycle.

bool TARGET_SCHED_IS_COSTLY_DEPENDENCE (*struct _dep *_dep,*   [Target Hook]
    int **cost**, *int* **distance**)

This hook is used to define which dependences are considered costly by the target, so costly that it is not advisable to schedule the insns that are involved in the dependence too close to one another. The parameters to this hook are as follows: The first parameter *_dep* is the dependence being evaluated. The second parameter *cost* is the cost of the dependence as estimated by the scheduler, and the third parameter *distance* is the distance in cycles between the two insns. The hook returns **true** if considering the distance between the two insns the dependence between them is considered costly by the target, and **false** otherwise.

Defining this hook can be useful in multiple-issue out-of-order machines, where (a) it's practically hopeless to predict the actual data/resource delays, however: (b) there's a better chance to predict the actual grouping that will be formed, and (c) correctly emulating the grouping can be very important. In such targets one may want to allow issuing dependent insns closer to one another—i.e., closer than the dependence distance; however, not in cases of "costly dependences", which this hooks allows to define.

void TARGET_SCHED_H_I_D_EXTENDED (*void*)   [Target Hook]

This hook is called by the insn scheduler after emitting a new instruction to the instruction stream. The hook notifies a target backend to extend its per instruction data structures.

void * TARGET_SCHED_ALLOC_SCHED_CONTEXT (*void*)   [Target Hook]

Return a pointer to a store large enough to hold target scheduling context.

void TARGET_SCHED_INIT_SCHED_CONTEXT (*void *tc, bool*   [Target Hook]
    clean_p)

Initialize store pointed to by *tc* to hold target scheduling context. It *clean_p* is true then initialize *tc* as if scheduler is at the beginning of the block. Otherwise, copy the current context into *tc*.

void TARGET_SCHED_SET_SCHED_CONTEXT (*void *tc*)   [Target Hook]

Copy target scheduling context pointed to by *tc* to the current context.

void TARGET_SCHED_CLEAR_SCHED_CONTEXT (*void *tc*)   [Target Hook]

Deallocate internal data in target scheduling context pointed to by *tc*.

void TARGET_SCHED_FREE_SCHED_CONTEXT (*void *tc*)   [Target Hook]

Deallocate a store for target scheduling context pointed to by *tc*.

int TARGET_SCHED_SPECULATE_INSN (*rtx_insn *insn, unsigned int*   [Target Hook]
    dep_status, *rtx *new_pat*)

This hook is called by the insn scheduler when *insn* has only speculative dependencies and therefore can be scheduled speculatively. The hook is used to check if the pattern of *insn* has a speculative version and, in case of successful check, to generate that speculative pattern. The hook should return 1, if the instruction has a speculative form, or −1, if it doesn't. *request* describes the type of requested speculation. If the return value equals 1 then *new_pat* is assigned the generated speculative pattern.

bool TARGET_SCHED_NEEDS_BLOCK_P (*unsigned int* **dep_status**)   [Target Hook]
This hook is called by the insn scheduler during generation of recovery code for *insn*. It should return **true**, if the corresponding check instruction should branch to recovery code, or **false** otherwise.

rtx TARGET_SCHED_GEN_SPEC_CHECK (*rtx_insn* ***insn**, *rtx_insn*   [Target Hook]
        *label, *unsigned int* **ds**)
This hook is called by the insn scheduler to generate a pattern for recovery check instruction. If *mutate_p* is zero, then *insn* is a speculative instruction for which the check should be generated. *label* is either a label of a basic block, where recovery code should be emitted, or a null pointer, when requested check doesn't branch to recovery code (a simple check). If *mutate_p* is nonzero, then a pattern for a branchy check corresponding to a simple check denoted by *insn* should be generated. In this case *label* can't be null.

void TARGET_SCHED_SET_SCHED_FLAGS (*struct spec_info_def*   [Target Hook]
        *spec_info)
This hook is used by the insn scheduler to find out what features should be enabled/used. The structure **spec_info* should be filled in by the target. The structure describes speculation types that can be used in the scheduler.

int TARGET_SCHED_SMS_RES_MII (*struct ddg* ***g**)   [Target Hook]
This hook is called by the swing modulo scheduler to calculate a resource-based lower bound which is based on the resources available in the machine and the resources required by each instruction. The target backend can use *g* to calculate such bound. A very simple lower bound will be used in case this hook is not implemented: the total number of instructions divided by the issue rate.

bool TARGET_SCHED_DISPATCH (*rtx_insn* ***insn**, *int* **x**)   [Target Hook]
This hook is called by Haifa Scheduler. It returns true if dispatch scheduling is supported in hardware and the condition specified in the parameter is true.

void TARGET_SCHED_DISPATCH_DO (*rtx_insn* ***insn**, *int* **x**)   [Target Hook]
This hook is called by Haifa Scheduler. It performs the operation specified in its second parameter.

bool TARGET_SCHED_EXPOSED_PIPELINE   [Target Hook]
True if the processor has an exposed pipeline, which means that not just the order of instructions is important for correctness when scheduling, but also the latencies of operations.

int TARGET_SCHED_REASSOCIATION_WIDTH (*unsigned int* **opc**,   [Target Hook]
        machine_mode **mode**)
This hook is called by tree reassociator to determine a level of parallelism required in output calculations chain.

void TARGET_SCHED_FUSION_PRIORITY (*rtx_insn *insn*, int   [Target Hook]
     max_pri, int *fusion_pri*, int *pri*)

This hook is called by scheduling fusion pass. It calculates fusion priorities for each
instruction passed in by parameter. The priorities are returned via pointer parameters.

insn is the instruction whose priorities need to be calculated. *max_pri* is the maximum
priority can be returned in any cases. *fusion_pri* is the pointer parameter through
which *insn*'s fusion priority should be calculated and returned. *pri* is the pointer
parameter through which *insn*'s priority should be calculated and returned.

Same *fusion_pri* should be returned for instructions which should be scheduled together. Different *pri* should be returned for instructions with same *fusion_pri*. *fu-
sion_pri* is the major sort key, *pri* is the minor sort key. All instructions will be
scheduled according to the two priorities. All priorities calculated should be between
0 (exclusive) and *max_pri* (inclusive). To avoid false dependencies, *fusion_pri* of instructions which need to be scheduled together should be smaller than *fusion_pri* of
irrelevant instructions.

Given below example:

```
ldr r10, [r1, 4]
add r4, r4, r10
ldr r15, [r2, 8]
sub r5, r5, r15
ldr r11, [r1, 0]
add r4, r4, r11
ldr r16, [r2, 12]
sub r5, r5, r16
```

On targets like ARM/AArch64, the two pairs of consecutive loads should be merged.
Since peephole2 pass can't help in this case unless consecutive loads are actually next
to each other in instruction flow. That's where this scheduling fusion pass works.
This hook calculates priority for each instruction based on its fustion type, like:

```
ldr r10, [r1, 4]   ; fusion_pri=99,  pri=96
add r4, r4, r10    ; fusion_pri=100, pri=100
ldr r15, [r2, 8]   ; fusion_pri=98,  pri=92
sub r5, r5, r15    ; fusion_pri=100, pri=100
ldr r11, [r1, 0]   ; fusion_pri=99,  pri=100
add r4, r4, r11    ; fusion_pri=100, pri=100
ldr r16, [r2, 12]  ; fusion_pri=98,  pri=88
sub r5, r5, r16    ; fusion_pri=100, pri=100
```

Scheduling fusion pass then sorts all ready to issue instructions according to the
priorities. As a result, instructions of same fusion type will be pushed together in
instruction flow, like:

```
ldr r11, [r1, 0]
ldr r10, [r1, 4]
ldr r15, [r2, 8]
ldr r16, [r2, 12]
add r4, r4, r10
sub r5, r5, r15
add r4, r4, r11
sub r5, r5, r16
```

Now peephole2 pass can simply merge the two pairs of loads.

Since scheduling fusion pass relies on peephole2 to do real fusion work, it is only enabled by default when peephole2 is in effect.

This is firstly introduced on ARM/AArch64 targets, please refer to the hook implementation for how different fusion types are supported.

void TARGET_EXPAND_DIVMOD_LIBFUNC (*rtx* **libfunc**,   [Target Hook]
      machine_mode **mode**, *rtx* **op0**, *rtx* **op1**, *rtx* ***quot**, *rtx* ***rem**)
    Define this hook for enabling divmod transform if the port does not have hardware divmod insn but defines target-specific divmod libfuncs.

17.18 Dividing the Output into Sections (Texts, Data, . . .)

An object file is divided into sections containing different types of data. In the most common case, there are three sections: the *text section*, which holds instructions and read-only data; the *data section*, which holds initialized writable data; and the *bss section*, which holds uninitialized data. Some systems have other kinds of sections.

'varasm.c' provides several well-known sections, such as text_section, data_section and bss_section. The normal way of controlling a foo_section variable is to define the associated *FOO_SECTION_ASM_OP* macro, as described below. The macros are only read once, when 'varasm.c' initializes itself, so their values must be run-time constants. They may however depend on command-line flags.

Note: Some run-time files, such 'crtstuff.c', also make use of the *FOO_SECTION_ASM_OP* macros, and expect them to be string literals.

Some assemblers require a different string to be written every time a section is selected. If your assembler falls into this category, you should define the TARGET_ASM_INIT_SECTIONS hook and use get_unnamed_section to set up the sections.

You must always create a text_section, either by defining TEXT_SECTION_ASM_OP or by initializing text_section in TARGET_ASM_INIT_SECTIONS. The same is true of data_section and DATA_SECTION_ASM_OP. If you do not create a distinct readonly_data_section, the default is to reuse text_section.

All the other 'varasm.c' sections are optional, and are null if the target does not provide them.

TEXT_SECTION_ASM_OP   [Macro]
    A C expression whose value is a string, including spacing, containing the assembler operation that should precede instructions and read-only data. Normally "\t.text" is right.

HOT_TEXT_SECTION_NAME   [Macro]
    If defined, a C string constant for the name of the section containing most frequently executed functions of the program. If not defined, GCC will provide a default definition if the target supports named sections.

UNLIKELY_EXECUTED_TEXT_SECTION_NAME   [Macro]
    If defined, a C string constant for the name of the section containing unlikely executed functions in the program.

DATA_SECTION_ASM_OP   [Macro]

    A C expression whose value is a string, including spacing, containing the assembler operation to identify the following data as writable initialized data. Normally `"\t.data"` is right.

SDATA_SECTION_ASM_OP   [Macro]

    If defined, a C expression whose value is a string, including spacing, containing the assembler operation to identify the following data as initialized, writable small data.

READONLY_DATA_SECTION_ASM_OP   [Macro]

    A C expression whose value is a string, including spacing, containing the assembler operation to identify the following data as read-only initialized data.

BSS_SECTION_ASM_OP   [Macro]

    If defined, a C expression whose value is a string, including spacing, containing the assembler operation to identify the following data as uninitialized global data. If not defined, and `ASM_OUTPUT_ALIGNED_BSS` not defined, uninitialized global data will be output in the data section if '`-fno-common`' is passed, otherwise `ASM_OUTPUT_COMMON` will be used.

SBSS_SECTION_ASM_OP   [Macro]

    If defined, a C expression whose value is a string, including spacing, containing the assembler operation to identify the following data as uninitialized, writable small data.

TLS_COMMON_ASM_OP   [Macro]

    If defined, a C expression whose value is a string containing the assembler operation to identify the following data as thread-local common data. The default is "`.tls_common`".

TLS_SECTION_ASM_FLAG   [Macro]

    If defined, a C expression whose value is a character constant containing the flag used to mark a section as a TLS section. The default is '`T`'.

INIT_SECTION_ASM_OP   [Macro]

    If defined, a C expression whose value is a string, including spacing, containing the assembler operation to identify the following data as initialization code. If not defined, GCC will assume such a section does not exist. This section has no corresponding `init_section` variable; it is used entirely in runtime code.

FINI_SECTION_ASM_OP   [Macro]

    If defined, a C expression whose value is a string, including spacing, containing the assembler operation to identify the following data as finalization code. If not defined, GCC will assume such a section does not exist. This section has no corresponding `fini_section` variable; it is used entirely in runtime code.

INIT_ARRAY_SECTION_ASM_OP   [Macro]

    If defined, a C expression whose value is a string, including spacing, containing the assembler operation to identify the following data as part of the `.init_array` (or equivalent) section. If not defined, GCC will assume such a section does not exist. Do not define both this macro and `INIT_SECTION_ASM_OP`.

FINI_ARRAY_SECTION_ASM_OP   [Macro]
> If defined, a C expression whose value is a string, including spacing, containing the assembler operation to identify the following data as part of the .fini_array (or equivalent) section. If not defined, GCC will assume such a section does not exist. Do not define both this macro and FINI_SECTION_ASM_OP.

MACH_DEP_SECTION_ASM_FLAG   [Macro]
> If defined, a C expression whose value is a character constant containing the flag used to mark a machine-dependent section. This corresponds to the SECTION_MACH_DEP section flag.

CRT_CALL_STATIC_FUNCTION (*section_op*, *function*)   [Macro]
> If defined, an ASM statement that switches to a different section via *section_op*, calls *function*, and switches back to the text section. This is used in 'crtstuff.c' if INIT_SECTION_ASM_OP or FINI_SECTION_ASM_OP to calls to initialization and finalization functions from the init and fini sections. By default, this macro uses a simple function call. Some ports need hand-crafted assembly code to avoid dependencies on registers initialized in the function prologue or to ensure that constant pools don't end up too far way in the text section.

TARGET_LIBGCC_SDATA_SECTION   [Macro]
> If defined, a string which names the section into which small variables defined in crtstuff and libgcc should go. This is useful when the target has options for optimizing access to small data, and you want the crtstuff and libgcc routines to be conservative in what they expect of your application yet liberal in what your application expects. For example, for targets with a .sdata section (like MIPS), you could compile crtstuff with -G 0 so that it doesn't require small data support from your application, but use this macro to put small data into .sdata so that your application can access these variables whether it uses small data or not.

FORCE_CODE_SECTION_ALIGN   [Macro]
> If defined, an ASM statement that aligns a code section to some arbitrary boundary. This is used to force all fragments of the .init and .fini sections to have to same alignment and thus prevent the linker from having to add any padding.

JUMP_TABLES_IN_TEXT_SECTION   [Macro]
> Define this macro to be an expression with a nonzero value if jump tables (for tablejump insns) should be output in the text section, along with the assembler instructions. Otherwise, the readonly data section is used.
>
> This macro is irrelevant if there is no separate readonly data section.

void TARGET_ASM_INIT_SECTIONS (*void*)   [Target Hook]
> Define this hook if you need to do something special to set up the 'varasm.c' sections, or if your target has some special sections of its own that you need to create.
>
> GCC calls this hook after processing the command line, but before writing any assembly code, and before calling any of the section-returning hooks described below.

int TARGET_ASM_RELOC_RW_MASK (*void*)   [Target Hook]

Return a mask describing how relocations should be treated when selecting sections. Bit 1 should be set if global relocations should be placed in a read-write section; bit 0 should be set if local relocations should be placed in a read-write section.

The default version of this function returns 3 when '-fpic' is in effect, and 0 otherwise. The hook is typically redefined when the target cannot support (some kinds of) dynamic relocations in read-only sections even in executables.

section * TARGET_ASM_SELECT_SECTION (*tree exp*, *int reloc*,   [Target Hook]
**   unsigned *HOST_WIDE_INT align*)**

Return the section into which *exp* should be placed. You can assume that *exp* is either a VAR_DECL node or a constant of some sort. *reloc* indicates whether the initial value of *exp* requires link-time relocations. Bit 0 is set when variable contains local relocations only, while bit 1 is set for global relocations. *align* is the constant alignment in bits.

The default version of this function takes care of putting read-only variables in readonly_data_section.

See also *USE_SELECT_SECTION_FOR_FUNCTIONS*.

USE_SELECT_SECTION_FOR_FUNCTIONS   [Macro]

Define this macro if you wish TARGET_ASM_SELECT_SECTION to be called for FUNCTION_DECLs as well as for variables and constants.

In the case of a FUNCTION_DECL, *reloc* will be zero if the function has been determined to be likely to be called, and nonzero if it is unlikely to be called.

void TARGET_ASM_UNIQUE_SECTION (*tree decl*, *int reloc*)   [Target Hook]

Build up a unique section name, expressed as a STRING_CST node, and assign it to 'DECL_SECTION_NAME (*decl*)'. As with TARGET_ASM_SELECT_SECTION, *reloc* indicates whether the initial value of *exp* requires link-time relocations.

The default version of this function appends the symbol name to the ELF section name that would normally be used for the symbol. For example, the function foo would be placed in .text.foo. Whatever the actual target object format, this is often good enough.

section * TARGET_ASM_FUNCTION_RODATA_SECTION (*tree decl*)   [Target Hook]

Return the readonly data section associated with 'DECL_SECTION_NAME (*decl*)'. The default version of this function selects .gnu.linkonce.r.name if the function's section is .gnu.linkonce.t.name, .rodata.name if function is in .text.name, and the normal readonly-data section otherwise.

const char * TARGET_ASM_MERGEABLE_RODATA_PREFIX   [Target Hook]

Usually, the compiler uses the prefix ".rodata" to construct section names for mergeable constant data. Define this macro to override the string if a different section name should be used.

section * TARGET_ASM_TM_CLONE_TABLE_SECTION (*void*)   [Target Hook]

Return the section that should be used for transactional memory clone tables.

section * TARGET_ASM_SELECT_RTX_SECTION (*machine_mode*   [Target Hook]
    mode, rtx *x*, unsigned *HOST_WIDE_INT* align)
> Return the section into which a constant *x*, of mode *mode*, should be placed. You can
> assume that *x* is some kind of constant in RTL. The argument *mode* is redundant
> except in the case of a const_int rtx. *align* is the constant alignment in bits.
>
> The default version of this function takes care of putting symbolic constants in flag_
> pic mode in data_section and everything else in readonly_data_section.

tree TARGET_MANGLE_DECL_ASSEMBLER_NAME (*tree* decl, *tree* id)   [Target Hook]
> Define this hook if you need to postprocess the assembler name generated by target-
> independent code. The *id* provided to this hook will be the computed name (e.g., the
> macro DECL_NAME of the *decl* in C, or the mangled name of the *decl* in C++). The
> return value of the hook is an IDENTIFIER_NODE for the appropriate mangled name
> on your target system. The default implementation of this hook just returns the *id*
> provided.

void TARGET_ENCODE_SECTION_INFO (*tree* decl, *rtx* **rtl**, *int*   [Target Hook]
    new_decl_p)
> Define this hook if references to a symbol or a constant must be treated differently
> depending on something about the variable or function named by the symbol (such
> as what section it is in).
>
> The hook is executed immediately after rtl has been created for *decl*, which may be
> a variable or function declaration or an entry in the constant pool. In either case, *rtl*
> is the rtl in question. Do *not* use DECL_RTL (decl) in this hook; that field may not
> have been initialized yet.
>
> In the case of a constant, it is safe to assume that the rtl is a mem whose address is a
> symbol_ref. Most decls will also have this form, but that is not guaranteed. Global
> register variables, for instance, will have a reg for their rtl. (Normally the right thing
> to do with such unusual rtl is leave it alone.)
>
> The *new_decl_p* argument will be true if this is the first time that TARGET_ENCODE_
> SECTION_INFO has been invoked on this decl. It will be false for subsequent invoca-
> tions, which will happen for duplicate declarations. Whether or not anything must
> be done for the duplicate declaration depends on whether the hook examines DECL_
> ATTRIBUTES. *new_decl_p* is always true when the hook is called for a constant.
>
> The usual thing for this hook to do is to record flags in the symbol_ref, using
> SYMBOL_REF_FLAG or SYMBOL_REF_FLAGS. Historically, the name string was modified
> if it was necessary to encode more than one bit of information, but this practice is
> now discouraged; use SYMBOL_REF_FLAGS.
>
> The default definition of this hook, default_encode_section_info in 'varasm.c',
> sets a number of commonly-useful bits in SYMBOL_REF_FLAGS. Check whether the
> default does what you need before overriding it.

const char * TARGET_STRIP_NAME_ENCODING (*const char* *name)   [Target Hook]
> Decode *name* and return the real name part, sans the characters that TARGET_ENCODE_
> SECTION_INFO may have added.

`bool` **`TARGET_IN_SMALL_DATA_P`** (*const_tree* **`exp`**)   [Target Hook]
> Returns true if *exp* should be placed into a "small data" section. The default version of this hook always returns false.

`bool` **`TARGET_HAVE_SRODATA_SECTION`**   [Target Hook]
> Contains the value true if the target places read-only "small data" into a separate section. The default value is false.

`bool` **`TARGET_PROFILE_BEFORE_PROLOGUE`** (*void*)   [Target Hook]
> It returns true if target wants profile code emitted before prologue.
>
> The default version of this hook use the target macro `PROFILE_BEFORE_PROLOGUE`.

`bool` **`TARGET_BINDS_LOCAL_P`** (*const_tree* **`exp`**)   [Target Hook]
> Returns true if *exp* names an object for which name resolution rules must resolve to the current "module" (dynamic shared library or executable image).
>
> The default version of this hook implements the name resolution rules for ELF, which has a looser model of global name binding than other currently supported object file formats.

`bool` **`TARGET_HAVE_TLS`**   [Target Hook]
> Contains the value true if the target supports thread-local storage. The default value is false.

17.19 Position Independent Code

This section describes macros that help implement generation of position independent code. Simply defining these macros is not enough to generate valid PIC; you must also add support to the hook `TARGET_LEGITIMATE_ADDRESS_P` and to the macro `PRINT_OPERAND_ADDRESS`, as well as `LEGITIMIZE_ADDRESS`. You must modify the definition of 'movsi' to do something appropriate when the source operand contains a symbolic address. You may also need to alter the handling of switch statements so that they use relative addresses.

`PIC_OFFSET_TABLE_REGNUM`   [Macro]
> The register number of the register used to address a table of static data addresses in memory. In some cases this register is defined by a processor's "application binary interface" (ABI). When this macro is defined, RTL is generated for this register once, as with the stack pointer and frame pointer registers. If this macro is not defined, it is up to the machine-dependent files to allocate such a register (if necessary). Note that this register must be fixed when in use (e.g. when `flag_pic` is true).

`PIC_OFFSET_TABLE_REG_CALL_CLOBBERED`   [Macro]
> A C expression that is nonzero if the register defined by `PIC_OFFSET_TABLE_REGNUM` is clobbered by calls. If not defined, the default is zero. Do not define this macro if `PIC_OFFSET_TABLE_REGNUM` is not defined.

`LEGITIMATE_PIC_OPERAND_P` (*x*)   [Macro]
> A C expression that is nonzero if *x* is a legitimate immediate operand on the target machine when generating position independent code. You can assume that *x* satisfies `CONSTANT_P`, so you need not check this. You can also assume *flag_pic* is true, so you need not check it either. You need not define this macro if all constants (including `SYMBOL_REF`) can be immediate operands when generating position independent code.

17.20 Defining the Output Assembler Language

This section describes macros whose principal purpose is to describe how to write instructions in assembler language—rather than what the instructions do.

17.20.1 The Overall Framework of an Assembler File

This describes the overall framework of an assembly file.

void TARGET_ASM_FILE_START (*void*)   [Target Hook]

> Output to `asm_out_file` any text which the assembler expects to find at the beginning of a file. The default behavior is controlled by two flags, documented below. Unless your target's assembler is quite unusual, if you override the default, you should call `default_file_start` at some point in your target hook. This lets other target files rely on these variables.

bool TARGET_ASM_FILE_START_APP_OFF   [Target Hook]

> If this flag is true, the text of the macro `ASM_APP_OFF` will be printed as the very first line in the assembly file, unless '`-fverbose-asm`' is in effect. (If that macro has been defined to the empty string, this variable has no effect.) With the normal definition of `ASM_APP_OFF`, the effect is to notify the GNU assembler that it need not bother stripping comments or extra whitespace from its input. This allows it to work a bit faster.

> The default is false. You should not set it to true unless you have verified that your port does not generate any extra whitespace or comments that will cause GAS to issue errors in NO_APP mode.

bool TARGET_ASM_FILE_START_FILE_DIRECTIVE   [Target Hook]

> If this flag is true, `output_file_directive` will be called for the primary source file, immediately after printing `ASM_APP_OFF` (if that is enabled). Most ELF assemblers expect this to be done. The default is false.

void TARGET_ASM_FILE_END (*void*)   [Target Hook]

> Output to `asm_out_file` any text which the assembler expects to find at the end of a file. The default is to output nothing.

void file_end_indicate_exec_stack ()   [Function]

> Some systems use a common convention, the '`.note.GNU-stack`' special section, to indicate whether or not an object file relies on the stack being executable. If your system uses this convention, you should define `TARGET_ASM_FILE_END` to this function. If you need to do other things in that hook, have your hook function call this function.

void TARGET_ASM_LTO_START (*void*)   [Target Hook]

> Output to `asm_out_file` any text which the assembler expects to find at the start of an LTO section. The default is to output nothing.

void TARGET_ASM_LTO_END (*void*)   [Target Hook]

> Output to `asm_out_file` any text which the assembler expects to find at the end of an LTO section. The default is to output nothing.

void `TARGET_ASM_CODE_END` (*void*)   [Target Hook]

> Output to `asm_out_file` any text which is needed before emitting unwind info and debug info at the end of a file. Some targets emit here PIC setup thunks that cannot be emitted at the end of file, because they couldn't have unwind info then. The default is to output nothing.

`ASM_COMMENT_START`   [Macro]

> A C string constant describing how to begin a comment in the target assembler language. The compiler assumes that the comment will end at the end of the line.

`ASM_APP_ON`   [Macro]

> A C string constant for text to be output before each `asm` statement or group of consecutive ones. Normally this is `"#APP"`, which is a comment that has no effect on most assemblers but tells the GNU assembler that it must check the lines that follow for all valid assembler constructs.

`ASM_APP_OFF`   [Macro]

> A C string constant for text to be output after each `asm` statement or group of consecutive ones. Normally this is `"#NO_APP"`, which tells the GNU assembler to resume making the time-saving assumptions that are valid for ordinary compiler output.

`ASM_OUTPUT_SOURCE_FILENAME` (*stream, name*)   [Macro]

> A C statement to output COFF information or DWARF debugging information which indicates that filename *name* is the current source file to the stdio stream *stream*.
>
> This macro need not be defined if the standard form of output for the file format in use is appropriate.

void `TARGET_ASM_OUTPUT_SOURCE_FILENAME` (*FILE *file*, *const*   [Target Hook]
  char *name)

> Output COFF information or DWARF debugging information which indicates that filename *name* is the current source file to the stdio stream *file*.
>
> This target hook need not be defined if the standard form of output for the file format in use is appropriate.

void `TARGET_ASM_OUTPUT_IDENT` (*const char *name*)   [Target Hook]

> Output a string based on *name*, suitable for the '#ident' directive, or the equivalent directive or pragma in non-C-family languages. If this hook is not defined, nothing is output for the '#ident' directive.

`OUTPUT_QUOTED_STRING` (*stream, string*)   [Macro]

> A C statement to output the string *string* to the stdio stream *stream*. If you do not call the function `output_quoted_string` in your config files, GCC will only call it to output filenames to the assembler source. So you can use it to canonicalize the format of the filename using this macro.

void `TARGET_ASM_NAMED_SECTION` (*const char *name*, *unsigned int*   [Target Hook]
  flags, *tree decl*)

> Output assembly directives to switch to section *name*. The section should have attributes as specified by *flags*, which is a bit mask of the `SECTION_*` flags defined in 'output.h'. If *decl* is non-NULL, it is the `VAR_DECL` or `FUNCTION_DECL` with which this section is associated.

bool **TARGET_ASM_ELF_FLAGS_NUMERIC** (*unsigned int* `flags`,   [Target Hook]
    unsigned int `*num`)
> This hook can be used to encode ELF section flags for which no letter code has been
> defined in the assembler. It is called by `default_asm_named_section` whenever the
> section flags need to be emitted in the assembler output. If the hook returns true,
> then the numerical value for ELF section flags should be calculated from *flags* and
> saved in **num*; the value is printed out instead of the normal sequence of letter codes.
> If the hook is not defined, or if it returns false, then *num* is ignored and the traditional
> letter sequence is emitted.

section * **TARGET_ASM_FUNCTION_SECTION** (*tree* `decl`, *enum*   [Target Hook]
    node_frequency `freq`, *bool* `startup`, *bool* `exit`)
> Return preferred text (sub)section for function *decl*. Main purpose of this function is
> to separate cold, normal and hot functions. *startup* is true when function is known to
> be used only at startup (from static constructors or it is `main()`). *exit* is true when
> function is known to be used only at exit (from static destructors). Return NULL if
> function should go to default text section.

void **TARGET_ASM_FUNCTION_SWITCHED_TEXT_SECTIONS** (*FILE*   [Target Hook]
    `*file`, *tree* `decl`, *bool* `new_is_cold`)
> Used by the target to emit any assembler directives or additional labels needed when
> a function is partitioned between different sections. Output should be written to *file*.
> The function decl is available as *decl* and the new section is 'cold' if *new_is_cold* is
> `true`.

bool **TARGET_HAVE_NAMED_SECTIONS**   [Common Target Hook]
> This flag is true if the target supports `TARGET_ASM_NAMED_SECTION`. It must not be
> modified by command-line option processing.

bool **TARGET_HAVE_SWITCHABLE_BSS_SECTIONS**   [Target Hook]
> This flag is true if we can create zeroed data by switching to a BSS section and then
> using `ASM_OUTPUT_SKIP` to allocate the space. This is true on most ELF targets.

unsigned int **TARGET_SECTION_TYPE_FLAGS** (*tree* `decl`, *const*   [Target Hook]
    char `*name`, *int* `reloc`)
> Choose a set of section attributes for use by `TARGET_ASM_NAMED_SECTION` based on
> a variable or function decl, a section name, and whether or not the declaration's
> initializer may contain runtime relocations. *decl* may be null, in which case read-
> write data should be assumed.
>
> The default version of this function handles choosing code vs data, read-only vs read-
> write data, and `flag_pic`. You should only need to override this if your target has
> special flags that might be set via `__attribute__`.

int **TARGET_ASM_RECORD_GCC_SWITCHES** (*print_switch_type* `type`,   [Target Hook]
    const char `*text`)
> Provides the target with the ability to record the gcc command line switches that
> have been passed to the compiler, and options that are enabled. The *type* argument
> specifies what is being recorded. It can take the following values:

SWITCH_TYPE_PASSED

> *text* is a command line switch that has been set by the user.

SWITCH_TYPE_ENABLED

> *text* is an option which has been enabled. This might be as a direct result of a command line switch, or because it is enabled by default or because it has been enabled as a side effect of a different command line switch. For example, the '-O2' switch enables various different individual optimization passes.

SWITCH_TYPE_DESCRIPTIVE

> *text* is either NULL or some descriptive text which should be ignored. If *text* is NULL then it is being used to warn the target hook that either recording is starting or ending. The first time *type* is SWITCH_TYPE_DESCRIPTIVE and *text* is NULL, the warning is for start up and the second time the warning is for wind down. This feature is to allow the target hook to make any necessary preparations before it starts to record switches and to perform any necessary tidying up after it has finished recording switches.

SWITCH_TYPE_LINE_START

> This option can be ignored by this target hook.

SWITCH_TYPE_LINE_END

> This option can be ignored by this target hook.

The hook's return value must be zero. Other return values may be supported in the future.

By default this hook is set to NULL, but an example implementation is provided for ELF based targets. Called *elf_record_gcc_switches*, it records the switches as ASCII text inside a new, string mergeable section in the assembler output file. The name of the new section is provided by the TARGET_ASM_RECORD_GCC_SWITCHES_SECTION target hook.

const char * TARGET_ASM_RECORD_GCC_SWITCHES_SECTION   [Target Hook]

> This is the name of the section that will be created by the example ELF implementation of the TARGET_ASM_RECORD_GCC_SWITCHES target hook.

17.20.2 Output of Data

const char * TARGET_ASM_BYTE_OP   [Target Hook]
const char * TARGET_ASM_ALIGNED_HI_OP   [Target Hook]
const char * TARGET_ASM_ALIGNED_SI_OP   [Target Hook]
const char * TARGET_ASM_ALIGNED_DI_OP   [Target Hook]
const char * TARGET_ASM_ALIGNED_TI_OP   [Target Hook]
const char * TARGET_ASM_UNALIGNED_HI_OP   [Target Hook]
const char * TARGET_ASM_UNALIGNED_SI_OP   [Target Hook]
const char * TARGET_ASM_UNALIGNED_DI_OP   [Target Hook]
const char * TARGET_ASM_UNALIGNED_TI_OP   [Target Hook]

> These hooks specify assembly directives for creating certain kinds of integer object. The TARGET_ASM_BYTE_OP directive creates a byte-sized object, the TARGET_ASM_

ALIGNED_HI_OP one creates an aligned two-byte object, and so on. Any of the hooks may be NULL, indicating that no suitable directive is available.

The compiler will print these strings at the start of a new line, followed immediately by the object's initial value. In most cases, the string should contain a tab, a pseudo-op, and then another tab.

bool TARGET_ASM_INTEGER (rtx x, unsigned int size, int   [Target Hook]
    aligned_p)

The assemble_integer function uses this hook to output an integer object. x is the object's value, size is its size in bytes and aligned_p indicates whether it is aligned. The function should return true if it was able to output the object. If it returns false, assemble_integer will try to split the object into smaller parts.

The default implementation of this hook will use the TARGET_ASM_BYTE_OP family of strings, returning false when the relevant string is NULL.

void TARGET_ASM_DECL_END (void)   [Target Hook]

Define this hook if the target assembler requires a special marker to terminate an initialized variable declaration.

bool TARGET_ASM_OUTPUT_ADDR_CONST_EXTRA (FILE *file, rtx x)   [Target Hook]

A target hook to recognize rtx patterns that output_addr_const can't deal with, and output assembly code to file corresponding to the pattern x. This may be used to allow machine-dependent UNSPECs to appear within constants.

If target hook fails to recognize a pattern, it must return false, so that a standard error message is printed. If it prints an error message itself, by calling, for example, output_operand_lossage, it may just return true.

ASM_OUTPUT_ASCII (stream, ptr, len)   [Macro]

A C statement to output to the stdio stream stream an assembler instruction to assemble a string constant containing the len bytes at ptr. ptr will be a C expression of type char * and len a C expression of type int.

If the assembler has a .ascii pseudo-op as found in the Berkeley Unix assembler, do not define the macro ASM_OUTPUT_ASCII.

ASM_OUTPUT_FDESC (stream, decl, n)   [Macro]

A C statement to output word n of a function descriptor for decl. This must be defined if TARGET_VTABLE_USES_DESCRIPTORS is defined, and is otherwise unused.

CONSTANT_POOL_BEFORE_FUNCTION   [Macro]

You may define this macro as a C expression. You should define the expression to have a nonzero value if GCC should output the constant pool for a function before the code for the function, or a zero value if GCC should output the constant pool after the function. If you do not define this macro, the usual case, GCC will output the constant pool before the function.

ASM_OUTPUT_POOL_PROLOGUE (file, funname, fundecl, size)   [Macro]

A C statement to output assembler commands to define the start of the constant pool for a function. funname is a string giving the name of the function. Should the return type of the function be required, it can be obtained via *fundecl*. *size* is the size, in bytes, of the constant pool that will be written immediately after this call.

If no constant-pool prefix is required, the usual case, this macro need not be defined.

ASM_OUTPUT_SPECIAL_POOL_ENTRY (*file*, *x*, *mode*, *align*, *labelno*,   [Macro]
  ***jumpto*)**

A C statement (with or without semicolon) to output a constant in the constant pool, if it needs special treatment. (This macro need not do anything for RTL expressions that can be output normally.)

The argument *file* is the standard I/O stream to output the assembler code on. *x* is the RTL expression for the constant to output, and *mode* is the machine mode (in case *x* is a 'const_int'). *align* is the required alignment for the value *x*; you should output an assembler directive to force this much alignment.

The argument *labelno* is a number to use in an internal label for the address of this pool entry. The definition of this macro is responsible for outputting the label definition at the proper place. Here is how to do this:

```
(*targetm.asm_out.internal_label) (file, "LC", labelno);
```

When you output a pool entry specially, you should end with a `goto` to the label *jumpto*. This will prevent the same pool entry from being output a second time in the usual manner.

You need not define this macro if it would do nothing.

ASM_OUTPUT_POOL_EPILOGUE (*file funname fundecl size*)   [Macro]

A C statement to output assembler commands to at the end of the constant pool for a function. *funname* is a string giving the name of the function. Should the return type of the function be required, you can obtain it via *fundecl*. *size* is the size, in bytes, of the constant pool that GCC wrote immediately before this call.

If no constant-pool epilogue is required, the usual case, you need not define this macro.

IS_ASM_LOGICAL_LINE_SEPARATOR (*C*, *STR*)   [Macro]

Define this macro as a C expression which is nonzero if *C* is used as a logical line separator by the assembler. *STR* points to the position in the string where *C* was found; this can be used if a line separator uses multiple characters.

If you do not define this macro, the default is that only the character ';' is treated as a logical line separator.

const char * TARGET_ASM_OPEN_PAREN   [Target Hook]
const char * TARGET_ASM_CLOSE_PAREN   [Target Hook]

These target hooks are C string constants, describing the syntax in the assembler for grouping arithmetic expressions. If not overridden, they default to normal parentheses, which is correct for most assemblers.

These macros are provided by 'real.h' for writing the definitions of ASM_OUTPUT_DOUBLE and the like:

REAL_VALUE_TO_TARGET_SINGLE (*x*, *l*)   [Macro]
REAL_VALUE_TO_TARGET_DOUBLE (*x*, *l*)   [Macro]

REAL_VALUE_TO_TARGET_LONG_DOUBLE (*x*, *l*)   [Macro]
REAL_VALUE_TO_TARGET_DECIMAL32 (*x*, *l*)   [Macro]
REAL_VALUE_TO_TARGET_DECIMAL64 (*x*, *l*)   [Macro]
REAL_VALUE_TO_TARGET_DECIMAL128 (*x*, *l*)   [Macro]

> These translate *x*, of type REAL_VALUE_TYPE, to the target's floating point representation, and store its bit pattern in the variable *l*. For REAL_VALUE_TO_TARGET_SINGLE and REAL_VALUE_TO_TARGET_DECIMAL32, this variable should be a simple long int. For the others, it should be an array of long int. The number of elements in this array is determined by the size of the desired target floating point data type: 32 bits of it go in each long int array element. Each array element holds 32 bits of the result, even if long int is wider than 32 bits on the host machine.
>
> The array element values are designed so that you can print them out using fprintf in the order they should appear in the target machine's memory.

17.20.3 Output of Uninitialized Variables

Each of the macros in this section is used to do the whole job of outputting a single uninitialized variable.

ASM_OUTPUT_COMMON (*stream*, *name*, *size*, *rounded*)   [Macro]

> A C statement (sans semicolon) to output to the stdio stream *stream* the assembler definition of a common-label named *name* whose size is *size* bytes. The variable *rounded* is the size rounded up to whatever alignment the caller wants. It is possible that *size* may be zero, for instance if a struct with no other member than a zero-length array is defined. In this case, the backend must output a symbol definition that allocates at least one byte, both so that the address of the resulting object does not compare equal to any other, and because some object formats cannot even express the concept of a zero-sized common symbol, as that is how they represent an ordinary undefined external.
>
> Use the expression assemble_name (*stream*, *name*) to output the name itself; before and after that, output the additional assembler syntax for defining the name, and a newline.
>
> This macro controls how the assembler definitions of uninitialized common global variables are output.

ASM_OUTPUT_ALIGNED_COMMON (*stream*, *name*, *size*, *alignment*)   [Macro]

> Like ASM_OUTPUT_COMMON except takes the required alignment as a separate, explicit argument. If you define this macro, it is used in place of ASM_OUTPUT_COMMON, and gives you more flexibility in handling the required alignment of the variable. The alignment is specified as the number of bits.

ASM_OUTPUT_ALIGNED_DECL_COMMON (*stream*, *decl*, *name*, *size*,   [Macro]
    alignment)

> Like ASM_OUTPUT_ALIGNED_COMMON except that *decl* of the variable to be output, if there is one, or NULL_TREE if there is no corresponding variable. If you define this macro, GCC will use it in place of both ASM_OUTPUT_COMMON and ASM_OUTPUT_ALIGNED_COMMON. Define this macro when you need to see the variable's decl in order to chose what to output.

ASM_OUTPUT_ALIGNED_BSS (*stream*, *decl*, *name*, *size*, *alignment*)   [Macro]

> A C statement (sans semicolon) to output to the stdio stream *stream* the assembler definition of uninitialized global *decl* named *name* whose size is *size* bytes. The variable *alignment* is the alignment specified as the number of bits.
>
> Try to use function `asm_output_aligned_bss` defined in file 'varasm.c' when defining this macro. If unable, use the expression `assemble_name (stream, name)` to output the name itself; before and after that, output the additional assembler syntax for defining the name, and a newline.
>
> There are two ways of handling global BSS. One is to define this macro. The other is to have `TARGET_ASM_SELECT_SECTION` return a switchable BSS section (see [TARGET_HAVE_SWITCHABLE_BSS_SECTIONS], page 547). You do not need to do both.
>
> Some languages do not have `common` data, and require a non-common form of global BSS in order to handle uninitialized globals efficiently. C++ is one example of this. However, if the target does not support global BSS, the front end may choose to make globals common in order to save space in the object file.

ASM_OUTPUT_LOCAL (*stream*, *name*, *size*, *rounded*)   [Macro]

> A C statement (sans semicolon) to output to the stdio stream *stream* the assembler definition of a local-common-label named *name* whose size is *size* bytes. The variable *rounded* is the size rounded up to whatever alignment the caller wants.
>
> Use the expression `assemble_name (stream, name)` to output the name itself; before and after that, output the additional assembler syntax for defining the name, and a newline.
>
> This macro controls how the assembler definitions of uninitialized static variables are output.

ASM_OUTPUT_ALIGNED_LOCAL (*stream*, *name*, *size*, *alignment*)   [Macro]

> Like `ASM_OUTPUT_LOCAL` except takes the required alignment as a separate, explicit argument. If you define this macro, it is used in place of `ASM_OUTPUT_LOCAL`, and gives you more flexibility in handling the required alignment of the variable. The alignment is specified as the number of bits.

ASM_OUTPUT_ALIGNED_DECL_LOCAL (*stream*, *decl*, *name*, *size*,   [Macro]
     alignment)

> Like `ASM_OUTPUT_ALIGNED_DECL` except that *decl* of the variable to be output, if there is one, or `NULL_TREE` if there is no corresponding variable. If you define this macro, GCC will use it in place of both `ASM_OUTPUT_DECL` and `ASM_OUTPUT_ALIGNED_DECL`. Define this macro when you need to see the variable's decl in order to chose what to output.

17.20.4 Output and Generation of Labels

This is about outputting labels.

ASM_OUTPUT_LABEL (*stream*, *name*)   [Macro]

> A C statement (sans semicolon) to output to the stdio stream *stream* the assembler definition of a label named *name*. Use the expression `assemble_name (stream,`

name) to output the name itself; before and after that, output the additional assembler syntax for defining the name, and a newline. A default definition of this macro is provided which is correct for most systems.

ASM_OUTPUT_FUNCTION_LABEL (*stream*, *name*, *decl*) [Macro]

A C statement (sans semicolon) to output to the stdio stream *stream* the assembler definition of a label named *name* of a function. Use the expression `assemble_name (stream, name)` to output the name itself; before and after that, output the additional assembler syntax for defining the name, and a newline. A default definition of this macro is provided which is correct for most systems.

If this macro is not defined, then the function name is defined in the usual manner as a label (by means of `ASM_OUTPUT_LABEL`).

ASM_OUTPUT_INTERNAL_LABEL (*stream*, *name*) [Macro]

Identical to `ASM_OUTPUT_LABEL`, except that *name* is known to refer to a compiler-generated label. The default definition uses `assemble_name_raw`, which is like `assemble_name` except that it is more efficient.

SIZE_ASM_OP [Macro]

A C string containing the appropriate assembler directive to specify the size of a symbol, without any arguments. On systems that use ELF, the default (in 'config/elfos.h') is '"\t.size\t"'; on other systems, the default is not to define this macro.

Define this macro only if it is correct to use the default definitions of `ASM_OUTPUT_SIZE_DIRECTIVE` and `ASM_OUTPUT_MEASURED_SIZE` for your system. If you need your own custom definitions of those macros, or if you do not need explicit symbol sizes at all, do not define this macro.

ASM_OUTPUT_SIZE_DIRECTIVE (*stream*, *name*, *size*) [Macro]

A C statement (sans semicolon) to output to the stdio stream *stream* a directive telling the assembler that the size of the symbol *name* is *size*. *size* is a `HOST_WIDE_INT`. If you define `SIZE_ASM_OP`, a default definition of this macro is provided.

ASM_OUTPUT_MEASURED_SIZE (*stream*, *name*) [Macro]

A C statement (sans semicolon) to output to the stdio stream *stream* a directive telling the assembler to calculate the size of the symbol *name* by subtracting its address from the current address.

If you define `SIZE_ASM_OP`, a default definition of this macro is provided. The default assumes that the assembler recognizes a special '.' symbol as referring to the current address, and can calculate the difference between this and another symbol. If your assembler does not recognize '.' or cannot do calculations with it, you will need to redefine `ASM_OUTPUT_MEASURED_SIZE` to use some other technique.

NO_DOLLAR_IN_LABEL [Macro]

Define this macro if the assembler does not accept the character '$' in label names. By default constructors and destructors in G++ have '$' in the identifiers. If this macro is defined, '.' is used instead.

NO_DOT_IN_LABEL   [Macro]

> Define this macro if the assembler does not accept the character '.' in label names. By default constructors and destructors in G++ have names that use '.'. If this macro is defined, these names are rewritten to avoid '.'.

TYPE_ASM_OP   [Macro]

> A C string containing the appropriate assembler directive to specify the type of a symbol, without any arguments. On systems that use ELF, the default (in 'config/elfos.h') is '"\t.type\t"'; on other systems, the default is not to define this macro.
>
> Define this macro only if it is correct to use the default definition of ASM_OUTPUT_TYPE_DIRECTIVE for your system. If you need your own custom definition of this macro, or if you do not need explicit symbol types at all, do not define this macro.

TYPE_OPERAND_FMT   [Macro]

> A C string which specifies (using printf syntax) the format of the second operand to TYPE_ASM_OP. On systems that use ELF, the default (in 'config/elfos.h') is '"@%s"'; on other systems, the default is not to define this macro.
>
> Define this macro only if it is correct to use the default definition of ASM_OUTPUT_TYPE_DIRECTIVE for your system. If you need your own custom definition of this macro, or if you do not need explicit symbol types at all, do not define this macro.

ASM_OUTPUT_TYPE_DIRECTIVE (*stream*, *type*)   [Macro]

> A C statement (sans semicolon) to output to the stdio stream *stream* a directive telling the assembler that the type of the symbol *name* is *type*. *type* is a C string; currently, that string is always either '"function"' or '"object"', but you should not count on this.
>
> If you define TYPE_ASM_OP and TYPE_OPERAND_FMT, a default definition of this macro is provided.

ASM_DECLARE_FUNCTION_NAME (*stream*, *name*, *decl*)   [Macro]

> A C statement (sans semicolon) to output to the stdio stream *stream* any text necessary for declaring the name *name* of a function which is being defined. This macro is responsible for outputting the label definition (perhaps using ASM_OUTPUT_FUNCTION_LABEL). The argument *decl* is the FUNCTION_DECL tree node representing the function.
>
> If this macro is not defined, then the function name is defined in the usual manner as a label (by means of ASM_OUTPUT_FUNCTION_LABEL).
>
> You may wish to use ASM_OUTPUT_TYPE_DIRECTIVE in the definition of this macro.

ASM_DECLARE_FUNCTION_SIZE (*stream*, *name*, *decl*)   [Macro]

> A C statement (sans semicolon) to output to the stdio stream *stream* any text necessary for declaring the size of a function which is being defined. The argument *name* is the name of the function. The argument *decl* is the FUNCTION_DECL tree node representing the function.
>
> If this macro is not defined, then the function size is not defined.
>
> You may wish to use ASM_OUTPUT_MEASURED_SIZE in the definition of this macro.

ASM_DECLARE_COLD_FUNCTION_NAME (*stream*, *name*, *decl*)   [Macro]

A C statement (sans semicolon) to output to the stdio stream *stream* any text necessary for declaring the name *name* of a cold function partition which is being defined. This macro is responsible for outputting the label definition (perhaps using `ASM_OUTPUT_FUNCTION_LABEL`). The argument *decl* is the `FUNCTION_DECL` tree node representing the function.

If this macro is not defined, then the cold partition name is defined in the usual manner as a label (by means of `ASM_OUTPUT_LABEL`).

You may wish to use `ASM_OUTPUT_TYPE_DIRECTIVE` in the definition of this macro.

ASM_DECLARE_COLD_FUNCTION_SIZE (*stream*, *name*, *decl*)   [Macro]

A C statement (sans semicolon) to output to the stdio stream *stream* any text necessary for declaring the size of a cold function partition which is being defined. The argument *name* is the name of the cold partition of the function. The argument *decl* is the `FUNCTION_DECL` tree node representing the function.

If this macro is not defined, then the partition size is not defined.

You may wish to use `ASM_OUTPUT_MEASURED_SIZE` in the definition of this macro.

ASM_DECLARE_OBJECT_NAME (*stream*, *name*, *decl*)   [Macro]

A C statement (sans semicolon) to output to the stdio stream *stream* any text necessary for declaring the name *name* of an initialized variable which is being defined. This macro must output the label definition (perhaps using `ASM_OUTPUT_LABEL`). The argument *decl* is the `VAR_DECL` tree node representing the variable.

If this macro is not defined, then the variable name is defined in the usual manner as a label (by means of `ASM_OUTPUT_LABEL`).

You may wish to use `ASM_OUTPUT_TYPE_DIRECTIVE` and/or `ASM_OUTPUT_SIZE_DIRECTIVE` in the definition of this macro.

void TARGET_ASM_DECLARE_CONSTANT_NAME (*FILE *file*, const   [Target Hook]
    char *name*, *const_tree* expr*, *HOST_WIDE_INT size*)

A target hook to output to the stdio stream *file* any text necessary for declaring the name *name* of a constant which is being defined. This target hook is responsible for outputting the label definition (perhaps using `assemble_label`). The argument *exp* is the value of the constant, and *size* is the size of the constant in bytes. The *name* will be an internal label.

The default version of this target hook, define the *name* in the usual manner as a label (by means of `assemble_label`).

You may wish to use `ASM_OUTPUT_TYPE_DIRECTIVE` in this target hook.

ASM_DECLARE_REGISTER_GLOBAL (*stream*, *decl*, *regno*, *name*)   [Macro]

A C statement (sans semicolon) to output to the stdio stream *stream* any text necessary for claiming a register *regno* for a global variable *decl* with name *name*.

If you don't define this macro, that is equivalent to defining it to do nothing.

ASM_FINISH_DECLARE_OBJECT (*stream*, *decl*, *toplevel*, *atend*)   [Macro]

A C statement (sans semicolon) to finish up declaring a variable name once the compiler has processed its initializer fully and thus has had a chance to determine the size of an array when controlled by an initializer. This is used on systems where it's necessary to declare something about the size of the object.

If you don't define this macro, that is equivalent to defining it to do nothing.

You may wish to use `ASM_OUTPUT_SIZE_DIRECTIVE` and/or `ASM_OUTPUT_MEASURED_SIZE` in the definition of this macro.

void **TARGET_ASM_GLOBALIZE_LABEL** (*FILE *stream*, const char   [Target Hook]
    *name)

This target hook is a function to output to the stdio stream *stream* some commands that will make the label *name* global; that is, available for reference from other files.

The default implementation relies on a proper definition of `GLOBAL_ASM_OP`.

void **TARGET_ASM_GLOBALIZE_DECL_NAME** (*FILE *stream*, tree   [Target Hook]
    decl)

This target hook is a function to output to the stdio stream *stream* some commands that will make the name associated with *decl* global; that is, available for reference from other files.

The default implementation uses the TARGET_ASM_GLOBALIZE_LABEL target hook.

void **TARGET_ASM_ASSEMBLE_UNDEFINED_DECL** (*FILE *stream*,   [Target Hook]
    const char **name*, const_tree *decl*)

This target hook is a function to output to the stdio stream *stream* some commands that will declare the name associated with *decl* which is not defined in the current translation unit. Most assemblers do not require anything to be output in this case.

ASM_WEAKEN_LABEL (*stream*, *name*)   [Macro]

A C statement (sans semicolon) to output to the stdio stream *stream* some commands that will make the label *name* weak; that is, available for reference from other files but only used if no other definition is available. Use the expression `assemble_name (stream, name)` to output the name itself; before and after that, output the additional assembler syntax for making that name weak, and a newline.

If you don't define this macro or `ASM_WEAKEN_DECL`, GCC will not support weak symbols and you should not define the `SUPPORTS_WEAK` macro.

ASM_WEAKEN_DECL (*stream*, *decl*, *name*, *value*)   [Macro]

Combines (and replaces) the function of `ASM_WEAKEN_LABEL` and `ASM_OUTPUT_WEAK_ALIAS`, allowing access to the associated function or variable decl. If *value* is not NULL, this C statement should output to the stdio stream *stream* assembler code which defines (equates) the weak symbol *name* to have the value *value*. If *value* is NULL, it should output commands to make *name* weak.

ASM_OUTPUT_WEAKREF (*stream*, *decl*, *name*, *value*)   [Macro]

Outputs a directive that enables *name* to be used to refer to symbol *value* with weak-symbol semantics. `decl` is the declaration of `name`.

SUPPORTS_WEAK   [Macro]

A preprocessor constant expression which evaluates to true if the target supports weak symbols.

If you don't define this macro, 'defaults.h' provides a default definition. If either ASM_WEAKEN_LABEL or ASM_WEAKEN_DECL is defined, the default definition is '1'; otherwise, it is '0'.

TARGET_SUPPORTS_WEAK [Macro]

A C expression which evaluates to true if the target supports weak symbols.

If you don't define this macro, 'defaults.h' provides a default definition. The default definition is '(SUPPORTS_WEAK)'. Define this macro if you want to control weak symbol support with a compiler flag such as '-melf'.

MAKE_DECL_ONE_ONLY (decl) [Macro]

A C statement (sans semicolon) to mark *decl* to be emitted as a public symbol such that extra copies in multiple translation units will be discarded by the linker. Define this macro if your object file format provides support for this concept, such as the 'COMDAT' section flags in the Microsoft Windows PE/COFF format, and this support requires changes to *decl*, such as putting it in a separate section.

SUPPORTS_ONE_ONLY [Macro]

A C expression which evaluates to true if the target supports one-only semantics.

If you don't define this macro, 'varasm.c' provides a default definition. If MAKE_DECL_ONE_ONLY is defined, the default definition is '1'; otherwise, it is '0'. Define this macro if you want to control one-only symbol support with a compiler flag, or if setting the DECL_ONE_ONLY flag is enough to mark a declaration to be emitted as one-only.

void TARGET_ASM_ASSEMBLE_VISIBILITY (tree decl, int visibility) [Target Hook]

This target hook is a function to output to *asm_out_file* some commands that will make the symbol(s) associated with *decl* have hidden, protected or internal visibility as specified by *visibility*.

TARGET_WEAK_NOT_IN_ARCHIVE_TOC [Macro]

A C expression that evaluates to true if the target's linker expects that weak symbols do not appear in a static archive's table of contents. The default is 0.

Leaving weak symbols out of an archive's table of contents means that, if a symbol will only have a definition in one translation unit and will have undefined references from other translation units, that symbol should not be weak. Defining this macro to be nonzero will thus have the effect that certain symbols that would normally be weak (explicit template instantiations, and vtables for polymorphic classes with noninline key methods) will instead be nonweak.

The C++ ABI requires this macro to be zero. Define this macro for targets where full C++ ABI compliance is impossible and where linker restrictions require weak symbols to be left out of a static archive's table of contents.

ASM_OUTPUT_EXTERNAL (stream, decl, name) [Macro]

A C statement (sans semicolon) to output to the stdio stream *stream* any text necessary for declaring the name of an external symbol named *name* which is referenced in this compilation but not defined. The value of *decl* is the tree node for the declaration.

This macro need not be defined if it does not need to output anything. The GNU assembler and most Unix assemblers don't require anything.

void TARGET_ASM_EXTERNAL_LIBCALL (*rtx* `symref`)   [Target Hook]
> This target hook is a function to output to *asm_out_file* an assembler pseudo-op to declare a library function name external. The name of the library function is given by *symref*, which is a `symbol_ref`.

void TARGET_ASM_MARK_DECL_PRESERVED (*const char* `*symbol`)   [Target Hook]
> This target hook is a function to output to *asm_out_file* an assembler directive to annotate *symbol* as used. The Darwin target uses the .no_dead_code_strip directive.

ASM_OUTPUT_LABELREF (`stream, name`)   [Macro]
> A C statement (sans semicolon) to output to the stdio stream *stream* a reference in assembler syntax to a label named *name*. This should add '_' to the front of the name, if that is customary on your operating system, as it is in most Berkeley Unix systems. This macro is used in `assemble_name`.

tree TARGET_MANGLE_ASSEMBLER_NAME (*const char* `*name`)   [Target Hook]
> Given a symbol *name*, perform same mangling as `varasm.c`'s `assemble_name`, but in memory rather than to a file stream, returning result as an `IDENTIFIER_NODE`. Required for correct LTO symtabs. The default implementation calls the `TARGET_STRIP_NAME_ENCODING` hook and then prepends the `USER_LABEL_PREFIX`, if any.

ASM_OUTPUT_SYMBOL_REF (`stream, sym`)   [Macro]
> A C statement (sans semicolon) to output a reference to `SYMBOL_REF` *sym*. If not defined, `assemble_name` will be used to output the name of the symbol. This macro may be used to modify the way a symbol is referenced depending on information encoded by `TARGET_ENCODE_SECTION_INFO`.

ASM_OUTPUT_LABEL_REF (`stream, buf`)   [Macro]
> A C statement (sans semicolon) to output a reference to *buf*, the result of `ASM_GENERATE_INTERNAL_LABEL`. If not defined, `assemble_name` will be used to output the name of the symbol. This macro is not used by `output_asm_label`, or the `%l` specifier that calls it; the intention is that this macro should be set when it is necessary to output a label differently when its address is being taken.

void TARGET_ASM_INTERNAL_LABEL (*FILE* `*stream`, *const char*   [Target Hook]
           `*prefix`, *unsigned long* `labelno`)
> A function to output to the stdio stream *stream* a label whose name is made from the string *prefix* and the number *labelno*.
>
> It is absolutely essential that these labels be distinct from the labels used for user-level functions and variables. Otherwise, certain programs will have name conflicts with internal labels.
>
> It is desirable to exclude internal labels from the symbol table of the object file. Most assemblers have a naming convention for labels that should be excluded; on many systems, the letter 'L' at the beginning of a label has this effect. You should find out what convention your system uses, and follow it.
>
> The default version of this function utilizes `ASM_GENERATE_INTERNAL_LABEL`.

ASM_OUTPUT_DEBUG_LABEL (*stream*, *prefix*, *num*)   [Macro]

A C statement to output to the stdio stream *stream* a debug info label whose name is made from the string *prefix* and the number *num*. This is useful for VLIW targets, where debug info labels may need to be treated differently than branch target labels. On some systems, branch target labels must be at the beginning of instruction bundles, but debug info labels can occur in the middle of instruction bundles.

If this macro is not defined, then (*targetm.asm_out.internal_label) will be used.

ASM_GENERATE_INTERNAL_LABEL (*string*, *prefix*, *num*)   [Macro]

A C statement to store into the string *string* a label whose name is made from the string *prefix* and the number *num*.

This string, when output subsequently by assemble_name, should produce the output that (*targetm.asm_out.internal_label) would produce with the same *prefix* and *num*.

If the string begins with '*', then assemble_name will output the rest of the string unchanged. It is often convenient for ASM_GENERATE_INTERNAL_LABEL to use '*' in this way. If the string doesn't start with '*', then ASM_OUTPUT_LABELREF gets to output the string, and may change it. (Of course, ASM_OUTPUT_LABELREF is also part of your machine description, so you should know what it does on your machine.)

ASM_FORMAT_PRIVATE_NAME (*outvar*, *name*, *number*)   [Macro]

A C expression to assign to *outvar* (which is a variable of type char *) a newly allocated string made from the string *name* and the number *number*, with some suitable punctuation added. Use alloca to get space for the string.

The string will be used as an argument to ASM_OUTPUT_LABELREF to produce an assembler label for an internal static variable whose name is *name*. Therefore, the string must be such as to result in valid assembler code. The argument *number* is different each time this macro is executed; it prevents conflicts between similarly-named internal static variables in different scopes.

Ideally this string should not be a valid C identifier, to prevent any conflict with the user's own symbols. Most assemblers allow periods or percent signs in assembler symbols; putting at least one of these between the name and the number will suffice.

If this macro is not defined, a default definition will be provided which is correct for most systems.

ASM_OUTPUT_DEF (*stream*, *name*, *value*)   [Macro]

A C statement to output to the stdio stream *stream* assembler code which defines (equates) the symbol *name* to have the value *value*.

If SET_ASM_OP is defined, a default definition is provided which is correct for most systems.

ASM_OUTPUT_DEF_FROM_DECLS (*stream*, *decl_of_name*,   [Macro]
      decl_of_value)

A C statement to output to the stdio stream *stream* assembler code which defines (equates) the symbol whose tree node is *decl_of_name* to have the value of the tree node *decl_of_value*. This macro will be used in preference to 'ASM_OUTPUT_DEF' if it is defined and if the tree nodes are available.

If `SET_ASM_OP` is defined, a default definition is provided which is correct for most systems.

TARGET_DEFERRED_OUTPUT_DEFS (*decl_of_name*, *decl_of_value*)   [Macro]

> A C statement that evaluates to true if the assembler code which defines (equates) the symbol whose tree node is *decl_of_name* to have the value of the tree node *decl_of_value* should be emitted near the end of the current compilation unit. The default is to not defer output of defines. This macro affects defines output by 'ASM_OUTPUT_DEF' and 'ASM_OUTPUT_DEF_FROM_DECLS'.

ASM_OUTPUT_WEAK_ALIAS (*stream*, *name*, *value*)   [Macro]

> A C statement to output to the stdio stream *stream* assembler code which defines (equates) the weak symbol *name* to have the value *value*. If *value* is `NULL`, it defines *name* as an undefined weak symbol.

> Define this macro if the target only supports weak aliases; define `ASM_OUTPUT_DEF` instead if possible.

OBJC_GEN_METHOD_LABEL (*buf*, *is_inst*, *class_name*, *cat_name*,   [Macro]
    sel_name)

> Define this macro to override the default assembler names used for Objective-C methods.

> The default name is a unique method number followed by the name of the class (e.g. '_1_Foo'). For methods in categories, the name of the category is also included in the assembler name (e.g. '_1_Foo_Bar').

> These names are safe on most systems, but make debugging difficult since the method's selector is not present in the name. Therefore, particular systems define other ways of computing names.

> *buf* is an expression of type `char *` which gives you a buffer in which to store the name; its length is as long as *class_name*, *cat_name* and *sel_name* put together, plus 50 characters extra.

> The argument *is_inst* specifies whether the method is an instance method or a class method; *class_name* is the name of the class; *cat_name* is the name of the category (or `NULL` if the method is not in a category); and *sel_name* is the name of the selector.

> On systems where the assembler can handle quoted names, you can use this macro to provide more human-readable names.

17.20.5 How Initialization Functions Are Handled

The compiled code for certain languages includes *constructors* (also called *initialization routines*)—functions to initialize data in the program when the program is started. These functions need to be called before the program is "started"—that is to say, before `main` is called.

Compiling some languages generates *destructors* (also called *termination routines*) that should be called when the program terminates.

To make the initialization and termination functions work, the compiler must output something in the assembler code to cause those functions to be called at the appropriate time. When you port the compiler to a new system, you need to specify how to do this.

There are two major ways that GCC currently supports the execution of initialization and termination functions. Each way has two variants. Much of the structure is common to all four variations.

The linker must build two lists of these functions—a list of initialization functions, called `__CTOR_LIST__`, and a list of termination functions, called `__DTOR_LIST__`.

Each list always begins with an ignored function pointer (which may hold 0, −1, or a count of the function pointers after it, depending on the environment). This is followed by a series of zero or more function pointers to constructors (or destructors), followed by a function pointer containing zero.

Depending on the operating system and its executable file format, either 'crtstuff.c' or 'libgcc2.c' traverses these lists at startup time and exit time. Constructors are called in reverse order of the list; destructors in forward order.

The best way to handle static constructors works only for object file formats which provide arbitrarily-named sections. A section is set aside for a list of constructors, and another for a list of destructors. Traditionally these are called '.ctors' and '.dtors'. Each object file that defines an initialization function also puts a word in the constructor section to point to that function. The linker accumulates all these words into one contiguous '.ctors' section. Termination functions are handled similarly.

This method will be chosen as the default by 'target-def.h' if `TARGET_ASM_NAMED_SECTION` is defined. A target that does not support arbitrary sections, but does support special designated constructor and destructor sections may define `CTORS_SECTION_ASM_OP` and `DTORS_SECTION_ASM_OP` to achieve the same effect.

When arbitrary sections are available, there are two variants, depending upon how the code in 'crtstuff.c' is called. On systems that support a *init* section which is executed at program startup, parts of 'crtstuff.c' are compiled into that section. The program is linked by the **gcc** driver like this:

```
ld -o output_file crti.o crtbegin.o ... -lgcc crtend.o crtn.o
```

The prologue of a function (`__init`) appears in the `.init` section of 'crti.o'; the epilogue appears in 'crtn.o'. Likewise for the function `__fini` in the *fini* section. Normally these files are provided by the operating system or by the GNU C library, but are provided by GCC for a few targets.

The objects 'crtbegin.o' and 'crtend.o' are (for most targets) compiled from 'crtstuff.c'. They contain, among other things, code fragments within the `.init` and `.fini` sections that branch to routines in the `.text` section. The linker will pull all parts of a section together, which results in a complete `__init` function that invokes the routines we need at startup.

To use this variant, you must define the `INIT_SECTION_ASM_OP` macro properly.

If no init section is available, when GCC compiles any function called **main** (or more accurately, any function designated as a program entry point by the language front end calling `expand_main_function`), it inserts a procedure call to `__main` as the first executable code after the function prologue. The `__main` function is defined in 'libgcc2.c' and runs the global constructors.

In file formats that don't support arbitrary sections, there are again two variants. In the simplest variant, the GNU linker (GNU **ld**) and an 'a.out' format must be used. In this case, `TARGET_ASM_CONSTRUCTOR` is defined to produce a `.stabs` entry of type 'N_SETT', referencing the name `__CTOR_LIST__`, and with the address of the void function containing the initialization code as its value. The GNU linker recognizes this as a request to add the value to a *set*; the values are accumulated, and are eventually placed in the executable as a vector in the format described above, with a leading (ignored) count and a trailing zero element. `TARGET_ASM_DESTRUCTOR` is handled similarly. Since no init section is available, the absence of `INIT_SECTION_ASM_OP` causes the compilation of **main** to call `__main` as above, starting the initialization process.

The last variant uses neither arbitrary sections nor the GNU linker. This is preferable when you want to do dynamic linking and when using file formats which the GNU linker does not support, such as 'ECOFF'. In this case, `TARGET_HAVE_CTORS_DTORS` is false, initialization and termination functions are recognized simply by their names. This requires an extra program in the linkage step, called `collect2`. This program pretends to be the linker, for use with GCC; it does its job by running the ordinary linker, but also arranges to include the vectors of initialization and termination functions. These functions are called via `__main` as described above. In order to use this method, `use_collect2` must be defined in the target in 'config.gcc'.

17.20.6 Macros Controlling Initialization Routines

Here are the macros that control how the compiler handles initialization and termination functions:

`INIT_SECTION_ASM_OP`   [Macro]
    If defined, a C string constant, including spacing, for the assembler operation to identify the following data as initialization code. If not defined, GCC will assume such a section does not exist. When you are using special sections for initialization and termination functions, this macro also controls how 'crtstuff.c' and 'libgcc2.c' arrange to run the initialization functions.

`HAS_INIT_SECTION`   [Macro]
    If defined, **main** will not call `__main` as described above. This macro should be defined for systems that control start-up code on a symbol-by-symbol basis, such as OSF/1, and should not be defined explicitly for systems that support `INIT_SECTION_ASM_OP`.

`LD_INIT_SWITCH`   [Macro]
    If defined, a C string constant for a switch that tells the linker that the following symbol is an initialization routine.

`LD_FINI_SWITCH`   [Macro]
    If defined, a C string constant for a switch that tells the linker that the following symbol is a finalization routine.

`COLLECT_SHARED_INIT_FUNC (stream, func)`   [Macro]
    If defined, a C statement that will write a function that can be automatically called when a shared library is loaded. The function should call *func*, which takes no arguments. If not defined, and the object format requires an explicit initialization function, then a function called `_GLOBAL__DI` will be generated.

This function and the following one are used by collect2 when linking a shared library that needs constructors or destructors, or has DWARF2 exception tables embedded in the code.

COLLECT_SHARED_FINI_FUNC (*stream*, *func*) [Macro]

If defined, a C statement that will write a function that can be automatically called when a shared library is unloaded. The function should call *func*, which takes no arguments. If not defined, and the object format requires an explicit finalization function, then a function called _GLOBAL__DD will be generated.

INVOKE__main [Macro]

If defined, main will call __main despite the presence of INIT_SECTION_ASM_OP. This macro should be defined for systems where the init section is not actually run automatically, but is still useful for collecting the lists of constructors and destructors.

SUPPORTS_INIT_PRIORITY [Macro]

If nonzero, the C++ init_priority attribute is supported and the compiler should emit instructions to control the order of initialization of objects. If zero, the compiler will issue an error message upon encountering an init_priority attribute.

bool TARGET_HAVE_CTORS_DTORS [Target Hook]

This value is true if the target supports some "native" method of collecting constructors and destructors to be run at startup and exit. It is false if we must use collect2.

void TARGET_ASM_CONSTRUCTOR (*rtx symbol*, *int priority*) [Target Hook]

If defined, a function that outputs assembler code to arrange to call the function referenced by *symbol* at initialization time.

Assume that *symbol* is a SYMBOL_REF for a function taking no arguments and with no return value. If the target supports initialization priorities, *priority* is a value between 0 and MAX_INIT_PRIORITY; otherwise it must be DEFAULT_INIT_PRIORITY.

If this macro is not defined by the target, a suitable default will be chosen if (1) the target supports arbitrary section names, (2) the target defines CTORS_SECTION_ASM_OP, or (3) USE_COLLECT2 is not defined.

void TARGET_ASM_DESTRUCTOR (*rtx symbol*, *int priority*) [Target Hook]

This is like TARGET_ASM_CONSTRUCTOR but used for termination functions rather than initialization functions.

If TARGET_HAVE_CTORS_DTORS is true, the initialization routine generated for the generated object file will have static linkage.

If your system uses collect2 as the means of processing constructors, then that program normally uses nm to scan an object file for constructor functions to be called.

On certain kinds of systems, you can define this macro to make collect2 work faster (and, in some cases, make it work at all):

OBJECT_FORMAT_COFF [Macro]

Define this macro if the system uses COFF (Common Object File Format) object files, so that collect2 can assume this format and scan object files directly for dynamic constructor/destructor functions.

This macro is effective only in a native compiler; `collect2` as part of a cross compiler always uses `nm` for the target machine.

REAL_NM_FILE_NAME   [Macro]

Define this macro as a C string constant containing the file name to use to execute `nm`. The default is to search the path normally for `nm`.

NM_FLAGS   [Macro]

`collect2` calls `nm` to scan object files for static constructors and destructors and LTO info. By default, '-n' is passed. Define `NM_FLAGS` to a C string constant if other options are needed to get the same output format as GNU `nm -n` produces.

If your system supports shared libraries and has a program to list the dynamic dependencies of a given library or executable, you can define these macros to enable support for running initialization and termination functions in shared libraries:

LDD_SUFFIX   [Macro]

Define this macro to a C string constant containing the name of the program which lists dynamic dependencies, like `ldd` under SunOS 4.

PARSE_LDD_OUTPUT (*ptr*)   [Macro]

Define this macro to be C code that extracts filenames from the output of the program denoted by `LDD_SUFFIX`. *ptr* is a variable of type `char *` that points to the beginning of a line of output from `LDD_SUFFIX`. If the line lists a dynamic dependency, the code must advance *ptr* to the beginning of the filename on that line. Otherwise, it must set *ptr* to `NULL`.

SHLIB_SUFFIX   [Macro]

Define this macro to a C string constant containing the default shared library extension of the target (e.g., '".so"'). `collect2` strips version information after this suffix when generating global constructor and destructor names. This define is only needed on targets that use `collect2` to process constructors and destructors.

17.20.7 Output of Assembler Instructions

This describes assembler instruction output.

REGISTER_NAMES   [Macro]

A C initializer containing the assembler's names for the machine registers, each one as a C string constant. This is what translates register numbers in the compiler into assembler language.

ADDITIONAL_REGISTER_NAMES   [Macro]

If defined, a C initializer for an array of structures containing a name and a register number. This macro defines additional names for hard registers, thus allowing the `asm` option in declarations to refer to registers using alternate names.

OVERLAPPING_REGISTER_NAMES   [Macro]

If defined, a C initializer for an array of structures containing a name, a register number and a count of the number of consecutive machine registers the name overlaps. This macro defines additional names for hard registers, thus allowing the `asm` option in declarations to refer to registers using alternate names. Unlike `ADDITIONAL_REGISTER_NAMES`, this macro should be used when the register name implies multiple underlying registers.

This macro should be used when it is important that a clobber in an `asm` statement clobbers all the underlying values implied by the register name. For example, on ARM, clobbering the double-precision VFP register "d0" implies clobbering both single-precision registers "s0" and "s1".

ASM_OUTPUT_OPCODE (*stream*, *ptr*) [Macro]

Define this macro if you are using an unusual assembler that requires different names for the machine instructions.

The definition is a C statement or statements which output an assembler instruction opcode to the stdio stream *stream*. The macro-operand *ptr* is a variable of type `char *` which points to the opcode name in its "internal" form—the form that is written in the machine description. The definition should output the opcode name to *stream*, performing any translation you desire, and increment the variable *ptr* to point at the end of the opcode so that it will not be output twice.

In fact, your macro definition may process less than the entire opcode name, or more than the opcode name; but if you want to process text that includes '%'-sequences to substitute operands, you must take care of the substitution yourself. Just be sure to increment *ptr* over whatever text should not be output normally.

If you need to look at the operand values, they can be found as the elements of `recog_data.operand`.

If the macro definition does nothing, the instruction is output in the usual way.

FINAL_PRESCAN_INSN (*insn*, *opvec*, *noperands*) [Macro]

If defined, a C statement to be executed just prior to the output of assembler code for *insn*, to modify the extracted operands so they will be output differently.

Here the argument *opvec* is the vector containing the operands extracted from *insn*, and *noperands* is the number of elements of the vector which contain meaningful data for this insn. The contents of this vector are what will be used to convert the insn template into assembler code, so you can change the assembler output by changing the contents of the vector.

This macro is useful when various assembler syntaxes share a single file of instruction patterns; by defining this macro differently, you can cause a large class of instructions to be output differently (such as with rearranged operands). Naturally, variations in assembler syntax affecting individual insn patterns ought to be handled by writing conditional output routines in those patterns.

If this macro is not defined, it is equivalent to a null statement.

void TARGET_ASM_FINAL_POSTSCAN_INSN (*FILE *file*, *rtx_insn* [Target Hook]
    *insn, *rtx *opvec*, *int noperands*)

If defined, this target hook is a function which is executed just after the output of assembler code for *insn*, to change the mode of the assembler if necessary.

Here the argument *opvec* is the vector containing the operands extracted from *insn*, and *noperands* is the number of elements of the vector which contain meaningful data for this insn. The contents of this vector are what was used to convert the insn template into assembler code, so you can change the assembler mode by checking the contents of the vector.

PRINT_OPERAND (*stream*, *x*, *code*)   [Macro]

> A C compound statement to output to stdio stream *stream* the assembler syntax for an instruction operand *x*. *x* is an RTL expression.
>
> *code* is a value that can be used to specify one of several ways of printing the operand. It is used when identical operands must be printed differently depending on the context. *code* comes from the '%' specification that was used to request printing of the operand. If the specification was just '%*digit*' then *code* is 0; if the specification was '%*ltr digit*' then *code* is the ASCII code for *ltr*.
>
> If *x* is a register, this macro should print the register's name. The names can be found in an array `reg_names` whose type is `char *[]`. `reg_names` is initialized from `REGISTER_NAMES`.
>
> When the machine description has a specification '%*punct*' (a '%' followed by a punctuation character), this macro is called with a null pointer for *x* and the punctuation character for *code*.

PRINT_OPERAND_PUNCT_VALID_P (*code*)   [Macro]

> A C expression which evaluates to true if *code* is a valid punctuation character for use in the `PRINT_OPERAND` macro. If `PRINT_OPERAND_PUNCT_VALID_P` is not defined, it means that no punctuation characters (except for the standard one, '%') are used in this way.

PRINT_OPERAND_ADDRESS (*stream*, *x*)   [Macro]

> A C compound statement to output to stdio stream *stream* the assembler syntax for an instruction operand that is a memory reference whose address is *x*. *x* is an RTL expression.
>
> On some machines, the syntax for a symbolic address depends on the section that the address refers to. On these machines, define the hook `TARGET_ENCODE_SECTION_INFO` to store the information into the `symbol_ref`, and then check for it here. See Section 17.20 [Assembler Format], page 545.

DBR_OUTPUT_SEQEND (*file*)   [Macro]

> A C statement, to be executed after all slot-filler instructions have been output. If necessary, call `dbr_sequence_length` to determine the number of slots filled in a sequence (zero if not currently outputting a sequence), to decide how many no-ops to output, or whatever.
>
> Don't define this macro if it has nothing to do, but it is helpful in reading assembly output if the extent of the delay sequence is made explicit (e.g. with white space).

Note that output routines for instructions with delay slots must be prepared to deal with not being output as part of a sequence (i.e. when the scheduling pass is not run, or when no slot fillers could be found.) The variable `final_sequence` is null when not processing a sequence, otherwise it contains the `sequence` rtx being output.

REGISTER_PREFIX   [Macro]
LOCAL_LABEL_PREFIX   [Macro]
USER_LABEL_PREFIX   [Macro]
IMMEDIATE_PREFIX   [Macro]

> If defined, C string expressions to be used for the '%R', '%L', '%U', and '%I' options of
> `asm_fprintf` (see 'final.c'). These are useful when a single 'md' file must support
> multiple assembler formats. In that case, the various 'tm.h' files can define these
> macros differently.

ASM_FPRINTF_EXTENSIONS (*file*, *argptr*, *format*)   [Macro]

> If defined this macro should expand to a series of `case` statements which will be
> parsed inside the `switch` statement of the `asm_fprintf` function. This allows targets
> to define extra printf formats which may useful when generating their assembler
> statements. Note that uppercase letters are reserved for future generic extensions
> to asm_fprintf, and so are not available to target specific code. The output file is
> given by the parameter *file*. The varargs input pointer is *argptr* and the rest of the
> format string, starting the character after the one that is being switched upon, is
> pointed to by *format*.

ASSEMBLER_DIALECT   [Macro]

> If your target supports multiple dialects of assembler language (such as different
> opcodes), define this macro as a C expression that gives the numeric index of the
> assembler language dialect to use, with zero as the first variant.

> If this macro is defined, you may use constructs of the form

>> '{option0|option1|option2...}'

> in the output templates of patterns (see Section 16.5 [Output Template], page 309) or
> in the first argument of `asm_fprintf`. This construct outputs 'option0', 'option1',
> 'option2', etc., if the value of ASSEMBLER_DIALECT is zero, one, two, etc. Any spe-
> cial characters within these strings retain their usual meaning. If there are fewer
> alternatives within the braces than the value of ASSEMBLER_DIALECT, the construct
> outputs nothing. If it's needed to print curly braces or '|' character in assembler
> output directly, '%{', '%}' and '%|' can be used.

> If you do not define this macro, the characters '{', '|' and '}' do not have any special
> meaning when used in templates or operands to `asm_fprintf`.

> Define the macros REGISTER_PREFIX, LOCAL_LABEL_PREFIX, USER_LABEL_PREFIX
> and IMMEDIATE_PREFIX if you can express the variations in assembler language syntax
> with that mechanism. Define ASSEMBLER_DIALECT and use the '{option0|option1}'
> syntax if the syntax variant are larger and involve such things as different opcodes
> or operand order.

ASM_OUTPUT_REG_PUSH (*stream*, *regno*)   [Macro]

> A C expression to output to *stream* some assembler code which will push hard register
> number *regno* onto the stack. The code need not be optimal, since this macro is used
> only when profiling.

ASM_OUTPUT_REG_POP (*stream*, *regno*)   [Macro]

    A C expression to output to *stream* some assembler code which will pop hard register number *regno* off of the stack. The code need not be optimal, since this macro is used only when profiling.

17.20.8 Output of Dispatch Tables

This concerns dispatch tables.

ASM_OUTPUT_ADDR_DIFF_ELT (*stream*, *body*, *value*, *rel*)   [Macro]

    A C statement to output to the stdio stream *stream* an assembler pseudo-instruction to generate a difference between two labels. *value* and *rel* are the numbers of two internal labels. The definitions of these labels are output using (*targetm.asm_out.internal_label), and they must be printed in the same way here. For example,

```
fprintf (stream, "\t.word L%d-L%d\n",
         value, rel)
```

    You must provide this macro on machines where the addresses in a dispatch table are relative to the table's own address. If defined, GCC will also use this macro on all machines when producing PIC. *body* is the body of the ADDR_DIFF_VEC; it is provided so that the mode and flags can be read.

ASM_OUTPUT_ADDR_VEC_ELT (*stream*, *value*)   [Macro]

    This macro should be provided on machines where the addresses in a dispatch table are absolute.

    The definition should be a C statement to output to the stdio stream *stream* an assembler pseudo-instruction to generate a reference to a label. *value* is the number of an internal label whose definition is output using (*targetm.asm_out.internal_label). For example,

```
fprintf (stream, "\t.word L%d\n", value)
```

ASM_OUTPUT_CASE_LABEL (*stream*, *prefix*, *num*, *table*)   [Macro]

    Define this if the label before a jump-table needs to be output specially. The first three arguments are the same as for (*targetm.asm_out.internal_label); the fourth argument is the jump-table which follows (a jump_table_data containing an addr_vec or addr_diff_vec).

    This feature is used on system V to output a swbeg statement for the table.

    If this macro is not defined, these labels are output with (*targetm.asm_out.internal_label).

ASM_OUTPUT_CASE_END (*stream*, *num*, *table*)   [Macro]

    Define this if something special must be output at the end of a jump-table. The definition should be a C statement to be executed after the assembler code for the table is written. It should write the appropriate code to stdio stream *stream*. The argument *table* is the jump-table insn, and *num* is the label-number of the preceding label.

    If this macro is not defined, nothing special is output at the end of the jump-table.

void TARGET_ASM_EMIT_UNWIND_LABEL (*FILE* *`stream`, *tree* `decl`,   [Target Hook]
      int `for_eh`, *int* `empty`)
> This target hook emits a label at the beginning of each FDE. It should be defined on targets where FDEs need special labels, and it should write the appropriate label, for the FDE associated with the function declaration *decl*, to the stdio stream *stream*. The third argument, *for_eh*, is a boolean: true if this is for an exception table. The fourth argument, *empty*, is a boolean: true if this is a placeholder label for an omitted FDE.
>
> The default is that FDEs are not given nonlocal labels.

void TARGET_ASM_EMIT_EXCEPT_TABLE_LABEL (*FILE* *`stream`)   [Target Hook]
> This target hook emits a label at the beginning of the exception table. It should be defined on targets where it is desirable for the table to be broken up according to function.
>
> The default is that no label is emitted.

void TARGET_ASM_EMIT_EXCEPT_PERSONALITY (*rtx* `personality`)   [Target Hook]
> If the target implements `TARGET_ASM_UNWIND_EMIT`, this hook may be used to emit a directive to install a personality hook into the unwind info. This hook should not be used if dwarf2 unwind info is used.

void TARGET_ASM_UNWIND_EMIT (*FILE* *`stream`, *rtx_insn* *`insn`)   [Target Hook]
> This target hook emits assembly directives required to unwind the given instruction. This is only used when `TARGET_EXCEPT_UNWIND_INFO` returns `UI_TARGET`.

bool TARGET_ASM_UNWIND_EMIT_BEFORE_INSN   [Target Hook]
> True if the `TARGET_ASM_UNWIND_EMIT` hook should be called before the assembly for *insn* has been emitted, false if the hook should be called afterward.

17.20.9 Assembler Commands for Exception Regions

This describes commands marking the start and the end of an exception region.

EH_FRAME_SECTION_NAME   [Macro]
> If defined, a C string constant for the name of the section containing exception handling frame unwind information. If not defined, GCC will provide a default definition if the target supports named sections. 'crtstuff.c' uses this macro to switch to the appropriate section.
>
> You should define this symbol if your target supports DWARF 2 frame unwind information and the default definition does not work.

EH_FRAME_THROUGH_COLLECT2   [Macro]
> If defined, DWARF 2 frame unwind information will identified by specially named labels. The collect2 process will locate these labels and generate code to register the frames.
>
> This might be necessary, for instance, if the system linker will not place the eh_frames in-between the sentinals from 'crtstuff.c', or if the system linker does garbage collection and sections cannot be marked as not to be collected.

EH_TABLES_CAN_BE_READ_ONLY   [Macro]

Define this macro to 1 if your target is such that no frame unwind information encoding used with non-PIC code will ever require a runtime relocation, but the linker may not support merging read-only and read-write sections into a single read-write section.

MASK_RETURN_ADDR   [Macro]

An rtx used to mask the return address found via **RETURN_ADDR_RTX**, so that it does not contain any extraneous set bits in it.

DWARF2_UNWIND_INFO   [Macro]

Define this macro to 0 if your target supports DWARF 2 frame unwind information, but it does not yet work with exception handling. Otherwise, if your target supports this information (if it defines **INCOMING_RETURN_ADDR_RTX** and **OBJECT_FORMAT_ELF**), GCC will provide a default definition of 1.

enum unwind_info_type TARGET_EXCEPT_UNWIND_INFO   [Common Target Hook]
      (*struct gcc_options *opts*)

This hook defines the mechanism that will be used for exception handling by the target. If the target has ABI specified unwind tables, the hook should return **UI_TARGET**. If the target is to use the **setjmp/longjmp**-based exception handling scheme, the hook should return **UI_SJLJ**. If the target supports DWARF 2 frame unwind information, the hook should return **UI_DWARF2**.

A target may, if exceptions are disabled, choose to return **UI_NONE**. This may end up simplifying other parts of target-specific code. The default implementation of this hook never returns **UI_NONE**.

Note that the value returned by this hook should be constant. It should not depend on anything except the command-line switches described by *opts*. In particular, the setting **UI_SJLJ** must be fixed at compiler start-up as C pre-processor macros and builtin functions related to exception handling are set up depending on this setting.

The default implementation of the hook first honors the '--enable-sjlj-exceptions' configure option, then **DWARF2_UNWIND_INFO**, and finally defaults to **UI_SJLJ**. If **DWARF2_UNWIND_INFO** depends on command-line options, the target must define this hook so that *opts* is used correctly.

bool TARGET_UNWIND_TABLES_DEFAULT   [Common Target Hook]

This variable should be set to **true** if the target ABI requires unwinding tables even when exceptions are not used. It must not be modified by command-line option processing.

DONT_USE_BUILTIN_SETJMP   [Macro]

Define this macro to 1 if the **setjmp/longjmp**-based scheme should use the **setjmp/longjmp** functions from the C library instead of the **__builtin_setjmp/__builtin_longjmp** machinery.

JMP_BUF_SIZE   [Macro]

This macro has no effect unless **DONT_USE_BUILTIN_SETJMP** is also defined. Define this macro if the default size of **jmp_buf** buffer for the **setjmp/longjmp**-based exception handling mechanism is not large enough, or if it is much too large. The default size is `FIRST_PSEUDO_REGISTER * sizeof(void *)`.

`DWARF_CIE_DATA_ALIGNMENT`   [Macro]
> This macro need only be defined if the target might save registers in the function prologue at an offset to the stack pointer that is not aligned to `UNITS_PER_WORD`. The definition should be the negative minimum alignment if `STACK_GROWS_DOWNWARD` is true, and the positive minimum alignment otherwise. See Section 17.21.5 [SDB and DWARF], page 577. Only applicable if the target supports DWARF 2 frame unwind information.

`bool TARGET_TERMINATE_DW2_EH_FRAME_INFO`   [Target Hook]
> Contains the value true if the target should add a zero word onto the end of a Dwarf-2 frame info section when used for exception handling. Default value is false if `EH_FRAME_SECTION_NAME` is defined, and true otherwise.

`rtx TARGET_DWARF_REGISTER_SPAN (rtx reg)`   [Target Hook]
> Given a register, this hook should return a parallel of registers to represent where to find the register pieces. Define this hook if the register and its mode are represented in Dwarf in non-contiguous locations, or if the register should be represented in more than one register in Dwarf. Otherwise, this hook should return `NULL_RTX`. If not defined, the default is to return `NULL_RTX`.

`machine_mode TARGET_DWARF_FRAME_REG_MODE (int regno)`   [Target Hook]
> Given a register, this hook should return the mode which the corresponding Dwarf frame register should have. This is normally used to return a smaller mode than the raw mode to prevent call clobbered parts of a register altering the frame register size

`void TARGET_INIT_DWARF_REG_SIZES_EXTRA (tree address)`   [Target Hook]
> If some registers are represented in Dwarf-2 unwind information in multiple pieces, define this hook to fill in information about the sizes of those pieces in the table used by the unwinder at runtime. It will be called by `expand_builtin_init_dwarf_reg_sizes` after filling in a single size corresponding to each hard register; *address* is the address of the table.

`bool TARGET_ASM_TTYPE (rtx sym)`   [Target Hook]
> This hook is used to output a reference from a frame unwinding table to the type_info object identified by *sym*. It should return `true` if the reference was output. Returning `false` will cause the reference to be output using the normal Dwarf2 routines.

`bool TARGET_ARM_EABI_UNWINDER`   [Target Hook]
> This flag should be set to `true` on targets that use an ARM EABI based unwinding library, and `false` on other targets. This effects the format of unwinding tables, and how the unwinder in entered after running a cleanup. The default is `false`.

17.20.10 Assembler Commands for Alignment

This describes commands for alignment.

JUMP_ALIGN (*label*)   [Macro]

>   The alignment (log base 2) to put in front of *label*, which is a common destination of
>   jumps and has no fallthru incoming edge.
>
>   This macro need not be defined if you don't want any special alignment to be done
>   at such a time. Most machine descriptions do not currently define the macro.
>
>   Unless it's necessary to inspect the *label* parameter, it is better to set the variable
>   *align_jumps* in the target's TARGET_OPTION_OVERRIDE. Otherwise, you should try to
>   honor the user's selection in *align_jumps* in a JUMP_ALIGN implementation.

int TARGET_ASM_JUMP_ALIGN_MAX_SKIP (*rtx_insn *label*)   [Target Hook]

>   The maximum number of bytes to skip before *label* when applying JUMP_ALIGN. This
>   works only if ASM_OUTPUT_MAX_SKIP_ALIGN is defined.

LABEL_ALIGN_AFTER_BARRIER (*label*)   [Macro]

>   The alignment (log base 2) to put in front of *label*, which follows a BARRIER.
>
>   This macro need not be defined if you don't want any special alignment to be done
>   at such a time. Most machine descriptions do not currently define the macro.

int TARGET_ASM_LABEL_ALIGN_AFTER_BARRIER_MAX_SKIP   [Target Hook]
>   (*rtx_insn *label*)
>
>   The maximum number of bytes to skip before *label* when applying LABEL_ALIGN_
>   AFTER_BARRIER. This works only if ASM_OUTPUT_MAX_SKIP_ALIGN is defined.

LOOP_ALIGN (*label*)   [Macro]

>   The alignment (log base 2) to put in front of *label* that heads a frequently executed
>   basic block (usually the header of a loop).
>
>   This macro need not be defined if you don't want any special alignment to be done
>   at such a time. Most machine descriptions do not currently define the macro.
>
>   Unless it's necessary to inspect the *label* parameter, it is better to set the variable
>   align_loops in the target's TARGET_OPTION_OVERRIDE. Otherwise, you should try
>   to honor the user's selection in align_loops in a LOOP_ALIGN implementation.

int TARGET_ASM_LOOP_ALIGN_MAX_SKIP (*rtx_insn *label*)   [Target Hook]

>   The maximum number of bytes to skip when applying LOOP_ALIGN to *label*. This
>   works only if ASM_OUTPUT_MAX_SKIP_ALIGN is defined.

LABEL_ALIGN (*label*)   [Macro]

>   The alignment (log base 2) to put in front of *label*. If LABEL_ALIGN_AFTER_BARRIER
>   / LOOP_ALIGN specify a different alignment, the maximum of the specified values is
>   used.
>
>   Unless it's necessary to inspect the *label* parameter, it is better to set the variable
>   align_labels in the target's TARGET_OPTION_OVERRIDE. Otherwise, you should try
>   to honor the user's selection in align_labels in a LABEL_ALIGN implementation.

int TARGET_ASM_LABEL_ALIGN_MAX_SKIP (*rtx_insn *label*)   [Target Hook]

>   The maximum number of bytes to skip when applying LABEL_ALIGN to *label*. This
>   works only if ASM_OUTPUT_MAX_SKIP_ALIGN is defined.

ASM_OUTPUT_SKIP (*stream*, *nbytes*)   [Macro]

>A C statement to output to the stdio stream *stream* an assembler instruction to advance the location counter by *nbytes* bytes. Those bytes should be zero when loaded. *nbytes* will be a C expression of type **unsigned HOST_WIDE_INT**.

ASM_NO_SKIP_IN_TEXT   [Macro]

>Define this macro if **ASM_OUTPUT_SKIP** should not be used in the text section because it fails to put zeros in the bytes that are skipped. This is true on many Unix systems, where the pseudo–op to skip bytes produces no-op instructions rather than zeros when used in the text section.

ASM_OUTPUT_ALIGN (*stream*, *power*)   [Macro]

>A C statement to output to the stdio stream *stream* an assembler command to advance the location counter to a multiple of 2 to the *power* bytes. *power* will be a C expression of type **int**.

ASM_OUTPUT_ALIGN_WITH_NOP (*stream*, *power*)   [Macro]

>Like **ASM_OUTPUT_ALIGN**, except that the "nop" instruction is used for padding, if necessary.

ASM_OUTPUT_MAX_SKIP_ALIGN (*stream*, *power*, *max_skip*)   [Macro]

>A C statement to output to the stdio stream *stream* an assembler command to advance the location counter to a multiple of 2 to the *power* bytes, but only if *max_skip* or fewer bytes are needed to satisfy the alignment request. *power* and *max_skip* will be a C expression of type **int**.

17.21 Controlling Debugging Information Format

This describes how to specify debugging information.

17.21.1 Macros Affecting All Debugging Formats

These macros affect all debugging formats.

DBX_REGISTER_NUMBER (*regno*)   [Macro]

>A C expression that returns the DBX register number for the compiler register number *regno*. In the default macro provided, the value of this expression will be *regno* itself. But sometimes there are some registers that the compiler knows about and DBX does not, or vice versa. In such cases, some register may need to have one number in the compiler and another for DBX.

>If two registers have consecutive numbers inside GCC, and they can be used as a pair to hold a multiword value, then they *must* have consecutive numbers after renumbering with **DBX_REGISTER_NUMBER**. Otherwise, debuggers will be unable to access such a pair, because they expect register pairs to be consecutive in their own numbering scheme.

>If you find yourself defining **DBX_REGISTER_NUMBER** in way that does not preserve register pairs, then what you must do instead is redefine the actual register numbering scheme.

DEBUGGER_AUTO_OFFSET (*x*)   [Macro]
> A C expression that returns the integer offset value for an automatic variable having address *x* (an RTL expression). The default computation assumes that *x* is based on the frame-pointer and gives the offset from the frame-pointer. This is required for targets that produce debugging output for DBX or COFF-style debugging output for SDB and allow the frame-pointer to be eliminated when the '-g' options is used.

DEBUGGER_ARG_OFFSET (*offset*, *x*)   [Macro]
> A C expression that returns the integer offset value for an argument having address *x* (an RTL expression). The nominal offset is *offset*.

PREFERRED_DEBUGGING_TYPE   [Macro]
> A C expression that returns the type of debugging output GCC should produce when the user specifies just '-g'. Define this if you have arranged for GCC to support more than one format of debugging output. Currently, the allowable values are DBX_DEBUG, SDB_DEBUG, DWARF_DEBUG, DWARF2_DEBUG, XCOFF_DEBUG, VMS_DEBUG, and VMS_AND_DWARF2_DEBUG.
>
> When the user specifies '-ggdb', GCC normally also uses the value of this macro to select the debugging output format, but with two exceptions. If DWARF2_DEBUGGING_INFO is defined, GCC uses the value DWARF2_DEBUG. Otherwise, if DBX_DEBUGGING_INFO is defined, GCC uses DBX_DEBUG.
>
> The value of this macro only affects the default debugging output; the user can always get a specific type of output by using '-gstabs', '-gcoff', '-gdwarf-2', '-gxcoff', or '-gvms'.

17.21.2 Specific Options for DBX Output

These are specific options for DBX output.

DBX_DEBUGGING_INFO   [Macro]
> Define this macro if GCC should produce debugging output for DBX in response to the '-g' option.

XCOFF_DEBUGGING_INFO   [Macro]
> Define this macro if GCC should produce XCOFF format debugging output in response to the '-g' option. This is a variant of DBX format.

DEFAULT_GDB_EXTENSIONS   [Macro]
> Define this macro to control whether GCC should by default generate GDB's extended version of DBX debugging information (assuming DBX-format debugging information is enabled at all). If you don't define the macro, the default is 1: always generate the extended information if there is any occasion to.

DEBUG_SYMS_TEXT   [Macro]
> Define this macro if all .stabs commands should be output while in the text section.

ASM_STABS_OP   [Macro]
> A C string constant, including spacing, naming the assembler pseudo op to use instead of "\t.stabs\t" to define an ordinary debugging symbol. If you don't define this macro, "\t.stabs\t" is used. This macro applies only to DBX debugging information format.

ASM_STABD_OP   [Macro]

A C string constant, including spacing, naming the assembler pseudo op to use instead of `"\t.stabd\t"` to define a debugging symbol whose value is the current location. If you don't define this macro, `"\t.stabd\t"` is used. This macro applies only to DBX debugging information format.

ASM_STABN_OP   [Macro]

A C string constant, including spacing, naming the assembler pseudo op to use instead of `"\t.stabn\t"` to define a debugging symbol with no name. If you don't define this macro, `"\t.stabn\t"` is used. This macro applies only to DBX debugging information format.

DBX_NO_XREFS   [Macro]

Define this macro if DBX on your system does not support the construct 'xs*tagname*'. On some systems, this construct is used to describe a forward reference to a structure named *tagname*. On other systems, this construct is not supported at all.

DBX_CONTIN_LENGTH   [Macro]

A symbol name in DBX-format debugging information is normally continued (split into two separate `.stabs` directives) when it exceeds a certain length (by default, 80 characters). On some operating systems, DBX requires this splitting; on others, splitting must not be done. You can inhibit splitting by defining this macro with the value zero. You can override the default splitting-length by defining this macro as an expression for the length you desire.

DBX_CONTIN_CHAR   [Macro]

Normally continuation is indicated by adding a '\' character to the end of a `.stabs` string when a continuation follows. To use a different character instead, define this macro as a character constant for the character you want to use. Do not define this macro if backslash is correct for your system.

DBX_STATIC_STAB_DATA_SECTION   [Macro]

Define this macro if it is necessary to go to the data section before outputting the '`.stabs`' pseudo-op for a non-global static variable.

DBX_TYPE_DECL_STABS_CODE   [Macro]

The value to use in the "code" field of the `.stabs` directive for a typedef. The default is N_LSYM.

DBX_STATIC_CONST_VAR_CODE   [Macro]

The value to use in the "code" field of the `.stabs` directive for a static variable located in the text section. DBX format does not provide any "right" way to do this. The default is N_FUN.

DBX_REGPARM_STABS_CODE   [Macro]

The value to use in the "code" field of the `.stabs` directive for a parameter passed in registers. DBX format does not provide any "right" way to do this. The default is N_RSYM.

DBX_REGPARM_STABS_LETTER   [Macro]
> The letter to use in DBX symbol data to identify a symbol as a parameter passed in registers. DBX format does not customarily provide any way to do this. The default is 'P'.

DBX_FUNCTION_FIRST   [Macro]
> Define this macro if the DBX information for a function and its arguments should precede the assembler code for the function. Normally, in DBX format, the debugging information entirely follows the assembler code.

DBX_BLOCKS_FUNCTION_RELATIVE   [Macro]
> Define this macro, with value 1, if the value of a symbol describing the scope of a block (N_LBRAC or N_RBRAC) should be relative to the start of the enclosing function. Normally, GCC uses an absolute address.

DBX_LINES_FUNCTION_RELATIVE   [Macro]
> Define this macro, with value 1, if the value of a symbol indicating the current line number (N_SLINE) should be relative to the start of the enclosing function. Normally, GCC uses an absolute address.

DBX_USE_BINCL   [Macro]
> Define this macro if GCC should generate N_BINCL and N_EINCL stabs for included header files, as on Sun systems. This macro also directs GCC to output a type number as a pair of a file number and a type number within the file. Normally, GCC does not generate N_BINCL or N_EINCL stabs, and it outputs a single number for a type number.

17.21.3 Open-Ended Hooks for DBX Format

These are hooks for DBX format.

DBX_OUTPUT_SOURCE_LINE (*stream*, *line*, *counter*)   [Macro]
> A C statement to output DBX debugging information before code for line number *line* of the current source file to the stdio stream *stream*. *counter* is the number of time the macro was invoked, including the current invocation; it is intended to generate unique labels in the assembly output.
>
> This macro should not be defined if the default output is correct, or if it can be made correct by defining DBX_LINES_FUNCTION_RELATIVE.

NO_DBX_FUNCTION_END   [Macro]
> Some stabs encapsulation formats (in particular ECOFF), cannot handle the .stabs "",N_FUN,,0,0,Lscope-function-1 gdb dbx extension construct. On those machines, define this macro to turn this feature off without disturbing the rest of the gdb extensions.

NO_DBX_BNSYM_ENSYM   [Macro]
> Some assemblers cannot handle the .stabd BNSYM/ENSYM,0,0 gdb dbx extension construct. On those machines, define this macro to turn this feature off without disturbing the rest of the gdb extensions.

17.21.4 File Names in DBX Format

This describes file names in DBX format.

DBX_OUTPUT_MAIN_SOURCE_FILENAME (*stream*, *name*)   [Macro]

> A C statement to output DBX debugging information to the stdio stream *stream*, which indicates that file *name* is the main source file—the file specified as the input file for compilation. This macro is called only once, at the beginning of compilation.
>
> This macro need not be defined if the standard form of output for DBX debugging information is appropriate.
>
> It may be necessary to refer to a label equal to the beginning of the text section. You can use 'assemble_name (stream, ltext_label_name)' to do so. If you do this, you must also set the variable *used_ltext_label_name* to true.

NO_DBX_MAIN_SOURCE_DIRECTORY   [Macro]

> Define this macro, with value 1, if GCC should not emit an indication of the current directory for compilation and current source language at the beginning of the file.

NO_DBX_GCC_MARKER   [Macro]

> Define this macro, with value 1, if GCC should not emit an indication that this object file was compiled by GCC. The default is to emit an N_OPT stab at the beginning of every source file, with 'gcc2_compiled.' for the string and value 0.

DBX_OUTPUT_MAIN_SOURCE_FILE_END (*stream*, *name*)   [Macro]

> A C statement to output DBX debugging information at the end of compilation of the main source file *name*. Output should be written to the stdio stream *stream*.
>
> If you don't define this macro, nothing special is output at the end of compilation, which is correct for most machines.

DBX_OUTPUT_NULL_N_SO_AT_MAIN_SOURCE_FILE_END   [Macro]

> Define this macro *instead of* defining DBX_OUTPUT_MAIN_SOURCE_FILE_END, if what needs to be output at the end of compilation is an N_SO stab with an empty string, whose value is the highest absolute text address in the file.

17.21.5 Macros for SDB and DWARF Output

Here are macros for SDB and DWARF output.

SDB_DEBUGGING_INFO   [Macro]

> Define this macro to 1 if GCC should produce COFF-style debugging output for SDB in response to the '-g' option.

DWARF2_DEBUGGING_INFO   [Macro]

> Define this macro if GCC should produce dwarf version 2 format debugging output in response to the '-g' option.

> **int TARGET_DWARF_CALLING_CONVENTION (*const_tree*   [Target Hook]
>   *function*)**
>
> > Define this to enable the dwarf attribute DW_AT_calling_convention to be emitted for each function. Instead of an integer return the enum value for the DW_CC_ tag.

To support optional call frame debugging information, you must also define `INCOMING_RETURN_ADDR_RTX` and either set `RTX_FRAME_RELATED_P` on the prologue insns if you use RTL for the prologue, or call `dwarf2out_def_cfa` and `dwarf2out_reg_save` as appropriate from `TARGET_ASM_FUNCTION_PROLOGUE` if you don't.

DWARF2_FRAME_INFO   [Macro]
    Define this macro to a nonzero value if GCC should always output Dwarf 2 frame information. If `TARGET_EXCEPT_UNWIND_INFO` (see Section 17.20.9 [Exception Region Output], page 569) returns `UI_DWARF2`, and exceptions are enabled, GCC will output this information not matter how you define `DWARF2_FRAME_INFO`.

enum unwind_info_type TARGET_DEBUG_UNWIND_INFO (*void*)   [Target Hook]
    This hook defines the mechanism that will be used for describing frame unwind information to the debugger. Normally the hook will return `UI_DWARF2` if DWARF 2 debug information is enabled, and return `UI_NONE` otherwise.

    A target may return `UI_DWARF2` even when DWARF 2 debug information is disabled in order to always output DWARF 2 frame information.

    A target may return `UI_TARGET` if it has ABI specified unwind tables. This will suppress generation of the normal debug frame unwind information.

DWARF2_ASM_LINE_DEBUG_INFO   [Macro]
    Define this macro to be a nonzero value if the assembler can generate Dwarf 2 line debug info sections. This will result in much more compact line number tables, and hence is desirable if it works.

bool TARGET_WANT_DEBUG_PUB_SECTIONS   [Target Hook]
    True if the `.debug_pubtypes` and `.debug_pubnames` sections should be emitted. These sections are not used on most platforms, and in particular GDB does not use them.

bool TARGET_DELAY_SCHED2   [Target Hook]
    True if sched2 is not to be run at its normal place. This usually means it will be run as part of machine-specific reorg.

bool TARGET_DELAY_VARTRACK   [Target Hook]
    True if vartrack is not to be run at its normal place. This usually means it will be run as part of machine-specific reorg.

bool TARGET_NO_REGISTER_ALLOCATION   [Target Hook]
    True if register allocation and the passes following it should not be run. Usually true only for virtual assembler targets.

ASM_OUTPUT_DWARF_DELTA (*stream, size, label1, label2*)   [Macro]
    A C statement to issue assembly directives that create a difference *lab1* minus *lab2*, using an integer of the given *size*.

ASM_OUTPUT_DWARF_VMS_DELTA (*stream, size, label1, label2*)   [Macro]
    A C statement to issue assembly directives that create a difference between the two given labels in system defined units, e.g. instruction slots on IA64 VMS, using an integer of the given size.

ASM_OUTPUT_DWARF_OFFSET (*stream*, *size*, *label*, *offset*, *section*)   [Macro]
>   A C statement to issue assembly directives that create a section-relative reference to
>   the given *label* plus *offset*, using an integer of the given *size*. The label is known to
>   be defined in the given *section*.

ASM_OUTPUT_DWARF_PCREL (*stream*, *size*, *label*)   [Macro]
>   A C statement to issue assembly directives that create a self-relative reference to the
>   given *label*, using an integer of the given *size*.

ASM_OUTPUT_DWARF_DATAREL (*stream*, *size*, *label*)   [Macro]
>   A C statement to issue assembly directives that create a reference to the given *label*
>   relative to the dbase, using an integer of the given *size*.

ASM_OUTPUT_DWARF_TABLE_REF (*label*)   [Macro]
>   A C statement to issue assembly directives that create a reference to the DWARF
>   table identifier *label* from the current section. This is used on some systems to avoid
>   garbage collecting a DWARF table which is referenced by a function.

void TARGET_ASM_OUTPUT_DWARF_DTPREL (*FILE *file*, *int size*,   [Target Hook]
     rtx x)
>   If defined, this target hook is a function which outputs a DTP-relative reference to
>   the given TLS symbol of the specified size.

PUT_SDB_...   [Macro]
>   Define these macros to override the assembler syntax for the special SDB assembler
>   directives. See 'sdbout.c' for a list of these macros and their arguments. If the
>   standard syntax is used, you need not define them yourself.

SDB_DELIM   [Macro]
>   Some assemblers do not support a semicolon as a delimiter, even between SDB as-
>   sembler directives. In that case, define this macro to be the delimiter to use (usually
>   '\n'). It is not necessary to define a new set of PUT_SDB_*op* macros if this is the only
>   change required.

SDB_ALLOW_UNKNOWN_REFERENCES   [Macro]
>   Define this macro to allow references to unknown structure, union, or enumeration
>   tags to be emitted. Standard COFF does not allow handling of unknown references,
>   MIPS ECOFF has support for it.

SDB_ALLOW_FORWARD_REFERENCES   [Macro]
>   Define this macro to allow references to structure, union, or enumeration tags that
>   have not yet been seen to be handled. Some assemblers choke if forward tags are
>   used, while some require it.

SDB_OUTPUT_SOURCE_LINE (*stream*, *line*)   [Macro]
>   A C statement to output SDB debugging information before code for line number
>   *line* of the current source file to the stdio stream *stream*. The default is to emit an
>   .ln directive.

17.21.6 Macros for VMS Debug Format

Here are macros for VMS debug format.

VMS_DEBUGGING_INFO [Macro]
> Define this macro if GCC should produce debugging output for VMS in response to the '-g' option. The default behavior for VMS is to generate minimal debug info for a traceback in the absence of '-g' unless explicitly overridden with '-g0'. This behavior is controlled by TARGET_OPTION_OPTIMIZATION and TARGET_OPTION_OVERRIDE.

17.22 Cross Compilation and Floating Point

While all modern machines use twos-complement representation for integers, there are a variety of representations for floating point numbers. This means that in a cross-compiler the representation of floating point numbers in the compiled program may be different from that used in the machine doing the compilation.

Because different representation systems may offer different amounts of range and precision, all floating point constants must be represented in the target machine's format. Therefore, the cross compiler cannot safely use the host machine's floating point arithmetic; it must emulate the target's arithmetic. To ensure consistency, GCC always uses emulation to work with floating point values, even when the host and target floating point formats are identical.

The following macros are provided by 'real.h' for the compiler to use. All parts of the compiler which generate or optimize floating-point calculations must use these macros. They may evaluate their operands more than once, so operands must not have side effects.

REAL_VALUE_TYPE [Macro]
> The C data type to be used to hold a floating point value in the target machine's format. Typically this is a struct containing an array of HOST_WIDE_INT, but all code should treat it as an opaque quantity.

HOST_WIDE_INT REAL_VALUE_FIX (_REAL_VALUE_TYPE_ x) [Macro]
> Truncates x to a signed integer, rounding toward zero.

unsigned HOST_WIDE_INT REAL_VALUE_UNSIGNED_FIX [Macro]
(_REAL_VALUE_TYPE_ x)
> Truncates x to an unsigned integer, rounding toward zero. If x is negative, returns zero.

REAL_VALUE_TYPE REAL_VALUE_ATOF (_const char_ *string, _machine_mode_ [Macro]
mode)
> Converts string into a floating point number in the target machine's representation for mode mode. This routine can handle both decimal and hexadecimal floating point constants, using the syntax defined by the C language for both.

int REAL_VALUE_NEGATIVE (_REAL_VALUE_TYPE_ x) [Macro]
> Returns 1 if x is negative (including negative zero), 0 otherwise.

int REAL_VALUE_ISINF (_REAL_VALUE_TYPE_ x) [Macro]
> Determines whether x represents infinity (positive or negative).

int REAL_VALUE_ISNAN (*REAL_VALUE_TYPE x*)   [Macro]
    Determines whether *x* represents a "NaN" (not-a-number).

REAL_VALUE_TYPE REAL_VALUE_NEGATE (*REAL_VALUE_TYPE x*)   [Macro]
    Returns the negative of the floating point value *x*.

REAL_VALUE_TYPE REAL_VALUE_ABS (*REAL_VALUE_TYPE x*)   [Macro]
    Returns the absolute value of *x*.

17.23 Mode Switching Instructions

The following macros control mode switching optimizations:

OPTIMIZE_MODE_SWITCHING (`entity`)   [Macro]
    Define this macro if the port needs extra instructions inserted for mode switching in
    an optimizing compilation.

    For an example, the SH4 can perform both single and double precision floating point
    operations, but to perform a single precision operation, the FPSCR PR bit has to be
    cleared, while for a double precision operation, this bit has to be set. Changing the
    PR bit requires a general purpose register as a scratch register, hence these FPSCR
    sets have to be inserted before reload, i.e. you can't put this into instruction emitting
    or TARGET_MACHINE_DEPENDENT_REORG.

    You can have multiple entities that are mode-switched, and select at run time which
    entities actually need it. OPTIMIZE_MODE_SWITCHING should return nonzero for any
    entity that needs mode-switching. If you define this macro, you also have to define
    NUM_MODES_FOR_MODE_SWITCHING, TARGET_MODE_NEEDED, TARGET_MODE_PRIORITY
    and TARGET_MODE_EMIT. TARGET_MODE_AFTER, TARGET_MODE_ENTRY, and
    TARGET_MODE_EXIT are optional.

NUM_MODES_FOR_MODE_SWITCHING   [Macro]
    If you define OPTIMIZE_MODE_SWITCHING, you have to define this as initializer for
    an array of integers. Each initializer element N refers to an entity that needs mode
    switching, and specifies the number of different modes that might need to be set
    for this entity. The position of the initializer in the initializer—starting counting
    at zero—determines the integer that is used to refer to the mode-switched entity in
    question. In macros that take mode arguments / yield a mode result, modes are
    represented as numbers $0 \ldots N - 1$. N is used to specify that no mode switch is
    needed / supplied.

void TARGET_MODE_EMIT (*int* `entity`, *int* `mode`, *int* `prev_mode`,   [Target Hook]
        HARD_REG_SET `regs_live`)
    Generate one or more insns to set *entity* to *mode*. *hard_reg_live* is the set of hard
    registers live at the point where the insn(s) are to be inserted. *prev_moxde* indicates
    the mode to switch from. Sets of a lower numbered entity will be emitted before sets
    of a higher numbered entity to a mode of the same or lower priority.

int TARGET_MODE_NEEDED (*int* `entity`, *rtx_insn* *`insn`)   [Target Hook]
    entity is an integer specifying a mode-switched entity. If OPTIMIZE_MODE_SWITCHING
    is defined, you must define this macro to return an integer value not larger than the

corresponding element in NUM_MODES_FOR_MODE_SWITCHING, to denote the mode that
entity must be switched into prior to the execution of *insn*.

int TARGET_MODE_AFTER (*int* entity, *int* mode, *rtx_insn* *insn)   [Target Hook]
> *entity* is an integer specifying a mode-switched entity. If this macro is defined, it is
> evaluated for every *insn* during mode switching. It determines the mode that an insn
> results in (if different from the incoming mode).

int TARGET_MODE_ENTRY (*int* entity)   [Target Hook]
> If this macro is defined, it is evaluated for every *entity* that needs mode switching. It
> should evaluate to an integer, which is a mode that *entity* is assumed to be switched
> to at function entry. If TARGET_MODE_ENTRY is defined then TARGET_MODE_EXIT must
> be defined.

int TARGET_MODE_EXIT (*int* entity)   [Target Hook]
> If this macro is defined, it is evaluated for every *entity* that needs mode switching. It
> should evaluate to an integer, which is a mode that *entity* is assumed to be switched
> to at function exit. If TARGET_MODE_EXIT is defined then TARGET_MODE_ENTRY must
> be defined.

int TARGET_MODE_PRIORITY (*int* entity, *int* n)   [Target Hook]
> This macro specifies the order in which modes for *entity* are processed. 0 is the high-
> est priority, NUM_MODES_FOR_MODE_SWITCHING[entity] - 1 the lowest. The value
> of the macro should be an integer designating a mode for *entity*. For any fixed
> *entity*, mode_priority (*entity*, *n*) shall be a bijection in 0 ... num_modes_for_mode_
> switching[entity] - 1.

17.24 Defining target-specific uses of __attribute__

Target-specific attributes may be defined for functions, data and types. These are described
using the following target hooks; they also need to be documented in 'extend.texi'.

const struct attribute_spec * TARGET_ATTRIBUTE_TABLE   [Target Hook]
> If defined, this target hook points to an array of 'struct attribute_spec' (defined in
> 'tree-core.h') specifying the machine specific attributes for this target and some of
> the restrictions on the entities to which these attributes are applied and the arguments
> they take.

bool TARGET_ATTRIBUTE_TAKES_IDENTIFIER_P (*const_tree* name)   [Target Hook]
> If defined, this target hook is a function which returns true if the machine-specific
> attribute named *name* expects an identifier given as its first argument to be passed on
> as a plain identifier, not subjected to name lookup. If this is not defined, the default
> is false for all machine-specific attributes.

int TARGET_COMP_TYPE_ATTRIBUTES (*const_tree* type1, *const_tree*   [Target Hook]
>   type2)
> If defined, this target hook is a function which returns zero if the attributes on *type1*
> and *type2* are incompatible, one if they are compatible, and two if they are nearly
> compatible (which causes a warning to be generated). If this is not defined, machine-
> specific attributes are supposed always to be compatible.

void TARGET_SET_DEFAULT_TYPE_ATTRIBUTES (*tree* **type**)   [Target Hook]
> If defined, this target hook is a function which assigns default attributes to the newly defined *type*.

tree TARGET_MERGE_TYPE_ATTRIBUTES (*tree* **type1**, *tree* **type2**)   [Target Hook]
> Define this target hook if the merging of type attributes needs special handling. If defined, the result is a list of the combined TYPE_ATTRIBUTES of *type1* and *type2*. It is assumed that comptypes has already been called and returned 1. This function may call merge_attributes to handle machine-independent merging.

tree TARGET_MERGE_DECL_ATTRIBUTES (*tree* **olddecl**, *tree*   [Target Hook]
>   **newdecl**)
> Define this target hook if the merging of decl attributes needs special handling. If defined, the result is a list of the combined DECL_ATTRIBUTES of *olddecl* and *newdecl*. *newdecl* is a duplicate declaration of *olddecl*. Examples of when this is needed are when one attribute overrides another, or when an attribute is nullified by a subsequent definition. This function may call merge_attributes to handle machine-independent merging.
>
> If the only target-specific handling you require is 'dllimport' for Microsoft Windows targets, you should define the macro TARGET_DLLIMPORT_DECL_ATTRIBUTES to 1. The compiler will then define a function called merge_dllimport_decl_attributes which can then be defined as the expansion of TARGET_MERGE_DECL_ATTRIBUTES. You can also add handle_dll_attribute in the attribute table for your port to perform initial processing of the 'dllimport' and 'dllexport' attributes. This is done in 'i386/cygwin.h' and 'i386/i386.c', for example.

bool TARGET_VALID_DLLIMPORT_ATTRIBUTE_P (*const_tree* **decl**)   [Target Hook]
> *decl* is a variable or function with __attribute__((dllimport)) specified. Use this hook if the target needs to add extra validation checks to handle_dll_attribute.

TARGET_DECLSPEC   [Macro]
> Define this macro to a nonzero value if you want to treat __declspec(X) as equivalent to __attribute((X)). By default, this behavior is enabled only for targets that define TARGET_DLLIMPORT_DECL_ATTRIBUTES. The current implementation of __declspec is via a built-in macro, but you should not rely on this implementation detail.

void TARGET_INSERT_ATTRIBUTES (*tree* **node**, *tree* ***attr_ptr**)   [Target Hook]
> Define this target hook if you want to be able to add attributes to a decl when it is being created. This is normally useful for back ends which wish to implement a pragma by using the attributes which correspond to the pragma's effect. The *node* argument is the decl which is being created. The *attr_ptr* argument is a pointer to the attribute list for this decl. The list itself should not be modified, since it may be shared with other decls, but attributes may be chained on the head of the list and *attr_ptr* modified to point to the new attributes, or a copy of the list may be made if further changes are needed.

bool TARGET_FUNCTION_ATTRIBUTE_INLINABLE_P (*const_tree*   [Target Hook]
        fndecl)
    This target hook returns **true** if it is OK to inline *fndecl* into the current function,
    despite its having target-specific attributes, **false** otherwise. By default, if a function
    has a target specific attribute attached to it, it will not be inlined.

bool TARGET_OPTION_VALID_ATTRIBUTE_P (*tree* **fndecl**, *tree*   [Target Hook]
        name, *tree* **args**, *int* **flags**)
    This hook is called to parse **attribute(target("..."))**, which allows setting target-
    specific options on individual functions. These function-specific options may differ
    from the options specified on the command line. The hook should return **true** if the
    options are valid.

    The hook should set the **DECL_FUNCTION_SPECIFIC_TARGET** field in the function dec-
    laration to hold a pointer to a target-specific **struct cl_target_option** structure.

void TARGET_OPTION_SAVE (*struct cl_target_option* ***ptr**, *struct*   [Target Hook]
        gcc_options ***opts**)
    This hook is called to save any additional target-specific information in the
    struct cl_target_option structure for function-specific options from the **struct
    gcc_options** structure. See Section 8.1 [Option file format], page 107.

void TARGET_OPTION_RESTORE (*struct gcc_options* ***opts**, *struct*   [Target Hook]
        cl_target_option ***ptr**)
    This hook is called to restore any additional target-specific information in the **struct
    cl_target_option** structure for function-specific options to the **struct gcc_options**
    structure.

void TARGET_OPTION_POST_STREAM_IN (*struct cl_target_option*   [Target Hook]
        *ptr)
    This hook is called to update target-specific information in the **struct cl_target_
    option** structure after it is streamed in from LTO bytecode.

void TARGET_OPTION_PRINT (*FILE* ***file**, *int* **indent**, *struct*   [Target Hook]
        cl_target_option ***ptr**)
    This hook is called to print any additional target-specific information in the **struct
    cl_target_option** structure for function-specific options.

bool TARGET_OPTION_PRAGMA_PARSE (*tree* **args**, *tree* **pop_target**)   [Target Hook]
    This target hook parses the options for **#pragma GCC target**, which sets the
    target-specific options for functions that occur later in the input stream. The
    options accepted should be the same as those handled by the **TARGET_OPTION_
    VALID_ATTRIBUTE_P** hook.

void TARGET_OPTION_OVERRIDE (*void*)   [Target Hook]
    Sometimes certain combinations of command options do not make sense on a partic-
    ular target machine. You can override the hook **TARGET_OPTION_OVERRIDE** to take
    account of this. This hooks is called once just after all the command options have
    been parsed.

Don't use this hook to turn on various extra optimizations for '-O'. That is what `TARGET_OPTION_OPTIMIZATION` is for.

If you need to do something whenever the optimization level is changed via the optimize attribute or pragma, see `TARGET_OVERRIDE_OPTIONS_AFTER_CHANGE`

bool `TARGET_OPTION_FUNCTION_VERSIONS` (*tree* `decl1`, *tree*   [Target Hook]
  `decl2`)

> This target hook returns **true** if *DECL1* and *DECL2* are versions of the same function. *DECL1* and *DECL2* are function versions if and only if they have the same function signature and different target specific attributes, that is, they are compiled for different target machines.

bool `TARGET_CAN_INLINE_P` (*tree* `caller`, *tree* `callee`)   [Target Hook]

> This target hook returns **false** if the *caller* function cannot inline *callee*, based on target specific information. By default, inlining is not allowed if the callee function has function specific target options and the caller does not use the same options.

void `TARGET_RELAYOUT_FUNCTION` (*tree* `fndecl`)   [Target Hook]

> This target hook fixes function *fndecl* after attributes are processed. Default does nothing. On ARM, the default function's alignment is updated with the attribute target.

17.25 Emulating TLS

For targets whose psABI does not provide Thread Local Storage via specific relocations and instruction sequences, an emulation layer is used. A set of target hooks allows this emulation layer to be configured for the requirements of a particular target. For instance the psABI may in fact specify TLS support in terms of an emulation layer.

The emulation layer works by creating a control object for every TLS object. To access the TLS object, a lookup function is provided which, when given the address of the control object, will return the address of the current thread's instance of the TLS object.

const char * `TARGET_EMUTLS_GET_ADDRESS`   [Target Hook]

> Contains the name of the helper function that uses a TLS control object to locate a TLS instance. The default causes libgcc's emulated TLS helper function to be used.

const char * `TARGET_EMUTLS_REGISTER_COMMON`   [Target Hook]

> Contains the name of the helper function that should be used at program startup to register TLS objects that are implicitly initialized to zero. If this is `NULL`, all TLS objects will have explicit initializers. The default causes libgcc's emulated TLS registration function to be used.

const char * `TARGET_EMUTLS_VAR_SECTION`   [Target Hook]

> Contains the name of the section in which TLS control variables should be placed. The default of `NULL` allows these to be placed in any section.

const char * `TARGET_EMUTLS_TMPL_SECTION`   [Target Hook]

> Contains the name of the section in which TLS initializers should be placed. The default of `NULL` allows these to be placed in any section.

`const char * TARGET_EMUTLS_VAR_PREFIX`   [Target Hook]
    Contains the prefix to be prepended to TLS control variable names. The default of
    `NULL` uses a target-specific prefix.

`const char * TARGET_EMUTLS_TMPL_PREFIX`   [Target Hook]
    Contains the prefix to be prepended to TLS initializer objects. The default of `NULL`
    uses a target-specific prefix.

`tree TARGET_EMUTLS_VAR_FIELDS (`*tree* `type`*, tree* `*name`)`   [Target Hook]
    Specifies a function that generates the FIELD_DECLs for a TLS control object type.
    type is the RECORD_TYPE the fields are for and *name* should be filled with the
    structure tag, if the default of `__emutls_object` is unsuitable. The default creates a
    type suitable for libgcc's emulated TLS function.

`tree TARGET_EMUTLS_VAR_INIT (`*tree* `var`*, tree* `decl`*, tree*   [Target Hook]
    `tmpl_addr`)
    Specifies a function that generates the CONSTRUCTOR to initialize a TLS control
    object. *var* is the TLS control object, *decl* is the TLS object and *tmpl_addr* is the
    address of the initializer. The default initializes libgcc's emulated TLS control object.

`bool TARGET_EMUTLS_VAR_ALIGN_FIXED`   [Target Hook]
    Specifies whether the alignment of TLS control variable objects is fixed and should
    not be increased as some backends may do to optimize single objects. The default is
    false.

`bool TARGET_EMUTLS_DEBUG_FORM_TLS_ADDRESS`   [Target Hook]
    Specifies whether a DWARF `DW_OP_form_tls_address` location descriptor may be
    used to describe emulated TLS control objects.

17.26 Defining coprocessor specifics for MIPS targets.

The MIPS specification allows MIPS implementations to have as many as 4 coprocessors,
each with as many as 32 private registers. GCC supports accessing these registers and
transferring values between the registers and memory using asm-ized variables. For example:

```
register unsigned int cp0count asm ("c0r1");
unsigned int d;

d = cp0count + 3;
```

("c0r1" is the default name of register 1 in coprocessor 0; alternate names may be
added as described below, or the default names may be overridden entirely in `SUBTARGET_`
`CONDITIONAL_REGISTER_USAGE`.)

Coprocessor registers are assumed to be epilogue-used; sets to them will be preserved
even if it does not appear that the register is used again later in the function.

Another note: according to the MIPS spec, coprocessor 1 (if present) is the FPU. One
accesses COP1 registers through standard mips floating-point support; they are not included
in this mechanism.

17.27 Parameters for Precompiled Header Validity Checking

void * TARGET_GET_PCH_VALIDITY (*size_t *sz*)   [Target Hook]

> This hook returns a pointer to the data needed by TARGET_PCH_VALID_P and sets
> '*sz' to the size of the data in bytes.

const char * TARGET_PCH_VALID_P (*const void *data*, *size_t sz*)   [Target Hook]

> This hook checks whether the options used to create a PCH file are compatible with
> the current settings. It returns NULL if so and a suitable error message if not. Error
> messages will be presented to the user and must be localized using '_(msg)'.
>
> *data* is the data that was returned by TARGET_GET_PCH_VALIDITY when the PCH file
> was created and *sz* is the size of that data in bytes. It's safe to assume that the data
> was created by the same version of the compiler, so no format checking is needed.
>
> The default definition of default_pch_valid_p should be suitable for most targets.

const char * TARGET_CHECK_PCH_TARGET_FLAGS (*int*   [Target Hook]
    pch_flags)

> If this hook is nonnull, the default implementation of TARGET_PCH_VALID_P will use
> it to check for compatible values of target_flags. *pch_flags* specifies the value that
> target_flags had when the PCH file was created. The return value is the same as
> for TARGET_PCH_VALID_P.

void TARGET_PREPARE_PCH_SAVE (*void*)   [Target Hook]

> Called before writing out a PCH file. If the target has some garbage-collected data
> that needs to be in a particular state on PCH loads, it can use this hook to enforce
> that state. Very few targets need to do anything here.

17.28 C++ ABI parameters

tree TARGET_CXX_GUARD_TYPE (*void*)   [Target Hook]

> Define this hook to override the integer type used for guard variables. These
> are used to implement one-time construction of static objects. The default is
> long_long_integer_type_node.

bool TARGET_CXX_GUARD_MASK_BIT (*void*)   [Target Hook]

> This hook determines how guard variables are used. It should return false (the
> default) if the first byte should be used. A return value of true indicates that only
> the least significant bit should be used.

tree TARGET_CXX_GET_COOKIE_SIZE (*tree type*)   [Target Hook]

> This hook returns the size of the cookie to use when allocating an array whose elements
> have the indicated *type*. Assumes that it is already known that a cookie is needed.
> The default is max(sizeof (size_t), alignof(type)), as defined in section 2.7 of
> the IA64/Generic C++ ABI.

bool TARGET_CXX_COOKIE_HAS_SIZE (*void*)   [Target Hook]

> This hook should return true if the element size should be stored in array cookies.
> The default is to return false.

int TARGET_CXX_IMPORT_EXPORT_CLASS (*tree* **type**, *int*   [Target Hook]
        import_export)

> If defined by a backend this hook allows the decision made to export class *type* to
> be overruled. Upon entry *import_export* will contain 1 if the class is going to be
> exported, −1 if it is going to be imported and 0 otherwise. This function should
> return the modified value and perform any other actions necessary to support the
> backend's targeted operating system.

bool TARGET_CXX_CDTOR_RETURNS_THIS (*void*)   [Target Hook]

> This hook should return **true** if constructors and destructors return the address of
> the object created/destroyed. The default is to return **false**.

bool TARGET_CXX_KEY_METHOD_MAY_BE_INLINE (*void*)   [Target Hook]

> This hook returns true if the key method for a class (i.e., the method which, if defined
> in the current translation unit, causes the virtual table to be emitted) may be an inline
> function. Under the standard Itanium C++ ABI the key method may be an inline
> function so long as the function is not declared inline in the class definition. Under
> some variants of the ABI, an inline function can never be the key method. The default
> is to return **true**.

void TARGET_CXX_DETERMINE_CLASS_DATA_VISIBILITY (*tree*   [Target Hook]
        decl)

> *decl* is a virtual table, virtual table table, typeinfo object, or other similar implicit
> class data object that will be emitted with external linkage in this translation unit. No
> ELF visibility has been explicitly specified. If the target needs to specify a visibility
> other than that of the containing class, use this hook to set DECL_VISIBILITY and
> DECL_VISIBILITY_SPECIFIED.

bool TARGET_CXX_CLASS_DATA_ALWAYS_COMDAT (*void*)   [Target Hook]

> This hook returns true (the default) if virtual tables and other similar implicit class
> data objects are always COMDAT if they have external linkage. If this hook returns
> false, then class data for classes whose virtual table will be emitted in only one
> translation unit will not be COMDAT.

bool TARGET_CXX_LIBRARY_RTTI_COMDAT (*void*)   [Target Hook]

> This hook returns true (the default) if the RTTI information for the basic types which
> is defined in the C++ runtime should always be COMDAT, false if it should not be
> COMDAT.

bool TARGET_CXX_USE_AEABI_ATEXIT (*void*)   [Target Hook]

> This hook returns true if __aeabi_atexit (as defined by the ARM EABI) should be
> used to register static destructors when '-fuse-cxa-atexit' is in effect. The default
> is to return false to use __cxa_atexit.

bool TARGET_CXX_USE_ATEXIT_FOR_CXA_ATEXIT (*void*)   [Target Hook]

> This hook returns true if the target atexit function can be used in the same man-
> ner as __cxa_atexit to register C++ static destructors. This requires that atexit-
> registered functions in shared libraries are run in the correct order when the libraries
> are unloaded. The default is to return false.

void TARGET_CXX_ADJUST_CLASS_AT_DEFINITION (*tree type*)   [Target Hook]
>   *type* is a C++ class (i.e., RECORD_TYPE or UNION_TYPE) that has just been
>   defined. Use this hook to make adjustments to the class (eg, tweak visibility or
>   perform any other required target modifications).

tree TARGET_CXX_DECL_MANGLING_CONTEXT (*const_tree decl*)   [Target Hook]
>   Return target-specific mangling context of *decl* or NULL_TREE.

17.29 Adding support for named address spaces

The draft technical report of the ISO/IEC JTC1 S22 WG14 N1275 standards committee,
Programming Languages - C - Extensions to support embedded processors, specifies a syntax for embedded processors to specify alternate address spaces. You can configure a GCC
port to support section 5.1 of the draft report to add support for address spaces other than
the default address space. These address spaces are new keywords that are similar to the
volatile and const type attributes.

Pointers to named address spaces can have a different size than pointers to the generic
address space.

For example, the SPU port uses the __ea address space to refer to memory in the host
processor, rather than memory local to the SPU processor. Access to memory in the __ea
address space involves issuing DMA operations to move data between the host processor
and the local processor memory address space. Pointers in the __ea address space are
either 32 bits or 64 bits based on the '-mea32' or '-mea64' switches (native SPU pointers
are always 32 bits).

Internally, address spaces are represented as a small integer in the range 0 to 15 with
address space 0 being reserved for the generic address space.

To register a named address space qualifier keyword with the C front end, the target may
call the c_register_addr_space routine. For example, the SPU port uses the following to
declare __ea as the keyword for named address space #1:

```
#define ADDR_SPACE_EA 1
c_register_addr_space ("__ea", ADDR_SPACE_EA);
```

machine_mode TARGET_ADDR_SPACE_POINTER_MODE (*addr_space_t*   [Target Hook]
>   *address_space*)
>   Define this to return the machine mode to use for pointers to *address_space* if the
>   target supports named address spaces. The default version of this hook returns ptr_
>   mode.

machine_mode TARGET_ADDR_SPACE_ADDRESS_MODE (*addr_space_t*   [Target Hook]
>   *address_space*)
>   Define this to return the machine mode to use for addresses in *address_space* if the
>   target supports named address spaces. The default version of this hook returns Pmode.

bool TARGET_ADDR_SPACE_VALID_POINTER_MODE (*machine_mode*   [Target Hook]
>   *mode*, *addr_space_t* as)
>   Define this to return nonzero if the port can handle pointers with machine mode *mode*
>   to address space as. This target hook is the same as the TARGET_VALID_POINTER_
>   MODE target hook, except that it includes explicit named address space support. The

default version of this hook returns true for the modes returned by either the `TARGET_ADDR_SPACE_POINTER_MODE` or `TARGET_ADDR_SPACE_ADDRESS_MODE` target hooks for the given address space.

bool **TARGET_ADDR_SPACE_LEGITIMATE_ADDRESS_P**   [Target Hook]
    (*machine_mode* `mode`, *rtx* `exp`, *bool* **strict**, *addr_space_t* **as**)
Define this to return true if *exp* is a valid address for mode *mode* in the named address space *as*. The *strict* parameter says whether strict addressing is in effect after reload has finished. This target hook is the same as the `TARGET_LEGITIMATE_ADDRESS_P` target hook, except that it includes explicit named address space support.

rtx **TARGET_ADDR_SPACE_LEGITIMIZE_ADDRESS** (*rtx* `x`, *rtx* `oldx`,   [Target Hook]
    machine_mode `mode`, *addr_space_t* **as**)
Define this to modify an invalid address *x* to be a valid address with mode *mode* in the named address space *as*. This target hook is the same as the `TARGET_LEGITIMIZE_ADDRESS` target hook, except that it includes explicit named address space support.

bool **TARGET_ADDR_SPACE_SUBSET_P** (*addr_space_t* **subset**,   [Target Hook]
    addr_space_t **superset**)
Define this to return whether the *subset* named address space is contained within the *superset* named address space. Pointers to a named address space that is a subset of another named address space will be converted automatically without a cast if used together in arithmetic operations. Pointers to a superset address space can be converted to pointers to a subset address space via explicit casts.

bool **TARGET_ADDR_SPACE_ZERO_ADDRESS_VALID** (*addr_space_t*   [Target Hook]
    as)
Define this to modify the default handling of address 0 for the address space. Return true if 0 should be considered a valid address.

rtx **TARGET_ADDR_SPACE_CONVERT** (*rtx* `op`, *tree* **from_type**, *tree*   [Target Hook]
    to_type)
Define this to convert the pointer expression represented by the RTL *op* with type *from_type* that points to a named address space to a new pointer expression with type *to_type* that points to a different named address space. When this hook it called, it is guaranteed that one of the two address spaces is a subset of the other, as determined by the `TARGET_ADDR_SPACE_SUBSET_P` target hook.

int **TARGET_ADDR_SPACE_DEBUG** (*addr_space_t* **as**)   [Target Hook]
Define this to define how the address space is encoded in dwarf. The result is the value to be used with `DW_AT_address_class`.

void **TARGET_ADDR_SPACE_DIAGNOSE_USAGE** (*addr_space_t* **as**,   [Target Hook]
    location_t **loc**)
Define this hook if the availability of an address space depends on command line options and some diagnostics should be printed when the address space is used. This hook is called during parsing and allows to emit a better diagnostic compared to the case where the address space was not registered with `c_register_addr_space`. *as* is the address space as registered with `c_register_addr_space`. *loc* is the location of the address space qualifier token. The default implementation does nothing.

17.30 Miscellaneous Parameters

Here are several miscellaneous parameters.

HAS_LONG_COND_BRANCH   [Macro]

> Define this boolean macro to indicate whether or not your architecture has conditional branches that can span all of memory. It is used in conjunction with an optimization that partitions hot and cold basic blocks into separate sections of the executable. If this macro is set to false, gcc will convert any conditional branches that attempt to cross between sections into unconditional branches or indirect jumps.

HAS_LONG_UNCOND_BRANCH   [Macro]

> Define this boolean macro to indicate whether or not your architecture has unconditional branches that can span all of memory. It is used in conjunction with an optimization that partitions hot and cold basic blocks into separate sections of the executable. If this macro is set to false, gcc will convert any unconditional branches that attempt to cross between sections into indirect jumps.

CASE_VECTOR_MODE   [Macro]

> An alias for a machine mode name. This is the machine mode that elements of a jump-table should have.

CASE_VECTOR_SHORTEN_MODE (min_offset, max_offset, body)   [Macro]

> Optional: return the preferred mode for an addr_diff_vec when the minimum and maximum offset are known. If you define this, it enables extra code in branch shortening to deal with addr_diff_vec. To make this work, you also have to define INSN_ALIGN and make the alignment for addr_diff_vec explicit. The body argument is provided so that the offset_unsigned and scale flags can be updated.

CASE_VECTOR_PC_RELATIVE   [Macro]

> Define this macro to be a C expression to indicate when jump-tables should contain relative addresses. You need not define this macro if jump-tables never contain relative addresses, or jump-tables should contain relative addresses only when '-fPIC' or '-fPIC' is in effect.

unsigned int TARGET_CASE_VALUES_THRESHOLD (void)   [Target Hook]

> This function return the smallest number of different values for which it is best to use a jump-table instead of a tree of conditional branches. The default is four for machines with a casesi instruction and five otherwise. This is best for most machines.

WORD_REGISTER_OPERATIONS   [Macro]

> Define this macro to 1 if operations between registers with integral mode smaller than a word are always performed on the entire register. Most RISC machines have this property and most CISC machines do not.

unsigned int TARGET_MIN_ARITHMETIC_PRECISION (void)   [Target Hook]

> On some RISC architectures with 64-bit registers, the processor also maintains 32-bit condition codes that make it possible to do real 32-bit arithmetic, although the operations are performed on the full registers.

On such architectures, defining this hook to 32 tells the compiler to try using 32-bit arithmetical operations setting the condition codes instead of doing full 64-bit arithmetic.

More generally, define this hook on RISC architectures if you want the compiler to try using arithmetical operations setting the condition codes with a precision lower than the word precision.

You need not define this hook if `WORD_REGISTER_OPERATIONS` is not defined to 1.

LOAD_EXTEND_OP (*mem_mode*)   [Macro]

Define this macro to be a C expression indicating when insns that read memory in *mem_mode*, an integral mode narrower than a word, set the bits outside of *mem_mode* to be either the sign-extension or the zero-extension of the data read. Return `SIGN_EXTEND` for values of *mem_mode* for which the insn sign-extends, `ZERO_EXTEND` for which it zero-extends, and `UNKNOWN` for other modes.

This macro is not called with *mem_mode* non-integral or with a width greater than or equal to `BITS_PER_WORD`, so you may return any value in this case. Do not define this macro if it would always return `UNKNOWN`. On machines where this macro is defined, you will normally define it as the constant `SIGN_EXTEND` or `ZERO_EXTEND`.

You may return a non-`UNKNOWN` value even if for some hard registers the sign extension is not performed, if for the `REGNO_REG_CLASS` of these hard registers `CANNOT_CHANGE_MODE_CLASS` returns nonzero when the *from* mode is *mem_mode* and the *to* mode is any integral mode larger than this but not larger than `word_mode`.

You must return `UNKNOWN` if for some hard registers that allow this mode, `CANNOT_CHANGE_MODE_CLASS` says that they cannot change to `word_mode`, but that they can change to another integral mode that is larger then *mem_mode* but still smaller than `word_mode`.

SHORT_IMMEDIATES_SIGN_EXTEND   [Macro]

Define this macro to 1 if loading short immediate values into registers sign extends.

unsigned int TARGET_MIN_DIVISIONS_FOR_RECIP_MUL   [Target Hook]
        (*machine_mode* **mode**)

When '`-ffast-math`' is in effect, GCC tries to optimize divisions by the same divisor, by turning them into multiplications by the reciprocal. This target hook specifies the minimum number of divisions that should be there for GCC to perform the optimization for a variable of mode *mode*. The default implementation returns 3 if the machine has an instruction for the division, and 2 if it does not.

MOVE_MAX   [Macro]

The maximum number of bytes that a single instruction can move quickly between memory and registers or between two memory locations.

MAX_MOVE_MAX   [Macro]

The maximum number of bytes that a single instruction can move quickly between memory and registers or between two memory locations. If this is undefined, the default is `MOVE_MAX`. Otherwise, it is the constant value that is the largest value that `MOVE_MAX` can have at run-time.

SHIFT_COUNT_TRUNCATED   [Macro]

A C expression that is nonzero if on this machine the number of bits actually used for the count of a shift operation is equal to the number of bits needed to represent the size of the object being shifted. When this macro is nonzero, the compiler will assume that it is safe to omit a sign-extend, zero-extend, and certain bitwise 'and' instructions that truncates the count of a shift operation. On machines that have instructions that act on bit-fields at variable positions, which may include 'bit test' instructions, a nonzero SHIFT_COUNT_TRUNCATED also enables deletion of truncations of the values that serve as arguments to bit-field instructions.

If both types of instructions truncate the count (for shifts) and position (for bit-field operations), or if no variable-position bit-field instructions exist, you should define this macro.

However, on some machines, such as the 80386 and the 680x0, truncation only applies to shift operations and not the (real or pretended) bit-field operations. Define SHIFT_COUNT_TRUNCATED to be zero on such machines. Instead, add patterns to the 'md' file that include the implied truncation of the shift instructions.

You need not define this macro if it would always have the value of zero.

unsigned HOST_WIDE_INT TARGET_SHIFT_TRUNCATION_MASK   [Target Hook]
     (machine_mode mode)

This function describes how the standard shift patterns for mode deal with shifts by negative amounts or by more than the width of the mode. See [shift patterns], page 365.

On many machines, the shift patterns will apply a mask m to the shift count, meaning that a fixed-width shift of x by y is equivalent to an arbitrary-width shift of x by y & m. If this is true for mode mode, the function should return m, otherwise it should return 0. A return value of 0 indicates that no particular behavior is guaranteed.

Note that, unlike SHIFT_COUNT_TRUNCATED, this function does not apply to general shift rtxes; it applies only to instructions that are generated by the named shift patterns.

The default implementation of this function returns GET_MODE_BITSIZE (mode) - 1 if SHIFT_COUNT_TRUNCATED and 0 otherwise. This definition is always safe, but if SHIFT_COUNT_TRUNCATED is false, and some shift patterns nevertheless truncate the shift count, you may get better code by overriding it.

TRULY_NOOP_TRUNCATION (outprec, inprec)   [Macro]

A C expression which is nonzero if on this machine it is safe to "convert" an integer of inprec bits to one of outprec bits (where outprec is smaller than inprec) by merely operating on it as if it had only outprec bits.

On many machines, this expression can be 1.

When TRULY_NOOP_TRUNCATION returns 1 for a pair of sizes for modes for which MODES_TIEABLE_P is 0, suboptimal code can result. If this is the case, making TRULY_NOOP_TRUNCATION return 0 in such cases may improve things.

int TARGET_MODE_REP_EXTENDED (*machine_mode* **mode**,   [Target Hook]
      machine_mode **rep_mode**)

> The representation of an integral mode can be such that the values are always ex-
> tended to a wider integral mode. Return SIGN_EXTEND if values of *mode* are rep-
> resented in sign-extended form to *rep_mode*. Return UNKNOWN otherwise. (Cur-
> rently, none of the targets use zero-extended representation this way so unlike LOAD_
> EXTEND_OP, TARGET_MODE_REP_EXTENDED is expected to return either SIGN_EXTEND
> or UNKNOWN. Also no target extends *mode* to *rep_mode* so that *rep_mode* is not the
> next widest integral mode and currently we take advantage of this fact.)
>
> Similarly to LOAD_EXTEND_OP you may return a non-UNKNOWN value even if the exten-
> sion is not performed on certain hard registers as long as for the REGNO_REG_CLASS
> of these hard registers CANNOT_CHANGE_MODE_CLASS returns nonzero.
>
> Note that TARGET_MODE_REP_EXTENDED and LOAD_EXTEND_OP describe two related
> properties. If you define TARGET_MODE_REP_EXTENDED (mode, word_mode) you prob-
> ably also want to define LOAD_EXTEND_OP (mode) to return the same type of extension.
>
> In order to enforce the representation of mode, TRULY_NOOP_TRUNCATION should return
> false when truncating to mode.

STORE_FLAG_VALUE   [Macro]

> A C expression describing the value returned by a comparison operator with an inte-
> gral mode and stored by a store-flag instruction ('cstore*mode*4') when the condition
> is true. This description must apply to *all* the 'cstore*mode*4' patterns and all the
> comparison operators whose results have a MODE_INT mode.
>
> A value of 1 or −1 means that the instruction implementing the comparison operator
> returns exactly 1 or −1 when the comparison is true and 0 when the comparison is
> false. Otherwise, the value indicates which bits of the result are guaranteed to be 1
> when the comparison is true. This value is interpreted in the mode of the comparison
> operation, which is given by the mode of the first operand in the 'cstore*mode*4'
> pattern. Either the low bit or the sign bit of STORE_FLAG_VALUE be on. Presently,
> only those bits are used by the compiler.
>
> If STORE_FLAG_VALUE is neither 1 or −1, the compiler will generate code that depends
> only on the specified bits. It can also replace comparison operators with equivalent
> operations if they cause the required bits to be set, even if the remaining bits are
> undefined. For example, on a machine whose comparison operators return an SImode
> value and where STORE_FLAG_VALUE is defined as '0x80000000', saying that just the
> sign bit is relevant, the expression
>
> > (ne:SI (and:SI x (const_int *power-of-2*)) (const_int 0))
>
> can be converted to
>
> > (ashift:SI x (const_int *n*))
>
> where *n* is the appropriate shift count to move the bit being tested into the sign bit.
>
> There is no way to describe a machine that always sets the low-order bit for a true
> value, but does not guarantee the value of any other bits, but we do not know of
> any machine that has such an instruction. If you are trying to port GCC to such a
> machine, include an instruction to perform a logical-and of the result with 1 in the
> pattern for the comparison operators and let us know at gcc@gcc.gnu.org.

Often, a machine will have multiple instructions that obtain a value from a comparison (or the condition codes). Here are rules to guide the choice of value for `STORE_FLAG_VALUE`, and hence the instructions to be used:

- Use the shortest sequence that yields a valid definition for `STORE_FLAG_VALUE`. It is more efficient for the compiler to "normalize" the value (convert it to, e.g., 1 or 0) than for the comparison operators to do so because there may be opportunities to combine the normalization with other operations.

- For equal-length sequences, use a value of 1 or −1, with −1 being slightly preferred on machines with expensive jumps and 1 preferred on other machines.

- As a second choice, choose a value of '0x80000001' if instructions exist that set both the sign and low-order bits but do not define the others.

- Otherwise, use a value of '0x80000000'.

Many machines can produce both the value chosen for `STORE_FLAG_VALUE` and its negation in the same number of instructions. On those machines, you should also define a pattern for those cases, e.g., one matching

```
(set A (neg:m (ne:m B C)))
```

Some machines can also perform **and** or **plus** operations on condition code values with less instructions than the corresponding 'cstoremode4' insn followed by **and** or **plus**. On those machines, define the appropriate patterns. Use the names **incscc** and **decscc**, respectively, for the patterns which perform **plus** or **minus** operations on condition code values. See 'rs6000.md' for some examples. The GNU Superoptimizer can be used to find such instruction sequences on other machines.

If this macro is not defined, the default value, 1, is used. You need not define `STORE_FLAG_VALUE` if the machine has no store-flag instructions, or if the value generated by these instructions is 1.

FLOAT_STORE_FLAG_VALUE (*mode*)   [Macro]
A C expression that gives a nonzero `REAL_VALUE_TYPE` value that is returned when comparison operators with floating-point results are true. Define this macro on machines that have comparison operations that return floating-point values. If there are no such operations, do not define this macro.

VECTOR_STORE_FLAG_VALUE (*mode*)   [Macro]
A C expression that gives a rtx representing the nonzero true element for vector comparisons. The returned rtx should be valid for the inner mode of *mode* which is guaranteed to be a vector mode. Define this macro on machines that have vector comparison operations that return a vector result. If there are no such operations, do not define this macro. Typically, this macro is defined as **const1_rtx** or **constm1_rtx**. This macro may return `NULL_RTX` to prevent the compiler optimizing such vector comparison operations for the given mode.

CLZ_DEFINED_VALUE_AT_ZERO (*mode, value*)   [Macro]
CTZ_DEFINED_VALUE_AT_ZERO (*mode, value*)   [Macro]
A C expression that indicates whether the architecture defines a value for **clz** or **ctz** with a zero operand. A result of 0 indicates the value is undefined. If the value is defined for only the RTL expression, the macro should evaluate to 1; if the value

applies also to the corresponding optab entry (which is normally the case if it expands directly into the corresponding RTL), then the macro should evaluate to 2. In the cases where the value is defined, *value* should be set to this value.

If this macro is not defined, the value of `clz` or `ctz` at zero is assumed to be undefined.

This macro must be defined if the target's expansion for `ffs` relies on a particular value to get correct results. Otherwise it is not necessary, though it may be used to optimize some corner cases, and to provide a default expansion for the `ffs` optab.

Note that regardless of this macro the "definedness" of `clz` and `ctz` at zero do *not* extend to the builtin functions visible to the user. Thus one may be free to adjust the value at will to match the target expansion of these operations without fear of breaking the API.

Pmode [Macro]

An alias for the machine mode for pointers. On most machines, define this to be the integer mode corresponding to the width of a hardware pointer; `SImode` on 32-bit machine or `DImode` on 64-bit machines. On some machines you must define this to be one of the partial integer modes, such as `PSImode`.

The width of `Pmode` must be at least as large as the value of `POINTER_SIZE`. If it is not equal, you must define the macro `POINTERS_EXTEND_UNSIGNED` to specify how pointers are extended to `Pmode`.

FUNCTION_MODE [Macro]

An alias for the machine mode used for memory references to functions being called, in `call` RTL expressions. On most CISC machines, where an instruction can begin at any byte address, this should be `QImode`. On most RISC machines, where all instructions have fixed size and alignment, this should be a mode with the same size and alignment as the machine instruction words - typically `SImode` or `HImode`.

STDC_0_IN_SYSTEM_HEADERS [Macro]

In normal operation, the preprocessor expands `__STDC__` to the constant 1, to signify that GCC conforms to ISO Standard C. On some hosts, like Solaris, the system compiler uses a different convention, where `__STDC__` is normally 0, but is 1 if the user specifies strict conformance to the C Standard.

Defining `STDC_0_IN_SYSTEM_HEADERS` makes GNU CPP follows the host convention when processing system header files, but when processing user files `__STDC__` will always expand to 1.

const char * TARGET_C_PREINCLUDE (*void*) [C Target Hook]

Define this hook to return the name of a header file to be included at the start of all compilations, as if it had been included with `#include <file>`. If this hook returns `NULL`, or is not defined, or the header is not found, or if the user specifies '`-ffreestanding`' or '`-nostdinc`', no header is included.

This hook can be used together with a header provided by the system C library to implement ISO C requirements for certain macros to be predefined that describe properties of the whole implementation rather than just the compiler.

bool **TARGET_CXX_IMPLICIT_EXTERN_C** (*const char**)   [C Target Hook]

>   Define this hook to add target-specific C++ implicit extern C functions. If this function returns true for the name of a file-scope function, that function implicitly gets extern "C" linkage rather than whatever language linkage the declaration would normally have. An example of such function is WinMain on Win32 targets.

NO_IMPLICIT_EXTERN_C   [Macro]

>   Define this macro if the system header files support C++ as well as C. This macro inhibits the usual method of using system header files in C++, which is to pretend that the file's contents are enclosed in 'extern "C" {...}'.

REGISTER_TARGET_PRAGMAS ()   [Macro]

>   Define this macro if you want to implement any target-specific pragmas. If defined, it is a C expression which makes a series of calls to c_register_pragma or c_register_pragma_with_expansion for each pragma. The macro may also do any setup required for the pragmas.

>   The primary reason to define this macro is to provide compatibility with other compilers for the same target. In general, we discourage definition of target-specific pragmas for GCC.

>   If the pragma can be implemented by attributes then you should consider defining the target hook 'TARGET_INSERT_ATTRIBUTES' as well.

>   Preprocessor macros that appear on pragma lines are not expanded. All '#pragma' directives that do not match any registered pragma are silently ignored, unless the user specifies '-Wunknown-pragmas'.

void **c_register_pragma** (*const char *space, const char *name, void*   [Function]
>   (**callback*) (*struct cpp_reader **))
void **c_register_pragma_with_expansion** (*const char *space, const*   [Function]
>   *char *name, void (*callback*) (*struct cpp_reader **))

>   Each call to c_register_pragma or c_register_pragma_with_expansion establishes one pragma. The *callback* routine will be called when the preprocessor encounters a pragma of the form

>   #pragma [space] name ...

>   *space* is the case-sensitive namespace of the pragma, or NULL to put the pragma in the global namespace. The callback routine receives *pfile* as its first argument, which can be passed on to cpplib's functions if necessary. You can lex tokens after the *name* by calling **pragma_lex**. Tokens that are not read by the callback will be silently ignored. The end of the line is indicated by a token of type CPP_EOF. Macro expansion occurs on the arguments of pragmas registered with c_register_pragma_with_expansion but not on the arguments of pragmas registered with c_register_pragma.

>   Note that the use of **pragma_lex** is specific to the C and C++ compilers. It will not work in the Java or Fortran compilers, or any other language compilers for that matter. Thus if **pragma_lex** is going to be called from target-specific code, it must only be done so when building the C and C++ compilers. This can be done by defining the variables c_target_objs and cxx_target_objs in the target entry in the 'config.gcc' file. These variables should name the target-specific, language-specific object file which contains the code that uses **pragma_lex**. Note it will also

be necessary to add a rule to the makefile fragment pointed to by `tmake_file` that shows how to build this object file.

HANDLE_PRAGMA_PACK_WITH_EXPANSION   [Macro]
Define this macro if macros should be expanded in the arguments of '`#pragma pack`'.

TARGET_DEFAULT_PACK_STRUCT   [Macro]
If your target requires a structure packing default other than 0 (meaning the machine default), define this macro to the necessary value (in bytes). This must be a value that would also be valid to use with '`#pragma pack()`' (that is, a small power of two).

DOLLARS_IN_IDENTIFIERS   [Macro]
Define this macro to control use of the character '`$`' in identifier names for the C family of languages. 0 means '`$`' is not allowed by default; 1 means it is allowed. 1 is the default; there is no need to define this macro in that case.

INSN_SETS_ARE_DELAYED (*insn*)   [Macro]
Define this macro as a C expression that is nonzero if it is safe for the delay slot scheduler to place instructions in the delay slot of *insn*, even if they appear to use a resource set or clobbered in *insn*. *insn* is always a `jump_insn` or an `insn`; GCC knows that every `call_insn` has this behavior. On machines where some `insn` or `jump_insn` is really a function call and hence has this behavior, you should define this macro.

You need not define this macro if it would always return zero.

INSN_REFERENCES_ARE_DELAYED (*insn*)   [Macro]
Define this macro as a C expression that is nonzero if it is safe for the delay slot scheduler to place instructions in the delay slot of *insn*, even if they appear to set or clobber a resource referenced in *insn*. *insn* is always a `jump_insn` or an `insn`. On machines where some `insn` or `jump_insn` is really a function call and its operands are registers whose use is actually in the subroutine it calls, you should define this macro. Doing so allows the delay slot scheduler to move instructions which copy arguments into the argument registers into the delay slot of *insn*.

You need not define this macro if it would always return zero.

MULTIPLE_SYMBOL_SPACES   [Macro]
Define this macro as a C expression that is nonzero if, in some cases, global symbols from one translation unit may not be bound to undefined symbols in another translation unit without user intervention. For instance, under Microsoft Windows symbols must be explicitly imported from shared libraries (DLLs).

You need not define this macro if it would always evaluate to zero.

rtx_insn * TARGET_MD_ASM_ADJUST (*vec<rtx>& outputs*,   [Target Hook]
         *vec<rtx>& inputs, vec<const char *>& constraints, vec<rtx>& clobbers,*
         HARD_REG_SET& clobbered_regs)
This target hook may add *clobbers* to *clobbers* and *clobbered_regs* for any hard regs the port wishes to automatically clobber for an asm. The *outputs* and *inputs* may be inspected to avoid clobbering a register that is already used by the asm.

It may modify the *outputs*, *inputs*, and *constraints* as necessary for other pre-processing. In this case the return value is a sequence of insns to emit after the asm.

MATH_LIBRARY [Macro]

Define this macro as a C string constant for the linker argument to link in the system math library, minus the initial '"-l"', or '""' if the target does not have a separate math library.

You need only define this macro if the default of '"m"' is wrong.

LIBRARY_PATH_ENV [Macro]

Define this macro as a C string constant for the environment variable that specifies where the linker should look for libraries.

You need only define this macro if the default of '"LIBRARY_PATH"' is wrong.

TARGET_POSIX_IO [Macro]

Define this macro if the target supports the following POSIX file functions, access, mkdir and file locking with fcntl / F_SETLKW. Defining `TARGET_POSIX_IO` will enable the test coverage code to use file locking when exiting a program, which avoids race conditions if the program has forked. It will also create directories at run-time for cross-profiling.

MAX_CONDITIONAL_EXECUTE [Macro]

A C expression for the maximum number of instructions to execute via conditional execution instructions instead of a branch. A value of `BRANCH_COST+1` is the default if the machine does not use cc0, and 1 if it does use cc0.

IFCVT_MODIFY_TESTS (*ce_info*, *true_expr*, *false_expr*) [Macro]

Used if the target needs to perform machine-dependent modifications on the conditionals used for turning basic blocks into conditionally executed code. *ce_info* points to a data structure, `struct ce_if_block`, which contains information about the currently processed blocks. *true_expr* and *false_expr* are the tests that are used for converting the then-block and the else-block, respectively. Set either *true_expr* or *false_expr* to a null pointer if the tests cannot be converted.

IFCVT_MODIFY_MULTIPLE_TESTS (*ce_info*, *bb*, *true_expr*, [Macro]
false_expr)

Like `IFCVT_MODIFY_TESTS`, but used when converting more complicated if-statements into conditions combined by **and** and **or** operations. *bb* contains the basic block that contains the test that is currently being processed and about to be turned into a condition.

IFCVT_MODIFY_INSN (*ce_info*, *pattern*, *insn*) [Macro]

A C expression to modify the *PATTERN* of an *INSN* that is to be converted to conditional execution format. *ce_info* points to a data structure, `struct ce_if_block`, which contains information about the currently processed blocks.

IFCVT_MODIFY_FINAL (*ce_info*) [Macro]

A C expression to perform any final machine dependent modifications in converting code to conditional execution. The involved basic blocks can be found in the `struct ce_if_block` structure that is pointed to by *ce_info*.

IFCVT_MODIFY_CANCEL (*ce_info*)   [Macro]
> A C expression to cancel any machine dependent modifications in converting code to conditional execution. The involved basic blocks can be found in the `struct ce_if_block` structure that is pointed to by *ce_info*.

IFCVT_MACHDEP_INIT (*ce_info*)   [Macro]
> A C expression to initialize any machine specific data for if-conversion of the if-block in the `struct ce_if_block` structure that is pointed to by *ce_info*.

void TARGET_MACHINE_DEPENDENT_REORG (*void*)   [Target Hook]
> If non-null, this hook performs a target-specific pass over the instruction stream. The compiler will run it at all optimization levels, just before the point at which it normally does delayed-branch scheduling.
>
> The exact purpose of the hook varies from target to target. Some use it to do transformations that are necessary for correctness, such as laying out in-function constant pools or avoiding hardware hazards. Others use it as an opportunity to do some machine-dependent optimizations.
>
> You need not implement the hook if it has nothing to do. The default definition is null.

void TARGET_INIT_BUILTINS (*void*)   [Target Hook]
> Define this hook if you have any machine-specific built-in functions that need to be defined. It should be a function that performs the necessary setup.
>
> Machine specific built-in functions can be useful to expand special machine instructions that would otherwise not normally be generated because they have no equivalent in the source language (for example, SIMD vector instructions or prefetch instructions).
>
> To create a built-in function, call the function `lang_hooks.builtin_function` which is defined by the language front end. You can use any type nodes set up by `build_common_tree_nodes`; only language front ends that use those two functions will call 'TARGET_INIT_BUILTINS'.

tree TARGET_BUILTIN_DECL (*unsigned* `code`, *bool* `initialize_p`)   [Target Hook]
> Define this hook if you have any machine-specific built-in functions that need to be defined. It should be a function that returns the builtin function declaration for the builtin function code *code*. If there is no such builtin and it cannot be initialized at this time if *initialize_p* is true the function should return `NULL_TREE`. If *code* is out of range the function should return `error_mark_node`.

rtx TARGET_EXPAND_BUILTIN (*tree* `exp`, *rtx* `target`, *rtx*   [Target Hook]
          `subtarget`, *machine_mode* `mode`, *int* `ignore`)
> Expand a call to a machine specific built-in function that was set up by 'TARGET_INIT_BUILTINS'. *exp* is the expression for the function call; the result should go to *target* if that is convenient, and have mode *mode* if that is convenient. *subtarget* may be used as the target for computing one of *exp*'s operands. *ignore* is nonzero if the value is to be ignored. This function should return the result of the call to the built-in function.

tree **TARGET_BUILTIN_CHKP_FUNCTION** (*unsigned* `fcode`)   [Target Hook]

This hook allows target to redefine built-in functions used by Pointer Bounds Checker for code instrumentation. Hook should return fndecl of function implementing generic builtin whose code is passed in *fcode*. Currently following built-in functions are obtained using this hook:

__bounds_type __chkp_bndmk (*const void* `*lb`, *size_t*   [Built-in Function]
            `size`)

Function code - BUILT_IN_CHKP_BNDMK. This built-in function is used by Pointer Bounds Checker to create bound values. *lb* holds low bound of the resulting bounds. *size* holds size of created bounds.

void __chkp_bndstx (*const void* `*ptr`, *__bounds_type* `b`,   [Built-in Function]
            const void `**loc`)

Function code - BUILT_IN_CHKP_BNDSTX. This built-in function is used by Pointer Bounds Checker to store bounds *b* for pointer *ptr* when *ptr* is stored by address *loc*.

__bounds_type __chkp_bndldx (*const void* `**loc`, *const*   [Built-in Function]
            void `*ptr`)

Function code - BUILT_IN_CHKP_BNDLDX. This built-in function is used by Pointer Bounds Checker to get bounds of pointer *ptr* loaded by address *loc*.

void __chkp_bndcl (*const void* `*ptr`, *__bounds_type* `b`)   [Built-in Function]

Function code - BUILT_IN_CHKP_BNDCL. This built-in function is used by Pointer Bounds Checker to perform check for pointer *ptr* against lower bound of bounds *b*.

void __chkp_bndcu (*const void* `*ptr`, *__bounds_type* `b`)   [Built-in Function]

Function code - BUILT_IN_CHKP_BNDCU. This built-in function is used by Pointer Bounds Checker to perform check for pointer *ptr* against upper bound of bounds *b*.

__bounds_type __chkp_bndret (*void* `*ptr`)   [Built-in Function]

Function code - BUILT_IN_CHKP_BNDRET. This built-in function is used by Pointer Bounds Checker to obtain bounds returned by a call statement. *ptr* passed to built-in is SSA_NAME returned by the call.

__bounds_type __chkp_intersect (*__bounds_type* `b1`,   [Built-in Function]
            __bounds_type `b2`)

Function code - BUILT_IN_CHKP_INTERSECT. This built-in function returns intersection of bounds *b1* and *b2*.

__bounds_type __chkp_narrow (*const void* `*ptr`,   [Built-in Function]
            __bounds_type `b`, *size_t* `s`)

Function code - BUILT_IN_CHKP_NARROW. This built-in function returns intersection of bounds *b* and [*ptr*, *ptr* + *s* - 1].

size_t __chkp_sizeof (*const void *ptr*)   [Built-in Function]
    Function code - BUILT_IN_CHKP_SIZEOF. This built-in function returns size of
    object referenced by *ptr*. *ptr* is always ADDR_EXPR of VAR_DECL. This built-in
    is used by Pointer Bounds Checker when bounds of object cannot be computed
    statically (e.g. object has incomplete type).

const void *__chkp_extract_lower (*__bounds_type* b)   [Built-in Function]
    Function code - BUILT_IN_CHKP_EXTRACT_LOWER. This built-in function returns
    lower bound of bounds *b*.

const void *__chkp_extract_upper (*__bounds_type* b)   [Built-in Function]
    Function code - BUILT_IN_CHKP_EXTRACT_UPPER. This built-in function returns
    upper bound of bounds *b*.

tree TARGET_CHKP_BOUND_TYPE (*void*)   [Target Hook]
    Return type to be used for bounds

enum machine_mode TARGET_CHKP_BOUND_MODE (*void*)   [Target Hook]
    Return mode to be used for bounds.

tree TARGET_CHKP_MAKE_BOUNDS_CONSTANT (*HOST_WIDE_INT*   [Target Hook]
    lb, *HOST_WIDE_INT* ub)
    Return constant used to statically initialize constant bounds with specified lower
    bound *lb* and upper bounds *ub*.

int TARGET_CHKP_INITIALIZE_BOUNDS (*tree* var, *tree* lb, *tree* ub,   [Target Hook]
    tree *stmts)
    Generate a list of statements *stmts* to initialize pointer bounds variable *var* with
    bounds *lb* and *ub*. Return the number of generated statements.

tree TARGET_RESOLVE_OVERLOADED_BUILTIN (*unsigned int* loc,   [Target Hook]
    tree fndecl, *void* *arglist)
    Select a replacement for a machine specific built-in function that was set up by
    'TARGET_INIT_BUILTINS'. This is done *before* regular type checking, and so allows
    the target to implement a crude form of function overloading. *fndecl* is the decla-
    ration of the built-in function. *arglist* is the list of arguments passed to the built-in
    function. The result is a complete expression that implements the operation, usually
    another CALL_EXPR. *arglist* really has type 'VEC(tree,gc)*'

tree TARGET_FOLD_BUILTIN (*tree* fndecl, *int* n_args, *tree* *argp,   [Target Hook]
    bool ignore)
    Fold a call to a machine specific built-in function that was set up by
    'TARGET_INIT_BUILTINS'. *fndecl* is the declaration of the built-in function. *n_args*
    is the number of arguments passed to the function; the arguments themselves
    are pointed to by *argp*. The result is another tree, valid for both GIMPLE and
    GENERIC, containing a simplified expression for the call's result. If *ignore* is true
    the value will be ignored.

bool TARGET_GIMPLE_FOLD_BUILTIN (*gimple_stmt_iterator *gsi*) [Target Hook]
Fold a call to a machine specific built-in function that was set up by 'TARGET_INIT_BUILTINS'. *gsi* points to the gimple statement holding the function call. Returns true if any change was made to the GIMPLE stream.

int TARGET_COMPARE_VERSION_PRIORITY (*tree decl1*, *tree decl2*) [Target Hook]
This hook is used to compare the target attributes in two functions to determine which function's features get higher priority. This is used during function multi-versioning to figure out the order in which two versions must be dispatched. A function version with a higher priority is checked for dispatching earlier. *decl1* and *decl2* are the two function decls that will be compared.

tree TARGET_GET_FUNCTION_VERSIONS_DISPATCHER (*void *decl*) [Target Hook]
This hook is used to get the dispatcher function for a set of function versions. The dispatcher function is called to invoke the right function version at run-time. *decl* is one version from a set of semantically identical versions.

tree TARGET_GENERATE_VERSION_DISPATCHER_BODY (*void *arg*) [Target Hook]
This hook is used to generate the dispatcher logic to invoke the right function version at run-time for a given set of function versions. *arg* points to the callgraph node of the dispatcher function whose body must be generated.

bool TARGET_CAN_USE_DOLOOP_P (*const widest_int &iterations*, [Target Hook]
 const widest_int &iterations_max, *unsigned int loop_depth*, *bool entered_at_top*)
Return true if it is possible to use low-overhead loops (`doloop_end` and `doloop_begin`) for a particular loop. *iterations* gives the exact number of iterations, or 0 if not known. *iterations_max* gives the maximum number of iterations, or 0 if not known. *loop_depth* is the nesting depth of the loop, with 1 for innermost loops, 2 for loops that contain innermost loops, and so on. *entered_at_top* is true if the loop is only entered from the top.

This hook is only used if `doloop_end` is available. The default implementation returns true. You can use `can_use_doloop_if_innermost` if the loop must be the innermost, and if there are no other restrictions.

const char * TARGET_INVALID_WITHIN_DOLOOP (*const rtx_insn* [Target Hook]
 *insn)
Take an instruction in *insn* and return NULL if it is valid within a low-overhead loop, otherwise return a string explaining why doloop could not be applied.

Many targets use special registers for low-overhead looping. For any instruction that clobbers these this function should return a string indicating the reason why the doloop could not be applied. By default, the RTL loop optimizer does not use a present doloop pattern for loops containing function calls or branch on table instructions.

bool TARGET_LEGITIMATE_COMBINED_INSN (*rtx_insn *insn*) [Target Hook]
Take an instruction in *insn* and return **false** if the instruction is not appropriate as a combination of two or more instructions. The default is to accept all instructions.

bool TARGET_CAN_FOLLOW_JUMP (*const rtx_insn **follower*, *const*   [Target Hook]
      *rtx_insn **followee*)

    FOLLOWER and FOLLOWEE are JUMP_INSN instructions; return true if FOL-
    LOWER may be modified to follow FOLLOWEE; false, if it can't. For example, on
    some targets, certain kinds of branches can't be made to follow through a hot/cold
    partitioning.

bool TARGET_COMMUTATIVE_P (*const_rtx x*, *int **outer_code*)   [Target Hook]

    This target hook returns **true** if x is considered to be commutative. Usually, this
    is just COMMUTATIVE_P (x), but the HP PA doesn't consider PLUS to be com-
    mutative inside a MEM. *outer_code* is the rtx code of the enclosing rtl, if known,
    otherwise it is UNKNOWN.

rtx TARGET_ALLOCATE_INITIAL_VALUE (*rtx **hard_reg*)   [Target Hook]

    When the initial value of a hard register has been copied in a pseudo register, it
    is often not necessary to actually allocate another register to this pseudo register,
    because the original hard register or a stack slot it has been saved into can be used.
    `TARGET_ALLOCATE_INITIAL_VALUE` is called at the start of register allocation once
    for each hard register that had its initial value copied by using `get_func_hard_reg_`
    `initial_val` or `get_hard_reg_initial_val`. Possible values are NULL_RTX, if you
    don't want to do any special allocation, a `REG` rtx—that would typically be the hard
    register itself, if it is known not to be clobbered—or a MEM. If you are returning a MEM,
    this is only a hint for the allocator; it might decide to use another register anyways.
    You may use `current_function_is_leaf` or `REG_N_SETS` in the hook to determine
    if the hard register in question will not be clobbered. The default value of this hook
    is NULL, which disables any special allocation.

int TARGET_UNSPEC_MAY_TRAP_P (*const_rtx x*, *unsigned **flags*)   [Target Hook]

    This target hook returns nonzero if x, an **unspec** or **unspec_volatile** operation,
    might cause a trap. Targets can use this hook to enhance precision of analysis for
    unspec and **unspec_volatile** operations. You may call `may_trap_p_1` to analyze
    inner elements of x in which case *flags* should be passed along.

void TARGET_SET_CURRENT_FUNCTION (*tree **decl*)   [Target Hook]

    The compiler invokes this hook whenever it changes its current function context
    (**cfun**). You can define this function if the back end needs to perform any initial-
    ization or reset actions on a per-function basis. For example, it may be used to
    implement function attributes that affect register usage or code generation patterns.
    The argument *decl* is the declaration for the new function context, and may be null
    to indicate that the compiler has left a function context and is returning to processing
    at the top level. The default hook function does nothing.

    GCC sets **cfun** to a dummy function context during initialization of some parts of
    the back end. The hook function is not invoked in this situation; you need not worry
    about the hook being invoked recursively, or when the back end is in a partially-
    initialized state. **cfun** might be NULL to indicate processing at top level, outside of
    any function scope.

TARGET_OBJECT_SUFFIX   [Macro]

  Define this macro to be a C string representing the suffix for object files on your
  target machine. If you do not define this macro, GCC will use '.o' as the suffix for
  object files.

TARGET_EXECUTABLE_SUFFIX   [Macro]

  Define this macro to be a C string representing the suffix to be automatically added
  to executable files on your target machine. If you do not define this macro, GCC will
  use the null string as the suffix for executable files.

COLLECT_EXPORT_LIST   [Macro]

  If defined, collect2 will scan the individual object files specified on its command line
  and create an export list for the linker. Define this macro for systems like AIX, where
  the linker discards object files that are not referenced from main and uses export lists.

MODIFY_JNI_METHOD_CALL (mdecl)   [Macro]

  Define this macro to a C expression representing a variant of the method call *mdecl*, if
  Java Native Interface (JNI) methods must be invoked differently from other methods
  on your target. For example, on 32-bit Microsoft Windows, JNI methods must be
  invoked using the stdcall calling convention and this macro is then defined as this
  expression:

```
build_type_attribute_variant (mdecl,
                              build_tree_list
                              (get_identifier ("stdcall"),
                              NULL))
```

bool TARGET_CANNOT_MODIFY_JUMPS_P (void)   [Target Hook]

  This target hook returns true past the point in which new jump instructions could
  be created. On machines that require a register for every jump such as the SHmedia
  ISA of SH5, this point would typically be reload, so this target hook should be defined
  to a function such as:

```
static bool
cannot_modify_jumps_past_reload_p ()
{
  return (reload_completed || reload_in_progress);
}
```

reg_class_t TARGET_BRANCH_TARGET_REGISTER_CLASS (void)   [Target Hook]

  This target hook returns a register class for which branch target register optimizations
  should be applied. All registers in this class should be usable interchangeably. After
  reload, registers in this class will be re-allocated and loads will be hoisted out of loops
  and be subjected to inter-block scheduling.

bool TARGET_BRANCH_TARGET_REGISTER_CALLEE_SAVED (bool   [Target Hook]
  after_prologue_epilogue_gen)

  Branch target register optimization will by default exclude callee-saved registers that
  are not already live during the current function; if this target hook returns true,
  they will be included. The target code must than make sure that all target registers in the class returned by 'TARGET_BRANCH_TARGET_REGISTER_CLASS' that might

need saving are saved. *after_prologue_epilogue_gen* indicates if prologues and epilogues have already been generated. Note, even if you only return true when *after_prologue_epilogue_gen* is false, you still are likely to have to make special provisions in `INITIAL_ELIMINATION_OFFSET` to reserve space for caller-saved target registers.

bool TARGET_HAVE_CONDITIONAL_EXECUTION (*void*)   [Target Hook]
    This target hook returns true if the target supports conditional execution. This target hook is required only when the target has several different modes and they have different conditional execution capability, such as ARM.

rtx TARGET_GEN_CCMP_FIRST (*rtx_insn* ****prep_seq**, *rtx_insn*   [Target Hook]
    ****gen_seq**, *int* **code**, *tree* **op0**, *tree* **op1**)
    This function prepares to emit a comparison insn for the first compare in a sequence of conditional comparisions. It returns an appropriate comparison with `CC` for passing to `gen_ccmp_next` or `cbranch_optab`. The insns to prepare the compare are saved in *prep_seq* and the compare insns are saved in *gen_seq*. They will be emitted when all the compares in the the conditional comparision are generated without error. *code* is the `rtx_code` of the compare for *op0* and *op1*.

rtx TARGET_GEN_CCMP_NEXT (*rtx_insn* ****prep_seq**, *rtx_insn*   [Target Hook]
    ****gen_seq**, *rtx* **prev**, *int* **cmp_code**, *tree* **op0**, *tree* **op1**, *int* **bit_code**)
    This function prepares to emit a conditional comparison within a sequence of conditional comparisons. It returns an appropriate comparison with `CC` for passing to `gen_ccmp_next` or `cbranch_optab`. The insns to prepare the compare are saved in *prep_seq* and the compare insns are saved in *gen_seq*. They will be emitted when all the compares in the conditional comparision are generated without error. The *prev* expression is the result of a prior call to `gen_ccmp_first` or `gen_ccmp_next`. It may return `NULL` if the combination of *prev* and this comparison is not supported, otherwise the result must be appropriate for passing to `gen_ccmp_next` or `cbranch_optab`. *code* is the `rtx_code` of the compare for *op0* and *op1*. *bit_code* is `AND` or `IOR`, which is the op on the compares.

unsigned TARGET_LOOP_UNROLL_ADJUST (*unsigned* **nunroll**, *struct*   [Target Hook]
    loop ***loop**)
    This target hook returns a new value for the number of times *loop* should be unrolled. The parameter *nunroll* is the number of times the loop is to be unrolled. The parameter *loop* is a pointer to the loop, which is going to be checked for unrolling. This target hook is required only when the target has special constraints like maximum number of memory accesses.

POWI_MAX_MULTS   [Macro]
    If defined, this macro is interpreted as a signed integer C expression that specifies the maximum number of floating point multiplications that should be emitted when expanding exponentiation by an integer constant inline. When this value is defined, exponentiation requiring more than this number of multiplications is implemented by calling the system library's `pow`, `powf` or `powl` routines. The default value places no upper bound on the multiplication count.

void TARGET_EXTRA_INCLUDES (*const char *sysroot, const char*   [Macro]
       *iprefix, int stdinc)

> This target hook should register any extra include files for the target. The parameter *stdinc* indicates if normal include files are present. The parameter *sysroot* is the system root directory. The parameter *iprefix* is the prefix for the gcc directory.

void TARGET_EXTRA_PRE_INCLUDES (*const char *sysroot, const char*   [Macro]
       *iprefix, int stdinc)

> This target hook should register any extra include files for the target before any standard headers. The parameter *stdinc* indicates if normal include files are present. The parameter *sysroot* is the system root directory. The parameter *iprefix* is the prefix for the gcc directory.

void TARGET_OPTF (*char *path*)   [Macro]

> This target hook should register special include paths for the target. The parameter *path* is the include to register. On Darwin systems, this is used for Framework includes, which have semantics that are different from '-I'.

bool *TARGET_USE_LOCAL_THUNK_ALIAS_P* (*tree* fndecl)   [Macro]

> This target macro returns true if it is safe to use a local alias for a virtual function *fndecl* when constructing thunks, false otherwise. By default, the macro returns true for all functions, if a target supports aliases (i.e. defines ASM_OUTPUT_DEF), false otherwise,

TARGET_FORMAT_TYPES   [Macro]

> If defined, this macro is the name of a global variable containing target-specific format checking information for the '-Wformat' option. The default is to have no target-specific format checks.

TARGET_N_FORMAT_TYPES   [Macro]

> If defined, this macro is the number of entries in TARGET_FORMAT_TYPES.

TARGET_OVERRIDES_FORMAT_ATTRIBUTES   [Macro]

> If defined, this macro is the name of a global variable containing target-specific format overrides for the '-Wformat' option. The default is to have no target-specific format overrides. If defined, TARGET_FORMAT_TYPES must be defined, too.

TARGET_OVERRIDES_FORMAT_ATTRIBUTES_COUNT   [Macro]

> If defined, this macro specifies the number of entries in TARGET_OVERRIDES_FORMAT_ATTRIBUTES.

TARGET_OVERRIDES_FORMAT_INIT   [Macro]

> If defined, this macro specifies the optional initialization routine for target specific customizations of the system printf and scanf formatter settings.

const char * TARGET_INVALID_ARG_FOR_UNPROTOTYPED_FN   [Target Hook]
      (*const_tree* typelist, *const_tree* funcdecl, *const_tree* val)

> If defined, this macro returns the diagnostic message when it is illegal to pass argument *val* to function *funcdecl* with prototype *typelist*.

const char * **TARGET_INVALID_CONVERSION** (*const_tree*   [Target Hook]
        fromtype, *const_tree* **totype**)

> If defined, this macro returns the diagnostic message when it is invalid to convert
> from *fromtype* to *totype*, or NULL if validity should be determined by the front end.

const char * **TARGET_INVALID_UNARY_OP** (*int* **op**, *const_tree*   [Target Hook]
        type)

> If defined, this macro returns the diagnostic message when it is invalid to apply
> operation *op* (where unary plus is denoted by CONVERT_EXPR) to an operand of type
> *type*, or NULL if validity should be determined by the front end.

const char * **TARGET_INVALID_BINARY_OP** (*int* **op**, *const_tree*   [Target Hook]
        type1, *const_tree* **type2**)

> If defined, this macro returns the diagnostic message when it is invalid to apply
> operation *op* to operands of types *type1* and *type2*, or NULL if validity should be
> determined by the front end.

tree **TARGET_PROMOTED_TYPE** (*const_tree* **type**)   [Target Hook]

> If defined, this target hook returns the type to which values of *type* should be pro-
> moted when they appear in expressions, analogous to the integer promotions, or
> NULL_TREE to use the front end's normal promotion rules. This hook is useful when
> there are target-specific types with special promotion rules. This is currently used
> only by the C and C++ front ends.

tree **TARGET_CONVERT_TO_TYPE** (*tree* **type**, *tree* **expr**)   [Target Hook]

> If defined, this hook returns the result of converting *expr* to *type*. It should return
> the converted expression, or NULL_TREE to apply the front end's normal conversion
> rules. This hook is useful when there are target-specific types with special conversion
> rules. This is currently used only by the C and C++ front ends.

OBJC_JBLEN   [Macro]

> This macro determines the size of the objective C jump buffer for the NeXT runtime.
> By default, OBJC_JBLEN is defined to an innocuous value.

LIBGCC2_UNWIND_ATTRIBUTE   [Macro]

> Define this macro if any target-specific attributes need to be attached to the functions
> in 'libgcc' that provide low-level support for call stack unwinding. It is used in
> declarations in 'unwind-generic.h' and the associated definitions of those functions.

void **TARGET_UPDATE_STACK_BOUNDARY** (*void*)   [Target Hook]

> Define this macro to update the current function stack boundary if necessary.

rtx **TARGET_GET_DRAP_RTX** (*void*)   [Target Hook]

> This hook should return an rtx for Dynamic Realign Argument Pointer (DRAP) if
> a different argument pointer register is needed to access the function's argument list
> due to stack realignment. Return NULL if no DRAP is needed.

bool **TARGET_ALLOCATE_STACK_SLOTS_FOR_ARGS** (*void*)   [Target Hook]

> When optimization is disabled, this hook indicates whether or not arguments should
> be allocated to stack slots. Normally, GCC allocates stacks slots for arguments when

not optimizing in order to make debugging easier. However, when a function is declared with `__attribute__((naked))`, there is no stack frame, and the compiler cannot safely move arguments from the registers in which they are passed to the stack. Therefore, this hook should return true in general, but false for naked functions. The default implementation always returns true.

unsigned HOST_WIDE_INT TARGET_CONST_ANCHOR   [Target Hook]

> On some architectures it can take multiple instructions to synthesize a constant. If there is another constant already in a register that is close enough in value then it is preferable that the new constant is computed from this register using immediate addition or subtraction. We accomplish this through CSE. Besides the value of the constant we also add a lower and an upper constant anchor to the available expressions. These are then queried when encountering new constants. The anchors are computed by rounding the constant up and down to a multiple of the value of `TARGET_CONST_ANCHOR`. `TARGET_CONST_ANCHOR` should be the maximum positive value accepted by immediate-add plus one. We currently assume that the value of `TARGET_CONST_ANCHOR` is a power of 2. For example, on MIPS, where add-immediate takes a 16-bit signed value, `TARGET_CONST_ANCHOR` is set to '0x8000'. The default value is zero, which disables this optimization.

unsigned HOST_WIDE_INT TARGET_ASAN_SHADOW_OFFSET (*void*)   [Target Hook]

> Return the offset bitwise ored into shifted address to get corresponding Address Sanitizer shadow memory address. NULL if Address Sanitizer is not supported by the target.

unsigned HOST_WIDE_INT TARGET_MEMMODEL_CHECK (*unsigned*   [Target Hook]
        HOST_WIDE_INT val)

> Validate target specific memory model mask bits. When NULL no target specific memory model bits are allowed.

unsigned char TARGET_ATOMIC_TEST_AND_SET_TRUEVAL   [Target Hook]

> This value should be set if the result written by `atomic_test_and_set` is not exactly 1, i.e. the `bool` `true`.

bool TARGET_HAS_IFUNC_P (*void*)   [Target Hook]

> It returns true if the target supports GNU indirect functions. The support includes the assembler, linker and dynamic linker. The default value of this hook is based on target's libc.

unsigned int TARGET_ATOMIC_ALIGN_FOR_MODE (*machine_mode*   [Target Hook]
        mode)

> If defined, this function returns an appropriate alignment in bits for an atomic object of machine_mode *mode*. If 0 is returned then the default alignment for the specified mode is used.

void TARGET_ATOMIC_ASSIGN_EXPAND_FENV (*tree* *hold, *tree*   [Target Hook]
        *clear, *tree* *update)

> ISO C11 requires atomic compound assignments that may raise floating-point exceptions to raise exceptions corresponding to the arithmetic operation whose result was

successfully stored in a compare-and-exchange sequence. This requires code equivalent to calls to `feholdexcept`, `feclearexcept` and `feupdateenv` to be generated at appropriate points in the compare-and-exchange sequence. This hook should set *`hold` to an expression equivalent to the call to `feholdexcept`, *`clear` to an expression equivalent to the call to `feclearexcept` and *`update` to an expression equivalent to the call to `feupdateenv`. The three expressions are `NULL_TREE` on entry to the hook and may be left as `NULL_TREE` if no code is required in a particular place. The default implementation leaves all three expressions as `NULL_TREE`. The `__atomic_feraiseexcept` function from `libatomic` may be of use as part of the code generated in *`update`.

void TARGET_RECORD_OFFLOAD_SYMBOL (*tree*)   [Target Hook]
Used when offloaded functions are seen in the compilation unit and no named sections are available. It is called once for each symbol that must be recorded in the offload function and variable table.

char * TARGET_OFFLOAD_OPTIONS (*void*)   [Target Hook]
Used when writing out the list of options into an LTO file. It should translate any relevant target-specific options (such as the ABI in use) into one of the '-foffload' options that exist as a common interface to express such options. It should return a string containing these options, separated by spaces, which the caller will free.

TARGET_SUPPORTS_WIDE_INT   [Macro]
On older ports, large integers are stored in `CONST_DOUBLE` rtl objects. Newer ports define `TARGET_SUPPORTS_WIDE_INT` to be nonzero to indicate that large integers are stored in `CONST_WIDE_INT` rtl objects. The `CONST_WIDE_INT` allows very large integer constants to be represented. `CONST_DOUBLE` is limited to twice the size of the host's `HOST_WIDE_INT` representation.

Converting a port mostly requires looking for the places where `CONST_DOUBLE`s are used with `VOIDmode` and replacing that code with code that accesses `CONST_WIDE_INT`s. '"grep -i const_double"' at the port level gets you to 95% of the changes that need to be made. There are a few places that require a deeper look.

- There is no equivalent to `hval` and `lval` for `CONST_WIDE_INT`s. This would be difficult to express in the md language since there are a variable number of elements.

  Most ports only check that `hval` is either 0 or -1 to see if the value is small. As mentioned above, this will no longer be necessary since small constants are always `CONST_INT`. Of course there are still a few exceptions, the alpha's constraint used by the zap instruction certainly requires careful examination by C code. However, all the current code does is pass the hval and lval to C code, so evolving the c code to look at the `CONST_WIDE_INT` is not really a large change.

- Because there is no standard template that ports use to materialize constants, there is likely to be some futzing that is unique to each port in this code.

- The rtx costs may have to be adjusted to properly account for larger constants that are represented as `CONST_WIDE_INT`.

All and all it does not take long to convert ports that the maintainer is familiar with.

void **TARGET_RUN_TARGET_SELFTESTS** (*void*)   [Target Hook]
> If selftests are enabled, run any selftests for this target.

18 Host Configuration

Most details about the machine and system on which the compiler is actually running are detected by the `configure` script. Some things are impossible for `configure` to detect; these are described in two ways, either by macros defined in a file named 'xm-*machine*.h' or by hook functions in the file specified by the *out_host_hook_obj* variable in 'config.gcc'. (The intention is that very few hosts will need a header file but nearly every fully supported host will need to override some hooks.)

If you need to define only a few macros, and they have simple definitions, consider using the `xm_defines` variable in your 'config.gcc' entry instead of creating a host configuration header. See Section 6.3.2.2 [System Config], page 64.

18.1 Host Common

Some things are just not portable, even between similar operating systems, and are too difficult for autoconf to detect. They get implemented using hook functions in the file specified by the *host_hook_obj* variable in 'config.gcc'.

void HOST_HOOKS_EXTRA_SIGNALS (*void*)   [Host Hook]
> This host hook is used to set up handling for extra signals. The most common thing to do in this hook is to detect stack overflow.

void * HOST_HOOKS_GT_PCH_GET_ADDRESS (*size_t* **size**, *int* **fd**)   [Host Hook]
> This host hook returns the address of some space that is likely to be free in some subsequent invocation of the compiler. We intend to load the PCH data at this address such that the data need not be relocated. The area should be able to hold *size* bytes. If the host uses `mmap`, *fd* is an open file descriptor that can be used for probing.

int HOST_HOOKS_GT_PCH_USE_ADDRESS (*void* * **address**, *size_t*   [Host Hook]
       size, *int* **fd**, *size_t* **offset**)
> This host hook is called when a PCH file is about to be loaded. We want to load *size* bytes from *fd* at *offset* into memory at *address*. The given address will be the result of a previous invocation of `HOST_HOOKS_GT_PCH_GET_ADDRESS`. Return −1 if we couldn't allocate *size* bytes at *address*. Return 0 if the memory is allocated but the data is not loaded. Return 1 if the hook has performed everything.

> If the implementation uses reserved address space, free any reserved space beyond *size*, regardless of the return value. If no PCH will be loaded, this hook may be called with *size* zero, in which case all reserved address space should be freed.

> Do not try to handle values of *address* that could not have been returned by this executable; just return −1. Such values usually indicate an out-of-date PCH file (built by some other GCC executable), and such a PCH file won't work.

size_t HOST_HOOKS_GT_PCH_ALLOC_GRANULARITY (*void*);   [Host Hook]
> This host hook returns the alignment required for allocating virtual memory. Usually this is the same as getpagesize, but on some hosts the alignment for reserving memory differs from the pagesize for committing memory.

18.2 Host Filesystem

GCC needs to know a number of things about the semantics of the host machine's filesystem. Filesystems with Unix and MS-DOS semantics are automatically detected. For other systems, you can define the following macros in 'xm-*machine*.h'.

HAVE_DOS_BASED_FILE_SYSTEM

> This macro is automatically defined by 'system.h' if the host file system obeys the semantics defined by MS-DOS instead of Unix. DOS file systems are case insensitive, file specifications may begin with a drive letter, and both forward slash and backslash ('/' and '\') are directory separators.

DIR_SEPARATOR
DIR_SEPARATOR_2

> If defined, these macros expand to character constants specifying separators for directory names within a file specification. 'system.h' will automatically give them appropriate values on Unix and MS-DOS file systems. If your file system is neither of these, define one or both appropriately in 'xm-*machine*.h'.
>
> However, operating systems like VMS, where constructing a pathname is more complicated than just stringing together directory names separated by a special character, should not define either of these macros.

PATH_SEPARATOR

> If defined, this macro should expand to a character constant specifying the separator for elements of search paths. The default value is a colon (':'). DOS-based systems usually, but not always, use semicolon (';').

VMS   Define this macro if the host system is VMS.

HOST_OBJECT_SUFFIX

> Define this macro to be a C string representing the suffix for object files on your host machine. If you do not define this macro, GCC will use '.o' as the suffix for object files.

HOST_EXECUTABLE_SUFFIX

> Define this macro to be a C string representing the suffix for executable files on your host machine. If you do not define this macro, GCC will use the null string as the suffix for executable files.

HOST_BIT_BUCKET

> A pathname defined by the host operating system, which can be opened as a file and written to, but all the information written is discarded. This is commonly known as a *bit bucket* or *null device*. If you do not define this macro, GCC will use '/dev/null' as the bit bucket. If the host does not support a bit bucket, define this macro to an invalid filename.

UPDATE_PATH_HOST_CANONICALIZE (*path*)

> If defined, a C statement (sans semicolon) that performs host-dependent canonicalization when a path used in a compilation driver or preprocessor is canonicalized. *path* is a malloc-ed path to be canonicalized. If the C statement does canonicalize *path* into a different buffer, the old path should be freed and the new buffer should have been allocated with malloc.

DUMPFILE_FORMAT

> Define this macro to be a C string representing the format to use for constructing the index part of debugging dump file names. The resultant string must fit in fifteen bytes. The full filename will be the concatenation of: the prefix of the assembler file name, the string resulting from applying this format to an index number, and a string unique to each dump file kind, e.g. 'rtl'.
>
> If you do not define this macro, GCC will use '.%02d.'. You should define this macro if using the default will create an invalid file name.

DELETE_IF_ORDINARY

> Define this macro to be a C statement (sans semicolon) that performs host-dependent removal of ordinary temp files in the compilation driver.
>
> If you do not define this macro, GCC will use the default version. You should define this macro if the default version does not reliably remove the temp file as, for example, on VMS which allows multiple versions of a file.

HOST_LACKS_INODE_NUMBERS

> Define this macro if the host filesystem does not report meaningful inode numbers in struct stat.

18.3 Host Misc

FATAL_EXIT_CODE

> A C expression for the status code to be returned when the compiler exits after serious errors. The default is the system-provided macro 'EXIT_FAILURE', or '1' if the system doesn't define that macro. Define this macro only if these defaults are incorrect.

SUCCESS_EXIT_CODE

> A C expression for the status code to be returned when the compiler exits without serious errors. (Warnings are not serious errors.) The default is the system-provided macro 'EXIT_SUCCESS', or '0' if the system doesn't define that macro. Define this macro only if these defaults are incorrect.

USE_C_ALLOCA

> Define this macro if GCC should use the C implementation of alloca provided by 'libiberty.a'. This only affects how some parts of the compiler itself allocate memory. It does not change code generation.
>
> When GCC is built with a compiler other than itself, the C alloca is always used. This is because most other implementations have serious bugs. You should define this macro only on a system where no stack-based alloca can possibly work. For instance, if a system has a small limit on the size of the stack, GCC's builtin alloca will not work reliably.

COLLECT2_HOST_INITIALIZATION

> If defined, a C statement (sans semicolon) that performs host-dependent initialization when collect2 is being initialized.

GCC_DRIVER_HOST_INITIALIZATION

> If defined, a C statement (sans semicolon) that performs host-dependent initialization when a compilation driver is being initialized.

HOST_LONG_LONG_FORMAT

> If defined, the string used to indicate an argument of type `long long` to functions like `printf`. The default value is `"ll"`.

HOST_LONG_FORMAT

> If defined, the string used to indicate an argument of type `long` to functions like `printf`. The default value is `"l"`.

HOST_PTR_PRINTF

> If defined, the string used to indicate an argument of type `void *` to functions like `printf`. The default value is `"%p"`.

In addition, if `configure` generates an incorrect definition of any of the macros in 'auto-host.h', you can override that definition in a host configuration header. If you need to do this, first see if it is possible to fix `configure`.

19 Makefile Fragments

When you configure GCC using the 'configure' script, it will construct the file 'Makefile' from the template file 'Makefile.in'. When it does this, it can incorporate makefile fragments from the 'config' directory. These are used to set Makefile parameters that are not amenable to being calculated by autoconf. The list of fragments to incorporate is set by 'config.gcc' (and occasionally 'config.build' and 'config.host'); See Section 6.3.2.2 [System Config], page 64.

Fragments are named either 't-*target*' or 'x-*host*', depending on whether they are relevant to configuring GCC to produce code for a particular target, or to configuring GCC to run on a particular host. Here *target* and *host* are mnemonics which usually have some relationship to the canonical system name, but no formal connection.

If these files do not exist, it means nothing needs to be added for a given target or host. Most targets need a few 't-*target*' fragments, but needing 'x-*host*' fragments is rare.

19.1 Target Makefile Fragments

Target makefile fragments can set these Makefile variables.

LIBGCC2_CFLAGS

>   Compiler flags to use when compiling 'libgcc2.c'.

LIB2FUNCS_EXTRA

>   A list of source file names to be compiled or assembled and inserted into 'libgcc.a'.

CRTSTUFF_T_CFLAGS

>   Special flags used when compiling 'crtstuff.c'. See Section 17.20.5 [Initialization], page 560.

CRTSTUFF_T_CFLAGS_S

>   Special flags used when compiling 'crtstuff.c' for shared linking. Used if you use 'crtbeginS.o' and 'crtendS.o' in EXTRA-PARTS. See Section 17.20.5 [Initialization], page 560.

MULTILIB_OPTIONS

>   For some targets, invoking GCC in different ways produces objects that can not be linked together. For example, for some targets GCC produces both big and little endian code. For these targets, you must arrange for multiple versions of 'libgcc.a' to be compiled, one for each set of incompatible options. When GCC invokes the linker, it arranges to link in the right version of 'libgcc.a', based on the command line options used.

>   The MULTILIB_OPTIONS macro lists the set of options for which special versions of 'libgcc.a' must be built. Write options that are mutually incompatible side by side, separated by a slash. Write options that may be used together separated by a space. The build procedure will build all combinations of compatible options.

>   For example, if you set MULTILIB_OPTIONS to 'm68000/m68020 msoft-float', 'Makefile' will build special versions of 'libgcc.a' using the following sets of

options: '-m68000', '-m68020', '-msoft-float', '-m68000 -msoft-float', and '-m68020 -msoft-float'.

MULTILIB_DIRNAMES

If `MULTILIB_OPTIONS` is used, this variable specifies the directory names that should be used to hold the various libraries. Write one element in `MULTILIB_DIRNAMES` for each element in `MULTILIB_OPTIONS`. If `MULTILIB_DIRNAMES` is not used, the default value will be `MULTILIB_OPTIONS`, with all slashes treated as spaces.

`MULTILIB_DIRNAMES` describes the multilib directories using GCC conventions and is applied to directories that are part of the GCC installation. When multilib-enabled, the compiler will add a subdirectory of the form *prefix*/*multilib* before each directory in the search path for libraries and crt files.

For example, if `MULTILIB_OPTIONS` is set to 'm68000/m68020 msoft-float', then the default value of `MULTILIB_DIRNAMES` is 'm68000 m68020 msoft-float'. You may specify a different value if you desire a different set of directory names.

MULTILIB_MATCHES

Sometimes the same option may be written in two different ways. If an option is listed in `MULTILIB_OPTIONS`, GCC needs to know about any synonyms. In that case, set `MULTILIB_MATCHES` to a list of items of the form 'option=option' to describe all relevant synonyms. For example, 'm68000=mc68000 m68020=mc68020'.

MULTILIB_EXCEPTIONS

Sometimes when there are multiple sets of `MULTILIB_OPTIONS` being specified, there are combinations that should not be built. In that case, set `MULTILIB_EXCEPTIONS` to be all of the switch exceptions in shell case syntax that should not be built.

For example the ARM processor cannot execute both hardware floating point instructions and the reduced size THUMB instructions at the same time, so there is no need to build libraries with both of these options enabled. Therefore `MULTILIB_EXCEPTIONS` is set to:

```
*mthumb/*mhard-float*
```

MULTILIB_REQUIRED

Sometimes when there are only a few combinations are required, it would be a big effort to come up with a `MULTILIB_EXCEPTIONS` list to cover all undesired ones. In such a case, just listing all the required combinations in `MULTILIB_REQUIRED` would be more straightforward.

The way to specify the entries in `MULTILIB_REQUIRED` is same with the way used for `MULTILIB_EXCEPTIONS`, only this time what are required will be specified. Suppose there are multiple sets of `MULTILIB_OPTIONS` and only two combinations are required, one for ARMv7-M and one for ARMv7-R with hard floating-point ABI and FPU, the `MULTILIB_REQUIRED` can be set to:

```
MULTILIB_REQUIRED =  mthumb/march=armv7-m
MULTILIB_REQUIRED += march=armv7-r/mfloat-abi=hard/mfpu=vfpv3-d16
```

The `MULTILIB_REQUIRED` can be used together with `MULTILIB_EXCEPTIONS`. The option combinations generated from `MULTILIB_OPTIONS` will be filtered by `MULTILIB_EXCEPTIONS` and then by `MULTILIB_REQUIRED`.

`MULTILIB_REUSE`

Sometimes it is desirable to reuse one existing multilib for different sets of options. Such kind of reuse can minimize the number of multilib variants. And for some targets it is better to reuse an existing multilib than to fall back to default multilib when there is no corresponding multilib. This can be done by adding reuse rules to `MULTILIB_REUSE`.

A reuse rule is comprised of two parts connected by equality sign. The left part is the option set used to build multilib and the right part is the option set that will reuse this multilib. Both parts should only use options specified in `MULTILIB_OPTIONS` and the equality signs found in options name should be replaced with periods. The order of options in the left part matters and should be same with those specified in `MULTILIB_REQUIRED` or aligned with the order in `MULTILIB_OPTIONS`. There is no such limitation for options in the right part as we don't build multilib from them.

`MULTILIB_REUSE` is different from `MULTILIB_MATCHES` in that it sets up relations between two option sets rather than two options. Here is an example to demo how we reuse libraries built in Thumb mode for applications built in ARM mode:

<code>MULTILIB_REUSE = mthumb/march.armv7-r=marm/march.armv7-r</code>

Before the advent of `MULTILIB_REUSE`, GCC select multilib by comparing command line options with options used to build multilib. The `MULTILIB_REUSE` is complementary to that way. Only when the original comparison matches nothing it will work to see if it is OK to reuse some existing multilib.

`MULTILIB_EXTRA_OPTS`

Sometimes it is desirable that when building multiple versions of 'libgcc.a' certain options should always be passed on to the compiler. In that case, set `MULTILIB_EXTRA_OPTS` to be the list of options to be used for all builds. If you set this, you should probably set `CRTSTUFF_T_CFLAGS` to a dash followed by it.

`MULTILIB_OSDIRNAMES`

If `MULTILIB_OPTIONS` is used, this variable specifies a list of subdirectory names, that are used to modify the search path depending on the chosen multilib. Unlike `MULTILIB_DIRNAMES`, `MULTILIB_OSDIRNAMES` describes the multilib directories using operating systems conventions, and is applied to the directories such as `lib` or those in the `LIBRARY_PATH` environment variable. The format is either the same as of `MULTILIB_DIRNAMES`, or a set of mappings. When it is the same as `MULTILIB_DIRNAMES`, it describes the multilib directories using operating system conventions, rather than GCC conventions. When it is a set of mappings of the form *gccdir*=*osdir*, the left side gives the GCC convention and the right gives the equivalent OS defined location. If the *osdir* part begins with a '!', GCC will not search in the non-multilib directory and use exclusively the multilib directory. Otherwise, the compiler will examine the search path for libraries and crt files twice; the first time it will add *multilib* to each directory in the search path, the second it will not.

For configurations that support both multilib and multiarch, `MULTILIB_OSDIRNAMES` also encodes the multiarch name, thus subsuming `MULTIARCH_DIRNAME`. The multiarch name is appended to each directory name, separated by a colon (e.g. '`../lib32:i386-linux-gnu`').

Each multiarch subdirectory will be searched before the corresponding OS multilib directory, for example '`/lib/i386-linux-gnu`' before '`/lib/../lib32`'. The multiarch name will also be used to modify the system header search path, as explained for `MULTIARCH_DIRNAME`.

`MULTIARCH_DIRNAME`

This variable specifies the multiarch name for configurations that are multiarch-enabled but not multilibbed configurations.

The multiarch name is used to augment the search path for libraries, crt files and system header files with additional locations. The compiler will add a multiarch subdirectory of the form *prefix*/*multiarch* before each directory in the library and crt search path. It will also add two directories `LOCAL_INCLUDE_DIR`/*multiarch* and `NATIVE_SYSTEM_HEADER_DIR`/*multiarch*) to the system header search path, respectively before `LOCAL_INCLUDE_DIR` and `NATIVE_SYSTEM_HEADER_DIR`.

`MULTIARCH_DIRNAME` is not used for configurations that support both multilib and multiarch. In that case, multiarch names are encoded in `MULTILIB_OSDIRNAMES` instead.

More documentation about multiarch can be found at `https://wiki.debian.org/Multiarch`.

`SPECS`   Unfortunately, setting `MULTILIB_EXTRA_OPTS` is not enough, since it does not affect the build of target libraries, at least not the build of the default multilib. One possible work-around is to use `DRIVER_SELF_SPECS` to bring options from the '`specs`' file as if they had been passed in the compiler driver command line. However, you don't want to be adding these options after the toolchain is installed, so you can instead tweak the '`specs`' file that will be used during the toolchain build, while you still install the original, built-in '`specs`'. The trick is to set `SPECS` to some other filename (say '`specs.install`'), that will then be created out of the built-in specs, and introduce a '`Makefile`' rule to generate the '`specs`' file that's going to be used at build time out of your '`specs.install`'.

`T_CFLAGS`   These are extra flags to pass to the C compiler. They are used both when building GCC, and when compiling things with the just-built GCC. This variable is deprecated and should not be used.

19.2 Host Makefile Fragments

The use of '`x-host`' fragments is discouraged. You should only use it for makefile dependencies.

20 `collect2`

GCC uses a utility called `collect2` on nearly all systems to arrange to call various initialization functions at start time.

The program `collect2` works by linking the program once and looking through the linker output file for symbols with particular names indicating they are constructor functions. If it finds any, it creates a new temporary '.c' file containing a table of them, compiles it, and links the program a second time including that file.

The actual calls to the constructors are carried out by a subroutine called `__main`, which is called (automatically) at the beginning of the body of `main` (provided `main` was compiled with GNU CC). Calling `__main` is necessary, even when compiling C code, to allow linking C and C++ object code together. (If you use '`-nostdlib`', you get an unresolved reference to `__main`, since it's defined in the standard GCC library. Include '`-lgcc`' at the end of your compiler command line to resolve this reference.)

The program `collect2` is installed as `ld` in the directory where the passes of the compiler are installed. When `collect2` needs to find the *real* `ld`, it tries the following file names:

- a hard coded linker file name, if GCC was configured with the '`--with-ld`' option.
- '`real-ld`' in the directories listed in the compiler's search directories.
- '`real-ld`' in the directories listed in the environment variable `PATH`.
- The file specified in the `REAL_LD_FILE_NAME` configuration macro, if specified.
- '`ld`' in the compiler's search directories, except that `collect2` will not execute itself recursively.
- '`ld`' in `PATH`.

"The compiler's search directories" means all the directories where `gcc` searches for passes of the compiler. This includes directories that you specify with '`-B`'.

Cross-compilers search a little differently:

- '`real-ld`' in the compiler's search directories.
- '`target-real-ld`' in `PATH`.
- The file specified in the `REAL_LD_FILE_NAME` configuration macro, if specified.
- '`ld`' in the compiler's search directories.
- '`target-ld`' in `PATH`.

`collect2` explicitly avoids running `ld` using the file name under which `collect2` itself was invoked. In fact, it remembers up a list of such names—in case one copy of `collect2` finds another copy (or version) of `collect2` installed as `ld` in a second place in the search path.

`collect2` searches for the utilities `nm` and `strip` using the same algorithm as above for `ld`.

21 Standard Header File Directories

`GCC_INCLUDE_DIR` means the same thing for native and cross. It is where GCC stores its private include files, and also where GCC stores the fixed include files. A cross compiled GCC runs `fixincludes` on the header files in '`$(tooldir)/include`'. (If the cross compilation header files need to be fixed, they must be installed before GCC is built. If the cross compilation header files are already suitable for GCC, nothing special need be done).

`GPLUSPLUS_INCLUDE_DIR` means the same thing for native and cross. It is where `g++` looks first for header files. The C++ library installs only target independent header files in that directory.

`LOCAL_INCLUDE_DIR` is used only by native compilers. GCC doesn't install anything there. It is normally '`/usr/local/include`'. This is where local additions to a packaged system should place header files.

`CROSS_INCLUDE_DIR` is used only by cross compilers. GCC doesn't install anything there.

`TOOL_INCLUDE_DIR` is used for both native and cross compilers. It is the place for other packages to install header files that GCC will use. For a cross-compiler, this is the equivalent of '`/usr/include`'. When you build a cross-compiler, `fixincludes` processes any header files in this directory.

22 Memory Management and Type Information

GCC uses some fairly sophisticated memory management techniques, which involve determining information about GCC's data structures from GCC's source code and using this information to perform garbage collection and implement precompiled headers.

A full C++ parser would be too complicated for this task, so a limited subset of C++ is interpreted and special markers are used to determine what parts of the source to look at. All **struct**, **union** and **template** structure declarations that define data structures that are allocated under control of the garbage collector must be marked. All global variables that hold pointers to garbage-collected memory must also be marked. Finally, all global variables that need to be saved and restored by a precompiled header must be marked. (The precompiled header mechanism can only save static variables if they're scalar. Complex data structures must be allocated in garbage-collected memory to be saved in a precompiled header.)

The full format of a marker is

```
GTY (([option] [(param)], [option] [(param)] ...))
```

but in most cases no options are needed. The outer double parentheses are still necessary, though: GTY(()). Markers can appear:

- In a structure definition, before the open brace;
- In a global variable declaration, after the keyword **static** or **extern**; and
- In a structure field definition, before the name of the field.

Here are some examples of marking simple data structures and globals.

```
struct GTY(()) tag
{
  fields...
};

typedef struct GTY(()) tag
{
  fields...
} *typename;

static GTY(()) struct tag *list;    /* points to GC memory */
static GTY(()) int counter;         /* save counter in a PCH */
```

The parser understands simple typedefs such as `typedef struct tag *name;` and `typedef int name;`. These don't need to be marked.

Since **gengtype**'s understanding of C++ is limited, there are several constructs and declarations that are not supported inside classes/structures marked for automatic GC code generation. The following C++ constructs produce a **gengtype** error on structures/classes marked for automatic GC code generation:

- Type definitions inside classes/structures are not supported.
- Enumerations inside classes/structures are not supported.

If you have a class or structure using any of the above constructs, you need to mark that class as GTY ((user)) and provide your own marking routines (see section Section 22.3 [User GC], page 630 for details).

It is always valid to include function definitions inside classes. Those are always ignored by **gengtype**, as it only cares about data members.

22.1 The Inside of a `GTY(())`

Sometimes the C code is not enough to fully describe the type structure. Extra information can be provided with GTY options and additional markers. Some options take a parameter, which may be either a string or a type name, depending on the parameter. If an option takes no parameter, it is acceptable either to omit the parameter entirely, or to provide an empty string as a parameter. For example, GTY ((skip)) and GTY ((skip (""))) are equivalent.

When the parameter is a string, often it is a fragment of C code. Four special escapes may be used in these strings, to refer to pieces of the data structure being marked:

%h   The current structure.

%1   The structure that immediately contains the current structure.

%0   The outermost structure that contains the current structure.

%a   A partial expression of the form [i1][i2]... that indexes the array item currently being marked.

For instance, suppose that you have a structure of the form

```
struct A {
  ...
};
struct B {
  struct A foo[12];
};
```

and b is a variable of type **struct** B. When marking 'b.foo[11]', %h would expand to 'b.foo[11]', %0 and %1 would both expand to 'b', and %a would expand to '[11]'.

As in ordinary C, adjacent strings will be concatenated; this is helpful when you have a complicated expression.

```
GTY ((chain_next ("TREE_CODE (&%h.generic) == INTEGER_TYPE"
              " ? TYPE_NEXT_VARIANT (&%h.generic)"
              " : TREE_CHAIN (&%h.generic)")))
```

The available options are:

`length ("expression")`

There are two places the type machinery will need to be explicitly told the length of an array of non-atomic objects. The first case is when a structure ends in a variable-length array, like this:

```
struct GTY(()) rtvec_def {
  int num_elem;        /* number of elements */
  rtx GTY ((length ("%h.num_elem"))) elem[1];
};
```

In this case, the `length` option is used to override the specified array length (which should usually be 1). The parameter of the option is a fragment of C code that calculates the length.

The second case is when a structure or a global variable contains a pointer to an array, like this:

```
struct gimple_omp_for_iter * GTY((length ("%h.collapse"))) iter;
```

In this case, `iter` has been allocated by writing something like

```
        x->iter = ggc_alloc_cleared_vec_gimple_omp_for_iter (collapse);
```

and the `collapse` provides the length of the field.

This second use of `length` also works on global variables, like:

```
static GTY((length("reg_known_value_size"))) rtx *reg_known_value;
```

Note that the `length` option is only meant for use with arrays of non-atomic objects, that is, objects that contain pointers pointing to other GTY-managed objects. For other GC-allocated arrays and strings you should use `atomic`.

`skip`

If `skip` is applied to a field, the type machinery will ignore it. This is somewhat dangerous; the only safe use is in a union when one field really isn't ever used.

`for_user`

Use this to mark types that need to be marked by user gc routines, but are not refered to in a template argument. So if you have some user gc type T1 and a non user gc type T2 you can give T2 the for_user option so that the marking functions for T1 can call non mangled functions to mark T2.

`desc ("expression")`
`tag ("constant")`
`default`

The type machinery needs to be told which field of a `union` is currently active. This is done by giving each field a constant `tag` value, and then specifying a discriminator using `desc`. The value of the expression given by `desc` is compared against each `tag` value, each of which should be different. If no `tag` is matched, the field marked with `default` is used if there is one, otherwise no field in the union will be marked.

In the `desc` option, the "current structure" is the union that it discriminates. Use `%1` to mean the structure containing it. There are no escapes available to the `tag` option, since it is a constant.

For example,

```
struct GTY(()) tree_binding
{
  struct tree_common common;
  union tree_binding_u {
    tree GTY ((tag ("0"))) scope;
    struct cp_binding_level * GTY ((tag ("1"))) level;
  } GTY ((desc ("BINDING_HAS_LEVEL_P ((tree)&%0)"))) xscope;
  tree value;
};
```

In this example, the value of BINDING_HAS_LEVEL_P when applied to a `struct tree_binding *` is presumed to be 0 or 1. If 1, the type mechanism will treat the field `level` as being present and if 0, will treat the field `scope` as being present.

The `desc` and `tag` options can also be used for inheritance to denote which subclass an instance is. See Section 22.2 [Inheritance and GTY], page 630 for more information.

`cache`

> When the `cache` option is applied to a global variable gt_clear_cache is called on that variable between the mark and sweep phases of garbage collection. The gt_clear_cache function is free to mark blocks as used, or to clear pointers in the variable.

`deletable`

> `deletable`, when applied to a global variable, indicates that when garbage collection runs, there's no need to mark anything pointed to by this variable, it can just be set to `NULL` instead. This is used to keep a list of free structures around for re-use.

`maybe_undef`

> When applied to a field, `maybe_undef` indicates that it's OK if the structure that this fields points to is never defined, so long as this field is always `NULL`. This is used to avoid requiring backends to define certain optional structures. It doesn't work with language frontends.

`nested_ptr (type, "to expression", "from expression")`

> The type machinery expects all pointers to point to the start of an object. Sometimes for abstraction purposes it's convenient to have a pointer which points inside an object. So long as it's possible to convert the original object to and from the pointer, such pointers can still be used. *type* is the type of the original object, the *to expression* returns the pointer given the original object, and the *from expression* returns the original object given the pointer. The pointer will be available using the %h escape.

`chain_next ("expression")`
`chain_prev ("expression")`
`chain_circular ("expression")`

> It's helpful for the type machinery to know if objects are often chained together in long lists; this lets it generate code that uses less stack space by iterating along the list instead of recursing down it. `chain_next` is an expression for the next item in the list, `chain_prev` is an expression for the previous item. For singly linked lists, use only `chain_next`; for doubly linked lists, use both. The machinery requires that taking the next item of the previous item gives the original item. `chain_circular` is similar to `chain_next`, but can be used for circular single linked lists.

`reorder ("function name")`

> Some data structures depend on the relative ordering of pointers. If the precompiled header machinery needs to change that ordering, it will call the function referenced by the `reorder` option, before changing the pointers in the object that's pointed to by the field the option applies to. The function must take four arguments, with the signature 'void *, void *, gt_pointer_operator, void *'. The first parameter is a pointer to the structure that contains the object being updated, or the object itself if there is no containing structure. The second parameter is a cookie that should be ignored. The third parameter is a routine that, given a pointer, will

update it to its correct new value. The fourth parameter is a cookie that must be passed to the second parameter.

PCH cannot handle data structures that depend on the absolute values of pointers. `reorder` functions can be expensive. When possible, it is better to depend on properties of the data, like an ID number or the hash of a string instead.

`atomic`

The `atomic` option can only be used with pointers. It informs the GC machinery that the memory that the pointer points to does not contain any pointers, and hence it should be treated by the GC and PCH machinery as an "atomic" block of memory that does not need to be examined when scanning memory for pointers. In particular, the machinery will not scan that memory for pointers to mark them as reachable (when marking pointers for GC) or to relocate them (when writing a PCH file).

The `atomic` option differs from the `skip` option. `atomic` keeps the memory under Garbage Collection, but makes the GC ignore the contents of the memory. `skip` is more drastic in that it causes the pointer and the memory to be completely ignored by the Garbage Collector. So, memory marked as `atomic` is automatically freed when no longer reachable, while memory marked as `skip` is not.

The `atomic` option must be used with great care, because all sorts of problem can occur if used incorrectly, that is, if the memory the pointer points to does actually contain a pointer.

Here is an example of how to use it:

```
struct GTY(()) my_struct {
  int number_of_elements;
  unsigned int * GTY ((atomic)) elements;
};
```

In this case, `elements` is a pointer under GC, and the memory it points to needs to be allocated using the Garbage Collector, and will be freed automatically by the Garbage Collector when it is no longer referenced. But the memory that the pointer points to is an array of `unsigned int` elements, and the GC must not try to scan it to find pointers to mark or relocate, which is why it is marked with the `atomic` option.

Note that, currently, global variables can not be marked with `atomic`; only fields of a struct can. This is a known limitation. It would be useful to be able to mark global pointers with `atomic` to make the PCH machinery aware of them so that they are saved and restored correctly to PCH files.

`special ("name")`

The `special` option is used to mark types that have to be dealt with by special case machinery. The parameter is the name of the special case. See 'gengtype.c' for further details. Avoid adding new special cases unless there is no other alternative.

`user`

The `user` option indicates that the code to mark structure fields is completely handled by user-provided routines. See section Section 22.3 [User GC], page 630 for details on what functions need to be provided.

22.2 Support for inheritance

gengtype has some support for simple class hierarchies. You can use this to have gengtype autogenerate marking routines, provided:

- There must be a concrete base class, with a discriminator expression that can be used to identify which subclass an instance is.

- Only single inheritance is used.

- None of the classes within the hierarchy are templates.

If your class hierarchy does not fit in this pattern, you must use Section 22.3 [User GC], page 630 instead.

The base class and its discriminator must be identified using the "desc" option. Each concrete subclass must use the "tag" option to identify which value of the discriminator it corresponds to.

Every class in the hierarchy must have a `GTY(())` marker, as gengtype will only attempt to parse classes that have such a marker[1].

```
class GTY((desc("%h.kind"), tag("0"))) example_base
{
public:
    int kind;
    tree a;
};

class GTY((tag("1"))) some_subclass : public example_base
{
public:
    tree b;
};

class GTY((tag("2"))) some_other_subclass : public example_base
{
public:
    tree c;
};
```

The generated marking routines for the above will contain a "switch" on "kind", visiting all appropriate fields. For example, if kind is 2, it will cast to "some_other_subclass" and visit fields a, b, and c.

22.3 Support for user-provided GC marking routines

The garbage collector supports types for which no automatic marking code is generated. For these types, the user is required to provide three functions: one to act as a marker for

---

[1] Classes lacking such a marker will not be identified as being part of the hierarchy, and so the marking routines will not handle them, leading to a assertion failure within the marking routines due to an unknown tag value (assuming that assertions are enabled).

garbage collection, and two functions to act as marker and pointer walker for pre-compiled headers.

Given a structure `struct GTY((user)) my_struct`, the following functions should be defined to mark `my_struct`:

```
void gt_ggc_mx (my_struct *p)
{
  /* This marks field 'fld'.  */
  gt_ggc_mx (p->fld);
}

void gt_pch_nx (my_struct *p)
{
  /* This marks field 'fld'.  */
  gt_pch_nx (tp->fld);
}

void gt_pch_nx (my_struct *p, gt_pointer_operator op, void *cookie)
{
  /* For every field 'fld', call the given pointer operator.  */
  op (&(tp->fld), cookie);
}
```

In general, each marker M should call M for every pointer field in the structure. Fields that are not allocated in GC or are not pointers must be ignored.

For embedded lists (e.g., structures with a **next** or **prev** pointer), the marker must follow the chain and mark every element in it.

Note that the rules for the pointer walker `gt_pch_nx (my_struct *, gt_pointer_operator, void *)` are slightly different. In this case, the operation `op` must be applied to the *address* of every pointer field.

22.3.1 User-provided marking routines for template types

When a template type TP is marked with `GTY`, all instances of that type are considered user-provided types. This means that the individual instances of TP do not need to be marked with `GTY`. The user needs to provide template functions to mark all the fields of the type.

The following code snippets represent all the functions that need to be provided. Note that type TP may reference to more than one type. In these snippets, there is only one type T, but there could be more.

```
template<typename T>
void gt_ggc_mx (TP<T> *tp)
{
  extern void gt_ggc_mx (T&);

  /* This marks field 'fld' of type 'T'.  */
  gt_ggc_mx (tp->fld);
}

template<typename T>
void gt_pch_nx (TP<T> *tp)
{
  extern void gt_pch_nx (T&);

  /* This marks field 'fld' of type 'T'.  */
  gt_pch_nx (tp->fld);
```

```
}

template<typename T>
void gt_pch_nx (TP<T *> *tp, gt_pointer_operator op, void *cookie)
{
  /* For every field 'fld' of 'tp' with type 'T *', call the given
     pointer operator.  */
  op (&(tp->fld), cookie);
}

template<typename T>
void gt_pch_nx (TP<T> *tp, gt_pointer_operator, void *cookie)
{
  extern void gt_pch_nx (T *, gt_pointer_operator, void *);

  /* For every field 'fld' of 'tp' with type 'T', call the pointer
     walker for all the fields of T.  */
  gt_pch_nx (&(tp->fld), op, cookie);
}
```

Support for user-defined types is currently limited. The following restrictions apply:

1. Type TP and all the argument types T must be marked with GTY.

2. Type TP can only have type names in its argument list.

3. The pointer walker functions are different for TP<T> and TP<T *>. In the case of TP<T>, references to T must be handled by calling gt_pch_nx (which will, in turn, walk all the pointers inside fields of T). In the case of TP<T *>, references to T * must be handled by calling the op function on the address of the pointer (see the code snippets above).

22.4 Marking Roots for the Garbage Collector

In addition to keeping track of types, the type machinery also locates the global variables (*roots*) that the garbage collector starts at. Roots must be declared using one of the following syntaxes:

- extern GTY(([options])) type name;
- static GTY(([options])) type name;

The syntax

- GTY(([options])) type name;

is *not* accepted. There should be an extern declaration of such a variable in a header somewhere—mark that, not the definition. Or, if the variable is only used in one file, make it static.

22.5 Source Files Containing Type Information

Whenever you add GTY markers to a source file that previously had none, or create a new source file containing GTY markers, there are three things you need to do:

1. You need to add the file to the list of source files the type machinery scans. There are four cases:

   a. For a back-end file, this is usually done automatically; if not, you should add it to target_gtfiles in the appropriate port's entries in 'config.gcc'.

b. For files shared by all front ends, add the filename to the `GTFILES` variable in 'Makefile.in'.

c. For files that are part of one front end, add the filename to the `gtfiles` variable defined in the appropriate 'config-lang.in'. Headers should appear before non-headers in this list.

d. For files that are part of some but not all front ends, add the filename to the `gtfiles` variable of *all* the front ends that use it.

2. If the file was a header file, you'll need to check that it's included in the right place to be visible to the generated files. For a back-end header file, this should be done automatically. For a front-end header file, it needs to be included by the same file that includes 'gtype-*lang*.h'. For other header files, it needs to be included in 'gtype-desc.c', which is a generated file, so add it to `ifiles` in `open_base_file` in 'gengtype.c'.

For source files that aren't header files, the machinery will generate a header file that should be included in the source file you just changed. The file will be called 'gt-*path*.h' where *path* is the pathname relative to the 'gcc' directory with slashes replaced by -, so for example the header file to be included in 'cp/parser.c' is called 'gt-cp-parser.c'. The generated header file should be included after everything else in the source file. Don't forget to mention this file as a dependency in the 'Makefile'!

For language frontends, there is another file that needs to be included somewhere. It will be called 'gtype-*lang*.h', where *lang* is the name of the subdirectory the language is contained in.

Plugins can add additional root tables. Run the **gengtype** utility in plugin mode as **gengtype -P pluginout.h** *source-dir file-list plugin*.c* with your plugin files *plugin*.c* using `GTY` to generate the *pluginout.h* file. The GCC build tree is needed to be present in that mode.

22.6 How to invoke the garbage collector

The GCC garbage collector GGC is only invoked explicitly. In contrast with many other garbage collectors, it is not implicitly invoked by allocation routines when a lot of memory has been consumed. So the only way to have GGC reclaim storage is to call the `ggc_collect` function explicitly. This call is an expensive operation, as it may have to scan the entire heap. Beware that local variables (on the GCC call stack) are not followed by such an invocation (as many other garbage collectors do): you should reference all your data from static or external `GTY`-ed variables, and it is advised to call `ggc_collect` with a shallow call stack. The GGC is an exact mark and sweep garbage collector (so it does not scan the call stack for pointers). In practice GCC passes don't often call `ggc_collect` themselves, because it is called by the pass manager between passes.

At the time of the `ggc_collect` call all pointers in the GC-marked structures must be valid or `NULL`. In practice this means that there should not be uninitialized pointer fields in the structures even if your code never reads or writes those fields at a particular instance. One way to ensure this is to use cleared versions of allocators unless all the fields are initialized manually immediately after allocation.

22.7 Troubleshooting the garbage collector

With the current garbage collector implementation, most issues should show up as GCC compilation errors. Some of the most commonly encountered issues are described below.

- Gengtype does not produce allocators for a GTY-marked type. Gengtype checks if there is at least one possible path from GC roots to at least one instance of each type before outputting allocators. If there is no such path, the GTY markers will be ignored and no allocators will be output. Solve this by making sure that there exists at least one such path. If creating it is unfeasible or raises a "code smell", consider if you really must use GC for allocating such type.

- Link-time errors about undefined `gt_ggc_r_foo_bar` and similarly-named symbols. Check if your 'foo_bar' source file has `#include "gt-foo_bar.h"` as its very last line.

23 Plugins

GCC plugins are loadable modules that provide extra features to the compiler. Like GCC itself they can be distributed in source and binary forms.

GCC plugins provide developers with a rich subset of the GCC API to allow them to extend GCC as they see fit. Whether it is writing an additional optimization pass, transforming code, or analyzing information, plugins can be quite useful.

23.1 Loading Plugins

Plugins are supported on platforms that support '-ldl -rdynamic'. They are loaded by the compiler using `dlopen` and invoked at pre-determined locations in the compilation process.

Plugins are loaded with

'-fplugin=/path/to/*name*.so' '-fplugin-arg-*name*-*key1*[=*value1*]'

The plugin arguments are parsed by GCC and passed to respective plugins as key-value pairs. Multiple plugins can be invoked by specifying multiple '-fplugin' arguments.

A plugin can be simply given by its short name (no dots or slashes). When simply passing '-fplugin=*name*', the plugin is loaded from the 'plugin' directory, so '-fplugin=*name*' is the same as '-fplugin=`gcc -print-file-name=plugin`/*name*.so', using backquote shell syntax to query the 'plugin' directory.

23.2 Plugin API

Plugins are activated by the compiler at specific events as defined in 'gcc-plugin.h'. For each event of interest, the plugin should call `register_callback` specifying the name of the event and address of the callback function that will handle that event.

The header 'gcc-plugin.h' must be the first gcc header to be included.

23.2.1 Plugin license check

Every plugin should define the global symbol `plugin_is_GPL_compatible` to assert that it has been licensed under a GPL-compatible license. If this symbol does not exist, the compiler will emit a fatal error and exit with the error message:

```
fatal error: plugin name is not licensed under a GPL-compatible license
name: undefined symbol: plugin_is_GPL_compatible
compilation terminated
```

The declared type of the symbol should be int, to match a forward declaration in 'gcc-plugin.h' that suppresses C++ mangling. It does not need to be in any allocated section, though. The compiler merely asserts that the symbol exists in the global scope. Something like this is enough:

```
int plugin_is_GPL_compatible;
```

23.2.2 Plugin initialization

Every plugin should export a function called `plugin_init` that is called right after the plugin is loaded. This function is responsible for registering all the callbacks required by the plugin and do any other required initialization.

This function is called from `compile_file` right before invoking the parser. The arguments to `plugin_init` are:

- `plugin_info`: Plugin invocation information.

- `version`: GCC version.

The `plugin_info` struct is defined as follows:

```
struct plugin_name_args
{
  char *base_name;              /* Short name of the plugin
                                    (filename without .so suffix). */
  const char *full_name;        /* Path to the plugin as specified with
                                    -fplugin=. */
  int argc;                     /* Number of arguments specified with
                                    -fplugin-arg-.... */
  struct plugin_argument *argv; /* Array of ARGC key-value pairs. */
  const char *version;          /* Version string provided by plugin. */
  const char *help;             /* Help string provided by plugin. */
}
```

If initialization fails, `plugin_init` must return a non-zero value. Otherwise, it should return 0.

The version of the GCC compiler loading the plugin is described by the following structure:

```
struct plugin_gcc_version
{
  const char *basever;
  const char *datestamp;
  const char *devphase;
  const char *revision;
  const char *configuration_arguments;
};
```

The function `plugin_default_version_check` takes two pointers to such structure and compare them field by field. It can be used by the plugin's `plugin_init` function.

The version of GCC used to compile the plugin can be found in the symbol `gcc_version` defined in the header 'plugin-version.h'. The recommended version check to perform looks like

```
#include "plugin-version.h"
...

int
plugin_init (struct plugin_name_args *plugin_info,
             struct plugin_gcc_version *version)
{
  if (!plugin_default_version_check (version, &gcc_version))
    return 1;

}
```

but you can also check the individual fields if you want a less strict check.

23.2.3 Plugin callbacks

Callback functions have the following prototype:

```
/* The prototype for a plugin callback function.
     gcc_data  - event-specific data provided by GCC
     user_data - plugin-specific data provided by the plug-in. */
typedef void (*plugin_callback_func)(void *gcc_data, void *user_data);
```

Callbacks can be invoked at the following pre-determined events:

```
enum plugin_event
{
  PLUGIN_START_PARSE_FUNCTION,  /* Called before parsing the body of a function. */
  PLUGIN_FINISH_PARSE_FUNCTION, /* After finishing parsing a function. */
  PLUGIN_PASS_MANAGER_SETUP,    /* To hook into pass manager.  */
  PLUGIN_FINISH_TYPE,           /* After finishing parsing a type.  */
  PLUGIN_FINISH_DECL,           /* After finishing parsing a declaration. */
  PLUGIN_FINISH_UNIT,           /* Useful for summary processing.  */
  PLUGIN_PRE_GENERICIZE,        /* Allows to see low level AST in C and C++ frontends.  */
  PLUGIN_FINISH,                /* Called before GCC exits.  */
  PLUGIN_INFO,                  /* Information about the plugin. */
  PLUGIN_GGC_START,             /* Called at start of GCC Garbage Collection. */
  PLUGIN_GGC_MARKING,           /* Extend the GGC marking. */
  PLUGIN_GGC_END,               /* Called at end of GGC. */
  PLUGIN_REGISTER_GGC_ROOTS,    /* Register an extra GGC root table. */
  PLUGIN_ATTRIBUTES,            /* Called during attribute registration */
  PLUGIN_START_UNIT,            /* Called before processing a translation unit.  */
  PLUGIN_PRAGMAS,               /* Called during pragma registration. */
  /* Called before first pass from all_passes.  */
  PLUGIN_ALL_PASSES_START,
  /* Called after last pass from all_passes.  */
  PLUGIN_ALL_PASSES_END,
  /* Called before first ipa pass.  */
  PLUGIN_ALL_IPA_PASSES_START,
  /* Called after last ipa pass.  */
  PLUGIN_ALL_IPA_PASSES_END,
  /* Allows to override pass gate decision for current_pass.  */
  PLUGIN_OVERRIDE_GATE,
  /* Called before executing a pass.  */
  PLUGIN_PASS_EXECUTION,
  /* Called before executing subpasses of a GIMPLE_PASS in
     execute_ipa_pass_list.  */
  PLUGIN_EARLY_GIMPLE_PASSES_START,
  /* Called after executing subpasses of a GIMPLE_PASS in
     execute_ipa_pass_list.  */
  PLUGIN_EARLY_GIMPLE_PASSES_END,
  /* Called when a pass is first instantiated.  */
  PLUGIN_NEW_PASS,
 /* Called when a file is #include-d or given via the #line directive.
    This could happen many times.  The event data is the included file path,
    as a const char* pointer.  */
  PLUGIN_INCLUDE_FILE,

  PLUGIN_EVENT_FIRST_DYNAMIC    /* Dummy event used for indexing callback
                                   array.  */
};
```

In addition, plugins can also look up the enumerator of a named event, and / or generate new events dynamically, by calling the function `get_named_event_id`.

To register a callback, the plugin calls `register_callback` with the arguments:

- `char *name`: Plugin name.

- `int event`: The event code.

- `plugin_callback_func callback`: The function that handles `event`.

- `void *user_data`: Pointer to plugin-specific data.

For the *PLUGIN_PASS_MANAGER_SETUP*, *PLUGIN_INFO*, and *PLU-GIN_REGISTER_GGC_ROOTS* pseudo-events the `callback` should be null, and the `user_data` is specific.

When the *PLUGIN_PRAGMAS* event is triggered (with a null pointer as data from GCC), plugins may register their own pragmas. Notice that pragmas are not available from 'lto1', so plugins used with -flto option to GCC during link-time optimization cannot use pragmas and do not even see functions like `c_register_pragma` or `pragma_lex`.

The *PLUGIN_INCLUDE_FILE* event, with a `const char*` file path as GCC data, is triggered for processing of `#include` or `#line` directives.

The *PLUGIN_FINISH* event is the last time that plugins can call GCC functions, notably emit diagnostics with `warning`, `error` etc.

23.3 Interacting with the pass manager

There needs to be a way to add/reorder/remove passes dynamically. This is useful for both analysis plugins (plugging in after a certain pass such as CFG or an IPA pass) and optimization plugins.

Basic support for inserting new passes or replacing existing passes is provided. A plugin registers a new pass with GCC by calling `register_callback` with the PLUGIN_PASS_MANAGER_SETUP event and a pointer to a `struct register_pass_info` object defined as follows

```
enum pass_positioning_ops
{
  PASS_POS_INSERT_AFTER,  // Insert after the reference pass.
  PASS_POS_INSERT_BEFORE, // Insert before the reference pass.
  PASS_POS_REPLACE        // Replace the reference pass.
};

struct register_pass_info
{
  struct opt_pass *pass;            /* New pass provided by the plugin.  */
  const char *reference_pass_name;  /* Name of the reference pass for hooking
                                       up the new pass.  */
  int ref_pass_instance_number;     /* Insert the pass at the specified
                                       instance number of the reference pass.  */
                                    /* Do it for every instance if it is 0.  */
  enum pass_positioning_ops pos_op; /* how to insert the new pass.  */
};


/* Sample plugin code that registers a new pass.  */
int
plugin_init (struct plugin_name_args *plugin_info,
             struct plugin_gcc_version *version)
{
  struct register_pass_info pass_info;

  ...

  /* Code to fill in the pass_info object with new pass information.  */

  ...
```

```
    /* Register the new pass.  */
    register_callback (plugin_info->base_name, PLUGIN_PASS_MANAGER_SETUP, NULL, &pass_info);█

    ...
}
```

23.4 Interacting with the GCC Garbage Collector

Some plugins may want to be informed when GGC (the GCC Garbage Collector) is running. They can register callbacks for the `PLUGIN_GGC_START` and `PLUGIN_GGC_END` events (for which the callback is called with a null `gcc_data`) to be notified of the start or end of the GCC garbage collection.

Some plugins may need to have GGC mark additional data. This can be done by registering a callback (called with a null `gcc_data`) for the `PLUGIN_GGC_MARKING` event. Such callbacks can call the `ggc_set_mark` routine, preferably through the `ggc_mark` macro (and conversely, these routines should usually not be used in plugins outside of the `PLUGIN_GGC_MARKING` event). Plugins that wish to hold weak references to gc data may also use this event to drop weak references when the object is about to be collected. The `ggc_marked_p` function can be used to tell if an object is marked, or is about to be collected. The `gt_clear_cache` overloads which some types define may also be of use in managing weak references.

Some plugins may need to add extra GGC root tables, e.g. to handle their own `GTY`-ed data. This can be done with the `PLUGIN_REGISTER_GGC_ROOTS` pseudo-event with a null callback and the extra root table (of type `struct ggc_root_tab*`) as `user_data`. Running the `gengtype -p` *source-dir file-list plugin*.c* ... utility generates these extra root tables.

You should understand the details of memory management inside GCC before using `PLUGIN_GGC_MARKING` or `PLUGIN_REGISTER_GGC_ROOTS`.

23.5 Giving information about a plugin

A plugin should give some information to the user about itself. This uses the following structure:

```
struct plugin_info
{
  const char *version;
  const char *help;
};
```

Such a structure is passed as the `user_data` by the plugin's init routine using `register_callback` with the `PLUGIN_INFO` pseudo-event and a null callback.

23.6 Registering custom attributes or pragmas

For analysis (or other) purposes it is useful to be able to add custom attributes or pragmas.

The `PLUGIN_ATTRIBUTES` callback is called during attribute registration. Use the `register_attribute` function to register custom attributes.

```
    /* Attribute handler callback */
    static tree
    handle_user_attribute (tree *node, tree name, tree args,
```

```
                              int flags, bool *no_add_attrs)
{
  return NULL_TREE;
}

/* Attribute definition */
static struct attribute_spec user_attr =
  { "user", 1, 1, false,  false, false, handle_user_attribute, false };

/* Plugin callback called during attribute registration.
Registered with register_callback (plugin_name, PLUGIN_ATTRIBUTES, register_attributes, NULL)
*/
static void
register_attributes (void *event_data, void *data)
{
  warning (0, G_("Callback to register attributes"));
  register_attribute (&user_attr);
}
```

The *PLUGIN_PRAGMAS* callback is called once during pragmas registration. Use the `c_register_pragma`, `c_register_pragma_with_data`, `c_register_pragma_with_expansion`, `c_register_pragma_with_expansion_and_data` functions to register custom pragmas and their handlers (which often want to call `pragma_lex`) from 'c-family/c-pragma.h'.

```
    /* Plugin callback called during pragmas registration. Registered with
        register_callback (plugin_name, PLUGIN_PRAGMAS,
                          register_my_pragma, NULL);
    */
    static void
    register_my_pragma (void *event_data, void *data)
    {
      warning (0, G_("Callback to register pragmas"));
      c_register_pragma ("GCCPLUGIN", "sayhello", handle_pragma_sayhello);
    }
```

It is suggested to pass `"GCCPLUGIN"` (or a short name identifying your plugin) as the "space" argument of your pragma.

Pragmas registered with `c_register_pragma_with_expansion` or `c_register_pragma_with_expansion_and_data` support preprocessor expansions. For example:

```
    #define NUMBER 10
    #pragma GCCPLUGIN foothreshold (NUMBER)
```

23.7 Recording information about pass execution

The event PLUGIN_PASS_EXECUTION passes the pointer to the executed pass (the same as current_pass) as `gcc_data` to the callback. You can also inspect cfun to find out about which function this pass is executed for. Note that this event will only be invoked if the gate check (if applicable, modified by PLUGIN_OVERRIDE_GATE) succeeds. You can use other hooks, like PLUGIN_ALL_PASSES_START, PLUGIN_ALL_PASSES_END, PLUGIN_ALL_IPA_PASSES_START, PLUGIN_ALL_IPA_PASSES_END, PLUGIN_EARLY_GIMPLE_PASSES_START, and/or PLUGIN_EARLY_GIMPLE_PASSES_END to manipulate global state in your plugin(s) in order to get context for the pass execution.

23.8 Controlling which passes are being run

After the original gate function for a pass is called, its result - the gate status - is stored as an integer. Then the event `PLUGIN_OVERRIDE_GATE` is invoked, with a pointer to the gate status in the `gcc_data` parameter to the callback function. A nonzero value of the gate status means that the pass is to be executed. You can both read and write the gate status via the passed pointer.

23.9 Keeping track of available passes

When your plugin is loaded, you can inspect the various pass lists to determine what passes are available. However, other plugins might add new passes. Also, future changes to GCC might cause generic passes to be added after plugin loading. When a pass is first added to one of the pass lists, the event `PLUGIN_NEW_PASS` is invoked, with the callback parameter `gcc_data` pointing to the new pass.

23.10 Building GCC plugins

If plugins are enabled, GCC installs the headers needed to build a plugin (somewhere in the installation tree, e.g. under '/usr/local'). In particular a 'plugin/include' directory is installed, containing all the header files needed to build plugins.

On most systems, you can query this `plugin` directory by invoking gcc -print-file-name=plugin (replace if needed `gcc` with the appropriate program path).

Inside plugins, this `plugin` directory name can be queried by calling `default_plugin_dir_name ()`.

Plugins may know, when they are compiled, the GCC version for which 'plugin-version.h' is provided. The constant macros GCCPLUGIN_VERSION_MAJOR, GCCPLUGIN_VERSION_MINOR, GCCPLUGIN_VERSION_PATCHLEVEL, GCCPLUGIN_VERSION are integer numbers, so a plugin could ensure it is built for GCC 4.7 with

```
#if GCCPLUGIN_VERSION != 4007
#error this GCC plugin is for GCC 4.7
#endif
```

The following GNU Makefile excerpt shows how to build a simple plugin:

```
HOST_GCC=g++
TARGET_GCC=gcc
PLUGIN_SOURCE_FILES= plugin1.c plugin2.cc
GCCPLUGINS_DIR:= $(shell $(TARGET_GCC) -print-file-name=plugin)
CXXFLAGS+= -I$(GCCPLUGINS_DIR)/include -fPIC -fno-rtti -O2

plugin.so: $(PLUGIN_SOURCE_FILES)
    $(HOST_GCC) -shared $(CXXFLAGS) $^ -o $@
```

A single source file plugin may be built with g++ -I`gcc -print-file-name=plugin`/include -fPIC -shared -fno-rtti -O2 plugin.c -o plugin.so, using backquote shell syntax to query the 'plugin' directory.

When a plugin needs to use `gengtype`, be sure that both 'gengtype' and 'gtype.state' have the same version as the GCC for which the plugin is built.

24 Link Time Optimization

Link Time Optimization (LTO) gives GCC the capability of dumping its internal representation (GIMPLE) to disk, so that all the different compilation units that make up a single executable can be optimized as a single module. This expands the scope of inter-procedural optimizations to encompass the whole program (or, rather, everything that is visible at link time).

24.1 Design Overview

Link time optimization is implemented as a GCC front end for a bytecode representation of GIMPLE that is emitted in special sections of .o files. Currently, LTO support is enabled in most ELF-based systems, as well as darwin, cygwin and mingw systems.

Since GIMPLE bytecode is saved alongside final object code, object files generated with LTO support are larger than regular object files. This "fat" object format makes it easy to integrate LTO into existing build systems, as one can, for instance, produce archives of the files. Additionally, one might be able to ship one set of fat objects which could be used both for development and the production of optimized builds. A, perhaps surprising, side effect of this feature is that any mistake in the toolchain that leads to LTO information not being used (e.g. an older libtool calling ld directly). This is both an advantage, as the system is more robust, and a disadvantage, as the user is not informed that the optimization has been disabled.

The current implementation only produces "fat" objects, effectively doubling compilation time and increasing file sizes up to 5x the original size. This hides the problem that some tools, such as ar and nm, need to understand symbol tables of LTO sections. These tools were extended to use the plugin infrastructure, and with these problems solved, GCC will also support "slim" objects consisting of the intermediate code alone.

At the highest level, LTO splits the compiler in two. The first half (the "writer") produces a streaming representation of all the internal data structures needed to optimize and generate code. This includes declarations, types, the callgraph and the GIMPLE representation of function bodies.

When '-flto' is given during compilation of a source file, the pass manager executes all the passes in all_lto_gen_passes. Currently, this phase is composed of two IPA passes:

- pass_ipa_lto_gimple_out This pass executes the function lto_output in 'lto-streamer-out.c', which traverses the call graph encoding every reachable declaration, type and function. This generates a memory representation of all the file sections described below.

- pass_ipa_lto_finish_out This pass executes the function produce_asm_for_decls in 'lto-streamer-out.c', which takes the memory image built in the previous pass and encodes it in the corresponding ELF file sections.

The second half of LTO support is the "reader". This is implemented as the GCC front end 'lto1' in 'lto/lto.c'. When 'collect2' detects a link set of .o/.a files with LTO information and the '-flto' is enabled, it invokes 'lto1' which reads the set of files and aggregates them into a single translation unit for optimization. The main entry point for the reader is 'lto/lto.c':lto_main.

24.1.1 LTO modes of operation

One of the main goals of the GCC link-time infrastructure was to allow effective compilation of large programs. For this reason GCC implements two link-time compilation modes.

1. *LTO mode*, in which the whole program is read into the compiler at link-time and optimized in a similar way as if it were a single source-level compilation unit.

2. *WHOPR or partitioned mode*, designed to utilize multiple CPUs and/or a distributed compilation environment to quickly link large applications. WHOPR stands for WHOle Program optimizeR (not to be confused with the semantics of '-fwhole-program'). It partitions the aggregated callgraph from many different .o files and distributes the compilation of the sub-graphs to different CPUs.

   Note that distributed compilation is not implemented yet, but since the parallelism is facilitated via generating a Makefile, it would be easy to implement.

WHOPR splits LTO into three main stages:

1. Local generation (LGEN) This stage executes in parallel. Every file in the program is compiled into the intermediate language and packaged together with the local callgraph and summary information. This stage is the same for both the LTO and WHOPR compilation mode.

2. Whole Program Analysis (WPA) WPA is performed sequentially. The global call-graph is generated, and a global analysis procedure makes transformation decisions. The global call-graph is partitioned to facilitate parallel optimization during phase 3. The results of the WPA stage are stored into new object files which contain the partitions of program expressed in the intermediate language and the optimization decisions.

3. Local transformations (LTRANS) This stage executes in parallel. All the decisions made during phase 2 are implemented locally in each partitioned object file, and the final object code is generated. Optimizations which cannot be decided efficiently during the phase 2 may be performed on the local call-graph partitions.

WHOPR can be seen as an extension of the usual LTO mode of compilation. In LTO, WPA and LTRANS are executed within a single execution of the compiler, after the whole program has been read into memory.

When compiling in WHOPR mode, the callgraph is partitioned during the WPA stage. The whole program is split into a given number of partitions of roughly the same size. The compiler tries to minimize the number of references which cross partition boundaries. The main advantage of WHOPR is to allow the parallel execution of LTRANS stages, which are the most time-consuming part of the compilation process. Additionally, it avoids the need to load the whole program into memory.

24.2 LTO file sections

LTO information is stored in several ELF sections inside object files. Data structures and enum codes for sections are defined in 'lto-streamer.h'.

These sections are emitted from 'lto-streamer-out.c' and mapped in all at once from 'lto/lto.c':lto_file_read. The individual functions dealing with the reading/writing of each section are described below.

- Command line options (`.gnu.lto_.opts`)

  This section contains the command line options used to generate the object files. This is used at link time to determine the optimization level and other settings when they are not explicitly specified at the linker command line.

  Currently, GCC does not support combining LTO object files compiled with different set of the command line options into a single binary. At link time, the options given on the command line and the options saved on all the files in a link-time set are applied globally. No attempt is made at validating the combination of flags (other than the usual validation done by option processing). This is implemented in '`lto/lto.c`':`lto_read_all_file_options`.

- Symbol table (`.gnu.lto_.symtab`)

  This table replaces the ELF symbol table for functions and variables represented in the LTO IL. Symbols used and exported by the optimized assembly code of "fat" objects might not match the ones used and exported by the intermediate code. This table is necessary because the intermediate code is less optimized and thus requires a separate symbol table.

  Additionally, the binary code in the "fat" object will lack a call to a function, since the call was optimized out at compilation time after the intermediate language was streamed out. In some special cases, the same optimization may not happen during link-time optimization. This would lead to an undefined symbol if only one symbol table was used.

  The symbol table is emitted in '`lto-streamer-out.c`':`produce_symtab`.

- Global declarations and types (`.gnu.lto_.decls`)

  This section contains an intermediate language dump of all declarations and types required to represent the callgraph, static variables and top-level debug info.

  The contents of this section are emitted in '`lto-streamer-out.c`':`produce_asm_for_decls`. Types and symbols are emitted in a topological order that preserves the sharing of pointers when the file is read back in ('`lto.c`':`read_cgraph_and_symbols`).

- The callgraph (`.gnu.lto_.cgraph`)

  This section contains the basic data structure used by the GCC inter-procedural optimization infrastructure. This section stores an annotated multi-graph which represents the functions and call sites as well as the variables, aliases and top-level **asm** statements.

  This section is emitted in '`lto-streamer-out.c`':`output_cgraph` and read in '`lto-cgraph.c`':`input_cgraph`.

- IPA references (`.gnu.lto_.refs`)

  This section contains references between function and static variables. It is emitted by '`lto-cgraph.c`':`output_refs` and read by '`lto-cgraph.c`':`input_refs`.

- Function bodies (`.gnu.lto_.function_body.<name>`)

  This section contains function bodies in the intermediate language representation. Every function body is in a separate section to allow copying of the section independently to different object files or reading the function on demand.

  Functions are emitted in '`lto-streamer-out.c`':`output_function` and read in '`lto-streamer-in.c`':`input_function`.

- Static variable initializers (`.gnu.lto_.vars`)

  This section contains all the symbols in the global variable pool. It is emitted by `'lto-cgraph.c':output_varpool` and read in `'lto-cgraph.c':input_cgraph`.

- Summaries and optimization summaries used by IPA passes (`.gnu.lto_.<xxx>`, where `<xxx>` is one of `jmpfuncs`, `pureconst` or `reference`)

  These sections are used by IPA passes that need to emit summary information during LTO generation to be read and aggregated at link time. Each pass is responsible for implementing two pass manager hooks: one for writing the summary and another for reading it in. The format of these sections is entirely up to each individual pass. The only requirement is that the writer and reader hooks agree on the format.

24.3 Using summary information in IPA passes

Programs are represented internally as a *callgraph* (a multi-graph where nodes are functions and edges are call sites) and a *varpool* (a list of static and external variables in the program).

The inter-procedural optimization is organized as a sequence of individual passes, which operate on the callgraph and the varpool. To make the implementation of WHOPR possible, every inter-procedural optimization pass is split into several stages that are executed at different times during WHOPR compilation:

- LGEN time

  1. *Generate summary* (`generate_summary` in `struct ipa_opt_pass_d`). This stage analyzes every function body and variable initializer is examined and stores relevant information into a pass-specific data structure.

  2. *Write summary* (`write_summary` in `struct ipa_opt_pass_d`). This stage writes all the pass-specific information generated by `generate_summary`. Summaries go into their own `LTO_section_*` sections that have to be declared in `'lto-streamer.h':enum lto_section_type`. A new section is created by calling `create_output_block` and data can be written using the `lto_output_*` routines.

- WPA time

  1. *Read summary* (`read_summary` in `struct ipa_opt_pass_d`). This stage reads all the pass-specific information in exactly the same order that it was written by `write_summary`.

  2. *Execute* (`execute` in `struct opt_pass`). This performs inter-procedural propagation. This must be done without actual access to the individual function bodies or variable initializers. Typically, this results in a transitive closure operation over the summary information of all the nodes in the callgraph.

  3. *Write optimization summary* (`write_optimization_summary` in `struct ipa_opt_pass_d`). This writes the result of the inter-procedural propagation into the object file. This can use the same data structures and helper routines used in `write_summary`.

- LTRANS time

  1. *Read optimization summary* (`read_optimization_summary` in `struct ipa_opt_pass_d`). The counterpart to `write_optimization_summary`. This reads the interprocedural optimization decisions in exactly the same format emitted by `write_optimization_summary`.

2. *Transform* (`function_transform` and `variable_transform` in `struct ipa_opt_pass_d`). The actual function bodies and variable initializers are updated based on the information passed down from the *Execute* stage.

The implementation of the inter-procedural passes are shared between LTO, WHOPR and classic non-LTO compilation.

- During the traditional file-by-file mode every pass executes its own *Generate summary*, *Execute*, and *Transform* stages within the single execution context of the compiler.

- In LTO compilation mode, every pass uses *Generate summary* and *Write summary* stages at compilation time, while the *Read summary*, *Execute*, and *Transform* stages are executed at link time.

- In WHOPR mode all stages are used.

To simplify development, the GCC pass manager differentiates between normal inter-procedural passes and small inter-procedural passes. A *small inter-procedural pass* (`SIMPLE_IPA_PASS`) is a pass that does everything at once and thus it can not be executed during WPA in WHOPR mode. It defines only the *Execute* stage and during this stage it accesses and modifies the function bodies. Such passes are useful for optimization at LGEN or LTRANS time and are used, for example, to implement early optimization before writing object files. The simple inter-procedural passes can also be used for easier prototyping and development of a new inter-procedural pass.

24.3.1 Virtual clones

One of the main challenges of introducing the WHOPR compilation mode was addressing the interactions between optimization passes. In LTO compilation mode, the passes are executed in a sequence, each of which consists of analysis (or *Generate summary*), propagation (or *Execute*) and *Transform* stages. Once the work of one pass is finished, the next pass sees the updated program representation and can execute. This makes the individual passes dependent on each other.

In WHOPR mode all passes first execute their *Generate summary* stage. Then summary writing marks the end of the LGEN stage. At WPA time, the summaries are read back into memory and all passes run the *Execute* stage. Optimization summaries are streamed and sent to LTRANS, where all the passes execute the *Transform* stage.

Most optimization passes split naturally into analysis, propagation and transformation stages. But some do not. The main problem arises when one pass performs changes and the following pass gets confused by seeing different callgraphs between the *Transform* stage and the *Generate summary* or *Execute* stage. This means that the passes are required to communicate their decisions with each other.

To facilitate this communication, the GCC callgraph infrastructure implements *virtual clones*, a method of representing the changes performed by the optimization passes in the callgraph without needing to update function bodies.

A *virtual clone* in the callgraph is a function that has no associated body, just a description of how to create its body based on a different function (which itself may be a virtual clone).

The description of function modifications includes adjustments to the function's signature (which allows, for example, removing or adding function arguments), substitutions to perform on the function body, and, for inlined functions, a pointer to the function that it will be inlined into.

It is also possible to redirect any edge of the callgraph from a function to its virtual clone. This implies updating of the call site to adjust for the new function signature.

Most of the transformations performed by inter-procedural optimizations can be represented via virtual clones. For instance, a constant propagation pass can produce a virtual clone of the function which replaces one of its arguments by a constant. The inliner can represent its decisions by producing a clone of a function whose body will be later integrated into a given function.

Using *virtual clones*, the program can be easily updated during the *Execute* stage, solving most of pass interactions problems that would otherwise occur during *Transform*.

Virtual clones are later materialized in the LTRANS stage and turned into real functions. Passes executed after the virtual clone were introduced also perform their *Transform* stage on new functions, so for a pass there is no significant difference between operating on a real function or a virtual clone introduced before its *Execute* stage.

Optimization passes then work on virtual clones introduced before their *Execute* stage as if they were real functions. The only difference is that clones are not visible during the *Generate Summary* stage.

To keep function summaries updated, the callgraph interface allows an optimizer to register a callback that is called every time a new clone is introduced as well as when the actual function or variable is generated or when a function or variable is removed. These hooks are registered in the *Generate summary* stage and allow the pass to keep its information intact until the *Execute* stage. The same hooks can also be registered during the *Execute* stage to keep the optimization summaries updated for the *Transform* stage.

24.3.2 IPA references

GCC represents IPA references in the callgraph. For a function or variable A, the *IPA reference* is a list of all locations where the address of A is taken and, when A is a variable, a list of all direct stores and reads to/from A. References represent an oriented multi-graph on the union of nodes of the callgraph and the varpool. See 'ipa-reference.c':ipa_reference_write_optimization_summary and 'ipa-reference.c':ipa_reference_read_optimization_summary for details.

24.3.3 Jump functions

Suppose that an optimization pass sees a function A and it knows the values of (some of) its arguments. The *jump function* describes the value of a parameter of a given function call in function A based on this knowledge.

Jump functions are used by several optimizations, such as the inter-procedural constant propagation pass and the devirtualization pass. The inliner also uses jump functions to perform inlining of callbacks.

24.4 Whole program assumptions, linker plugin and symbol visibilities

Link-time optimization gives relatively minor benefits when used alone. The problem is that propagation of inter-procedural information does not work well across functions and variables that are called or referenced by other compilation units (such as from a dynamically linked library). We say that such functions and variables are *externally visible*.

To make the situation even more difficult, many applications organize themselves as a set of shared libraries, and the default ELF visibility rules allow one to overwrite any externally visible symbol with a different symbol at runtime. This basically disables any optimizations across such functions and variables, because the compiler cannot be sure that the function body it is seeing is the same function body that will be used at runtime. Any function or variable not declared `static` in the sources degrades the quality of inter-procedural optimization.

To avoid this problem the compiler must assume that it sees the whole program when doing link-time optimization. Strictly speaking, the whole program is rarely visible even at link-time. Standard system libraries are usually linked dynamically or not provided with the link-time information. In GCC, the whole program option ('`-fwhole-program`') asserts that every function and variable defined in the current compilation unit is static, except for function `main` (note: at link time, the current unit is the union of all objects compiled with LTO). Since some functions and variables need to be referenced externally, for example by another DSO or from an assembler file, GCC also provides the function and variable attribute `externally_visible` which can be used to disable the effect of '`-fwhole-program`' on a specific symbol.

The whole program mode assumptions are slightly more complex in C++, where inline functions in headers are put into *COMDAT* sections. COMDAT function and variables can be defined by multiple object files and their bodies are unified at link-time and dynamic link-time. COMDAT functions are changed to local only when their address is not taken and thus un-sharing them with a library is not harmful. COMDAT variables always remain externally visible, however for readonly variables it is assumed that their initializers cannot be overwritten by a different value.

GCC provides the function and variable attribute `visibility` that can be used to specify the visibility of externally visible symbols (or alternatively an '`-fdefault-visibility`' command line option). ELF defines the `default`, `protected`, `hidden` and `internal` visibilities.

The most commonly used is visibility is `hidden`. It specifies that the symbol cannot be referenced from outside of the current shared library. Unfortunately, this information cannot be used directly by the link-time optimization in the compiler since the whole shared library also might contain non-LTO objects and those are not visible to the compiler.

GCC solves this problem using linker plugins. A *linker plugin* is an interface to the linker that allows an external program to claim the ownership of a given object file. The linker then performs the linking procedure by querying the plugin about the symbol table of the claimed objects and once the linking decisions are complete, the plugin is allowed to provide the final object file before the actual linking is made. The linker plugin obtains the symbol resolution information which specifies which symbols provided by the claimed objects are bound from the rest of a binary being linked.

GCC is designed to be independent of the rest of the toolchain and aims to support linkers without plugin support. For this reason it does not use the linker plugin by default. Instead, the object files are examined by `collect2` before being passed to the linker and objects found to have LTO sections are passed to `lto1` first. This mode does not work for library archives.

The decision on what object files from the archive are needed depends on the actual linking and thus GCC would have to implement the linker itself. The resolution information is missing too and thus GCC needs to make an educated guess based on '-fwhole-program'. Without the linker plugin GCC also assumes that symbols are declared hidden and not referred by non-LTO code by default.

24.5 Internal flags controlling lto1

The following flags are passed into lto1 and are not meant to be used directly from the command line.

- -fwpa This option runs the serial part of the link-time optimizer performing the inter-procedural propagation (WPA mode). The compiler reads in summary information from all inputs and performs an analysis based on summary information only. It generates object files for subsequent runs of the link-time optimizer where individual object files are optimized using both summary information from the WPA mode and the actual function bodies. It then drives the LTRANS phase.

- -fltrans This option runs the link-time optimizer in the local-transformation (LTRANS) mode, which reads in output from a previous run of the LTO in WPA mode. In the LTRANS mode, LTO optimizes an object and produces the final assembly.

- -fltrans-output-list=file This option specifies a file to which the names of LTRANS output files are written. This option is only meaningful in conjunction with '-fwpa'.

- -fresolution=file This option specifies the linker resolution file. This option is only meaningful in conjunction with '-fwpa' and as option to pass through to the LTO linker plugin.

25 Match and Simplify

The GIMPLE and GENERIC pattern matching project match-and-simplify tries to address several issues.

1. unify expression simplifications currently spread and duplicated over separate files like fold-const.c, gimple-fold.c and builtins.c

2. allow for a cheap way to implement building and simplifying non-trivial GIMPLE expressions, avoiding the need to go through building and simplifying GENERIC via fold_buildN and then gimplifying via force_gimple_operand

To address these the project introduces a simple domain specific language to write expression simplifications from which code targeting GIMPLE and GENERIC is auto-generated. The GENERIC variant follows the fold_buildN API while for the GIMPLE variant and to address 2) new APIs are introduced.

25.1 GIMPLE API

tree gimple_simplify (*enum tree_code, tree, tree, gimple_seq*   [GIMPLE function]
        *, tree (*)(tree))

tree gimple_simplify (*enum tree_code, tree, tree, tree,*   [GIMPLE function]
        gimple_seq *, tree (*)(tree))

tree gimple_simplify (*enum tree_code, tree, tree, tree, tree,*   [GIMPLE function]
        gimple_seq *, tree (*)(tree))

tree gimple_simplify (*enum built_in_function, tree, tree,*   [GIMPLE function]
        gimple_seq *, tree (*)(tree))

tree gimple_simplify (*enum built_in_function, tree, tree,*   [GIMPLE function]
        tree, gimple_seq *, tree (*)(tree))

tree gimple_simplify (*enum built_in_function, tree, tree,*   [GIMPLE function]
        tree, tree, gimple_seq *, tree (*)(tree))

    The main GIMPLE API entry to the expression simplifications mimicing that of the GENERIC fold_{unary,binary,ternary} functions.

thus providing n-ary overloads for operation or function. The additional arguments are a gimple_seq where built statements are inserted on (if NULL then simplifications requiring new statements are not performed) and a valueization hook that can be used to tie simplifications to a SSA lattice.

In addition to those APIs fold_stmt is overloaded with a valueization hook:

fold_stmt (gimple_stmt_iterator *, tree (*)(tree));   [bool]

    Ontop of these a fold_buildN-like API for GIMPLE is introduced:

tree gimple_build (*gimple_seq *, location_t, enum tree_code,*   [GIMPLE function]
        tree, tree, tree (*valueize) (tree) = NULL);

tree gimple_build (*gimple_seq *, location_t, enum tree_code,*   [GIMPLE function]
        tree, tree, tree, tree (*valueize) (tree) = NULL);

tree gimple_build (*gimple_seq *, location_t, enum tree_code,*   [GIMPLE function]
        tree, tree, tree, tree, tree (*valueize) (tree) = NULL);

`tree gimple_build` (*gimple_seq* *, *location_t, enum*   [GIMPLE function]
        built_in_function, tree, tree, tree (*valueize) (*tree*) = *NULL*);
`tree gimple_build` (*gimple_seq* *, *location_t, enum*   [GIMPLE function]
        built_in_function, tree, tree, tree, tree (*valueize) (*tree*) = *NULL*);
`tree gimple_build` (*gimple_seq* *, *location_t, enum*   [GIMPLE function]
        built_in_function, tree, tree, tree, tree, tree (*valueize) (*tree*) = *NULL*);
`tree gimple_convert` (*gimple_seq* *, *location_t, tree, tree*);   [GIMPLE function]

which is supposed to replace `force_gimple_operand (fold_buildN (...), ...)` and calls to `fold_convert`. Overloads without the `location_t` argument exist. Built statements are inserted on the provided sequence and simplification is performed using the optional valueization hook.

25.2 The Language

The language to write expression simplifications in resembles other domain-specific languages GCC uses. Thus it is lispy. Lets start with an example from the match.pd file:

```
(simplify
 (bit_and @0 integer_all_onesp)
 @0)
```

This example contains all required parts of an expression simplification. A simplification is wrapped inside a (`simplify ...`) expression. That contains at least two operands - an expression that is matched with the GIMPLE or GENERIC IL and a replacement expression that is returned if the match was successful.

Expressions have an operator ID, `bit_and` in this case. Expressions can be lower-case tree codes with `_expr` stripped off or builtin function code names in all-caps, like `BUILT_IN_SQRT`.

`@n` denotes a so-called capture. It captures the operand and lets you refer to it in other places of the match-and-simplify. In the above example it is refered to in the replacement expression. Captures are `@` followed by a number or an identifier.

```
(simplify
 (bit_xor @0 @0)
 { build_zero_cst (type); })
```

In this example `@0` is mentioned twice which constrains the matched expression to have two equal operands. Usually matches are constraint to equal types. If operands may be constants and conversions are involved matching by value might be preferred in which case use `@@0` to denote a by value match and the specific operand you want to refer to in the result part. This example also introduces operands written in C code. These can be used in the expression replacements and are supposed to evaluate to a tree node which has to be a valid GIMPLE operand (so you cannot generate expressions in C code).

```
(simplify
 (trunc_mod integer_zerop@0 @1)
 (if (!integer_zerop (@1))
  @0))
```

Here `@0` captures the first operand of the trunc_mod expression which is also predicated with `integer_zerop`. Expression operands may be either expressions, predicates or captures. Captures can be unconstrained or capture expresions or predicates.

This example introduces an optional operand of simplify, the if-expression. This condition is evaluated after the expression matched in the IL and is required to evaluate to true to

enable the replacement expression in the second operand position. The expression operand
of the `if` is a standard C expression which may contain references to captures. The `if` has
an optional third operand which may contain the replacement expression that is enabled
when the condition evaluates to false.

A `if` expression can be used to specify a common condition for multiple simplify patterns,
avoiding the need to repeat that multiple times:

```
(if (!TYPE_SATURATING (type)
     && !FLOAT_TYPE_P (type) && !FIXED_POINT_TYPE_P (type))
 (simplify
  (minus (plus @0 @1) @0)
  @1)
 (simplify
  (minus (minus @0 @1) @0)
  (negate @1)))
```

Note that `if`s in outer position do not have the optional else clause but instead have
multiple then clauses.

Ifs can be nested.

There exists a `switch` expression which can be used to chain conditions avoiding nesting
`if`s too much:

```
(simplify
 (simple_comparison @0 REAL_CST@1)
 (switch
  /* a CMP (-0) -> a CMP 0  */
  (if (REAL_VALUE_MINUS_ZERO (TREE_REAL_CST (@1)))
   (cmp @0 { build_real (TREE_TYPE (@1), dconst0); }))
  /* x != NaN is always true, other ops are always false.  */
  (if (REAL_VALUE_ISNAN (TREE_REAL_CST (@1))
       && ! HONOR_SNANS (@1))
   { constant_boolean_node (cmp == NE_EXPR, type); })))
```

Is equal to

```
(simplify
 (simple_comparison @0 REAL_CST@1)
 (switch
  /* a CMP (-0) -> a CMP 0  */
  (if (REAL_VALUE_MINUS_ZERO (TREE_REAL_CST (@1)))
   (cmp @0 { build_real (TREE_TYPE (@1), dconst0); })
   /* x != NaN is always true, other ops are always false.  */
   (if (REAL_VALUE_ISNAN (TREE_REAL_CST (@1))
        && ! HONOR_SNANS (@1))
    { constant_boolean_node (cmp == NE_EXPR, type); }))))
```

which has the second `if` in the else operand of the first. The `switch` expression takes
`if` expressions as operands (which may not have else clauses) and as a last operand a
replacement expression which should be enabled by default if no other condition evaluated
to true.

Captures can also be used for capturing results of sub-expressions.

```
#if GIMPLE
(simplify
 (pointer_plus (addr@2 @0) INTEGER_CST_P@1)
 (if (is_gimple_min_invariant (@2)))
 {
   HOST_WIDE_INT off;
```

```
    tree base = get_addr_base_and_unit_offset (@0, &off);
    off += tree_to_uhwi (@1);
    /* Now with that we should be able to simply write
       (addr (mem_ref (addr @base) (plus @off @1))) */
    build1 (ADDR_EXPR, type,
             build2 (MEM_REF, TREE_TYPE (TREE_TYPE (@2)),
                     build_fold_addr_expr (base),
                     build_int_cst (ptr_type_node, off)));
  })
#endif
```

In the above example, @2 captures the result of the expression (addr @0). For outermost expression only its type can be captured, and the keyword type is reserved for this purpose. The above example also gives a way to conditionalize patterns to only apply to GIMPLE or GENERIC by means of using the pre-defined preprocessor macros GIMPLE and GENERIC and using preprocessor directives.

```
(simplify
 (bit_and:c integral_op_p@0 (bit_ior:c (bit_not @0) @1))
 (bit_and @1 @0))
```

Here we introduce flags on match expressions. The flag used above, c, denotes that the expression should be also matched commutated. Thus the above match expression is really the following four match expressions:

```
(bit_and integral_op_p@0 (bit_ior (bit_not @0) @1))
(bit_and (bit_ior (bit_not @0) @1) integral_op_p@0)
(bit_and integral_op_p@0 (bit_ior @1 (bit_not @0)))
(bit_and (bit_ior @1 (bit_not @0)) integral_op_p@0)
```

Usual canonicalizations you know from GENERIC expressions are applied before matching, so for example constant operands always come second in commutative expressions.

The second supported flag is s which tells the code generator to fail the pattern if the expression marked with s does have more than one use. For example in

```
(simplify
 (pointer_plus (pointer_plus:s @0 @1) @3)
 (pointer_plus @0 (plus @1 @3)))
```

this avoids the association if (pointer_plus @0 @1) is used outside of the matched expression and thus it would stay live and not trivially removed by dead code elimination.

More features exist to avoid too much repetition.

```
(for op (plus pointer_plus minus bit_ior bit_xor)
 (simplify
  (op @0 integer_zerop)
  @0))
```

A for expression can be used to repeat a pattern for each operator specified, substituting op. for can be nested and a for can have multiple operators to iterate.

```
(for opa (plus minus)
     opb (minus plus)
 (for opc (plus minus)
  (simplify...
```

In this example the pattern will be repeated four times with opa, opb, opc being plus, minus, plus, plus, minus, minus, minus, plus, plus, minus, plus, minus.

To avoid repeating operator lists in for you can name them via

```
(define_operator_list pmm plus minus mult)
```

and use them in `for` operator lists where they get expanded.

```
(for opa (pmm trunc_div)
 (simplify...
```

So this example iterates over `plus`, `minus`, `mult` and `trunc_div`.

Using operator lists can also remove the need to explicitly write a `for`. All operator list uses that appear in a `simplify` or `match` pattern in operator positions will implicitly be added to a new `for`. For example

```
(define_operator_list SQRT BUILT_IN_SQRTF BUILT_IN_SQRT BUILT_IN_SQRTL)
(define_operator_list POW BUILT_IN_POWF BUILT_IN_POW BUILT_IN_POWL)
(simplify
 (SQRT (POW @0 @1))
 (POW (abs @0) (mult @1 { built_real (TREE_TYPE (@1), dconsthalf); })))
```

is the same as

```
(for SQRT (BUILT_IN_SQRTF BUILT_IN_SQRT BUILT_IN_SQRTL)
     POW (BUILT_IN_POWF BUILT_IN_POW BUILT_IN_POWL)
 (simplify
  (SQRT (POW @0 @1))
  (POW (abs @0) (mult @1 { built_real (TREE_TYPE (@1), dconsthalf); }))))
```

`for`s and operator lists can include the special identifier `null` that matches nothing and can never be generated. This can be used to pad an operator list so that it has a standard form, even if there isn't a suitable operator for every form.

Another building block are `with` expressions in the result expression which nest the generated code in a new C block followed by its argument:

```
(simplify
 (convert (mult @0 @1))
 (with { tree utype = unsigned_type_for (type); }
 (convert (mult (convert:utype @0) (convert:utype @1)))))
```

This allows code nested in the `with` to refer to the declared variables. In the above case we use the feature to specify the type of a generated expression with the `:type` syntax where `type` needs to be an identifier that refers to the desired type. Usually the types of the generated result expressions are determined from the context, but sometimes like in the above case it is required that you specify them explicitly.

As intermediate conversions are often optional there is a way to avoid the need to repeat patterns both with and without such conversions. Namely you can mark a conversion as being optional with a ?:

```
(simplify
 (eq (convert@0 @1) (convert? @2))
 (eq @1 (convert @2)))
```

which will match both `(eq (convert @1) (convert @2))` and `(eq (convert @1) @2)`. The optional converts are supposed to be all either present or not, thus `(eq (convert? @1) (convert? @2))` will result in two patterns only. If you want to match all four combinations you have access to two additional conditional converts as in `(eq (convert1? @1) (convert2? @2))`.

Predicates available from the GCC middle-end need to be made available explicitly via `define_predicates`:

```
(define_predicates
 integer_onep integer_zerop integer_all_onesp)
```

You can also define predicates using the pattern matching language and the `match` form:

```
(match negate_expr_p
 INTEGER_CST
 (if (TYPE_OVERFLOW_WRAPS (type)
      || may_negate_without_overflow_p (t))))
(match negate_expr_p
 (negate @0))
```

This shows that for `match` expressions there is t available which captures the outermost expression (something not possible in the `simplify` context). As you can see `match` has an identifier as first operand which is how you refer to the predicate in patterns. Multiple `match` for the same identifier add additional cases where the predicate matches.

Predicates can also match an expression in which case you need to provide a template specifying the identifier and where to get its operands from:

```
(match (logical_inverted_value @0)
 (eq @0 integer_zerop))
(match (logical_inverted_value @0)
 (bit_not truth_valued_p@0))
```

You can use the above predicate like

```
(simplify
 (bit_and @0 (logical_inverted_value @0))
 { build_zero_cst (type); })
```

Which will match a bitwise and of an operand with its logical inverted value.

Funding Free Software

If you want to have more free software a few years from now, it makes sense for you to help encourage people to contribute funds for its development. The most effective approach known is to encourage commercial redistributors to donate.

Users of free software systems can boost the pace of development by encouraging for-a-fee distributors to donate part of their selling price to free software developers—the Free Software Foundation, and others.

The way to convince distributors to do this is to demand it and expect it from them. So when you compare distributors, judge them partly by how much they give to free software development. Show distributors they must compete to be the one who gives the most.

To make this approach work, you must insist on numbers that you can compare, such as, "We will donate ten dollars to the Frobnitz project for each disk sold." Don't be satisfied with a vague promise, such as "A portion of the profits are donated," since it doesn't give a basis for comparison.

Even a precise fraction "of the profits from this disk" is not very meaningful, since creative accounting and unrelated business decisions can greatly alter what fraction of the sales price counts as profit. If the price you pay is $50, ten percent of the profit is probably less than a dollar; it might be a few cents, or nothing at all.

Some redistributors do development work themselves. This is useful too; but to keep everyone honest, you need to inquire how much they do, and what kind. Some kinds of development make much more long-term difference than others. For example, maintaining a separate version of a program contributes very little; maintaining the standard version of a program for the whole community contributes much. Easy new ports contribute little, since someone else would surely do them; difficult ports such as adding a new CPU to the GNU Compiler Collection contribute more; major new features or packages contribute the most.

By establishing the idea that supporting further development is "the proper thing to do" when distributing free software for a fee, we can assure a steady flow of resources into making more free software.

The GNU Project and GNU/Linux

The GNU Project was launched in 1984 to develop a complete Unix-like operating system which is free software: the GNU system. (GNU is a recursive acronym for "GNU's Not Unix"; it is pronounced "guh-NEW".) Variants of the GNU operating system, which use the kernel Linux, are now widely used; though these systems are often referred to as "Linux", they are more accurately called GNU/Linux systems.

For more information, see:

```
http://www.gnu.org/
http://www.gnu.org/gnu/linux-and-gnu.html
```

GNU General Public License

Version 3, 29 June 2007

Copyright © 2007 Free Software Foundation, Inc. http://fsf.org/

Preamble

The GNU General Public License is a free, copyleft license for software and other kinds of works.

The licenses for most software and other practical works are designed to take away your freedom to share and change the works. By contrast, the GNU General Public License is intended to guarantee your freedom to share and change all versions of a program–to make sure it remains free software for all its users. We, the Free Software Foundation, use the GNU General Public License for most of our software; it applies also to any other work released this way by its authors. You can apply it to your programs, too.

When we speak of free software, we are referring to freedom, not price. Our General Public Licenses are designed to make sure that you have the freedom to distribute copies of free software (and charge for them if you wish), that you receive source code or can get it if you want it, that you can change the software or use pieces of it in new free programs, and that you know you can do these things.

To protect your rights, we need to prevent others from denying you these rights or asking you to surrender the rights. Therefore, you have certain responsibilities if you distribute copies of the software, or if you modify it: responsibilities to respect the freedom of others.

For example, if you distribute copies of such a program, whether gratis or for a fee, you must pass on to the recipients the same freedoms that you received. You must make sure that they, too, receive or can get the source code. And you must show them these terms so they know their rights.

Developers that use the GNU GPL protect your rights with two steps: (1) assert copyright on the software, and (2) offer you this License giving you legal permission to copy, distribute and/or modify it.

For the developers' and authors' protection, the GPL clearly explains that there is no warranty for this free software. For both users' and authors' sake, the GPL requires that modified versions be marked as changed, so that their problems will not be attributed erroneously to authors of previous versions.

Some devices are designed to deny users access to install or run modified versions of the software inside them, although the manufacturer can do so. This is fundamentally incompatible with the aim of protecting users' freedom to change the software. The systematic pattern of such abuse occurs in the area of products for individuals to use, which is precisely where it is most unacceptable. Therefore, we have designed this version of the GPL to prohibit the practice for those products. If such problems arise substantially in other domains, we stand ready to extend this provision to those domains in future versions of the GPL, as needed to protect the freedom of users.

Finally, every program is threatened constantly by software patents. States should not allow patents to restrict development and use of software on general-purpose computers, but in those that do, we wish to avoid the special danger that patents applied to a free program could make it effectively proprietary. To prevent this, the GPL assures that patents cannot be used to render the program non-free.

The precise terms and conditions for copying, distribution and modification follow.

TERMS AND CONDITIONS

0. Definitions.

   "This License" refers to version 3 of the GNU General Public License.

   "Copyright" also means copyright-like laws that apply to other kinds of works, such as semiconductor masks.

   "The Program" refers to any copyrightable work licensed under this License. Each licensee is addressed as "you". "Licensees" and "recipients" may be individuals or organizations.

   To "modify" a work means to copy from or adapt all or part of the work in a fashion requiring copyright permission, other than the making of an exact copy. The resulting work is called a "modified version" of the earlier work or a work "based on" the earlier work.

   A "covered work" means either the unmodified Program or a work based on the Program.

   To "propagate" a work means to do anything with it that, without permission, would make you directly or secondarily liable for infringement under applicable copyright law, except executing it on a computer or modifying a private copy. Propagation includes copying, distribution (with or without modification), making available to the public, and in some countries other activities as well.

   To "convey" a work means any kind of propagation that enables other parties to make or receive copies. Mere interaction with a user through a computer network, with no transfer of a copy, is not conveying.

   An interactive user interface displays "Appropriate Legal Notices" to the extent that it includes a convenient and prominently visible feature that (1) displays an appropriate copyright notice, and (2) tells the user that there is no warranty for the work (except to the extent that warranties are provided), that licensees may convey the work under this License, and how to view a copy of this License. If the interface presents a list of user commands or options, such as a menu, a prominent item in the list meets this criterion.

1. Source Code.

   The "source code" for a work means the preferred form of the work for making modifications to it. "Object code" means any non-source form of a work.

   A "Standard Interface" means an interface that either is an official standard defined by a recognized standards body, or, in the case of interfaces specified for a particular programming language, one that is widely used among developers working in that language.

The "System Libraries" of an executable work include anything, other than the work as a whole, that (a) is included in the normal form of packaging a Major Component, but which is not part of that Major Component, and (b) serves only to enable use of the work with that Major Component, or to implement a Standard Interface for which an implementation is available to the public in source code form. A "Major Component", in this context, means a major essential component (kernel, window system, and so on) of the specific operating system (if any) on which the executable work runs, or a compiler used to produce the work, or an object code interpreter used to run it.

The "Corresponding Source" for a work in object code form means all the source code needed to generate, install, and (for an executable work) run the object code and to modify the work, including scripts to control those activities. However, it does not include the work's System Libraries, or general-purpose tools or generally available free programs which are used unmodified in performing those activities but which are not part of the work. For example, Corresponding Source includes interface definition files associated with source files for the work, and the source code for shared libraries and dynamically linked subprograms that the work is specifically designed to require, such as by intimate data communication or control flow between those subprograms and other parts of the work.

The Corresponding Source need not include anything that users can regenerate automatically from other parts of the Corresponding Source.

The Corresponding Source for a work in source code form is that same work.

2. Basic Permissions.

All rights granted under this License are granted for the term of copyright on the Program, and are irrevocable provided the stated conditions are met. This License explicitly affirms your unlimited permission to run the unmodified Program. The output from running a covered work is covered by this License only if the output, given its content, constitutes a covered work. This License acknowledges your rights of fair use or other equivalent, as provided by copyright law.

You may make, run and propagate covered works that you do not convey, without conditions so long as your license otherwise remains in force. You may convey covered works to others for the sole purpose of having them make modifications exclusively for you, or provide you with facilities for running those works, provided that you comply with the terms of this License in conveying all material for which you do not control copyright. Those thus making or running the covered works for you must do so exclusively on your behalf, under your direction and control, on terms that prohibit them from making any copies of your copyrighted material outside their relationship with you.

Conveying under any other circumstances is permitted solely under the conditions stated below. Sublicensing is not allowed; section 10 makes it unnecessary.

3. Protecting Users' Legal Rights From Anti-Circumvention Law.

No covered work shall be deemed part of an effective technological measure under any applicable law fulfilling obligations under article 11 of the WIPO copyright treaty adopted on 20 December 1996, or similar laws prohibiting or restricting circumvention of such measures.

When you convey a covered work, you waive any legal power to forbid circumvention of technological measures to the extent such circumvention is effected by exercising rights under this License with respect to the covered work, and you disclaim any intention to limit operation or modification of the work as a means of enforcing, against the work's users, your or third parties' legal rights to forbid circumvention of technological measures.

4. Conveying Verbatim Copies.

You may convey verbatim copies of the Program's source code as you receive it, in any medium, provided that you conspicuously and appropriately publish on each copy an appropriate copyright notice; keep intact all notices stating that this License and any non-permissive terms added in accord with section 7 apply to the code; keep intact all notices of the absence of any warranty; and give all recipients a copy of this License along with the Program.

You may charge any price or no price for each copy that you convey, and you may offer support or warranty protection for a fee.

5. Conveying Modified Source Versions.

You may convey a work based on the Program, or the modifications to produce it from the Program, in the form of source code under the terms of section 4, provided that you also meet all of these conditions:

  a. The work must carry prominent notices stating that you modified it, and giving a relevant date.

  b. The work must carry prominent notices stating that it is released under this License and any conditions added under section 7. This requirement modifies the requirement in section 4 to "keep intact all notices".

  c. You must license the entire work, as a whole, under this License to anyone who comes into possession of a copy. This License will therefore apply, along with any applicable section 7 additional terms, to the whole of the work, and all its parts, regardless of how they are packaged. This License gives no permission to license the work in any other way, but it does not invalidate such permission if you have separately received it.

  d. If the work has interactive user interfaces, each must display Appropriate Legal Notices; however, if the Program has interactive interfaces that do not display Appropriate Legal Notices, your work need not make them do so.

A compilation of a covered work with other separate and independent works, which are not by their nature extensions of the covered work, and which are not combined with it such as to form a larger program, in or on a volume of a storage or distribution medium, is called an "aggregate" if the compilation and its resulting copyright are not used to limit the access or legal rights of the compilation's users beyond what the individual works permit. Inclusion of a covered work in an aggregate does not cause this License to apply to the other parts of the aggregate.

6. Conveying Non-Source Forms.

You may convey a covered work in object code form under the terms of sections 4 and 5, provided that you also convey the machine-readable Corresponding Source under the terms of this License, in one of these ways:

a. Convey the object code in, or embodied in, a physical product (including a physical distribution medium), accompanied by the Corresponding Source fixed on a durable physical medium customarily used for software interchange.

b. Convey the object code in, or embodied in, a physical product (including a physical distribution medium), accompanied by a written offer, valid for at least three years and valid for as long as you offer spare parts or customer support for that product model, to give anyone who possesses the object code either (1) a copy of the Corresponding Source for all the software in the product that is covered by this License, on a durable physical medium customarily used for software interchange, for a price no more than your reasonable cost of physically performing this conveying of source, or (2) access to copy the Corresponding Source from a network server at no charge.

c. Convey individual copies of the object code with a copy of the written offer to provide the Corresponding Source. This alternative is allowed only occasionally and noncommercially, and only if you received the object code with such an offer, in accord with subsection 6b.

d. Convey the object code by offering access from a designated place (gratis or for a charge), and offer equivalent access to the Corresponding Source in the same way through the same place at no further charge. You need not require recipients to copy the Corresponding Source along with the object code. If the place to copy the object code is a network server, the Corresponding Source may be on a different server (operated by you or a third party) that supports equivalent copying facilities, provided you maintain clear directions next to the object code saying where to find the Corresponding Source. Regardless of what server hosts the Corresponding Source, you remain obligated to ensure that it is available for as long as needed to satisfy these requirements.

e. Convey the object code using peer-to-peer transmission, provided you inform other peers where the object code and Corresponding Source of the work are being offered to the general public at no charge under subsection 6d.

A separable portion of the object code, whose source code is excluded from the Corresponding Source as a System Library, need not be included in conveying the object code work.

A "User Product" is either (1) a "consumer product", which means any tangible personal property which is normally used for personal, family, or household purposes, or (2) anything designed or sold for incorporation into a dwelling. In determining whether a product is a consumer product, doubtful cases shall be resolved in favor of coverage. For a particular product received by a particular user, "normally used" refers to a typical or common use of that class of product, regardless of the status of the particular user or of the way in which the particular user actually uses, or expects or is expected to use, the product. A product is a consumer product regardless of whether the product has substantial commercial, industrial or non-consumer uses, unless such uses represent the only significant mode of use of the product.

"Installation Information" for a User Product means any methods, procedures, authorization keys, or other information required to install and execute modified versions of a covered work in that User Product from a modified version of its Corresponding Source.

The information must suffice to ensure that the continued functioning of the modified object code is in no case prevented or interfered with solely because modification has been made.

If you convey an object code work under this section in, or with, or specifically for use in, a User Product, and the conveying occurs as part of a transaction in which the right of possession and use of the User Product is transferred to the recipient in perpetuity or for a fixed term (regardless of how the transaction is characterized), the Corresponding Source conveyed under this section must be accompanied by the Installation Information. But this requirement does not apply if neither you nor any third party retains the ability to install modified object code on the User Product (for example, the work has been installed in ROM).

The requirement to provide Installation Information does not include a requirement to continue to provide support service, warranty, or updates for a work that has been modified or installed by the recipient, or for the User Product in which it has been modified or installed. Access to a network may be denied when the modification itself materially and adversely affects the operation of the network or violates the rules and protocols for communication across the network.

Corresponding Source conveyed, and Installation Information provided, in accord with this section must be in a format that is publicly documented (and with an implementation available to the public in source code form), and must require no special password or key for unpacking, reading or copying.

7. Additional Terms.

"Additional permissions" are terms that supplement the terms of this License by making exceptions from one or more of its conditions. Additional permissions that are applicable to the entire Program shall be treated as though they were included in this License, to the extent that they are valid under applicable law. If additional permissions apply only to part of the Program, that part may be used separately under those permissions, but the entire Program remains governed by this License without regard to the additional permissions.

When you convey a copy of a covered work, you may at your option remove any additional permissions from that copy, or from any part of it. (Additional permissions may be written to require their own removal in certain cases when you modify the work.) You may place additional permissions on material, added by you to a covered work, for which you have or can give appropriate copyright permission.

Notwithstanding any other provision of this License, for material you add to a covered work, you may (if authorized by the copyright holders of that material) supplement the terms of this License with terms:

a. Disclaiming warranty or limiting liability differently from the terms of sections 15 and 16 of this License; or

b. Requiring preservation of specified reasonable legal notices or author attributions in that material or in the Appropriate Legal Notices displayed by works containing it; or

c. Prohibiting misrepresentation of the origin of that material, or requiring that modified versions of such material be marked in reasonable ways as different from the original version; or

    d. Limiting the use for publicity purposes of names of licensors or authors of the material; or

    e. Declining to grant rights under trademark law for use of some trade names, trademarks, or service marks; or

    f. Requiring indemnification of licensors and authors of that material by anyone who conveys the material (or modified versions of it) with contractual assumptions of liability to the recipient, for any liability that these contractual assumptions directly impose on those licensors and authors.

All other non-permissive additional terms are considered "further restrictions" within the meaning of section 10. If the Program as you received it, or any part of it, contains a notice stating that it is governed by this License along with a term that is a further restriction, you may remove that term. If a license document contains a further restriction but permits relicensing or conveying under this License, you may add to a covered work material governed by the terms of that license document, provided that the further restriction does not survive such relicensing or conveying.

If you add terms to a covered work in accord with this section, you must place, in the relevant source files, a statement of the additional terms that apply to those files, or a notice indicating where to find the applicable terms.

Additional terms, permissive or non-permissive, may be stated in the form of a separately written license, or stated as exceptions; the above requirements apply either way.

8. Termination.

You may not propagate or modify a covered work except as expressly provided under this License. Any attempt otherwise to propagate or modify it is void, and will automatically terminate your rights under this License (including any patent licenses granted under the third paragraph of section 11).

However, if you cease all violation of this License, then your license from a particular copyright holder is reinstated (a) provisionally, unless and until the copyright holder explicitly and finally terminates your license, and (b) permanently, if the copyright holder fails to notify you of the violation by some reasonable means prior to 60 days after the cessation.

Moreover, your license from a particular copyright holder is reinstated permanently if the copyright holder notifies you of the violation by some reasonable means, this is the first time you have received notice of violation of this License (for any work) from that copyright holder, and you cure the violation prior to 30 days after your receipt of the notice.

Termination of your rights under this section does not terminate the licenses of parties who have received copies or rights from you under this License. If your rights have been terminated and not permanently reinstated, you do not qualify to receive new licenses for the same material under section 10.

9. Acceptance Not Required for Having Copies.

You are not required to accept this License in order to receive or run a copy of the Program. Ancillary propagation of a covered work occurring solely as a consequence of using peer-to-peer transmission to receive a copy likewise does not require acceptance.

However, nothing other than this License grants you permission to propagate or modify any covered work. These actions infringe copyright if you do not accept this License. Therefore, by modifying or propagating a covered work, you indicate your acceptance of this License to do so.

10. Automatic Licensing of Downstream Recipients.

Each time you convey a covered work, the recipient automatically receives a license from the original licensors, to run, modify and propagate that work, subject to this License. You are not responsible for enforcing compliance by third parties with this License.

An "entity transaction" is a transaction transferring control of an organization, or substantially all assets of one, or subdividing an organization, or merging organizations. If propagation of a covered work results from an entity transaction, each party to that transaction who receives a copy of the work also receives whatever licenses to the work the party's predecessor in interest had or could give under the previous paragraph, plus a right to possession of the Corresponding Source of the work from the predecessor in interest, if the predecessor has it or can get it with reasonable efforts.

You may not impose any further restrictions on the exercise of the rights granted or affirmed under this License. For example, you may not impose a license fee, royalty, or other charge for exercise of rights granted under this License, and you may not initiate litigation (including a cross-claim or counterclaim in a lawsuit) alleging that any patent claim is infringed by making, using, selling, offering for sale, or importing the Program or any portion of it.

11. Patents.

A "contributor" is a copyright holder who authorizes use under this License of the Program or a work on which the Program is based. The work thus licensed is called the contributor's "contributor version".

A contributor's "essential patent claims" are all patent claims owned or controlled by the contributor, whether already acquired or hereafter acquired, that would be infringed by some manner, permitted by this License, of making, using, or selling its contributor version, but do not include claims that would be infringed only as a consequence of further modification of the contributor version. For purposes of this definition, "control" includes the right to grant patent sublicenses in a manner consistent with the requirements of this License.

Each contributor grants you a non-exclusive, worldwide, royalty-free patent license under the contributor's essential patent claims, to make, use, sell, offer for sale, import and otherwise run, modify and propagate the contents of its contributor version.

In the following three paragraphs, a "patent license" is any express agreement or commitment, however denominated, not to enforce a patent (such as an express permission to practice a patent or covenant not to sue for patent infringement). To "grant" such a patent license to a party means to make such an agreement or commitment not to enforce a patent against the party.

If you convey a covered work, knowingly relying on a patent license, and the Corresponding Source of the work is not available for anyone to copy, free of charge and under the terms of this License, through a publicly available network server or other readily accessible means, then you must either (1) cause the Corresponding Source to be so available, or (2) arrange to deprive yourself of the benefit of the patent license for this particular work, or (3) arrange, in a manner consistent with the requirements of this License, to extend the patent license to downstream recipients. "Knowingly relying" means you have actual knowledge that, but for the patent license, your conveying the covered work in a country, or your recipient's use of the covered work in a country, would infringe one or more identifiable patents in that country that you have reason to believe are valid.

If, pursuant to or in connection with a single transaction or arrangement, you convey, or propagate by procuring conveyance of, a covered work, and grant a patent license to some of the parties receiving the covered work authorizing them to use, propagate, modify or convey a specific copy of the covered work, then the patent license you grant is automatically extended to all recipients of the covered work and works based on it.

A patent license is "discriminatory" if it does not include within the scope of its coverage, prohibits the exercise of, or is conditioned on the non-exercise of one or more of the rights that are specifically granted under this License. You may not convey a covered work if you are a party to an arrangement with a third party that is in the business of distributing software, under which you make payment to the third party based on the extent of your activity of conveying the work, and under which the third party grants, to any of the parties who would receive the covered work from you, a discriminatory patent license (a) in connection with copies of the covered work conveyed by you (or copies made from those copies), or (b) primarily for and in connection with specific products or compilations that contain the covered work, unless you entered into that arrangement, or that patent license was granted, prior to 28 March 2007.

Nothing in this License shall be construed as excluding or limiting any implied license or other defenses to infringement that may otherwise be available to you under applicable patent law.

12. No Surrender of Others' Freedom.

If conditions are imposed on you (whether by court order, agreement or otherwise) that contradict the conditions of this License, they do not excuse you from the conditions of this License. If you cannot convey a covered work so as to satisfy simultaneously your obligations under this License and any other pertinent obligations, then as a consequence you may not convey it at all. For example, if you agree to terms that obligate you to collect a royalty for further conveying from those to whom you convey the Program, the only way you could satisfy both those terms and this License would be to refrain entirely from conveying the Program.

13. Use with the GNU Affero General Public License.

Notwithstanding any other provision of this License, you have permission to link or combine any covered work with a work licensed under version 3 of the GNU Affero General Public License into a single combined work, and to convey the resulting work. The terms of this License will continue to apply to the part which is the covered work, but the special requirements of the GNU Affero General Public License, section 13, concerning interaction through a network will apply to the combination as such.

14. Revised Versions of this License.

The Free Software Foundation may publish revised and/or new versions of the GNU General Public License from time to time. Such new versions will be similar in spirit to the present version, but may differ in detail to address new problems or concerns.

Each version is given a distinguishing version number. If the Program specifies that a certain numbered version of the GNU General Public License "or any later version" applies to it, you have the option of following the terms and conditions either of that numbered version or of any later version published by the Free Software Foundation. If the Program does not specify a version number of the GNU General Public License, you may choose any version ever published by the Free Software Foundation.

If the Program specifies that a proxy can decide which future versions of the GNU General Public License can be used, that proxy's public statement of acceptance of a version permanently authorizes you to choose that version for the Program.

Later license versions may give you additional or different permissions. However, no additional obligations are imposed on any author or copyright holder as a result of your choosing to follow a later version.

15. Disclaimer of Warranty.

THERE IS NO WARRANTY FOR THE PROGRAM, TO THE EXTENT PERMITTED BY APPLICABLE LAW. EXCEPT WHEN OTHERWISE STATED IN WRITING THE COPYRIGHT HOLDERS AND/OR OTHER PARTIES PROVIDE THE PROGRAM "AS IS" WITHOUT WARRANTY OF ANY KIND, EITHER EXPRESSED OR IMPLIED, INCLUDING, BUT NOT LIMITED TO, THE IMPLIED WARRANTIES OF MERCHANTABILITY AND FITNESS FOR A PARTICULAR PURPOSE. THE ENTIRE RISK AS TO THE QUALITY AND PERFORMANCE OF THE PROGRAM IS WITH YOU. SHOULD THE PROGRAM PROVE DEFECTIVE, YOU ASSUME THE COST OF ALL NECESSARY SERVICING, REPAIR OR CORRECTION.

16. Limitation of Liability.

IN NO EVENT UNLESS REQUIRED BY APPLICABLE LAW OR AGREED TO IN WRITING WILL ANY COPYRIGHT HOLDER, OR ANY OTHER PARTY WHO MODIFIES AND/OR CONVEYS THE PROGRAM AS PERMITTED ABOVE, BE LIABLE TO YOU FOR DAMAGES, INCLUDING ANY GENERAL, SPECIAL, INCIDENTAL OR CONSEQUENTIAL DAMAGES ARISING OUT OF THE USE OR INABILITY TO USE THE PROGRAM (INCLUDING BUT NOT LIMITED TO LOSS OF DATA OR DATA BEING RENDERED INACCURATE OR LOSSES SUSTAINED BY YOU OR THIRD PARTIES OR A FAILURE OF THE PROGRAM TO OPERATE WITH ANY OTHER PROGRAMS), EVEN IF SUCH HOLDER OR OTHER PARTY HAS BEEN ADVISED OF THE POSSIBILITY OF SUCH DAMAGES.

17. Interpretation of Sections 15 and 16.

If the disclaimer of warranty and limitation of liability provided above cannot be given local legal effect according to their terms, reviewing courts shall apply local law that most closely approximates an absolute waiver of all civil liability in connection with the Program, unless a warranty or assumption of liability accompanies a copy of the Program in return for a fee.

END OF TERMS AND CONDITIONS

How to Apply These Terms to Your New Programs

If you develop a new program, and you want it to be of the greatest possible use to the public, the best way to achieve this is to make it free software which everyone can redistribute and change under these terms.

To do so, attach the following notices to the program. It is safest to attach them to the start of each source file to most effectively state the exclusion of warranty; and each file should have at least the "copyright" line and a pointer to where the full notice is found.

```
one line to give the program's name and a brief idea of what it does.
Copyright (C) year name of author

This program is free software: you can redistribute it and/or modify
it under the terms of the GNU General Public License as published by
the Free Software Foundation, either version 3 of the License, or (at
your option) any later version.

This program is distributed in the hope that it will be useful, but
WITHOUT ANY WARRANTY; without even the implied warranty of
MERCHANTABILITY or FITNESS FOR A PARTICULAR PURPOSE.  See the GNU
General Public License for more details.

You should have received a copy of the GNU General Public License
along with this program.  If not, see http://www.gnu.org/licenses/.
```

Also add information on how to contact you by electronic and paper mail.

If the program does terminal interaction, make it output a short notice like this when it starts in an interactive mode:

```
program Copyright (C) year name of author
This program comes with ABSOLUTELY NO WARRANTY; for details type 'show w'.
This is free software, and you are welcome to redistribute it
under certain conditions; type 'show c' for details.
```

The hypothetical commands 'show w' and 'show c' should show the appropriate parts of the General Public License. Of course, your program's commands might be different; for a GUI interface, you would use an "about box".

You should also get your employer (if you work as a programmer) or school, if any, to sign a "copyright disclaimer" for the program, if necessary. For more information on this, and how to apply and follow the GNU GPL, see http://www.gnu.org/licenses/.

The GNU General Public License does not permit incorporating your program into proprietary programs. If your program is a subroutine library, you may consider it more useful to permit linking proprietary applications with the library. If this is what you want to do, use the GNU Lesser General Public License instead of this License. But first, please read http://www.gnu.org/philosophy/why-not-lgpl.html.

GNU Free Documentation License

Version 1.3, 3 November 2008

Copyright © 2000, 2001, 2002, 2007, 2008 Free Software Foundation, Inc.
http://fsf.org/

Everyone is permitted to copy and distribute verbatim copies
of this license document, but changing it is not allowed.

0. PREAMBLE

The purpose of this License is to make a manual, textbook, or other functional and useful document *free* in the sense of freedom: to assure everyone the effective freedom to copy and redistribute it, with or without modifying it, either commercially or non-commercially. Secondarily, this License preserves for the author and publisher a way to get credit for their work, while not being considered responsible for modifications made by others.

This License is a kind of "copyleft", which means that derivative works of the document must themselves be free in the same sense. It complements the GNU General Public License, which is a copyleft license designed for free software.

We have designed this License in order to use it for manuals for free software, because free software needs free documentation: a free program should come with manuals providing the same freedoms that the software does. But this License is not limited to software manuals; it can be used for any textual work, regardless of subject matter or whether it is published as a printed book. We recommend this License principally for works whose purpose is instruction or reference.

1. APPLICABILITY AND DEFINITIONS

This License applies to any manual or other work, in any medium, that contains a notice placed by the copyright holder saying it can be distributed under the terms of this License. Such a notice grants a world-wide, royalty-free license, unlimited in duration, to use that work under the conditions stated herein. The "Document", below, refers to any such manual or work. Any member of the public is a licensee, and is addressed as "you". You accept the license if you copy, modify or distribute the work in a way requiring permission under copyright law.

A "Modified Version" of the Document means any work containing the Document or a portion of it, either copied verbatim, or with modifications and/or translated into another language.

A "Secondary Section" is a named appendix or a front-matter section of the Document that deals exclusively with the relationship of the publishers or authors of the Document to the Document's overall subject (or to related matters) and contains nothing that could fall directly within that overall subject. (Thus, if the Document is in part a textbook of mathematics, a Secondary Section may not explain any mathematics.) The relationship could be a matter of historical connection with the subject or with related matters, or of legal, commercial, philosophical, ethical or political position regarding them.

The "Invariant Sections" are certain Secondary Sections whose titles are designated, as being those of Invariant Sections, in the notice that says that the Document is released under this License. If a section does not fit the above definition of Secondary then it is not allowed to be designated as Invariant. The Document may contain zero Invariant Sections. If the Document does not identify any Invariant Sections then there are none.

The "Cover Texts" are certain short passages of text that are listed, as Front-Cover Texts or Back-Cover Texts, in the notice that says that the Document is released under this License. A Front-Cover Text may be at most 5 words, and a Back-Cover Text may be at most 25 words.

A "Transparent" copy of the Document means a machine-readable copy, represented in a format whose specification is available to the general public, that is suitable for revising the document straightforwardly with generic text editors or (for images composed of pixels) generic paint programs or (for drawings) some widely available drawing editor, and that is suitable for input to text formatters or for automatic translation to a variety of formats suitable for input to text formatters. A copy made in an otherwise Transparent file format whose markup, or absence of markup, has been arranged to thwart or discourage subsequent modification by readers is not Transparent. An image format is not Transparent if used for any substantial amount of text. A copy that is not "Transparent" is called "Opaque".

Examples of suitable formats for Transparent copies include plain ASCII without markup, Texinfo input format, LaTeX input format, SGML or XML using a publicly available DTD, and standard-conforming simple HTML, PostScript or PDF designed for human modification. Examples of transparent image formats include PNG, XCF and JPG. Opaque formats include proprietary formats that can be read and edited only by proprietary word processors, SGML or XML for which the DTD and/or processing tools are not generally available, and the machine-generated HTML, PostScript or PDF produced by some word processors for output purposes only.

The "Title Page" means, for a printed book, the title page itself, plus such following pages as are needed to hold, legibly, the material this License requires to appear in the title page. For works in formats which do not have any title page as such, "Title Page" means the text near the most prominent appearance of the work's title, preceding the beginning of the body of the text.

The "publisher" means any person or entity that distributes copies of the Document to the public.

A section "Entitled XYZ" means a named subunit of the Document whose title either is precisely XYZ or contains XYZ in parentheses following text that translates XYZ in another language. (Here XYZ stands for a specific section name mentioned below, such as "Acknowledgements", "Dedications", "Endorsements", or "History".) To "Preserve the Title" of such a section when you modify the Document means that it remains a section "Entitled XYZ" according to this definition.

The Document may include Warranty Disclaimers next to the notice which states that this License applies to the Document. These Warranty Disclaimers are considered to be included by reference in this License, but only as regards disclaiming warranties: any other implication that these Warranty Disclaimers may have is void and has no effect on the meaning of this License.

2. VERBATIM COPYING

You may copy and distribute the Document in any medium, either commercially or noncommercially, provided that this License, the copyright notices, and the license notice saying this License applies to the Document are reproduced in all copies, and that you add no other conditions whatsoever to those of this License. You may not use technical measures to obstruct or control the reading or further copying of the copies you make or distribute. However, you may accept compensation in exchange for copies. If you distribute a large enough number of copies you must also follow the conditions in section 3.

You may also lend copies, under the same conditions stated above, and you may publicly display copies.

3. COPYING IN QUANTITY

If you publish printed copies (or copies in media that commonly have printed covers) of the Document, numbering more than 100, and the Document's license notice requires Cover Texts, you must enclose the copies in covers that carry, clearly and legibly, all these Cover Texts: Front-Cover Texts on the front cover, and Back-Cover Texts on the back cover. Both covers must also clearly and legibly identify you as the publisher of these copies. The front cover must present the full title with all words of the title equally prominent and visible. You may add other material on the covers in addition. Copying with changes limited to the covers, as long as they preserve the title of the Document and satisfy these conditions, can be treated as verbatim copying in other respects.

If the required texts for either cover are too voluminous to fit legibly, you should put the first ones listed (as many as fit reasonably) on the actual cover, and continue the rest onto adjacent pages.

If you publish or distribute Opaque copies of the Document numbering more than 100, you must either include a machine-readable Transparent copy along with each Opaque copy, or state in or with each Opaque copy a computer-network location from which the general network-using public has access to download using public-standard network protocols a complete Transparent copy of the Document, free of added material. If you use the latter option, you must take reasonably prudent steps, when you begin distribution of Opaque copies in quantity, to ensure that this Transparent copy will remain thus accessible at the stated location until at least one year after the last time you distribute an Opaque copy (directly or through your agents or retailers) of that edition to the public.

It is requested, but not required, that you contact the authors of the Document well before redistributing any large number of copies, to give them a chance to provide you with an updated version of the Document.

4. MODIFICATIONS

You may copy and distribute a Modified Version of the Document under the conditions of sections 2 and 3 above, provided that you release the Modified Version under precisely this License, with the Modified Version filling the role of the Document, thus licensing distribution and modification of the Modified Version to whoever possesses a copy of it. In addition, you must do these things in the Modified Version:

A. Use in the Title Page (and on the covers, if any) a title distinct from that of the Document, and from those of previous versions (which should, if there were any, be listed in the History section of the Document). You may use the same title as a previous version if the original publisher of that version gives permission.

B. List on the Title Page, as authors, one or more persons or entities responsible for authorship of the modifications in the Modified Version, together with at least five of the principal authors of the Document (all of its principal authors, if it has fewer than five), unless they release you from this requirement.

C. State on the Title page the name of the publisher of the Modified Version, as the publisher.

D. Preserve all the copyright notices of the Document.

E. Add an appropriate copyright notice for your modifications adjacent to the other copyright notices.

F. Include, immediately after the copyright notices, a license notice giving the public permission to use the Modified Version under the terms of this License, in the form shown in the Addendum below.

G. Preserve in that license notice the full lists of Invariant Sections and required Cover Texts given in the Document's license notice.

H. Include an unaltered copy of this License.

I. Preserve the section Entitled "History", Preserve its Title, and add to it an item stating at least the title, year, new authors, and publisher of the Modified Version as given on the Title Page. If there is no section Entitled "History" in the Document, create one stating the title, year, authors, and publisher of the Document as given on its Title Page, then add an item describing the Modified Version as stated in the previous sentence.

J. Preserve the network location, if any, given in the Document for public access to a Transparent copy of the Document, and likewise the network locations given in the Document for previous versions it was based on. These may be placed in the "History" section. You may omit a network location for a work that was published at least four years before the Document itself, or if the original publisher of the version it refers to gives permission.

K. For any section Entitled "Acknowledgements" or "Dedications", Preserve the Title of the section, and preserve in the section all the substance and tone of each of the contributor acknowledgements and/or dedications given therein.

L. Preserve all the Invariant Sections of the Document, unaltered in their text and in their titles. Section numbers or the equivalent are not considered part of the section titles.

M. Delete any section Entitled "Endorsements". Such a section may not be included in the Modified Version.

N. Do not retitle any existing section to be Entitled "Endorsements" or to conflict in title with any Invariant Section.

O. Preserve any Warranty Disclaimers.

If the Modified Version includes new front-matter sections or appendices that qualify as Secondary Sections and contain no material copied from the Document, you may at your option designate some or all of these sections as invariant. To do this, add their titles to the list of Invariant Sections in the Modified Version's license notice. These titles must be distinct from any other section titles.

You may add a section Entitled "Endorsements", provided it contains nothing but endorsements of your Modified Version by various parties—for example, statements of peer review or that the text has been approved by an organization as the authoritative definition of a standard.

You may add a passage of up to five words as a Front-Cover Text, and a passage of up to 25 words as a Back-Cover Text, to the end of the list of Cover Texts in the Modified Version. Only one passage of Front-Cover Text and one of Back-Cover Text may be added by (or through arrangements made by) any one entity. If the Document already includes a cover text for the same cover, previously added by you or by arrangement made by the same entity you are acting on behalf of, you may not add another; but you may replace the old one, on explicit permission from the previous publisher that added the old one.

The author(s) and publisher(s) of the Document do not by this License give permission to use their names for publicity for or to assert or imply endorsement of any Modified Version.

5. COMBINING DOCUMENTS

You may combine the Document with other documents released under this License, under the terms defined in section 4 above for modified versions, provided that you include in the combination all of the Invariant Sections of all of the original documents, unmodified, and list them all as Invariant Sections of your combined work in its license notice, and that you preserve all their Warranty Disclaimers.

The combined work need only contain one copy of this License, and multiple identical Invariant Sections may be replaced with a single copy. If there are multiple Invariant Sections with the same name but different contents, make the title of each such section unique by adding at the end of it, in parentheses, the name of the original author or publisher of that section if known, or else a unique number. Make the same adjustment to the section titles in the list of Invariant Sections in the license notice of the combined work.

In the combination, you must combine any sections Entitled "History" in the various original documents, forming one section Entitled "History"; likewise combine any sections Entitled "Acknowledgements", and any sections Entitled "Dedications". You must delete all sections Entitled "Endorsements."

6. COLLECTIONS OF DOCUMENTS

You may make a collection consisting of the Document and other documents released under this License, and replace the individual copies of this License in the various documents with a single copy that is included in the collection, provided that you follow the rules of this License for verbatim copying of each of the documents in all other respects.

You may extract a single document from such a collection, and distribute it individually under this License, provided you insert a copy of this License into the extracted document, and follow this License in all other respects regarding verbatim copying of that document.

7. AGGREGATION WITH INDEPENDENT WORKS

A compilation of the Document or its derivatives with other separate and independent documents or works, in or on a volume of a storage or distribution medium, is called an "aggregate" if the copyright resulting from the compilation is not used to limit the legal rights of the compilation's users beyond what the individual works permit. When the Document is included in an aggregate, this License does not apply to the other works in the aggregate which are not themselves derivative works of the Document.

If the Cover Text requirement of section 3 is applicable to these copies of the Document, then if the Document is less than one half of the entire aggregate, the Document's Cover Texts may be placed on covers that bracket the Document within the aggregate, or the electronic equivalent of covers if the Document is in electronic form. Otherwise they must appear on printed covers that bracket the whole aggregate.

8. TRANSLATION

Translation is considered a kind of modification, so you may distribute translations of the Document under the terms of section 4. Replacing Invariant Sections with translations requires special permission from their copyright holders, but you may include translations of some or all Invariant Sections in addition to the original versions of these Invariant Sections. You may include a translation of this License, and all the license notices in the Document, and any Warranty Disclaimers, provided that you also include the original English version of this License and the original versions of those notices and disclaimers. In case of a disagreement between the translation and the original version of this License or a notice or disclaimer, the original version will prevail.

If a section in the Document is Entitled "Acknowledgements", "Dedications", or "History", the requirement (section 4) to Preserve its Title (section 1) will typically require changing the actual title.

9. TERMINATION

You may not copy, modify, sublicense, or distribute the Document except as expressly provided under this License. Any attempt otherwise to copy, modify, sublicense, or distribute it is void, and will automatically terminate your rights under this License.

However, if you cease all violation of this License, then your license from a particular copyright holder is reinstated (a) provisionally, unless and until the copyright holder explicitly and finally terminates your license, and (b) permanently, if the copyright holder fails to notify you of the violation by some reasonable means prior to 60 days after the cessation.

Moreover, your license from a particular copyright holder is reinstated permanently if the copyright holder notifies you of the violation by some reasonable means, this is the first time you have received notice of violation of this License (for any work) from that copyright holder, and you cure the violation prior to 30 days after your receipt of the notice.

Termination of your rights under this section does not terminate the licenses of parties who have received copies or rights from you under this License. If your rights have been terminated and not permanently reinstated, receipt of a copy of some or all of the same material does not give you any rights to use it.

10. FUTURE REVISIONS OF THIS LICENSE

The Free Software Foundation may publish new, revised versions of the GNU Free Documentation License from time to time. Such new versions will be similar in spirit to the present version, but may differ in detail to address new problems or concerns. See http://www.gnu.org/copyleft/.

Each version of the License is given a distinguishing version number. If the Document specifies that a particular numbered version of this License "or any later version" applies to it, you have the option of following the terms and conditions either of that specified version or of any later version that has been published (not as a draft) by the Free Software Foundation. If the Document does not specify a version number of this License, you may choose any version ever published (not as a draft) by the Free Software Foundation. If the Document specifies that a proxy can decide which future versions of this License can be used, that proxy's public statement of acceptance of a version permanently authorizes you to choose that version for the Document.

11. RELICENSING

"Massive Multiauthor Collaboration Site" (or "MMC Site") means any World Wide Web server that publishes copyrightable works and also provides prominent facilities for anybody to edit those works. A public wiki that anybody can edit is an example of such a server. A "Massive Multiauthor Collaboration" (or "MMC") contained in the site means any set of copyrightable works thus published on the MMC site.

"CC-BY-SA" means the Creative Commons Attribution-Share Alike 3.0 license published by Creative Commons Corporation, a not-for-profit corporation with a principal place of business in San Francisco, California, as well as future copyleft versions of that license published by that same organization.

"Incorporate" means to publish or republish a Document, in whole or in part, as part of another Document.

An MMC is "eligible for relicensing" if it is licensed under this License, and if all works that were first published under this License somewhere other than this MMC, and subsequently incorporated in whole or in part into the MMC, (1) had no cover texts or invariant sections, and (2) were thus incorporated prior to November 1, 2008.

The operator of an MMC Site may republish an MMC contained in the site under CC-BY-SA on the same site at any time before August 1, 2009, provided the MMC is eligible for relicensing.

ADDENDUM: How to use this License for your documents

To use this License in a document you have written, include a copy of the License in the document and put the following copyright and license notices just after the title page:

```
Copyright (C)  year  your name.
Permission is granted to copy, distribute and/or modify this document
under the terms of the GNU Free Documentation License, Version 1.3
or any later version published by the Free Software Foundation;
with no Invariant Sections, no Front-Cover Texts, and no Back-Cover
Texts.  A copy of the license is included in the section entitled ''GNU
Free Documentation License''.
```

If you have Invariant Sections, Front-Cover Texts and Back-Cover Texts, replace the "with...Texts." line with this:

```
with the Invariant Sections being list their titles, with
the Front-Cover Texts being list, and with the Back-Cover Texts
being list.
```

If you have Invariant Sections without Cover Texts, or some other combination of the three, merge those two alternatives to suit the situation.

If your document contains nontrivial examples of program code, we recommend releasing these examples in parallel under your choice of free software license, such as the GNU General Public License, to permit their use in free software.

Contributors to GCC

The GCC project would like to thank its many contributors. Without them the project would not have been nearly as successful as it has been. Any omissions in this list are accidental. Feel free to contact law@redhat.com or gerald@pfeifer.com if you have been left out or some of your contributions are not listed. Please keep this list in alphabetical order.

- Analog Devices helped implement the support for complex data types and iterators.
- John David Anglin for threading-related fixes and improvements to libstdc++-v3, and the HP-UX port.
- James van Artsdalen wrote the code that makes efficient use of the Intel 80387 register stack.
- Abramo and Roberto Bagnara for the SysV68 Motorola 3300 Delta Series port.
- Alasdair Baird for various bug fixes.
- Giovanni Bajo for analyzing lots of complicated C++ problem reports.
- Peter Barada for his work to improve code generation for new ColdFire cores.
- Gerald Baumgartner added the signature extension to the C++ front end.
- Godmar Back for his Java improvements and encouragement.
- Scott Bambrough for help porting the Java compiler.
- Wolfgang Bangerth for processing tons of bug reports.
- Jon Beniston for his Microsoft Windows port of Java and port to Lattice Mico32.
- Daniel Berlin for better DWARF 2 support, faster/better optimizations, improved alias analysis, plus migrating GCC to Bugzilla.
- Geoff Berry for his Java object serialization work and various patches.
- David Binderman tests weekly snapshots of GCC trunk against Fedora Rawhide for several architectures.
- Laurynas Biveinis for memory management work and DJGPP port fixes.
- Uros Bizjak for the implementation of x87 math built-in functions and for various middle end and i386 back end improvements and bug fixes.
- Eric Blake for helping to make GCJ and libgcj conform to the specifications.
- Janne Blomqvist for contributions to GNU Fortran.
- Segher Boessenkool for various fixes.
- Hans-J. Boehm for his garbage collector, IA-64 libffi port, and other Java work.
- Neil Booth for work on cpplib, lang hooks, debug hooks and other miscellaneous cleanups.
- Steven Bosscher for integrating the GNU Fortran front end into GCC and for contributing to the tree-ssa branch.
- Eric Botcazou for fixing middle- and backend bugs left and right.
- Per Bothner for his direction via the steering committee and various improvements to the infrastructure for supporting new languages. Chill front end implementation. Initial implementations of cpplib, fix-header, config.guess, libio, and past C++ library (libg++) maintainer. Dreaming up, designing and implementing much of GCJ.

- Devon Bowen helped port GCC to the Tahoe.
- Don Bowman for mips-vxworks contributions.
- James Bowman for the FT32 port.
- Dave Brolley for work on cpplib and Chill.
- Paul Brook for work on the ARM architecture and maintaining GNU Fortran.
- Robert Brown implemented the support for Encore 32000 systems.
- Christian Bruel for improvements to local store elimination.
- Herman A.J. ten Brugge for various fixes.
- Joerg Brunsmann for Java compiler hacking and help with the GCJ FAQ.
- Joe Buck for his direction via the steering committee from its creation to 2013.
- Craig Burley for leadership of the G77 Fortran effort.
- Tobias Burnus for contributions to GNU Fortran.
- Stephan Buys for contributing Doxygen notes for libstdc++.
- Paolo Carlini for libstdc++ work: lots of efficiency improvements to the C++ strings, streambufs and formatted I/O, hard detective work on the frustrating localization issues, and keeping up with the problem reports.
- John Carr for his alias work, SPARC hacking, infrastructure improvements, previous contributions to the steering committee, loop optimizations, etc.
- Stephane Carrez for 68HC11 and 68HC12 ports.
- Steve Chamberlain for support for the Renesas SH and H8 processors and the PicoJava processor, and for GCJ config fixes.
- Glenn Chambers for help with the GCJ FAQ.
- John-Marc Chandonia for various libgcj patches.
- Denis Chertykov for contributing and maintaining the AVR port, the first GCC port for an 8-bit architecture.
- Scott Christley for his Objective-C contributions.
- Eric Christopher for his Java porting help and clean-ups.
- Branko Cibej for more warning contributions.
- The GNU Classpath project for all of their merged runtime code.
- Nick Clifton for arm, mcore, fr30, v850, m32r, msp430 rx work, '`--help`', and other random hacking.
- Michael Cook for libstdc++ cleanup patches to reduce warnings.
- R. Kelley Cook for making GCC buildable from a read-only directory as well as other miscellaneous build process and documentation clean-ups.
- Ralf Corsepius for SH testing and minor bug fixing.
- François-Xavier Coudert for contributions to GNU Fortran.
- Stan Cox for care and feeding of the x86 port and lots of behind the scenes hacking.
- Alex Crain provided changes for the 3b1.
- Ian Dall for major improvements to the NS32k port.
- Paul Dale for his work to add uClinux platform support to the m68k backend.

- Dario Dariol contributed the four varieties of sample programs that print a copy of their source.

- Russell Davidson for fstream and stringstream fixes in libstdc++.

- Bud Davis for work on the G77 and GNU Fortran compilers.

- Mo DeJong for GCJ and libgcj bug fixes.

- Jerry DeLisle for contributions to GNU Fortran.

- DJ Delorie for the DJGPP port, build and libiberty maintenance, various bug fixes, and the M32C, MeP, MSP430, and RL78 ports.

- Arnaud Desitter for helping to debug GNU Fortran.

- Gabriel Dos Reis for contributions to G++, contributions and maintenance of GCC diagnostics infrastructure, libstdc++-v3, including `valarray<>`, `complex<>`, maintaining the numerics library (including that pesky `<limits>` :-) and keeping up-to-date anything to do with numbers.

- Ulrich Drepper for his work on glibc, testing of GCC using glibc, ISO C99 support, CFG dumping support, etc., plus support of the C++ runtime libraries including for all kinds of C interface issues, contributing and maintaining `complex<>`, sanity checking and disbursement, configuration architecture, libio maintenance, and early math work.

- François Dumont for his work on libstdc++-v3, especially maintaining and improving `debug-mode` and associative and unordered containers.

- Zdenek Dvorak for a new loop unroller and various fixes.

- Michael Eager for his work on the Xilinx MicroBlaze port.

- Richard Earnshaw for his ongoing work with the ARM.

- David Edelsohn for his direction via the steering committee, ongoing work with the RS6000/PowerPC port, help cleaning up Haifa loop changes, doing the entire AIX port of libstdc++ with his bare hands, and for ensuring GCC properly keeps working on AIX.

- Kevin Ediger for the floating point formatting of num_put::do_put in libstdc++.

- Phil Edwards for libstdc++ work including configuration hackery, documentation maintainer, chief breaker of the web pages, the occasional iostream bug fix, and work on shared library symbol versioning.

- Paul Eggert for random hacking all over GCC.

- Mark Elbrecht for various DJGPP improvements, and for libstdc++ configuration support for locales and fstream-related fixes.

- Vadim Egorov for libstdc++ fixes in strings, streambufs, and iostreams.

- Christian Ehrhardt for dealing with bug reports.

- Ben Elliston for his work to move the Objective-C runtime into its own subdirectory and for his work on autoconf.

- Revital Eres for work on the PowerPC 750CL port.

- Marc Espie for OpenBSD support.

- Doug Evans for much of the global optimization framework, arc, m32r, and SPARC work.

- Christopher Faylor for his work on the Cygwin port and for caring and feeding the gcc.gnu.org box and saving its users tons of spam.
- Fred Fish for BeOS support and Ada fixes.
- Ivan Fontes Garcia for the Portuguese translation of the GCJ FAQ.
- Peter Gerwinski for various bug fixes and the Pascal front end.
- Kaveh R. Ghazi for his direction via the steering committee, amazing work to make '-W -Wall -W* -Werror' useful, and testing GCC on a plethora of platforms. Kaveh extends his gratitude to the CAIP Center at Rutgers University for providing him with computing resources to work on Free Software from the late 1980s to 2010.
- John Gilmore for a donation to the FSF earmarked improving GNU Java.
- Judy Goldberg for c++ contributions.
- Torbjorn Granlund for various fixes and the c-torture testsuite, multiply- and divide-by-constant optimization, improved long long support, improved leaf function register allocation, and his direction via the steering committee.
- Jonny Grant for improvements to collect2's '--help' documentation.
- Anthony Green for his '-Os' contributions, the moxie port, and Java front end work.
- Stu Grossman for gdb hacking, allowing GCJ developers to debug Java code.
- Michael K. Gschwind contributed the port to the PDP-11.
- Richard Biener for his ongoing middle-end contributions and bug fixes and for release management.
- Ron Guilmette implemented the protoize and unprotoize tools, the support for DWARF 1 symbolic debugging information, and much of the support for System V Release 4. He has also worked heavily on the Intel 386 and 860 support.
- Sumanth Gundapaneni for contributing the CR16 port.
- Mostafa Hagog for Swing Modulo Scheduling (SMS) and post reload GCSE.
- Bruno Haible for improvements in the runtime overhead for EH, new warnings and assorted bug fixes.
- Andrew Haley for his amazing Java compiler and library efforts.
- Chris Hanson assisted in making GCC work on HP-UX for the 9000 series 300.
- Michael Hayes for various thankless work he's done trying to get the c30/c40 ports functional. Lots of loop and unroll improvements and fixes.
- Dara Hazeghi for wading through myriads of target-specific bug reports.
- Kate Hedstrom for staking the G77 folks with an initial testsuite.
- Richard Henderson for his ongoing SPARC, alpha, ia32, and ia64 work, loop opts, and generally fixing lots of old problems we've ignored for years, flow rewrite and lots of further stuff, including reviewing tons of patches.
- Aldy Hernandez for working on the PowerPC port, SIMD support, and various fixes.
- Nobuyuki Hikichi of Software Research Associates, Tokyo, contributed the support for the Sony NEWS machine.
- Kazu Hirata for caring and feeding the Renesas H8/300 port and various fixes.
- Katherine Holcomb for work on GNU Fortran.

- Manfred Hollstein for his ongoing work to keep the m88k alive, lots of testing and bug fixing, particularly of GCC configury code.

- Steve Holmgren for MachTen patches.

- Mat Hostetter for work on the TILE-Gx and TILEPro ports.

- Jan Hubicka for his x86 port improvements.

- Falk Hueffner for working on C and optimization bug reports.

- Bernardo Innocenti for his m68k work, including merging of ColdFire improvements and uClinux support.

- Christian Iseli for various bug fixes.

- Kamil Iskra for general m68k hacking.

- Lee Iverson for random fixes and MIPS testing.

- Balaji V. Iyer for Cilk+ development and merging.

- Andreas Jaeger for testing and benchmarking of GCC and various bug fixes.

- Martin Jambor for his work on inter-procedural optimizations, the switch conversion pass, and scalar replacement of aggregates.

- Jakub Jelinek for his SPARC work and sibling call optimizations as well as lots of bug fixes and test cases, and for improving the Java build system.

- Janis Johnson for ia64 testing and fixes, her quality improvement sidetracks, and web page maintenance.

- Kean Johnston for SCO OpenServer support and various fixes.

- Tim Josling for the sample language treelang based originally on Richard Kenner's "toy" language.

- Nicolai Josuttis for additional libstdc++ documentation.

- Klaus Kaempf for his ongoing work to make alpha-vms a viable target.

- Steven G. Kargl for work on GNU Fortran.

- David Kashtan of SRI adapted GCC to VMS.

- Ryszard Kabatek for many, many libstdc++ bug fixes and optimizations of strings, especially member functions, and for auto_ptr fixes.

- Geoffrey Keating for his ongoing work to make the PPC work for GNU/Linux and his automatic regression tester.

- Brendan Kehoe for his ongoing work with G++ and for a lot of early work in just about every part of libstdc++.

- Oliver M. Kellogg of Deutsche Aerospace contributed the port to the MIL-STD-1750A.

- Richard Kenner of the New York University Ultracomputer Research Laboratory wrote the machine descriptions for the AMD 29000, the DEC Alpha, the IBM RT PC, and the IBM RS/6000 as well as the support for instruction attributes. He also made changes to better support RISC processors including changes to common subexpression elimination, strength reduction, function calling sequence handling, and condition code support, in addition to generalizing the code for frame pointer elimination and delay slot scheduling. Richard Kenner was also the head maintainer of GCC for several years.

- Mumit Khan for various contributions to the Cygwin and Mingw32 ports and maintaining binary releases for Microsoft Windows hosts, and for massive libstdc++ porting work to Cygwin/Mingw32.

- Robin Kirkham for cpu32 support.

- Mark Klein for PA improvements.

- Thomas Koenig for various bug fixes.

- Bruce Korb for the new and improved fixincludes code.

- Benjamin Kosnik for his G++ work and for leading the libstdc++-v3 effort.

- Maxim Kuvyrkov for contributions to the instruction scheduler, the Android and m68k/Coldfire ports, and optimizations.

- Charles LaBrec contributed the support for the Integrated Solutions 68020 system.

- Asher Langton and Mike Kumbera for contributing Cray pointer support to GNU Fortran, and for other GNU Fortran improvements.

- Jeff Law for his direction via the steering committee, coordinating the entire egcs project and GCC 2.95, rolling out snapshots and releases, handling merges from GCC2, reviewing tons of patches that might have fallen through the cracks else, and random but extensive hacking.

- Walter Lee for work on the TILE-Gx and TILEPro ports.

- Marc Lehmann for his direction via the steering committee and helping with analysis and improvements of x86 performance.

- Victor Leikehman for work on GNU Fortran.

- Ted Lemon wrote parts of the RTL reader and printer.

- Kriang Lerdsuwanakij for C++ improvements including template as template parameter support, and many C++ fixes.

- Warren Levy for tremendous work on libgcj (Java Runtime Library) and random work on the Java front end.

- Alain Lichnewsky ported GCC to the MIPS CPU.

- Oskar Liljeblad for hacking on AWT and his many Java bug reports and patches.

- Robert Lipe for OpenServer support, new testsuites, testing, etc.

- Chen Liqin for various S+core related fixes/improvement, and for maintaining the S+core port.

- Weiwen Liu for testing and various bug fixes.

- Manuel López-Ibáñez for improving '-Wconversion' and many other diagnostics fixes and improvements.

- Dave Love for his ongoing work with the Fortran front end and runtime libraries.

- Martin von Löwis for internal consistency checking infrastructure, various C++ improvements including namespace support, and tons of assistance with libstdc++/compiler merges.

- H.J. Lu for his previous contributions to the steering committee, many x86 bug reports, prototype patches, and keeping the GNU/Linux ports working.

- Greg McGary for random fixes and (someday) bounded pointers.

- Andrew MacLeod for his ongoing work in building a real EH system, various code generation improvements, work on the global optimizer, etc.
- Vladimir Makarov for hacking some ugly i960 problems, PowerPC hacking improvements to compile-time performance, overall knowledge and direction in the area of instruction scheduling, and design and implementation of the automaton based instruction scheduler.
- Bob Manson for his behind the scenes work on dejagnu.
- John Marino for contributing the DragonFly BSD port.
- Philip Martin for lots of libstdc++ string and vector iterator fixes and improvements, and string clean up and testsuites.
- Michael Matz for his work on dominance tree discovery, the x86-64 port, link-time optimization framework and general optimization improvements.
- All of the Mauve project contributors, for Java test code.
- Bryce McKinlay for numerous GCJ and libgcj fixes and improvements.
- Adam Megacz for his work on the Microsoft Windows port of GCJ.
- Michael Meissner for LRS framework, ia32, m32r, v850, m88k, MIPS, powerpc, haifa, ECOFF debug support, and other assorted hacking.
- Jason Merrill for his direction via the steering committee and leading the G++ effort.
- Martin Michlmayr for testing GCC on several architectures using the entire Debian archive.
- David Miller for his direction via the steering committee, lots of SPARC work, improvements in jump.c and interfacing with the Linux kernel developers.
- Gary Miller ported GCC to Charles River Data Systems machines.
- Alfred Minarik for libstdc++ string and ios bug fixes, and turning the entire libstdc++ testsuite namespace-compatible.
- Mark Mitchell for his direction via the steering committee, mountains of C++ work, load/store hoisting out of loops, alias analysis improvements, ISO C restrict support, and serving as release manager from 2000 to 2011.
- Alan Modra for various GNU/Linux bits and testing.
- Toon Moene for his direction via the steering committee, Fortran maintenance, and his ongoing work to make us make Fortran run fast.
- Jason Molenda for major help in the care and feeding of all the services on the gcc.gnu.org (formerly egcs.cygnus.com) machine—mail, web services, ftp services, etc etc. Doing all this work on scrap paper and the backs of envelopes would have been... difficult.
- Catherine Moore for fixing various ugly problems we have sent her way, including the haifa bug which was killing the Alpha & PowerPC Linux kernels.
- Mike Moreton for his various Java patches.
- David Mosberger-Tang for various Alpha improvements, and for the initial IA-64 port.
- Stephen Moshier contributed the floating point emulator that assists in cross-compilation and permits support for floating point numbers wider than 64 bits and for ISO C99 support.

- Bill Moyer for his behind the scenes work on various issues.
- Philippe De Muyter for his work on the m68k port.
- Joseph S. Myers for his work on the PDP-11 port, format checking and ISO C99 support, and continuous emphasis on (and contributions to) documentation.
- Nathan Myers for his work on libstdc++-v3: architecture and authorship through the first three snapshots, including implementation of locale infrastructure, string, shadow C headers, and the initial project documentation (DESIGN, CHECKLIST, and so forth). Later, more work on MT-safe string and shadow headers.
- Felix Natter for documentation on porting libstdc++.
- Nathanael Nerode for cleaning up the configuration/build process.
- NeXT, Inc. donated the front end that supports the Objective-C language.
- Hans-Peter Nilsson for the CRIS and MMIX ports, improvements to the search engine setup, various documentation fixes and other small fixes.
- Geoff Noer for his work on getting cygwin native builds working.
- Diego Novillo for his work on Tree SSA, OpenMP, SPEC performance tracking web pages, GIMPLE tuples, and assorted fixes.
- David O'Brien for the FreeBSD/alpha, FreeBSD/AMD x86-64, FreeBSD/ARM, FreeBSD/PowerPC, and FreeBSD/SPARC64 ports and related infrastructure improvements.
- Alexandre Oliva for various build infrastructure improvements, scripts and amazing testing work, including keeping libtool issues sane and happy.
- Stefan Olsson for work on mt_alloc.
- Melissa O'Neill for various NeXT fixes.
- Rainer Orth for random MIPS work, including improvements to GCC's o32 ABI support, improvements to dejagnu's MIPS support, Java configuration clean-ups and porting work, and maintaining the IRIX, Solaris 2, and Tru64 UNIX ports.
- Hartmut Penner for work on the s390 port.
- Paul Petersen wrote the machine description for the Alliant FX/8.
- Alexandre Petit-Bianco for implementing much of the Java compiler and continued Java maintainership.
- Matthias Pfaller for major improvements to the NS32k port.
- Gerald Pfeifer for his direction via the steering committee, pointing out lots of problems we need to solve, maintenance of the web pages, and taking care of documentation maintenance in general.
- Andrew Pinski for processing bug reports by the dozen.
- Ovidiu Predescu for his work on the Objective-C front end and runtime libraries.
- Jerry Quinn for major performance improvements in C++ formatted I/O.
- Ken Raeburn for various improvements to checker, MIPS ports and various cleanups in the compiler.
- Rolf W. Rasmussen for hacking on AWT.
- David Reese of Sun Microsystems contributed to the Solaris on PowerPC port.

- Volker Reichelt for keeping up with the problem reports.
- Joern Rennecke for maintaining the sh port, loop, regmove & reload hacking and developing and maintaining the Epiphany port.
- Loren J. Rittle for improvements to libstdc++-v3 including the FreeBSD port, threading fixes, thread-related configury changes, critical threading documentation, and solutions to really tricky I/O problems, as well as keeping GCC properly working on FreeBSD and continuous testing.
- Craig Rodrigues for processing tons of bug reports.
- Ola Rönnerup for work on mt_alloc.
- Gavin Romig-Koch for lots of behind the scenes MIPS work.
- David Ronis inspired and encouraged Craig to rewrite the G77 documentation in texinfo format by contributing a first pass at a translation of the old 'g77-0.5.16/f/DOC' file.
- Ken Rose for fixes to GCC's delay slot filling code.
- Ira Rosen for her contributions to the auto-vectorizer.
- Paul Rubin wrote most of the preprocessor.
- Pétur Runólfsson for major performance improvements in C++ formatted I/O and large file support in C++ filebuf.
- Chip Salzenberg for libstdc++ patches and improvements to locales, traits, Makefiles, libio, libtool hackery, and "long long" support.
- Juha Sarlin for improvements to the H8 code generator.
- Greg Satz assisted in making GCC work on HP-UX for the 9000 series 300.
- Roger Sayle for improvements to constant folding and GCC's RTL optimizers as well as for fixing numerous bugs.
- Bradley Schatz for his work on the GCJ FAQ.
- Peter Schauer wrote the code to allow debugging to work on the Alpha.
- William Schelter did most of the work on the Intel 80386 support.
- Tobias Schlüter for work on GNU Fortran.
- Bernd Schmidt for various code generation improvements and major work in the reload pass, serving as release manager for GCC 2.95.3, and work on the Blackfin and C6X ports.
- Peter Schmid for constant testing of libstdc++—especially application testing, going above and beyond what was requested for the release criteria—and libstdc++ header file tweaks.
- Jason Schroeder for jcf-dump patches.
- Andreas Schwab for his work on the m68k port.
- Lars Segerlund for work on GNU Fortran.
- Dodji Seketeli for numerous C++ bug fixes and debug info improvements.
- Tim Shen for major work on <regex>.
- Joel Sherrill for his direction via the steering committee, RTEMS contributions and RTEMS testing.
- Nathan Sidwell for many C++ fixes/improvements.

- Jeffrey Siegal for helping RMS with the original design of GCC, some code which handles the parse tree and RTL data structures, constant folding and help with the original VAX & m68k ports.

- Kenny Simpson for prompting libstdc++ fixes due to defect reports from the LWG (thereby keeping GCC in line with updates from the ISO).

- Franz Sirl for his ongoing work with making the PPC port stable for GNU/Linux.

- Andrey Slepuhin for assorted AIX hacking.

- Trevor Smigiel for contributing the SPU port.

- Christopher Smith did the port for Convex machines.

- Danny Smith for his major efforts on the Mingw (and Cygwin) ports. Retired from GCC maintainership August 2010, having mentored two new maintainers into the role.

- Randy Smith finished the Sun FPA support.

- Ed Smith-Rowland for his continuous work on libstdc++-v3, special functions, `<random>`, and various improvements to C++11 features.

- Scott Snyder for queue, iterator, istream, and string fixes and libstdc++ testsuite entries. Also for providing the patch to G77 to add rudimentary support for `INTEGER*1`, `INTEGER*2`, and `LOGICAL*1`.

- Zdenek Sojka for running automated regression testing of GCC and reporting numerous bugs.

- Jayant Sonar for contributing the CR16 port.

- Brad Spencer for contributions to the GLIBCPP_FORCE_NEW technique.

- Richard Stallman, for writing the original GCC and launching the GNU project.

- Jan Stein of the Chalmers Computer Society provided support for Genix, as well as part of the 32000 machine description.

- Nigel Stephens for various mips16 related fixes/improvements.

- Jonathan Stone wrote the machine description for the Pyramid computer.

- Graham Stott for various infrastructure improvements.

- John Stracke for his Java HTTP protocol fixes.

- Mike Stump for his Elxsi port, G++ contributions over the years and more recently his vxworks contributions

- Jeff Sturm for Java porting help, bug fixes, and encouragement.

- Shigeya Suzuki for this fixes for the bsdi platforms.

- Ian Lance Taylor for the Go frontend, the initial mips16 and mips64 support, general configury hacking, fixincludes, etc.

- Holger Teutsch provided the support for the Clipper CPU.

- Gary Thomas for his ongoing work to make the PPC work for GNU/Linux.

- Paul Thomas for contributions to GNU Fortran.

- Philipp Thomas for random bug fixes throughout the compiler

- Jason Thorpe for thread support in libstdc++ on NetBSD.

- Kresten Krab Thorup wrote the run time support for the Objective-C language and the fantastic Java bytecode interpreter.

- Michael Tiemann for random bug fixes, the first instruction scheduler, initial C++ support, function integration, NS32k, SPARC and M88k machine description work, delay slot scheduling.
- Andreas Tobler for his work porting libgcj to Darwin.
- Teemu Torma for thread safe exception handling support.
- Leonard Tower wrote parts of the parser, RTL generator, and RTL definitions, and of the VAX machine description.
- Daniel Towner and Hariharan Sandanagobalane contributed and maintain the picoChip port.
- Tom Tromey for internationalization support and for his many Java contributions and libgcj maintainership.
- Lassi Tuura for improvements to config.guess to determine HP processor types.
- Petter Urkedal for libstdc++ CXXFLAGS, math, and algorithms fixes.
- Andy Vaught for the design and initial implementation of the GNU Fortran front end.
- Brent Verner for work with the libstdc++ cshadow files and their associated configure steps.
- Todd Vierling for contributions for NetBSD ports.
- Jonathan Wakely for contributing libstdc++ Doxygen notes and XHTML guidance.
- Dean Wakerley for converting the install documentation from HTML to texinfo in time for GCC 3.0.
- Krister Walfridsson for random bug fixes.
- Feng Wang for contributions to GNU Fortran.
- Stephen M. Webb for time and effort on making libstdc++ shadow files work with the tricky Solaris 8+ headers, and for pushing the build-time header tree. Also, for starting and driving the `<regex>` effort.
- John Wehle for various improvements for the x86 code generator, related infrastructure improvements to help x86 code generation, value range propagation and other work, WE32k port.
- Ulrich Weigand for work on the s390 port.
- Janus Weil for contributions to GNU Fortran.
- Zack Weinberg for major work on cpplib and various other bug fixes.
- Matt Welsh for help with Linux Threads support in GCJ.
- Urban Widmark for help fixing java.io.
- Mark Wielaard for new Java library code and his work integrating with Classpath.
- Dale Wiles helped port GCC to the Tahoe.
- Bob Wilson from Tensilica, Inc. for the Xtensa port.
- Jim Wilson for his direction via the steering committee, tackling hard problems in various places that nobody else wanted to work on, strength reduction and other loop optimizations.
- Paul Woegerer and Tal Agmon for the CRX port.
- Carlo Wood for various fixes.

- Tom Wood for work on the m88k port.
- Chung-Ju Wu for his work on the Andes NDS32 port.
- Canqun Yang for work on GNU Fortran.
- Masanobu Yuhara of Fujitsu Laboratories implemented the machine description for the Tron architecture (specifically, the Gmicro).
- Kevin Zachmann helped port GCC to the Tahoe.
- Ayal Zaks for Swing Modulo Scheduling (SMS).
- Xiaoqiang Zhang for work on GNU Fortran.
- Gilles Zunino for help porting Java to Irix.

The following people are recognized for their contributions to GNAT, the Ada front end of GCC:

- Bernard Banner
- Romain Berrendonner
- Geert Bosch
- Emmanuel Briot
- Joel Brobecker
- Ben Brosgol
- Vincent Celier
- Arnaud Charlet
- Chien Chieng
- Cyrille Comar
- Cyrille Crozes
- Robert Dewar
- Gary Dismukes
- Robert Duff
- Ed Falis
- Ramon Fernandez
- Sam Figueroa
- Vasiliy Fofanov
- Michael Friess
- Franco Gasperoni
- Ted Giering
- Matthew Gingell
- Laurent Guerby
- Jerome Guitton
- Olivier Hainque
- Jerome Hugues
- Hristian Kirtchev
- Jerome Lambourg

- Bruno Leclerc
- Albert Lee
- Sean McNeil
- Javier Miranda
- Laurent Nana
- Pascal Obry
- Dong-Ik Oh
- Laurent Pautet
- Brett Porter
- Thomas Quinot
- Nicolas Roche
- Pat Rogers
- Jose Ruiz
- Douglas Rupp
- Sergey Rybin
- Gail Schenker
- Ed Schonberg
- Nicolas Setton
- Samuel Tardieu

The following people are recognized for their contributions of new features, bug reports, testing and integration of classpath/libgcj for GCC version 4.1:

- Lillian Angel for `JTree` implementation and lots Free Swing additions and bug fixes.
- Wolfgang Baer for `GapContent` bug fixes.
- Anthony Balkissoon for `JList`, Free Swing 1.5 updates and mouse event fixes, lots of Free Swing work including `JTable` editing.
- Stuart Ballard for RMI constant fixes.
- Goffredo Baroncelli for `HTTPURLConnection` fixes.
- Gary Benson for `MessageFormat` fixes.
- Daniel Bonniot for `Serialization` fixes.
- Chris Burdess for lots of gnu.xml and http protocol fixes, `StAX` and `DOM` `xml:id` support.
- Ka-Hing Cheung for `TreePath` and `TreeSelection` fixes.
- Archie Cobbs for build fixes, VM interface updates, `URLClassLoader` updates.
- Kelley Cook for build fixes.
- Martin Cordova for Suggestions for better `SocketTimeoutException`.
- David Daney for `BitSet` bug fixes, `HttpURLConnection` rewrite and improvements.
- Thomas Fitzsimmons for lots of upgrades to the gtk+ AWT and Cairo 2D support. Lots of imageio framework additions, lots of AWT and Free Swing bug fixes.
- Jeroen Frijters for `ClassLoader` and nio cleanups, serialization fixes, better `Proxy` support, bug fixes and IKVM integration.

- Santiago Gala for `AccessControlContext` fixes.

- Nicolas Geoffray for `VMClassLoader` and `AccessController` improvements.

- David Gilbert for `basic` and `metal` icon and plaf support and lots of documenting, Lots of Free Swing and metal theme additions. `MetalIconFactory` implementation.

- Anthony Green for `MIDI` framework, `ALSA` and `DSSI` providers.

- Andrew Haley for `Serialization` and `URLClassLoader` fixes, gcj build speedups.

- Kim Ho for `JFileChooser` implementation.

- Andrew John Hughes for `Locale` and net fixes, URI RFC2986 updates, `Serialization` fixes, `Properties` XML support and generic branch work, VMIntegration guide update.

- Bastiaan Huisman for `TimeZone` bug fixing.

- Andreas Jaeger for mprec updates.

- Paul Jenner for better '`-Werror`' support.

- Ito Kazumitsu for `NetworkInterface` implementation and updates.

- Roman Kennke for `BoxLayout`, `GrayFilter` and `SplitPane`, plus bug fixes all over. Lots of Free Swing work including styled text.

- Simon Kitching for `String` cleanups and optimization suggestions.

- Michael Koch for configuration fixes, `Locale` updates, bug and build fixes.

- Guilhem Lavaux for configuration, thread and channel fixes and Kaffe integration. JCL native `Pointer` updates. Logger bug fixes.

- David Lichteblau for JCL support library global/local reference cleanups.

- Aaron Luchko for JDWP updates and documentation fixes.

- Ziga Mahkovec for `Graphics2D` upgraded to Cairo 0.5 and new regex features.

- Sven de Marothy for BMP imageio support, CSS and `TextLayout` fixes. `GtkImage` rewrite, 2D, awt, free swing and date/time fixes and implementing the Qt4 peers.

- Casey Marshall for crypto algorithm fixes, `FileChannel` lock, `SystemLogger` and `FileHandler` rotate implementations, NIO `FileChannel.map` support, security and policy updates.

- Bryce McKinlay for RMI work.

- Audrius Meskauskas for lots of Free Corba, RMI and HTML work plus testing and documenting.

- Kalle Olavi Niemitalo for build fixes.

- Rainer Orth for build fixes.

- Andrew Overholt for `File` locking fixes.

- Ingo Proetel for `Image`, `Logger` and `URLClassLoader` updates.

- Olga Rodimina for `MenuSelectionManager` implementation.

- Jan Roehrich for `BasicTreeUI` and `JTree` fixes.

- Julian Scheid for documentation updates and gjdoc support.

- Christian Schlichtherle for zip fixes and cleanups.

- Robert Schuster for documentation updates and beans fixes, `TreeNode` enumerations and `ActionCommand` and various fixes, XML and URL, AWT and Free Swing bug fixes.

- Keith Seitz for lots of JDWP work.
- Christian Thalinger for 64-bit cleanups, Configuration and VM interface fixes and `CACAO` integration, `fdlibm` updates.
- Gael Thomas for `VMClassLoader` boot packages support suggestions.
- Andreas Tobler for Darwin and Solaris testing and fixing, `Qt4` support for Darwin/OS X, `Graphics2D` support, `gtk+` updates.
- Dalibor Topic for better `DEBUG` support, build cleanups and Kaffe integration. `Qt4` build infrastructure, `SHA1PRNG` and `GdkPixbugDecoder` updates.
- Tom Tromey for Eclipse integration, generics work, lots of bug fixes and gcj integration including coordinating The Big Merge.
- Mark Wielaard for bug fixes, packaging and release management, `Clipboard` implementation, system call interrupts and network timeouts and `GdkPixpufDecoder` fixes.

In addition to the above, all of which also contributed time and energy in testing GCC, we would like to thank the following for their contributions to testing:

- Michael Abd-El-Malek
- Thomas Arend
- Bonzo Armstrong
- Steven Ashe
- Chris Baldwin
- David Billinghurst
- Jim Blandy
- Stephane Bortzmeyer
- Horst von Brand
- Frank Braun
- Rodney Brown
- Sidney Cadot
- Bradford Castalia
- Robert Clark
- Jonathan Corbet
- Ralph Doncaster
- Richard Emberson
- Levente Farkas
- Graham Fawcett
- Mark Fernyhough
- Robert A. French
- Jörgen Freyh
- Mark K. Gardner
- Charles-Antoine Gauthier
- Yung Shing Gene

- David Gilbert
- Simon Gornall
- Fred Gray
- John Griffin
- Patrik Hagglund
- Phil Hargett
- Amancio Hasty
- Takafumi Hayashi
- Bryan W. Headley
- Kevin B. Hendricks
- Joep Jansen
- Christian Joensson
- Michel Kern
- David Kidd
- Tobias Kuipers
- Anand Krishnaswamy
- A. O. V. Le Blanc
- llewelly
- Damon Love
- Brad Lucier
- Matthias Klose
- Martin Knoblauch
- Rick Lutowski
- Jesse Macnish
- Stefan Morrell
- Anon A. Mous
- Matthias Mueller
- Pekka Nikander
- Rick Niles
- Jon Olson
- Magnus Persson
- Chris Pollard
- Richard Polton
- Derk Reefman
- David Rees
- Paul Reilly
- Tom Reilly
- Torsten Rueger
- Danny Sadinoff

- Marc Schifer
- Erik Schnetter
- Wayne K. Schroll
- David Schuler
- Vin Shelton
- Tim Souder
- Adam Sulmicki
- Bill Thorson
- George Talbot
- Pedro A. M. Vazquez
- Gregory Warnes
- Ian Watson
- David E. Young
- And many others

And finally we'd like to thank everyone who uses the compiler, provides feedback and generally reminds us why we're doing this work in the first place.

Option Index

GCC's command line options are indexed here without any initial '-' or '--'. Where an option has both positive and negative forms (such as '-foption' and '-fno-option'), relevant entries in the manual are indexed under the most appropriate form; it may sometimes be useful to look up both forms.

Concept Index

H

I

N

S

U

W

X

www.ingramcontent.com/pod-product-compliance
Lightning Source LLC
Chambersburg PA
CBHW080352060326
40689CB00019B/3979